Lucy's Bones, Sacred Stones, & Einstein's Brain

ALSO BY HARVEY RACHLIN

The Making of a Detective (1995)

The Making of a Cop (1991)

The Songwriter's Workshop (editor) (1991)

The TV and Movie Business (1991)

*The Songwriter's and Musician's Guide
to Making Great Demos* (1988)

The Kennedys: A Chronological History: 1823–Present (1986)

The Money Encyclopedia (editor) (1984)

Love Grams (1983)

The Encyclopedia of the Music Business (1981)

The Songwriter's Handbook (1977)

The

Remarkable

Stories Behind the

Great Objects

and Artifacts

of History,

from Antiquity

to the

Modern Era

Lucy's Bones,

SACRED STONES,

& Einstein's Brain

An Owl Book

Henry Holt and Company
New York

Henry Holt and Company, LLC
Publishers since 1866
115 West 18th Street
New York, New York 10011

Henry Holt ® is a registered
trademark of Henry Holt and Company, LLC.

Published in Canada by Fitzhenry & Whiteside Ltd.,
195 Allstate Parkway, Markham, Ontario L3R 4T8.

Library of Congress Cataloging-in-Publication Data
Rachlin, Harvey.
Lucy's bones, sacred stones, and Einstein's brain: the
remarkable stories behind the great objects and artifacts of
history, from antiquity to the modern era / Harvey Rachlin.
p.   cm.
ISBN 0-8050-6406-0
Includes bibliographical references and index.
1. History—Miscellanea.   2. Antiquities.   I. Title.   II. Series.
D10.R335   1996   95-19935
909—dc20   CIP

Henry Holt books are available for special promotions and
premiums. For details contact: Director, Special Markets.

First published in hardcover in 1996 by
Henry Holt and Company

First Owl Books Edition 1996

DESIGNED BY BETTY LEW

Printed in the United States of America

10   9   8   7   6   5   4

To the memory
of my friend
Steven Schulman

Contents

Lucy's Bones, Sacred Stones, & Einstein's Brain

INTRODUCTION

Historical artifacts make physically manifest the dreams and ideas, the great deeds and events, of human history. They symbolize the glorious triumphs of human endeavor, its humiliating defeats, and just about everything in between. Steeped in legend, artifacts forge an indelible link with the past. Imagine, if you will, holding in your hands Tutankhamen's gold face mask, Columbus's Book of Privileges, or Horatio Nelson's uniform coat. Nothing quite approaches the thrill of coming face-to-face in the present with an object associated with a famous figure of the past. Some artifacts signify gallant and heroic deeds. Others are instruments of evil or the focal points of sacred or bizarre occurrences. Each has a tale to tell, whether an epic chapter or a footnote. Such artifacts open a window on the past, helping us to understand our heritage and ultimately ourselves.

Even if we can't go back in time to witness the first power-driven heavier-than-air flight, the signing by representatives of the American colonies of the document declaring their freedom from the British realm, or the Judeans' construction of an ingeniously conceived rock tunnel to thwart the invading Assyrians, we can today still seek out the Wright brothers' *Flyer*, the Declaration of Independence, and the Siloam Inscription. Or we can contemplate relics like Marie Antoinette's slipper (Museum of Fine Art, Caen, France), George Washington's schoolboy copybooks (Library of Congress, Washington, D.C.), Lewis and Clark's journals (American Philosophical Society, Philadelphia), Jules Verne's globe (Jules Verne Museum, Nantes, France), or Sigmund Freud's couch (Freud Museum, London).

What about the toothbrush of Napoleon (Science Museum, London) or the shaving mug of Honest Abe (Ford's Theatre National Historic Site, Washington, D.C.)? Such relics remind us that these mythic figures were flesh-and-blood mortals, too. But mortals succumb; artifacts (properly preserved and cared for) can survive for thousands, if not millions, of years. The sundry bas-reliefs, baked clay tablets, papyrus letters, pottery, figurines, and tools of the ancient past provide invaluable insights into the evolution of civilization. Some stellar artifacts remain, too—for example, the Code of Hammurabi (Louvre Museum, Paris) and the Dead Sea Scrolls (most of the scrolls are in the Israel Museum and the Rockefeller Museum, both in Jerusalem).

That these things still exist, having endured destructive natural processes, capricious human behavior, and the ravages of time, is incredible. But the discovery of an artifact marks only the beginning of a long process of scholarly research. Sometimes it is a challenge for experts to determine just what an artifact is. After all, relics of antiquity do not come with labels attached. If you found the cup from which Christ drank at the Last Supper, or the tablets Moses brought down from Mount Sinai, they would not be inscribed "The Holy Grail," or "The Ten Commandments." Painstaking study, analysis, and debate attend the identification of artifacts. And at the end of the process, our conclusions remain conjecture, more or less.

Over the past centuries, the work of many archaeologists has centered on biblical sites. Humans have been endlessly fascinated by God and, of course, by whether the archaeological record can be said to confirm the theological record. We find that many seventeenth- and eighteenth-century archaeologists often too hastily interpreted ancient inscriptions to fit their preconceptions. Perhaps this is still true today. Yet the brilliant work of the pioneers of the past, such as Heinrich Schliemann, Jean-François Champollion, Henry Creswicke Rawlinson, Charles Leonard Woolley, Austen Layard, and Flinders Petrie, established modern archaeology as a science, a discipline, and an art. Modern society owes them a deep debt.

The search for artifacts is not a simple affair, and I often found myself led into endless loops and down blind alleys with no object in sight. Where, one might ask, is the first lightbulb of Thomas Edison? Edison conducted a series of experiments in which different materials were progressively used to achieve increasingly better results. In 1878 and 1879, Edison worked with bulbs over many months, gradually moving them from unusable short-lived filaments to a filament-and-bulb design that was long-lived enough to patent. At each stage the bulbs were taken apart to be examined. I learned that the very first lightbulb that Edison experimented with was probably long ago discarded. But not all of Edison's original inventions have disappeared. His original phonograph mechanism, the machine that marked the advent of the sound recording era and the one on which the nursery rhyme "Mary Had a Little Lamb" was recorded and played back on tinfoil mounted to it, does still exist (Edison National Historic Site, West Orange, New Jersey); unfortunately, the tinfoil was probably also long ago thrown away.

Of all the hundreds of thousands of words written by William Shakespeare, only a few are known to survive in his own hand: six signatures and the words *by me,* which precede one of them. Four signatures are at the Public Record Office in London, three on a will (which has the *by me* preface), and one on a deposition. The Guildhall Library and the British Library, both also in London, have one signature each on a deed. And it is widely believed that the manuscript of a play at the British Library, *The Book of Sir Thomas More,* is written, in part, in his hand (several people cooperated in its authorship). Since there is no identification of Shakespeare as an author of the play and there are no known signed letters or manuscripts of Shakespeare against which the handwriting could be compared, it is difficult to prove this, but by comparing the use of language and style, some have said that the manuscript in question might be an early work of Shakespeare.

In Shakespeare's day, discarded sheets of paper would often be used in binding books. That means that some printed books of the time might literally have contained Shakespeare's work between their covers! Alas, my zeal in tracking down relics of Shakespeare's hand did not extend to ungluing sixteenth-century books. In any case, if any of Shakespeare's manuscripts remained at his printer's shop, they would probably have been destroyed in the great fire of London in 1666.

None of Gutenberg's printing presses or the equipment from his workshop are extant. It is not known when the original Gutenberg printing press was destroyed or how it actually looked, or even if it was destroyed. But it's possible that Gutenberg's original printing press was destroyed during his lifetime, around 1462, when, during a conflict between Adolf of Nassau and Diether of Isenburg, many houses were torched; Gutenberg's workshop and the equipment therein could have been among the casualties. At the Gutenberg-Museum in Mainz, Germany, which has two of the forty-eight surviving Gutenberg bibles—the Solms-Lauback and the Shuckburg, named after their previous owners—there is a reconstructed Gutenberg press, but it is not a perfect model, as nothing of certainty is known about Gutenberg's original printing presses. The first prints of his workshop were not made until 1499, thirty-one years after the inventor of movable type died.

Man is a relative newcomer among Earth's creatures. But, endowed with a brain like no other before him, he quickly learned to express himself. He soon discovered he had a musical soul (a flute has been found that is thirty-two thousand years old) and a taste for painting (cave art dates back twenty-nine thousand years). It would be only a few thousand years more before he would begin to sculpt figures and fashion weapons, tools, and other implements. As human history unfolded and societies became more complex, artifacts became more dramatic, more representative of human needs, drives, emotions, and introspection.

Over time, some artifacts attained special significance, gradually growing in historical value until they became national, even international, treasures. In the meantime, however, many important relics were handled rather haphazardly. Often their significance went unrecognized for centuries. Around the world today are numerous extant artifacts having wonderful provenances and histories. They are housed in museums, libraries, archives, and other institutions as well as collections in the private domain.*

Some artifacts exist only because at times in the past, people specifically created and preserved some objects to serve as relics. It was a custom of the past, for instance, to preserve locks of hair and to make life and death masks. Today we have locks from George Washington (Pierpont Morgan Library, New York, New York), Thomas Jefferson (Library of Congress, Washington, D.C.), John Keats (Pierpont Morgan Library), and *Frankenstein* author Mary Shelley (New York Public Library, New York, New York) as well as life masks of such people as Thomas Jefferson and Dolley Madison (New York State Historical Association, Cooperstown, New York) and Beethoven (Beethoven-Haus, Bonn, Germany), and death masks of such figures as John Keats (National Portrait Gallery, London), Walt Whitman (Harvard University, Cambridge, Massachu-

---

*Some museums and institutions house casts or replicas of bones and artifacts, and these are not to be confused with the original objects or artifacts, whose locations are given at the end of each chapter of this book.

setts), and Clara Barton (National Portrait Gallery, Washington, D.C.).

I have endeavored to find artifacts with striking, colorful backgrounds. The selection here ranges from the offbeat to the famous and includes lesser-known objects with histories of mystery, massacre, and marauding—what I call cloak-and-dagger artifacts. In all cases, however, I picked objects whose stories I found absorbing—enough, I hope, to inspire the reader to undertake his or her own voyage of discovery.

All the artifacts described here are the originals or at least are said to be the original. Does it matter if they are real? The authenticity of liturgical relics may be less important than what they symbolize. Believing such relics can work miracles, people have venerated them over long periods.

Traditionally, according to the canon of the Roman Catholic Church, liturgical relics are classified as first, second, and third class. A first-class relic is something that was part of a holy person, such as a bone, hair, limb, or finger, or his or her blood. A second-class relic is an object that belonged to the person in life. And a third-class relic is something that touched the holy person but that he or she did not own. The dates for liturgical relics are those of popular tradition, which of course may or may not be true.

Various biblical and liturgical artifacts were thought by people of the past (and some of the present) to have fearsome military power. Such objects, associated with figures in the Bible, were deemed holy relics, ordained by God to bring power to the bearer and calamity upon his target. This was the thesis of the popular motion picture *Raiders of the Lost Ark,* the lost ark being the biblical Ark of the Covenant.

Part of the labor—and fun—of writing this book was trying to track down the locations of noteworthy artifacts, if indeed they still existed. One, for example, that I very much wanted to find was the letter that spawned America's most famous newspaper editorial: Virginia O'Hanlon's "Is There a Santa Claus?" letter. The eight-year-old New York City girl's innocent letter in 1897 to the editor of the *New York Sun* and the wistful editorial response were reprinted in the *Sun* a couple of times and have been quoted the world over. They are a symbol of hope for all things people believe in.

So what happened to the letter? The *New York Sun* shut down many years ago. I imagined that somewhere, cartons of the newspaper's files were piled in a warehouse, with the letter, a bit crushed, in an old file just waiting to be discovered. When I finally found the *Sun*'s archives, however, the letter was nowhere to be found.

In tracking down artifacts, I became a sort of detective. As one who has always enjoyed scavenger hunts and puzzles, I embraced the challenge of searching for artifacts. Each case I solved led me to seek out another one that might be even more difficult to find.

There is a great story about the siege of Plattsburgh, New York, during the War of 1812. The American general Alexander Macomb, while commanding the Champlain Department, called for volunteers to assist in defending approaches to the area against the invading British. A number of schoolboys, mostly fifteen years of age, volunteered with a group commanded by Captain Martin J. Aitkin. One can imagine the trepidation with which these tender youths entered into battle with the professional redcoats, but they fought heroically and successfully, fending the British off a crucial bridge. I was told one of their muskets still existed, and I searched for it but couldn't find it. What I did turn up, however, was one of the Model 1819 Hall breech-loading rifles (National Museum of American History, Washington, D.C.) that Congress presented years later in lieu of a medal or other citation to members of the volunteer corps for their "gallantry and patriotic services" during the siege. This rifle was awarded to Gustavus A. Bird, one of the schoolboys under Captain Aitkin's command, but none of the weapons the boys held during the battle seems to have survived.

Then there was the roller coaster of excitement and letdown when I heard that Crazy Horse's "scalp shirt" was at the Nebraska State Historical Society in Lincoln. Crazy Horse was the Sioux war leader who led American Indians in the massacre of Custer and some of his men at the Little Bighorn River in Montana in 1876, and who fought earlier in the Fetterman Massacre, the Battle of the Rosebud, and the Wagon-Box Fight. Scalp shirts contained locks of hair of tribal members and were made by Plains Indians to symbolically represent the tribe for whom the wearer was responsible.

One day, one of the historical society's curators realized the shirt was machine-made and decided to check into its history. After examining original letters from the donors, he found that the "scalp shirt" wasn't even manufactured until a year after Crazy Horse's death in 1877. Shortly before, Crazy Horse had taken a third wife. Upon his death she took a second husband. The second husband took the name of his wife's famous first husband and became known as Crazy Horse of Pine Ridge Agency. Thus this garment is simply a shirt worn by Crazy Horse's third wife's second husband. Got that?

What of Neville Chamberlain's black umbrella, the famous prop from his infamous sojourn to Munich, where he was duped by Hitler in September 1938? Everyone interested in World War II has seen photographs of the tall, mustachioed man in black top hat leaning on a closed umbrella—a kind of tall, somber Chaplin. The celebrated umbrella was the subject of the 1938 French hit song by Ray Ventura et ses Collegiens, "La Chamberlaine: Polka Parapluie" ("The Umbrella Polka"), as well as "The Umbrella Man" by Flanagan and Allen in England. Many of the prime minister's papers and letters went to the University of Birmingham in England, and a large quantity of his unwanted clothing and paraphernalia, including some of his everyday umbrellas, was given away to deserving causes after his death. The celebrated umbrella, however, has probably long since disintegrated at a municipal dump.

One gruesome relic that has never been found is the head of the famous Mexican revolutionary leader Pancho Villa. His head was severed from his corpse in Chihuahua in 1926, three years after his murder, and remains missing.

At the Mütter Museum of the College of Physicians of Philadelphia are plaster casts of the torsos of the original Siamese twins, Chang and Eng, along with their preserved connected livers; and a tumor secretly removed from President Grover Cleveland's jaw. At the National Museum of Health and Medicine in Washington, D.C., is a wax model of the groin area of Two-Pistol Pete, John Baptist Dos Santos, who had two penises, four testicles, and three legs. On the subject of penises, let it be said that John Dillinger was buried with his penis. The widely circulated story of Dillinger's penis existing separate from his body is spurious and probably originated as gossip because Dillinger's brain was in fact removed during his autopsy. Another possibility comes from a photograph of Dillinger's corpse in the morgue, taken from the side, where something is sticking up from under the sheet, perhaps a brace on the side of the table. Incidentally, Dillinger's brain, which had been at Northwestern University, is now presumably lost.

The Royal Society in London has an instrument that was traditionally believed to be a reflecting telescope constructed by the immortal Sir Isaac Newton. Now there is considerable doubt about this; it may be an old replica, and Newton's optical telescope may have disappeared sometime in the late seventeenth or early eighteenth century.

Animals become artifacts too, when preserved in skins or mounted after death. Indeed, some famous horses or horses of famous people have been preserved for posterity. Included in this book is the story of Stonewall Jackson's charger, Little Sorrel. Other eminent equestrian remains include Civil War general Philip Henry Sheridan's Winchester (National Museum of American History), Little Bighorn captain Myles Keogh's Comanche (Museum of Natural History, University of Kansas, Lawrence), Napoleon's favorite charger, Vizir (Museum of the Army, Paris, on loan from the Louvre), the poisoned world racing champion thoroughbred of the 1930s, Phar Lap (Museum of Victoria, Melbourne, Australia), and singing cowboy and television star Roy Rogers's Trigger (Roy Rogers–Dale Evans Museum, Victorville, California). Also extant is the preserved head of Civil War general George Meade's horse, Old Baldy (Civil War Library and Museum, Philadelphia).

The bones of Robert E. Lee's Traveller had long been on exhibit (Washington and Lee University, Lexington, Virginia) but were disarticulated in the early 1960s and buried in May 1971 because they had gotten rather decrepit. Traveller's hide was never preserved, but hair from his tail has been saved at the museum underneath Lee Chapel, Washington and Lee University. During the Civil War, people were known to pluck or cut off hairs from the manes and tails of famous animals for souvenirs.

When I finished writing this book, it suddenly occurred to me that it was not just a collection of objects but a series of historical vignettes that illuminated the continuing drama of humankind—its events, beliefs, hopes, and deeds. From the shinbone of Major General Daniel Edgar Sickles to the diary of Anne Frank, from the Siloam Inscription to *Voyager 1* and *Voyager 2*'s gold-plated record, these artifacts and their stories document the boundless spirit of humanity.

Somewhere on this Earth—under the desert sands, deep in the ocean, or maybe even in somebody's attic—lie artifacts just waiting to be discovered, with their cryptic yet revealing clues to the mysteries of humankind.

The Black Stone of the Ka'bah

DATE: Before the creation of humankind (by tradition).

WHAT IT IS: The black stone is a revered object set in a corner wall of the Ka'bah, a sanctuary Muslims believe to be the holiest place on Earth.

WHAT IT LOOKS LIKE: The stone, having been sundered, is composed of several pieces and fragments, bound together by a silver ligature. It is semicircular and measures about 10 inches horizontally and 12 inches vertically.

A mysterious object of unimaginable antiquity and possibly of extraterrestrial origin is revered today by Muslims around the world as being consummately holy, as coming from the Supreme Being, Allah, and as having been touched through the millennia by holy men from Abraham to Mohammed. This is Alhajar Al-Aswad, the Black Stone, and it is lodged in a wall of a sanctuary on grounds that are strictly forbidden to non-Muslims.

According to Islamic tradition, the stone came to Earth aeons ago from heaven, where numerous angels linked in a chain worshiped Allah by chanting and praying as they continually circled Al-baitul Ma'moor, the House Meant for the Worship of Allah by Angels, built under the throne of Allah. Allah wanted humankind to have a similar shrine from which to worship him, and he gave Adam a bright and pure white stone to bring to Earth from Paradise to set in the Ka'bah, the shrine he would build. The stone was called Alhajar Alsad, the Happiest Stone, because of all the stones in Paradise it alone had been chosen for the Ka'bah.

With Alhajar Alsad in his arms, Adam descended from Heaven to the island off India known today as Sri Lanka, and Allah guided him to Mecca, a site directly below his throne in heaven. Adam placed the stone in the ground and built the Ka'bah for it to be mounted in.

Sometime later, when the Deluge, or Great Flood, swept over Earth's surface, the Ka'bah was severely damaged and its holy stone was taken away by divine power to a safe place. It remained hidden from human eyes until Allah told Abraham, the father of all prophets after him, to re-build the Ka'bah. The angel Gabriel led Abraham to the site in Mecca where the Ka'bah was to be erected; Abraham built the House of Allah, and Gabriel gave him the holy stone to place in it.

The people of the land joined Abraham in revering the stone by touch-ing and kissing it. They also sacrificed lambs and cows and other animals near the sacred house and put the blood of the animals on the stone. Over time the stone began to darken.

As the centuries passed, the Ka'bah was frequently damaged by natural calamities and rebuilt by whichever Arab tribe held it as property at that particular time. Eventually it became a place of worship for Arab tribes from all over the region.

In the early seventh century a fire ravaged the Ka'bah, and the people rebuilt it this time with higher walls and the door several feet off the ground so sentinels could better regulate those who entered the house. But the Arab tribes, who had erected the sacred house jointly, disagreed about who should have the right to install the Black Stone. They decided to let the first person who entered the courtyard be the judge, to render a decision on who would have the right.

It happened that the first person to come from the outside was Mo-hammed. At this time Mohammed was not a prophet, but he did have a reputation of being a faithful, trustful young man. After hearing the prob-lem, Mohammed wisely came up with a plan that would satisfy and honor all concerned. He placed a piece of cloth on the ground and set the Black Stone at the center. Then he asked each of the tribes to select a dele-gate to gather around the cloth. Together they lifted the cloth with the Black Stone off the ground and carried it to the Ka'bah, where Mo-hammed himself set the stone in place.

Around A.D. 610 the Islamic religion was formally regenerated when this same Mohammed, who had opposed his countrymen's practice of worshiping idols, received a revelation from Allah and began preaching his word as revealed to him through Gabriel, the same angel who gave

Muslims are seen making a tawāf *(circuit) around the Kaʻbah. It is recommended that when possible they kiss and touch the Black Stone.*

revelation to all the prophets and who guided Abraham and his son Ishmael in the reconstruction of the Kaʻbah.*

Mohammed's outspokenness against idolatry stirred the rancor of the disbelieving tribes of Mecca. This rancor gradually grew to the point where the Prophet's life was in danger, and in 622, on receipt of instruction from Allah, he migrated to Medina. His journey is called the Hegira, and the year 622 marks the start of the Muslim calendar.

With the spread of Islam came the eruption of battles, but eventually the people of Mecca accepted the religion, believing that Mohammed was a prophet and the Koran, the Muslim sacred scriptures, the final revelations sent by Allah. The Kaʻbah became the Muslim sanctuary, and the stone idols that had been placed inside were discarded. The Black Stone was left untouched.

*Islam, which means "peaceful, willing, and total submission to the will of Allah," teaches that Mohammed was the last prophet sent to humankind. The prophets of Islam who came before him, including Adam, Noah, Abraham, Moses, and Jesus, are the very same people who appear in the Judeo-Christian traditions, but Islam continued the chain of prophecy where these other religions left off.

The Ka'bah (Sacred House), with the Black Stone set in its southeast corner in a silver casing a few feet off the ground, surrounded by the faithful.

After Mohammed died, his companions led the Muslim nation under the laws set forth by Allah as revealed to the prophet Mohammed. The caliph Omar, who originally opposed Mohammed, gave faith to the people that the Black Stone was not an idol, saying to it, "I know you are incapable of doing good or harm. Had I not seen the messenger of Allah kissing you, I would not have done so."

Mohammed's companions inaugurated sweeping changes, which resulted in sectarian conflict and eventually an attack on Mecca. In an assault in 682 the House of Allah was again damaged, and the Black Stone was broken into pieces. After the invaders retreated, many of the local population fled, fearing Allah would punish them for permitting the sanctuary to be destroyed. But the caliph commenced reconstruction, and the townspeople joined him when they saw Allah did not punish him. Stones from around the countryside were used as the building materials. The ruler had the pieces of the Black Stone composed and bound with a silver ring and had this object implanted in a corner wall.

Since the time of Mohammed, the Ka'bah has been occasionally damaged but never completely destroyed. Muslims believe the sacred building is indestructible, protected along with the Koran exclusively and ultimately by Allah from annihilation on Earth. In the same year Mohammed was born, the king of Ethiopia and his soldiers came to attack the sacred house but were, tradition holds, completely destroyed by armies of yellow pigeonlike birds called *ab aabeels* that dropped stones on them by the order of Allah.

Day and night throughout the year, Muslims perform a ritual at the Ka'bah called a *tawāf*. Recalling the angels in heaven circling Al-baitul Ma'moor, it is a ritual in which Muslims walk quickly around the Ka'bah seven times and make their devotions. During the *tawāf* they kiss or touch the Black Stone (or point at it if the Ka'bah is crowded and they cannot get close to it).

Once a year Muslims from around the world make a pilgrimage to Masjid Al-Haraam, the largest and most sacred mosque in the world, in whose open middle the Ka'bah is located. On specific days in the month of Zilhujja, the last month in the Arab calendar, they perform the rituals of the pilgrimage which include their *tawāf* around the Ka'bah. A *tawāf* always begins at the Black Stone.

The Black Stone is set about three feet from the ground into the exterior southeastern corner of the Ka'bah, a stone building shaped like a huge cube. It is the centuries-old tradition of Muslims to touch and kiss the stone because this was the prophet Mohammed's practice. Muslims claim the Prophet taught that if one kisses the stone with conviction from the heart and walks around the Ka'bah praying to Allah, the stone will bear witness to one's supplication on the Day of Judgment, when the stone will be given vision and the power to talk.

The Black Stone is set in a hole, so those wishing to touch or kiss it must insert their hand or face. The stone, which feels smooth and soothing, also has a pleasant fragrance, which it is said to have emitted since the time of Abraham.

In making a *tawāf*, at certain sections of the walls Muslims will make prayers according to the Islamic commandments. Opposite the Black Stone is the Maqam Ibrahim (Spot of Abraham) corner. As the pilgrims move from this corner to the Black Stone to complete a circuit, Allah is said to forgive, if he wishes, some of their sins.

Several feet in front of the Black Stone is the Zamzam well, which has an unusual provenance. While Abraham was away from his second wife, Hagar, and their newborn son, Ishmael, to visit his wife Sarah at Mecca,

Hagar needed water, and she ran up and down between two mountains, Safā and Marwah, in extreme thirst, until the angel Gabriel hit the ground with his wings and brought forth a flow of clear water from under the feet of Ishmael. There seemed to be no man-made source for this water since no drilling had been done in the ground. Water still comes from the Zamzam well today, and Muslims believe it shall continue until the Day of Judgment.

The Ka'bah interior itself is open only two or three times per year. On these occasions the king (or the king's representative) and the Muslim heads of the diplomatic missions of other countries sweep and clean the inside of the Ka'bah. It is considered an honor to be invited to the sanctuary for these events.

Only Muslims are permitted to pray at the Ka'bah. Few non-Muslim Westerners have ever set eyes upon it, but one who did was the English Orientalist Sir Richard Francis Burton; he dressed as a Muslim to conceal his identity and was able to enter Masjid Al-Haraam, the "sacred" mosque. In describing the emotional experience of Muslims who made their devotions at the Ka'bah and pressed their hearts against the Black Stone, Burton wrote, "It was as if the poetical legends of the Arab spoke truth, and that the waving wings of angels, not the sweet breeze of morning, were agitating and swelling the black covering of the shrine . . . theirs was the high feeling of religious enthusiasm."

From descriptions of its substance and color, modern Western scientists have agreed that the Black Stone probably did not originate on this planet. But they surmise that rather than having been brought down by Adam from a celestial paradise, it is most likely a fragment of a meteor that fell to Earth uncounted aeons ago.

LOCATION: Mecca, Saudi Arabia.

Lucy the Hominid

DATE: Circa 3.2 million B.C.

WHAT IT IS: The skeletal remains of an *Australopithecus afarensis,* one of the earliest known humanlike ancestors and forerunners of the human race. Lucy was a transitional creature between ape and human.

WHAT IT LOOKS LIKE: Dozens of bones and fragments exist, comprising almost half of a complete skeleton. The skeleton reveals that Lucy was about 3½ feet tall.

Lucy is one of the most extraordinary finds in paleoanthropological history, perched in the pantheon of hominid discoveries with those from Neanderthal, Java, Mauer, Zhoukoudian, and Taung. Her discovery is all the more remarkable in light of the auspicious circumstances that attended it. Serendipity always plays a major role in the laborious endeavor of finding fossils, but the finding of Lucy was so unlikely as to verge on the miraculous. Lucy was reposing in an area where fossils, once exposed to the surface, erode or are destroyed completely unless found within a few years. If a young American paleoanthropologist hadn't been there to meet her, Lucy might have disappeared into oblivion and humankind's further understanding of its origins delayed for an unknown period.

At least five million years ago, a dramatic change was taking place in the area we now know as Africa: an apelike species of creatures was evolving into our human ancestors. This species roamed certain areas of the land, through lush, verdant forests, across meandering streams teeming with aquatic organisms, past ferociously active volcanoes, large predatory beasts, and deadly quicksand bogs. The climate was warm and favorable to an astonishing variety of animal and plant life. The *hom-inids*—the term for the human race including its distant progenitors—lived on the forest ground before moving out to the savannas, expansive open grasslands where the environment was equally perilous. They had small brains and V-shaped jaws with no chins and resembled apes except in one extremely significant respect. Rather than perambulating on four limbs, they walked erect on two feet. Being bipedal freed their hands, enabling them to carry out simple functions that would grow more complex as future species developed.

The unearthing in the mid-1970s of this predecessor of humankind had the amazing effect of compelling scientists to revise their conception of the evolution of the human race.

Since the first great hominid discovery in the mid–nineteenth century, the quest for humankind's origin has been a spirited endeavor in which paleoanthropologists seek out and piece together fossil finds, postulate new species and genus names and evolutionary chains, debate these, and continually reformulate their ideas. Mammal and reptile fossils from eras far deeper in time than those of hominids have been found, but it is the hominid pieces that have been the greatest anthropological treasures.

Exotic names have been attached to the disinterred remains, reflecting the sites where they have been found. In 1856 the first discovery of a Neanderthal (Rheinisches Landesmuseum, Bonn, Germany) in the Neander Valley of Germany revealed a primitive human who lived fifty thousand to one hundred thousand years ago. The discovery of the Neanderthal, with its low sloping forehead, heavy eyebrow ridges, and large jaw, jarred those who doubted human roots extended so far back in time. A younger ancestor was found next, Cro-Magnon (Musée de l'Homme, Paris), in the Dordogne region of France, estimated to be less than thirty thousand years old. This was an example of *Homo sapiens,* or a modern human. These individuals painted pictures on the walls of caves, hunted animals for food, and even dabbled in religion. They were tall and had modern faces and large brains.

With the discovery of the Java specimen, or *Homo erectus,* in Indonesia in 1891 by Eugène Dubois, scientists had to stretch the age of humankind back to half a million years or more. The Java specimen (Rijksmuseum van Natuurlijke Historie, Leiden, Netherlands) was described as an "ape-man." Disturbing as the idea of evolving from such a primitive creature was to some people, Java Man walked upright and undeniably represented an important phase in human evolutionary development.

Neither ape nor human, Australopithecus afarensis *is considered to be an ancestor of modern human beings because of its bipedal locomotion. On average, females weighed sixty to sixty-five pounds and were three and a half to four feet tall; males, ninety to 120 pounds and four and a half to five feet tall.*

The finding of other bones, skulls, and teeth—the fossil remnants from which earlier beings are identified—added more, and sometimes older, hominids to the "family tree." The Mauer mandible (Geologisch-Palaeontologisches Institut, University of Heidelberg), discovered near Heidelberg, Germany, in 1907, had a massive jaw with humanlike teeth and is estimated to be as old as seven hundred thousand years. Peking Man (Institute of Vertebrate Paleontology and Paleoanthropology, Beijing, China; Paleontological Institute, Uppsala, Sweden), found at Zhoukoudian, China, in 1927, handled fire and made stone tools and was thought to have lived from a quarter million to a half million years ago. Taung Infant (University of the Witwatersrand, Johannesburg, South Africa), found in an area called Taung in Cape Province, South Africa, and identified in 1924 by Raymond Dart, an Australian anatomist living in South Africa, was proclaimed a "missing link." More than three decades later, after much doubt was cast by the British anthropological establishment, which said the creature was an ape—skulls of young apes are difficult to distinguish from those of hominids—evidence revealed that it was a two-million-year-old hominid. The 1959 discovery of a very robust australopithecine skull at Olduvai (National Museum, Dar es Salaam, Tanzania), by Mary Leakey in Tanganyika, Africa (now Tanzania), revealed another creature who lived 1.75 million years ago; the then-new method of potassium-argon dating made the previously laborious and often inaccurate process of determining the age of fossils virtually conclusive.

The dilemma, and the source of contention for paleoanthropologists, was whether hominid fossils were *Homo* or *Australopithecus* (a pre-human genus named by Dart), and further, in what species of the chosen genus a fossil should be placed, or whether a new one needed to be created. *Homo* species were established, and earlier hominids fit in neatly. Australopithecines were at first categorized as either *robustus*, stout and vegetarian, or *africanus*, gracile (slender) and omnivorous. But confusion still existed, complicated when the bogus Piltdown Man (see page 297) was thought to be genuine. It would take new hominid discoveries and years of debating and investigating, utilizing modern technologies, to clear up the confusion and establish a generally agreed-upon evolutionary scheme and explanation.

In 1974 a young American paleoanthropologist of Swedish descent named Donald Johanson was looking for hominid fossils in Hadar, a site in the Afar region of Ethiopia. This was one of many sites in the Great Rift Valley of eastern Africa where paleoanthropologists concentrated their searches for hominid fossils from the Pliocene and Pleistocene epochs (five million years ago until ten thousand years ago). This was Johanson's second field season in as many years.

On the last day of November, Johanson's assistant, Tom Gray, a graduate student, went over his itinerary for the day. He was uncertain of the location of a particular site for a fossil map being composed and needed some guidance. Johanson was overloaded with work at the camp, but he had a gut feeling that something important had emerged from the ground and was waiting to be discovered, before erosion destroyed it forever. He agreed to help.

They made their way to the fossil site and searched it thoroughly, but nothing remarkable turned up. It was blazing hot; Gray was tired and wanted to return to camp. Johanson obliged, but he chose a circuitous route that would bring them to a desiccated ravine he wanted to canvass. This proved more rewarding than he could ever have imagined. Johanson spotted a bone that he instantly recognized as hominid. Forgetting the heat and their fatigue, the two combed the immediate area, turning up dozens of bones.

The men were incredulous. Paleoanthropologists consider themselves

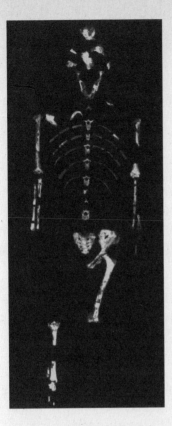

The skeleton of "Lucy." Shortly after finding the bones, Donald Johanson heard the Beatles' song "Lucy in the Sky with Diamonds" and adopted the girl's name in the title for his ancient creature.

fortunate if they find a single tooth or fragment of bone, lucky indeed if they turn up a fragment of a hominid skull. Johanson and Gray were looking at enough ancient bones to assemble into a skeleton! This was unprecedented.

When the field season ended, Johanson headed back to his home base, Case Western Reserve University in Cleveland, Ohio. Now he had the considerable challenge of determining exactly what he had found. From the shape of the pelvic bone, he knew the skeleton was that of a female. It was apparent that Lucy—the nickname he gave the creature—was very, very old. But was she *Homo* (more closely related to living humans) or *Australopithecus* (from an extinct branch of the human family tree)? Or ape? The answer would shed light on the course of human evolution.

Johanson delighted in his quarry; he knew he had something special. Lucy's brain was too small and her jaw wasn't rounded enough for *Homo*. And although she was apelike, her knee joint indicated she walked upright and her teeth were humanlike. She was hominid, not an anthropoid ape. An australopithecine, but which species? *Africanus? Robustus?* Perhaps something else?

Over the next four years (with two more field seasons at Hadar, one of which yielded the important "First Family," the skeletal remains of more than a dozen australopithecine children and adults found at one site), Johanson dedicated himself to determining Lucy's significance. As a specimen, Lucy was unique because her multiple bones permitted the approximation of not only her height and weight but also her body proportions, or the relative sizes of her arms, legs, and other parts of her body. Bone reconstruction also revealed much about the creature's functional anatomy, particularly locomotion, or the way the bones and muscles moved. But perhaps the most fascinating finding was what Lucy revealed not as an individual specimen but as part of a species.

Johanson engaged specialists in radiometric dating to make an exhaustive examination, and their results were breathtaking. Lucy was more than three million years old and an older australopithecine than the robust and gracile creatures. Indeed, she was ancestral to both *Homo* and *Australopithecus,* which is to say, she was an ancestor of all later hominids, including modern humans, and all australopithecines.

Lucy was an entirely different species. What to name her? Because she had been reposing in Ethiopia's Afar region, Johanson, Tim White, an assistant anthropology professor at the University of California, Berkeley, and Yves Coppens, the director of the Laboratoire d'Anthropologie at the Musée de l'Homme in Paris, settled on the name *Australopithecus afarensis.*

Johanson's assertion that Lucy was a new species was naturally challenged by some of his colleagues, but it was eventually accepted by most of the paleoanthropological community. Then other questions popped up. Who came before Lucy? How far back did hominids go? Past Lucy, the evidence is sketchy. In 1994 a new hominid fossil species was discovered in Ethiopia in rocks about 4.4 million years old. Named *Ardipithicus ramidus,* the species is even more apelike than Lucy but is barely humanlike because of the anatomy of its teeth. It fills the gap between apes and hominids and is about as primitive a hominid as could be expected as well as the oldest hominid species known today. Another newly discovered species, *Australopithecus anamensis*, was announced by anthropologist Meave Leakey and her colleagues in 1995. More than four million years old, *anamensis* walked bipedally and might be ancestral to Lucy.

Exploring around Lake Victoria in eastern Africa in the 1940s, Louis Leakey (the husband of Mary Leakey) reached far back in time. Remarkably, he discovered fragments of apes from the Miocene epoch, twenty million years in the past. Evidently various types of primitive apes flourished during this epoch, but except for the line that eventually produced human beings, most became extinct (the ancestors of living chimps and gorillas also left descendants). Today there are fossils of primates known to be as old as sixty-five million years.

The enduring Miocene line filtered into various primates of uncertain identity, but sixteen or seventeen million years later *Australopithecus afarensis* emerged. And it was australopithecines like Lucy who nurtured the seeds that gave rise to *Homo habilis*, who spawned *Homo erectus*, from whom in turn sprang *Homo sapiens*.

Johanson believes that Lucy lived near a lake and weighed about sixty pounds. Sometime when she was in her twenties, more than three million years in Earth's past, the diminutive hominid was down by the edge of the lake, where for some unknown reason she died, only to become entombed in the ground, her repose undisturbed through the ages, until she was serendipitously found in our own modern era.

LOCATION: National Museum, Addis Ababa, Ethiopia.

The Code of Hammurabi

DATE: Eighteenth century B.C.

WHAT IT IS: A stele, or stone pillar, on which are inscribed the legal provisions of the Babylonian king Hammurabi. The code is one of the great documents of ancient jurisprudence and one of the most complete collections of laws to survive. Other ancient codes that have survived include the laws of King Ur-Nammu, the reforms of Urukagina, the Hittite laws, and the biblical codes.

WHAT IT LOOKS LIKE: The code is inscribed on a black basalt stele over 8 feet high depicting King Hammurabi standing before Shamash, the Sun God, who is seated on a throne atop a mountain, receiving the sacred laws. Below him is engraved the code, comprising forty-nine columns of cuneiform text.

By 3500 B.C., on a verdant and fertile plain cradled by the Tigris and Euphrates Rivers in Mesopotamia (an area now known as Iraq), an advanced civilization had developed. Here, to a degree hitherto unknown in ancient societies, a sophisticated form of written communication accessible to and used widely by the people enabled the spread of information and the development of a complex commerce and culture.

During the course of the third millennium B.C., the Sumerians dominated the region, ruling over several city-states. But by about 2350 B.C., their power began to erode, and a new breed of warriors managed to unite Mesopotamia under the rule of the Akkadian kings.

Two centuries after the start of the dynasty, the empire began to crumble. The city-states reverted to their old rivalries, and once again blood began to spill. So it was a most formidable task for Ur-Nammu, king of the Third Dynasty of Ur around 2000 B.C., and later, Hammurabi, an Amorite whose reign began in the eighteenth century B.C., to reunite the warring towns and villages. With fierce determination, Hammurabi was able not only to reestablish the city-state alliances secured by his forebears but, leading his army to the north against the city of Mari, was able to expand his empire to the whole of Mesopotamia.

During his forty-two years as king, Hammurabi continually had to fight rising coalitions vying for power and city-states seeking autonomy. But his military prowess and his strong political leadership enabled him to maintain an extraordinary degree of social harmony.

Hammurabi's system of rules for conduct and punishment in his kingdom was set down in his law code, his greatest accomplishment. The code addressed nearly every aspect of life in Babylonian society, including property ownership, trading, loans, partnerships, contracts, marriage, adultery, divorce, adoption, children's rights, inheritance, religion, military service, perjury, burglary, looting, robbery, rape, assault, and murder. The cuneiform canons were designed to prescribe justice for abused parties. Depending on the crime, a variety of punishments could be inflicted, ranging from fines, forfeiture of property, flogging and public ridicule, to severing the hands, to death by burning or drowning. The code's provisions represented nothing less than Hammurabi's blueprint for the proper running and administering of a society.

After Hammurabi died around 1750 B.C., his son Samsuiluna inherited the kingdom but was barely able to keep order. One century later, Babylonia was no longer capable of repelling invaders. The Hittites were the first to maraud the area, followed by the Kassites, who settled there. It is not known where the stele of the Code of Hammurabi was sequestered during this time.

Babylon's demise came around 1160 B.C. when the truculent Elamites, led by King Shutruk-Nahhunte, initiated a series of military operations. The Elamites marched into the cities of Babylonia and slew hundreds, if not thousands, of people at a time. The most frequently used form of execution was impalement, although other macabre means such as burning

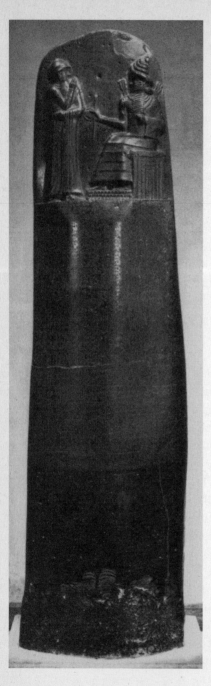

The Code of Hammurabi

or clubbing were undoubtedly employed. After pillaging and looting, the Elamites eventually returned to their capital in Susa with the Babylonian statue of Marduk (the god of Babylonia) and other famous Mesopotamian sculptures including the victory stele of King Naram-Sin of Akkad and the Code of Hammurabi. In time, Babylonian resistance prevented the Elamites from ever fully conquering the region, and the statue of Marduk was finally returned as a symbol of good faith. The Elamites would not give up the Code of Hammurabi, however.

In accord with their practice of defacing inscriptions of captured monuments and etching on their own dedications, the Elamites obliterated some of the script on the code, but for some reason—perhaps because of the stele's warning that defacers would be cursed—a new inscription was never written. The monumental stone pillar, which required great labors in its making and presumably in its transport, was placed in a temple in Susa, where it was certain to have been treasured. After the Elamite civilization declined several hundred years later, the last traces of reference to the code were lost.

In early 1902 French archaeologists excavating in Iran around the site of the old Elam capital of Susa discovered a cache of artifacts, one of the greatest of which was the stele bearing the Code of Hammurabi. The code not only offered a revealing portrait of the righteous king but also provided invaluable insight into the law and culture of Babylonia, one of the oldest civilizations of recorded history.

LOCATION:　The Louvre Museum, Paris, France.

The Contents of King Tutankhamen's Tomb

DATE: Circa 1352 B.C.

WHAT IT IS: The contents of the burial chambers of the ancient Egyptian boy-king Tutankhamen.

WHAT IT LOOKS LIKE: The cache of royal burial treasures found in the antechamber, annex, sepulchral chamber, treasury, and corridors includes the king's gold mask, golden throne, couches, royal robes, golden shrine, wishing cup, perfume vases, necklaces, decorative pectoral, gold pendants, alabaster vases, caskets, chests, stools, chairs, hassocks, weapons, chariots, statues, figurines, faience cups, corselets, sandals, ornate sticks, whips, bows, gloves, fruit baskets, model boats, paintings, boomerangs, and games.

Were it not for the pertinacity and dogged detective work of archaeologist Howard Carter, one of ancient Egypt's greatest treasures might still be buried. Carter's fellow archaeologists had for years scoffed at his conviction that one or more of the sepulchres of the dynastic pharaohs located in the Valley of the Kings might remain chaste and undiscovered. But Carter was convinced that none of the previously discovered tombs was that of King Tut, and that he must still slumber somewhere beneath the mounds and rubble of the plundered valley.

It had been the practice of ancient Egyptian pharaohs to be buried in royal tombs with the bulk of their resplendent earthly belongings to ensure safe passage to, and well-being in, the afterworld. Elaborate measures were taken to fortify their death chambers and protect them from grave robbers bold enough to risk the vengeance of the spirits. Burial galleries were mined in secrecy, false passages constructed, rubble piled floor-to-ceiling against the ponderous doors to the burial chambers, interior rooms bolted shut, and statues of feared animal-gods placed to guard the doors. Over time, however, the royal treasures fell prey to determined plunderers. Tomb robbers would raid at night, tunneling by the light of a flickering candle while sentries stood guard at the entrance.

Eventually, virtually all the kings' tombs were foraged. But the tomb of Tutankhamen, a king who at the age of nine or ten began a reign that was to last nine years, somehow managed to elude the most skillful poachers. Tut's tomb even remained undetected by the hermits and bandits who in later centuries sought shelter and refuge in the royal necropolis, and later by scientists employing modern devices and techniques.

The existence of Tutankhamen had been unequivocally established, but his tomb and mummy had never been conclusively documented, as had been done for the other pharaohs. In the early 1800s such famed archaeologists as the Italian Giovanni Battista Belzoni and the German Karl Richard Lepsius surveyed the valley, cleared whatever tombs still lay untouched, and pronounced the area exhausted. In the early 1900s, however, Theodore Davis, an American, received permission to explore the valley and spent many seasons digging. Some tombs were found, including those of Yuya and Thuya, ancestors of Tutankhamen's wife. Davis declared the boy-king mystery solved when he found a small vault containing relics inscribed with the names of Tutankhamen and his queen. Satisfied that he had found Tut's tomb, Davis terminated his concession from the Egyptian government to excavate the valley.

Howard Carter, who had long been interested in King Tutankhamen, questioned Davis's claim. Few archaeologists of the day were more qualified than Carter to take such a position and—as it turned out—to undertake a painstaking search to find Tut's royal subterranean graveyard.

Born in Norfolk, England, in 1873, Carter received his initiation into archaeology at an early age. When he was seventeen, he worked in Egypt as a draftsman for the Archaeological Survey of Egypt. The next year, he trained in excavating under the renowned archaeologist Flinders Petrie. By the time he was thirty, Carter had a command of the Arabic language and had excavated extensively in Egypt. His career came to an abrupt halt in the early 1900s, however, when, as an inspector in the Egyptian government's antiquities department, he became embroiled in an altercation involving some belligerent tourists and, believing he had acted properly, refused to render an apology. Carter was fired from his job and slunk into early retirement.

At about the same time that Carter's professional career in archaeology was coming to an end, an aristocratic Englishman's interest in the subject was starting to blossom. Respiratory problems forced Lord Carnarvon, born George Edward Stanhope Molyneux Herbert, son of the fourth earl of Carnarvon, to seek refuge from England's harsh winters in a more salubrious climate, and for that he chose Egypt. There he developed an interest in archaeology that bloomed into a full passion for digging for and collecting Egyptian antiquities. Lord Carnarvon was but an amateur in excavating, however, and if he was going to take his interest seriously, he needed the help of a professional. A friend suggested he solicit Howard Carter, and in 1907 the two joined forces, Lord Carnarvon providing the money, Carter the expertise.

The collaboration resulted in the discoveries of many tombs, including that of King Amenophis I. Three years after the two began working together, the concession rights to the Valley of the Kings passed to Lord Carnarvon and Howard Carter.

Although Theodore Davis asserted that the valley had been emptied, Carter thought otherwise. The cramped pit that Davis uncovered would have been an unfit sepulchre for an Egyptian pharaoh, and having explored the area, Carter believed there were sections that had escaped thorough investigation.

Although King Tutankhamen came into power at a very young age, he did indeed preside over a nation as a ruler in the Eighteenth Dynasty of Pharaohs. He became pharaoh by familial succession, through his marriage to the third daughter of King Akhenaton. After the king died in 1362 B.C., Tutankhaton, as he was known as a prince, succeeded him. The new king and queen were both about nine or ten years old. Tutankhamen ruled unremarkably until his death, nine years later, at the age of eighteen (he reigned from 1361 to 1352 B.C.) and would have been to modern society an obscure pharaoh but for two factors: his tomb, though pillaged shortly after his death, escaped wholesale liquidation by later plunderers; and Howard Carter, in the twentieth century, held to the belief that Tut's tomb lay undiscovered.

Carter was convinced that the Valley of the Kings, near Luxor, must indeed be the burial site of King Tut, since a nest of shattered pottery and linen found there that had been dismissed by Davis was later found to bear Tutankhamen's name. Believing that the burial chambers of King Tut lay around the middle of the valley, Carter began planning his excavation, only to be interrupted by World War I.

Digging began after the war but bore no fruit after six seasons. Carter felt work should continue as long as there was land that remained unexcavated. "It is true that you may find less in more time in The Valley than in any other site in Egypt," he wrote in *The Tomb of Tut-Ankh-Amen*, his account of the search cowritten with A. C. Mace, "but, on the other hand, if a lucky strike be made, you will be repaid for years and years of dull and unprofitable work." Although he continued excavating, coming up empty after six seasons had left him depressed and discouraged. "We had almost made up our minds that we were beaten, and were preparing to leave The Valley and try our luck elsewhere; and then—hardly had we set hoe to ground in our last despairing effort than we made a discovery that far exceeded our wildest dreams."

The digging had halted the previous season by the northeast corner of Ramses VI's tomb. This time Carter directed his men to excavate south. The area they would come upon, Carter recalled, had ancient huts; these were typically used by a pharaoh's laborers when building a tomb and could mean a tomb was nearby.

On the morning of November 4, 1922, Carter reported to the excavation site. He was immediately struck by the silence. Where were the clamoring of hammers and the chattering of human voices? Carter was told that the workmen had ceased activity earlier when a step cut had been discovered beneath an ancient hut. Further digging revealed a stairway and, as the thrilling possibilities ran through the minds of all present, a large corridor was found to lead to a sealed doorway. Carter bored a hole through the door, put in a flare, and observed stones piled ceiling-high. This subterranean necropolis was chaste!

Carter summoned Lord Carnarvon in England to join him for the

Howard Carter, left, and A. C. Mace at the closed entrance to Tutankhamen's burial chamber.

entering of what appeared to be Tut's royal tomb. As he waited a fort-
night for his arrival, word about the possibility spread, and soon people's
attention everywhere was fixed on the Valley of the Kings.

After Carnarvon arrived in Egypt, workmen began clearing the stones
beyond the sealed door. They cleared a passageway and, on the afternoon
of the twenty-sixth of November 1922, found another sealed door. Royal
cachets on this door revealed it was indeed the tomb of Tutankhamen.
What lay beyond the door? With Carnarvon, Carnarvon's daughter, and
workmen behind him, Carter, shaking with excitement, made a hole.
Then he introduced a light into the blackness. Let Carter tell you what he
saw: "At first I could see nothing, the hot air escaping from the chamber
causing the candle flame to flicker, but presently, as my eyes grew accustomed to the light, details of the room within emerged slowly from the
mist, strange animals, statues, and gold—everywhere the glint of gold."
Carter and the others became the first human beings in three thousand
years to enter King Tutankhamen's royal gallery, uncovering the richest
archaeological find in modern history.

Over the next few months, they found priceless ancient treasures. But
they were also reluctant to violate sacred rooms that had seen no living
human for three millennia. Those present have recorded their palpable
sense of fear in passing through the sealed door to the burial room, which
reached its highest pitch as they raised the lid of King Tut's sarcophagus.

The searchers found Tutankhamen's mummy (which is still in his tomb
in the Valley of the Kings at Luxor) and the mummies of two babies (Museum of the Faculty of Medicine, Cairo University). Carter also found
fruit, grains, and honey in the tomb.

Much of ancient Egyptian life was based on superstition and idol worship; the society was organized around the constant need to placate
Egypt's fierce and wrathful gods. But after the exhumation of King Tut's
tomb, a sequence of tragic occurrences caused many to wonder if those
gods had been disturbed.

Only five months after the discovery, Lord Carnarvon, patron of the
expedition, had a bitter argument with Carter over the disposition of the
chamber's treasures. Carter demanded that they become possessions of
the Egyptian government. Lord Carnarvon, insisting that they be moved
to England, was then bitten on the cheek by a mosquito and died in Cairo
from the resulting infection. (An autopsy performed later on the mummy
revealed a similar insect bite in the same area of Tut's face.) Two strange
phenomena were observed at the precise moment of Carnarvon's death:

the lights in Cairo suddenly and inexplicably went dark, and Carnarvon's dog, back in England, had a howling fit and expired for no apparent reason.

A string of deaths ensued. A specialist in Egyptian antiquities in Paris who had inventoried the burial treasure suddenly died, then Carter's literary collaborator on the expedition, A. C. Mace of the Metropolitan Museum of Art in New York City. More inexplicable deaths of people connected to the expedition followed, as well as suicides and an assassination. The number of fatalities eventually surpassed two dozen.

Was the mummy cursed? To many, such a theory is preposterous. Sensationalized press reports and the public's thirst for incredible

The posthumous symbol of the ancient Egyptian boy-king.

and gruesome events are cited as the reasons for the propagation of tales of the mummy's curse.* Yet while the sequence of calamitous events surely seems uncanny to a reasonable mind, it must be considered that many of the protagonists and minor players did live out normal lives; Carter himself lived to the age of sixty-five.

Indeed, the fantastic notion of a curse should not supplant the incredible fact that an abundant treasure reposed intact and undisturbed through the ages in a sculpted subterranean time capsule as all history marched on, as civilizations took root, as wars were unleashed, as the

---

*In September 1993 an Italian medical investigator named Nicola De Paola announced that a poisonous microscopic fungus, whose germination in sealed ancient tombs is enabled by moisture and air that seep through narrow cracks of stone, may be responsible for the fatalities of those who mysteriously died after entering King Tutankhamen's tomb or coming into contact with mummies or other objects from it. But given the quantity of deaths ascribed to Tut's curse, as well as the decades that have passed since the victims' interments and the geographic diversity of their graves, conclusive proof that the fungus killed all the victims is unlikely.

course of human events in its plenary dramas unfolded. For today we have not just the personal possessions of an ancient forebear but the imposing, magnificent royal cache of a king who led a nation more than thirty-three hundred years ago—before Moses delivered the Israelites from Egyptian bondage and took them to the Promised Land, before David became the king of the united Hebrew nation of Judah and Israel, and long before the birth of Christ and the start of the common era.

LOCATION: Egyptian Museum, Cairo, Egypt.

The Black Obelisk

DATE: Circa 827 B.C.

WHAT IT IS: A magnificent biographical monument depicting battles and other events during the reign of Shalmaneser III, king of Assyria from 858 to 824 B.C. The structure adds credence to the Bible with its mention of Jehu, the Israelite king who is written about in 1 and 2 Kings of the Old Testament.

WHAT IT LOOKS LIKE: The four-sided obelisk is made of black limestone and measures almost 7 feet in length. There are 190 lines of cuneiform text, and on each side, five rows of relief sculptures (twenty panels in all).

The wrath of God was about to be unleashed.

According to biblical tradition, it was the middle of the ninth century B.C. in the kingdom of Israel, and sacrilege was rampant among the people. Jezebel, the wife of King Ahab, had introduced worship of the pagan god Baal during her husband's reign. The children of Israel had destroyed their altars, slain by sword all the prophets of the Lord (save the one hundred who had been hidden in the caves), and forsaken their covenant with the Lord.

Around 842 B.C., Elisha the prophet instructed a young student*

---

*The Bible literally refers to the student as the *son* of a prophet but that term is generally recognized by talmudic literature and Bible scholars to mean a student prophet. Furthermore, according to the Talmud, the student prophet was Jonah, of the well-known biblical whale story.

prophet to journey to Ramoth Gilead, find an army captain named Jehu, and anoint him king of Israel. The young man went and anointed Jehu, telling him the Lord had ordered him to strike the house of his master, Ahab, and avenge the blood of all the servants of the Lord slaughtered at the hands of Jezebel (2 Kings 9:7). Jehu told his men of the Lord's decree, and they immediately declared him king.

In the city of Jezreel, Joram, Ahab and Jezebel's son who had inherited the crown of Israel, was convalescing from wounds received in battle with the Aramaeans. Ahaziah, the king of Judah, was visiting with him. A tower watchman spotted Jehu's company of soldiers outside the city and alerted Joram, who sent a messenger to inquire if Jehu came in peace. When the messenger didn't return, Joram dispatched yet another, who also never returned. And so Joram and Ahaziah prepared their chariots and rode out to confront Jehu. When Joram asked if his mission was peaceful, Jehu responded that there could be no peace as long as the harlotries and witchcrafts of Joram's mother, Jezebel, were so bountiful.

Joram proclaimed to Ahaziah that this was treachery and dashed off in his chariot, but Jehu aimed his bow at him and shot with such force that the arrow went through his heart and came out the other side of his body. Jehu ordered his captain to cast Joram's corpse onto the field of Naboth. Naboth was an Israelite who refused to sell his vineyard to Ahab. In response Jezebel had spread lies that Naboth was sacrilegious, and he was killed. When Ahaziah saw Joram's remains on the field, he too tried to flee in his chariot but was shot by Jehu's men and later died at Megiddo. There was still more vengeance for the new king of Israel to take.

Jehu entered Jezreel and sought out Jezebel, whom he found at her window with her eyes painted and her head attired. Jezebel castigated Jehu for what he had done, but Jehu ignored her; he found several men in the royal residence who were on his side, and ordered them to throw Jezebel out the window. They did, and Jehu then rode his chariot over Jezebel, killing her. Before she could be buried, her corpse, in fulfillment of a prophecy, was eaten by dogs in the moat of Jezreel (1 Kings 21:23).

Jehu finished his commission from the Lord by slaughtering Ahab's seventy remaining sons, as well as all the friends and priests and wise men of the house of Ahab, whereupon he established himself as ruler. As a reward for having carried out what was right in the Lord's eyes, the Lord promised Jehu a dynasty of four generations. But in ruling Israel, Jehu never put a stop to the sacrilegious practices introduced by Jeroboam, the founder of the kingdom of Israel, and the people continued to sin.

Jehu's kingdom was threatened by the Aramaeans, neighbors in Damascus, so he obtained protection from the Assyrians, led by Shalmaneser III, by paying heavy tribute. Along with other events occurring during Shalmaneser III's reign, Jehu's obeisance was inscribed on a magnificent monument, which over the course of time became buried and lost.

Late October 1845, Mosul, Ottoman Empire (later part of modern Iraq). Having departed Constantinople by steamer and traversing mountains on foot and valleys and plains on horseback, Austen Henry Layard, a twenty-eight-year-old French-born Englishman, arrived at this city on the west bank of the Tigris. Layard was trained to be a barrister but submitted to a keener penchant for traveling and exploring archaeological ruins. Inspired by the Assyrian discoveries of the Frenchman Paul Emile Botta at Khorsabad, Layard secured limited funds from British diplomat Sir Stratford Canning to carry on excavations at the site of Nimrud, which he had long desired to do. On earlier journeys he had seen huge mounds in the deserts that seemed to promise the remains of ancient civilizations somewhere within their depths. Arab inhabitants of the land reported that in digging foundations for their homes they had unearthed many of the kinds of objects that Europeans came to search for so passionately. Proper excavation could yield dramatic results.

At that time the Ottoman Empire was in precipitous decline. Saved from conquest by Egypt some years earlier by a treaty prompted by international powers, the sultan embarked on a series of reforms. Yet deep within the empire, corruption among local officials was still viciously rampant, with marauding armies supplementing the terror the officials used to govern the people, or rather to extricate people's property at their whim. Just two years earlier Beder Khan Bey at Tryari Province slaughtered ten thousand men, women, and children.

At Mosul, Layard proffered letters of introduction from the British embassy at Constantinople to the governor, Mohammed Pasha, a disfigured tyrant who levied tariffs upon tribes of the territory to pay for the care of his teeth, decayed by the food he lowered himself to accept from them. It would have been dangerous for Layard to reveal the true nature of his mission; ostensibly he was there to hunt wild boars. The people were so terror-stricken by the pasha (the Turkish title for a governor) that the mere presence of a foreigner offered hope. But the pasha was cunning and mindful that a stranger could stir thoughts of rebellion within the souls of the discontented, and so in a test of their loyalty he feigned his own death. The pasha's reported passing was naturally cause for celebration by the inhabitants, who were oblivious to the pasha's moles around them. The pasha grinningly emerged in the broad light of day to the shock of the people and used the insult of their bliss over his reported passing to usurp property he somehow previously overlooked.

Such was the climate of politics and the oppressed conditions of the territory in which Layard traveled. On November 8 Layard and a small party, armed with an arsenal of weapons, ventured on a raft down the Tigris for Nimrud. Several hours later the group arrived at Naifa, a small village. It was dark, with little sign of life, when Layard spotted a flicker of light emanating from a wretched hut. The party quietly walked over, and Layard observed through a split in a wall a turbaned Arab with three women whose heads were covered with black handkerchiefs, naked children, and a couple of dogs.

When Layard introduced himself, the man, recognizing him as a European, was honest and forthright, telling him that the villagers, as a result of the pasha's pillaging, had dispersed. Layard took a liking to the man, obviously of intelligence, and offered him a job gathering and supervising a crew of men for excavating. The man in turn entertained Layard with tales about the buried ruins; it was here, for example, that the prophet Abraham shattered the idols, and when the heathen Nimrod sought to kill him, Abraham prayed to God for protection and asked not for his deliverance by armies, the mightiest of which Nimrod could cut down, but by a tiny creature. So God sent a gnat to Nimrod, which entered his ear and ate away at his brain for four centuries while his servants beat drums to mitigate the excruciating pain.

The next morning, Awad II, the host of Layard and his party, awakened Layard and presented six villagers for his crew. They walked to Nimrud, about a mile away, to the largest mound. Broken pottery abounded, and in the rubbish were all sorts of old fragments. Layard summoned the workers to start excavating, commencing the operations that could lead to the ancient city of Calah, capital of Assyria.

After several days, as a diplomatic move, Layard returned to Mosul to report on his findings to the pasha, who without a doubt had been spying on his excavations. Gossip of momentous finds was already circulating among the townspeople of Mosul, and Layard feared interruption of his work by the insatiable pasha. But that did not happen, and Layard suggested to the pasha that he have one of his soldiers represent him at the excavations.

Layard returned to Nimrud, where he increased his crew to thirty, consisting of both Arabs and the robust mountain-reared Chaldeans. Layard's excavations continued before the watchful eyes of a notorious band of hundreds of horsemen who plundered villages and sometimes did the dirty work of the pasha for remuneration and booty. Soon the pasha did attempt to stop the excavation under the pretense that Layard was disturbing ancient burial grounds, but Layard was able to prevail. The fires of his quest burned deeply inside him, and he would not allow bureaucracy and political prevarication to thwart him. He knew that the most marvelous finds were still ahead.

Several huge animal and human figures were uncovered, and it appeared that submerged deeper were even larger buildings. Layard notified Sir Stratford Canning about his findings and requested a decree from the Porte (the Ottoman government) to enable him to continue his work without further interruption. The week before Christmas Layard returned to Mosul and found the people there exultant; the pasha had been removed and replaced by a young and fair-minded general. Still, the country's turbulent political situation made further excavation impossible, and Layard traveled to Baghdad to arrange for the removal of the objects he had already uncovered.

Layard returned to Mosul early in 1846 and was happy to see that numerous reforms had been made by the new pasha. The population was increasing to former levels as villagers who had fled were returning. Excavation continued, and out of the rubble in deep pits came magnificently sculptured objects: huge winged bulls, human heads, lions with human heads, winged humans.

November 1846, Nimrud. After a blistering summer when 115-degree-plus temperatures even in the darkened confines of the trenches brought work to a halt, the excavation continued, and on a greater scale than before. Layard now employed numerous Arabs and dozens of Nestorian Chaldeans, with the benefit of assistance from their families. With armed guards and a communal system of living, it was a very sophisticated operation.

The mound—encompassing more than sixty acres—was by now di-

The Black Obelisk

vided into several alphabetically designated chambers. Inscribed slabs with interesting bas-reliefs were uncovered, as well as a pavement six feet below the rubble in one chamber.

Around the mound's middle, where huge bulls with wings had previously been found, Layard directed a search for a building whose entrance he believed the bulls guarded. A trench was cut and some large slabs with inscriptions were found, but no walls yet. The workers cut the trench deeper but with no results as the days passed on. Just as Layard was about to discontinue the search, one of the workers uncovered the corner of a column of marble. They quickly uncovered the rest of the object, and soon a black obelisk was fully exposed to view in the trench.

Layard didn't quite know what to make of this remarkable object. "From the nature, therefore, of the bas-reliefs," he wrote, "it is natural to conjecture that the monument was erected to commemorate the conquest of India, or of some other country far to the east of Assyria, and on the confines of the Indian peninsula. The name of the king, whose deeds it appears to record, is the same as that on the centre bulls; and it is introduced by a genealogical list containing many other royal names."

It would be up to scholars to decipher the approximately two hundred lines of inscriptions. Layard immediately copied the lines and the bas-reliefs and had a team of his most honest workers guard it when the camp was asleep.

By December a sufficient number of sculptures and objects had been collected to warrant another shipment to England. Early in the month, Layard traveled to Mosul to purchase materials to build another raft and securely pack the antiquities that were to be taken. He entrusted the transport of these skins, ropes, mats, felts, and other items to a team of Arabs who traveled with them by raft but camped at darkness so they could wait until daylight to cross a particular dam. A gang from a feared tribe sprang upon them during the night, beat them, and took their goods. When Layard heard of this, he went to the authorities, who said they could not help recover the materials from a desert tribe.

After some investigating over the course of a few days, Layard determined who the thieves were and took a few of his soldiers into the desert. The tribesmen gathered as the men rode into their camp, and Layard boldly entered the sheik's tent and asked for the return of the stolen items. While movements in other areas of the tent could be heard—obviously, Layard thought, a hasty attempt to conceal the swag—the sheik feigned ignorance of the matter. With a gesture to his formidable dragoon, Layard initiated a prearranged plan. The man grabbed the sheik and tied him to a horse, while Layard's other men held off the tribesmen with pistols. The sheik was dragged all the way to Nimrud, where he confessed to the plundering and sent a message to his people requesting the goods be returned, with some animals for goodwill. After another stern reprimand Layard discharged the sheik, who was to cause no further problems.

In mid-December the obelisk and several bas-reliefs were ready to be transported. Quite ponderous and capacious, they were taken to the river courtesy of the pasha's heavy buffalo carts. Soon twenty-three cases of the ancient objects were on their way by raft, leaving the area where they had been made long, long ago.

Layard's satisfaction at rendering these antiquities to his sponsors in England was a bit premature, unfortunately. From Baghdad they were sent to a port city, where they remained for a year before a vessel came to take them. Then they were shipped to Bombay, where an English editor and inspector of laboratories exhibited them before the public. In April 1848 they were placed on another boat. Almost six months later they arrived in England, where they were greeted by Layard himself. More than a year later, decipherings of the cryptic message of the obelisk poured in, beginning with that of Edward Hincks, the rector of Killyleagh and an Orientalist, and the famous Assyriologist Henry Creswicke Rawlinson. (Hincks and Rawlinson deciphered the vowel system of Persian cuneiform.)

Recorded on the obelisk were important events of the reign of the Assyrian ruler Shalmaneser III. The inscription recounts operations of the Assyrian army and tells about tributes paid to the king by leaders from other nations. There are pictorial renderings of people carrying gifts and bowing down before the king. There are illustrations of various kinds of animals given to the king. And there is a description of Jehu, the same Israelite king of the Old Testament, offering precious metals and other valuable objects to Shalmaneser.

Approximately twenty-seven hundred years after Shalmaneser III's scribes documented his reign, it became public information for the ages and made a most valuable addition to the garland of biblical antiquities.

LOCATION: British Museum, London, England.

The Siloam Inscription

DATE: Circa 700 B.C.

WHAT IT IS: A stone inscribed in Hebrew from Hezekiah's water tunnel in Jerusalem describing how the tunnel was cut. According to the Bible, the subterranean conduit was hewn through solid rock to channel water into the city when its external water source faced being blocked off by the advancing Assyrian armies of Sennacherib.

WHAT IT LOOKS LIKE: The stone is somewhat rectangular and bears six lines of inscription.

And when Hezekiah saw that Sennacherib was come, and that he was purposed to fight against Jerusalem, he took counsel with his princes and his mighty men to stop the waters of the fountains which were without the city; and they helped him . . . and they stopped all the fountains, and the brook that flowed together through the midst of the land, saying: "Why should the kings of Assyria come, and find much water?"

—2 Chronicles 32:2–4

The attack was imminent. The Assyrians were on the rampage, determined to crush Jerusalem after the recalcitrant King Hezekiah boldly terminated his country's subservience to the mightier pagan empire. Knowing his forces were no match for his tyrannical enemy, Hezekiah desperately needed a stratagem to save his city, his people.

The basic facts of this historical episode are as follows: At one time Israel was a united kingdom made up of twelve tribes. But under the heavy-handed leadership of Rehoboam, King Solomon's son, ten tribes seceded, forming the northern kingdom known as Israel. Two tribes, those of Judah and Benjamin, remained in the south, forming the kingdom of Judah. Hezekiah was the thirteenth king of Judah.

After the split, the separate kingdoms of Israel to the north and Judah to the south were both besieged by the powerful Assyrians, led by Sennacherib. Israel fell first, shortly before 720 B.C., but Judah, brought under Assyrian control, refused to yield completely.

For years, Judah was essentially a satellite nation, with King Ahaz, Hezekiah's father, paying tribute to the Assyrians. This practice began after Ahaz appealed to Assyria for protection against Israel and Aram (Syria), who were threatening Judah with military invasion. Ahaz's appeal for protection to the king of Assyria brought upon him an obligation to present tribute in the form of considerable amounts of gold and silver.

When Ahaz died and Hezekiah became ruler, the son refused to follow in the ways of his irreverent and ignoble father. He wanted to eliminate Assyrian control and join Israel and Judah in a single independent state once again. Hezekiah destroyed the Assyrian altars and invited all Israel and Judah to come to Jerusalem to the house of the Lord, the God of Israel, to celebrate Passover: "Ye children of Israel, turn back unto the Lord, the God of Abraham, Isaac, and Israel, that He may return to the remnant that are escaped of you out of the hand of the kings of Assyria" (2 Chronicles 30:6).

Hezekiah became deathly ill and was told by Isaiah the prophet that he would die. Hezekiah then prayed to the Lord, weeping bitterly. The Lord told Isaiah the king's prayer was heard, and that he would heal Hezekiah, and more: "And I will add unto thy days fifteen years; and I will deliver thee and this city out of the hand of the king of Assyria" (2 Kings 20:6).

Sennacherib began his assault on Judah by methodically overtaking the cities in the kingdom. It was an Assyrian tactic to conquer a city by cutting off its food and water resources, and it worked quite well. Now before the fortress city of Lachish, King Sennacherib dispatched servants to Jerusalem to urge its inhabitants not to let Hezekiah persuade them "to die by famine and thirst" with the promise that the Lord would deliver the people from the Assyrians.

To prepare Jerusalem for Sennacherib's attack, Hezekiah fortified the city and armed his soldiers with new weapons. He also prepared for the Assyrian food impedance by storing large amounts of grain within the city walls. But how could he stop the Assyrians from cutting off the water supply? Nothing short of rearranging nature would save the inhabitants of Jerusalem.

Enacting a bold strategy to prevent Sennacherib's armies from cutting off Jerusalem's water supply, Hezekiah stopped up the fountains outside the walls and had two teams of men, one at the Gihon Spring, which lay east of Jerusalem, the other at the Siloam Pool, inside the city walls, dig underground toward one another. Once they were connected, water could be piped into the city, and the spring could be obstructed from view by stones and rubble. Meanwhile, the warring Assyrians would be stopping up the old canal, thinking the city's inhabitants would eventually capitulate before they died of dehydration. But the people would actually be enjoying an unending supply of water channeled underground: "He made the pool and the conduit and brought water into the city" (2 Kings 20:20).

Now, putting the scriptures aside, we move to A.D. 1838, when the first serious investigation of an amazing man-made, rock-cut underground canal in the Holy Land commenced. The tunnel, running from the Gihon Spring to the Siloam Pool in Jerusalem, had been known of since at least the seventeenth century and was considered highly intriguing, but no serious study had been made of it. American biblical scholar Edward Robinson, a forty-four-year-old professor at Union Theological Seminary, decided to measure the tunnel to get a precise picture of ancient engineering principles. Entering at the pool, where the tunnel's height reached twenty feet, Robinson and a companion began traversing the dark, wet passageway shoeless and by candlelight. About eight hundred feet through the black corridor, the tunnel ceiling became so low that the only way to move was on hands and knees. They were not prepared for this type of exploration, so with their clothes wet and muddy, they marked the spot where they had stopped and returned outside.

When Robinson and his companion continued their exploration three days later, they entered the tunnel from the Gihon side. At certain points the opening was so small that they could move forward only by propelling themselves prostrate with arms and feet. They forded winding passages until they came to the spot they had marked at the time they had entered on the opposite side.

Robinson made some peculiar observations. Above the surface, the two ends of the tunnel were 1,200 feet directly apart. But by Robinson's measurements, the underground passage was about 1,750 feet long. The extra footage was the result of the winding nature of the passage—there was

The Gihon Spring

The Siloam Pool, into which water flowed from the Gihon Spring via the Siloam tunnel.

also an S-shaped curve as the two passageways converged—but why did the hewers cut through this way? They would have been perfectly capable of cutting in a direct line, which certainly would have been more expedient, especially in light of Sennacherib's impending attack. No definitive answer has ever been given for this, although explanations that the workmen were following rock faults or trying to avoid hitting the tombs of embedded kings have been offered.

Robinson also observed chisel marks going in opposite directions at the opposite ends of the tunnel. This led him to conclude that the tunnel was not quarried straight through at one end but dug by two separate teams who had begun at opposite ends and were working toward each other.

In the world of archaeology, the keen eyes of professional explorers occasionally miss significant artifacts—sometimes owing to happenstance, other times to the random forces of nature shielding the reposing treasures—and their discovery is eventually made by unwitting civilians.

One day in 1880 some children were wading in the Siloam Pool when one ventured into the canal and fell. Touching the wall as he clambered to his feet, he felt some unusual impressions. They looked like writing. When he got out he reported what he had found, and his discovery immediately became a source of great interest. A scholar copied the inscription and made a cast of it. There were six lines. Enough of the original text remained to learn its raison d'être. The inscription had been made to commemorate the jubilation that two teams, cleaving the tunnel from opposite ends, had felt when they finally cut through to each other. It is translated thus in *The Ancient Near East: An Anthology of Texts and Pictures*, edited by James B. Pritchard:

> [. . . when] (the tunnel) was driven through. And this was the way in which it was cut through:—While [. . .] (were) still [. . .] axe(s), each man toward his fellow, and while there were still three cubits to be cut through, [there was heard] the voice of a man calling to his fellow, for there was *an overlap* in the rock on the right [and on the left]. And when the tunnel was driven through, the quarrymen hewed (the rock), each man toward his fellow, axe against axe; and the water flowed from the spring toward the reservoir for 1,200 cubits, and the height of the rock above the head(s) of the quarrymen was 100 cubits.

The inscription was confirmed to be in old Hebrew. Its characters belonged to a Semitic alphabet also used by the Phoenicians and Moabites. Not only was it a superb example of ancient Hebrew writing, but it is the oldest known example of Hebrew writing save the Gezer Calendar, which predates it by about a couple of centuries.

From the writing, scholars were able to determine that the inscription was in fact made about the time Hezekiah was king of Judah. That it was found in a water tunnel appears to support the biblical passages about King Hezekiah building a pool and a conduit to bring the waters of the Gihon Spring down into the city.

There was one odd thing about the inscription on the tunnel wall: its location. Instead of being roughly halfway between the two end points, the writing was engraved near the tunnel's Siloam entrance.

In 1890, after it had lain undisturbed for centuries, a plunderer cut the rock bearing the ancient engraving from the tunnel. It was later found in Jerusalem in the possession of a Greek, broken into sections. Turkish officers, who occupied the land at the time, seized the damaged relic and dispatched it to a museum in their country.

Returning to the Old Testament: Sennacherib was on his way with a

The Siloam Inscription. Ancient quarrymen probably never imagined their subterranean wall memorial engraving would endure for thousands of years.

huge Assyrian army to annihilate ancient Jerusalem. But the Lord would not permit it to happen, saying he would defend the city for his sake and his servant David's: "And it came to pass that night, that the angel of the Lord went forth, and smote in the camp of the Assyrians a hundred fourscore and five thousand [185,000] men; and when men arose early in the morning, behold, they were all dead corpses" (2 Kings 19:35). Sennacherib departed and never returned, and Jerusalem, for the time being at least, was saved, as was the tunnel and its glorious inscription.

LOCATION: Archaeological Museum, Istanbul, Turkey.

The Rosetta Stone

DATE: 196 B.C.

WHAT IT IS: A stone tablet bearing three inscriptions in two languages. It became the key for unlocking the lost language of hieroglyphs and provided a portal to the ancient world of Egypt.

WHAT IT LOOKS LIKE: It is a black basalt slab that measures almost 45 inches in height, 28½ inches in width, and 11 inches in thickness. Its weight is estimated to be 1,676 pounds. It is largely but not wholly intact, with portions of the upper left, upper right, and lower right missing.

In the final years of the eighteenth century, France had a new hero, a young warrior who had demonstrated military virtuosity leading conquests in Italy. Now at home and restless, Napoleon Bonaparte was seeking another campaign. He wanted further to secure the support of his compatriots but was also wary of his own personal safety. France was in the hands of a corrupt government, the Directory, and conspiracies abounded.

Napoleon wanted to strike at France's great enemy, England. A direct attack on the island would be futile, however, for the English navy was far superior to France's. Where to land a blow against England? Egypt.

Napoleon believed that English trade, which encroached upon French merchants, would be disrupted. In addition, Egypt, which was part of the Ottoman Empire, could provide a strategic point from which to attack England's prized colony, India (the British governor of India had just signed a trade treaty with the beys, or local governors, in Egypt).

With the approval of the Directory—which quietly hoped the campaign would cause the demise of this potential usurper of power—Napoleon prepared for this complex venture. As he pondered the destiny of his military machinations, he could not have imagined that the expedition would yield this by-product: a priceless treasure discovered by the French, which, in one of the great ironies of archaeology, would be whisked away by the enemy with nary a drop of blood spilled, as exasperated French soldiers looked on helplessly.

Shortly after sunrise on May 19, 1798, several hundred French warships sailed out of Toulon. More than fifty thousand soldiers embarked on the voyage, along with hundreds of horses. On board the vessels also was the Commission of Science and Art, an elite corps of engineers, geologists, antiquarians, mathematicians, and poets, handpicked by Napoleon to conduct an exhaustive survey of the historical and mysterious land of Egypt, as well as to edify its impoverished citizens.

On July 1, 1798, in the darkness of the early morning hours, several thousand French soldiers disembarked at Marabout, eight miles west of Alexandria, and on the following day, July 2, stormed the port city. On the way to Cairo, near the pyramids, the French encountered thousands of Mamelukes, a renowned Egyptian cavalry of professionally trained soldiers, awaiting them.

Before going into battle, Napoleon rode his horse through the ranks of his men, standing at attention in the golden sand as the blistering sun beat down on them. After scrutinizing his troops, the general pointed to the ancient structures, weather-beaten but resplendent in the near distance, and issued his famous declaration: "Soldiers, from the heights of the pyramids, forty centuries are looking down on you." The French, outnumbered but better equipped than their foe, cut down the Mamelukes. Napoleon continued to sweep through Egypt, rejoicing in victory, until Vice Admiral Horatio Nelson destroyed the French fleet in the Mediterranean in the Battle of the Nile.

Trapped in the northeast African land, the soldiers worked to fortify their positions, and Napoleon's band of savants toiled assiduously on a variety of projects. Despite the long history of Egypt, little was actually known about the area, and the French civilians set themselves to investigating its resources scientifically.

In August 1799, just over a year after Napoleon launched his invasion of Egypt at Alexandria, a great discovery was made. French soldiers were building up their defenses around the area of Fort St. Julien, near the northern city of Rosetta, or Rashid (which is near the mouth of the western branch of the Nile), when a soldier or engineer found in the ruins an ancient stone. With its cryptic inscriptions, it was immediately recognized as an object of great importance. It was sent to Cairo, where it was housed in the Institut d'Egypte. Members of Napoleon's special civilian corps dispersed around the country were requested to go there at once. Perhaps this mysterious stone held great secrets of the distant past.

On the stone were three parallel inscriptions. The top two, hieroglyphic and demotic (a form of cursive writing), were in the Egyptian language; the bottom one was Greek. Although the number of lines of each inscription varied, increasing in each section going down the stone, the three sections of inscriptions were roughly the same size. Could they bear the same message? Greek was known, but hieroglyphs had fallen into oblivion some thirteen centuries earlier. Scholars hoped the Greek could be used as the basis to translate the hieroglyphs. An alphabet and grammar could be established, and the meaning of hieroglyphic inscriptions on other antiquities could finally be derived. The ramifications were astounding. Great secrets of the past and new stories of the Bible would be unraveled, all by virtue of this single stone!

Intense excitement about the stone swiftly traveled to Europe. Napoleon himself saw the "Pierre de Rosette," as the French called it, and marveled. Two printers, Marc Aurel and Jean Joseph Marcel, made impressions, and a member of the Commission of Science and Art made casts—all for distribution to scholars in Europe.

Although all the lines of the Greek (as well as the other inscriptions) exhibited some damage, the Greek text on the stone was readily translated. The stone was presumably one of several that had been inscribed following an assembly of priests at Memphis around 200 B.C. The priests had passed a decree on the ninth anniversary of the reign of Ptolemy V Epiphanes, who had succeeded his father as king. Under the decree, recorded in the inscription, the deeds that Ptolemy, not yet thirteen but ruling under the tutelage of wise counselors, had performed during his reign to bring prosperity to Egypt were to be "inscribed upon stelae of hard stone in holy, and native, and Greek characters and set up in each of the temples of the first, second and third class close to the image of the King." The benefactions of Ptolemy V included adorning and repairing temples, freeing prisoners, stopping impressment into the navy, using a system of equal justice, preventing floods by building dams, and destroying impious individuals.

The initial high hopes that the Rosetta Stone would be a long-awaited key to ancient languages were thwarted for some time. Because some portions of the stone were missing, translating the hieroglyphic and demotic texts by comparing them with the Greek would be difficult. It was still not certain that the three texts bore the same message. Hieroglyphic, or pictorial, script was the most ancient form of Egyptian writing. It was usually chiseled into stone. As papyrus came to be used as the writing medium, it was succeeded by other forms of writing: hieratic, a cursive form, which eventually led to demotic, a simpler cursive form.

Efforts to unravel the philological mystery of ancient Egyptian writing did not begin with the discovery of the Rosetta Stone. Since the sixteenth century, scholars had made dedicated attempts to decipher hieroglyphs. The German Jesuit Anthonasius Kircher, the English bishop William Warburton, and the French scholar Nicolas Freret were among the most prominent early Egyptologists. Because of the mistakenly held view that hieroglyphs were simply and purely a system of picture writing, however, they came up with rather far-fetched translations.

Hieroglyphic writing, which consists of various kinds of symbols, strained the minds of the Egyptologists. Some pictures were apparent, like those of animals, but others, having strange shapes, were mysterious and unknown. Furthermore, for the familiar pictures or symbols, were their meanings what they seemed to be?

Did a single symbol express a simple thought? Or could several symbols represent a single idea? In which direction were the characters read? By what logic did the ancient scribes set down symbols to express their thoughts and ideas?

One of the first to take up the challenge of deciphering the demotic inscription of the Rosetta Stone was a renowned Orientalist, Antoine Isaac Silvestre de Sacy of France. He uncovered some proper names mentioned in the text. Later, in 1802, the Swedish scholar Johan David Acherblad identified more names, as well as some Coptic-style words. Acherblad's findings ended here; the words he identified were alphabetical, and he held the view that demotic writing was purely alphabetical. This view would eventually be shown to be false, but a complete translation of the demotic inscription wouldn't be made public for about half a century.

The enigmatic stone reposed quietly for years in the British Museum—how it got there is a process we shall return to in a moment—while the general public continued to speculate on the substance of its inscrutable hieroglyphic writing, and scholars labored assiduously to break the code. The first breakthrough came around 1816 from a British physicist and medical doctor who had been examining a copy of the Rosetta Stone.

Thomas Young advanced the idea that hieroglyphic characters could have a phonetic value—that is, the symbols represented sounds of the language. This was not a novel idea but one of which he may not have previously been aware, and he made a convincing argument for it. It was commonly believed that in hieroglyphic writing the elliptical figures in which symbols were enclosed, called cartouches, represented royal names. Young attempted to identify the phonetic value of the symbols in the single cartouche that appears several times in the hieroglyphs of the Rosetta, which he believed to signify the name Ptolemy, and successfully identified several of them.

It wasn't until the French scholar Jean-François Champollion set himself to the task of deciphering the Rosetta Stone that the riddle of hieroglyphs was finally solved. Champollion had developed a zealous interest in Egyptology as a student. When he was seventeen he studied Oriental languages in Paris and started compiling a Coptic dictionary, which he maintained was a later form of the Egyptian language using Greek characters. In 1812, at the age of twenty-two, he was made a professor.

Using Young's work, his own knowledge of the Coptic language, and other hieroglyphic inscriptions, Champollion was able to determine the phonetic values of other hieroglyphic characters and decipher other royal names. Champollion determined that in a cartouche certain symbols represented one or two different letters and that a particular symbol was used after a female name. The value of unknown symbols in the cartouches of royal names could be deduced with accuracy by guessing their Greek letter equivalent.

Champollion concluded that the ancient Egyptian language had three forms—hieroglyphic, hieratic, and demotic—and that hieroglyphs were not just symbols signifying ideas but phonetic as well. His assertions were published in 1822 in his *Lettre à M. Dacier, relative à l'alphabet des hiéroglyphes phonétiques*. Champollion's remarkable accomplishment, made with only fourteen incomplete lines of hieroglyphs on the Rosetta Stone, opened the alphabet of ancient Egypt and all the hieroglyphic writings of the people.

In early 1799, after more than half a year in Egypt, Napoleon faced a great military challenge. A massive Turkish army had gathered in Syria, preparing to seize control of Egypt from France. Confronting Turkey's army was something Napoleon wanted to avoid; in fact, a precondition of his Egyptian campaign was to secure a promise from the French minister of foreign affairs, Charles Maurice de Talleyrand-Périgord, to go to Turkey and negotiate peaceful relations between the two countries. But Talleyrand deceived him, and Napoleon was forced to confront this dire situation.

In an effort to thwart the Turkish invasion, Napoleon led thousands of French soldiers to the Turks. On his way to Acre the French defeated contingents at El 'Arish, Gaza, and Jaffa. At Acre awaited tens of thousands of Turkish soldiers whose ranks were supplemented by English troops. The Turks repelled the French advance and forced Napoleon to retreat. Eight thousand French soldiers began the trek back through the Sinai Desert. Healthy soldiers carried sick ones, many so ravaged by the plague that Napoleon wanted them euthanized with opium, although the expedition's surgeon objected. Shortly after, the Turks invaded Aboukir by sea, but in a fierce battle they were defeated by the French.

With sweeping changes now taking place in Europe—several countries had declared war on France, and France itself was in a desperate state of affairs—and Egypt now a dead-end stop, Napoleon decided to return home. In August 1799 he quietly boarded the *Muiron*, not even conferring with General Jean-Baptiste Kléber, who would assume control of the French army in Egypt after he left. The *Muiron* and another ship managed to slip through the British men-of-war, setting the stage for sweeping changes in French history.

As Napoleon, who had been greeted upon his arrival with hysterical cheers, led a coup d'état to expel the Directory, the English and Turks mounted assaults on the French that were to end their occupation in Egypt. During the siege, the Rosetta Stone was transported from Cairo to Alexandria to prevent the British from seizing it. But under the terms of the Alexandria capitulation treaty, in which the French surrendered to the British, the French in that city were forced to turn over the antiquities they had collected in Egypt. The Rosetta Stone, the prized French discovery, had by now caused a sensation throughout Europe and was, needless to say, coveted by the English.

The French at first refused to deliver the antiquities, but then relented. General J. F. Menou, who had the stone carefully preserved in his house, wrote the following to the British lieutenant-colonel Christopher Hely-Hutchinson: "You want it Monsieur le général? You can have it since you are the stronger of us two—. You may pick it up whenever you please."

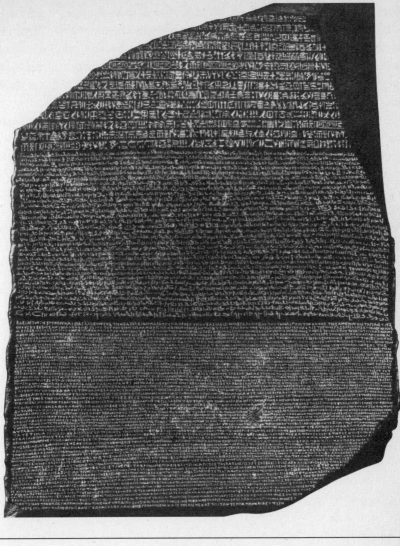

The Rosetta Stone

In September 1801 English brevet colonel Tomkyns Hilgrove Turner, who had fought at Aboukir Bay and Alexandria, went to visit Menou to procure the stone. Turner cited the sixteenth article of the treaty, and General Menou handed it over grudgingly.

A squad of artillerymen seized the stone without resistance. As they carted the magnificent ancient treasure through Alexandria, French soldiers and civilians collected on the streets and sputtered insults at them.

In the spasmodic voyage from Egypt to England, many of the Egyptian antiquities were damaged. Because of the importance of the Rosetta Stone, however, Colonel Turner personally accompanied this precious cargo on its journey aboard a frigate. The Rosetta Stone left Egypt from Alexandria and sailed into the English Channel in February 1802.

At Deptford the stone was placed in a small boat and taken through customs. It was lodged at the quarters of the Society of Antiquaries so it could be examined by experts before being dispatched to its permanent station of public exhibition, where, Turner later wrote, "I trust it will long remain, a most valuable relic of antiquity, the feeble but only yet discovered link of the Egyptian to the known languages, a proud trophy of the arms of Britain (I could almost say *spolia opima*), not plundered from defenceless inhabitants, but honourably acquired by the fortune of war."

LOCATION: British Museum, London, England.

The Portland Vase

DATE: Circa the end of the first century B.C. to the beginning of the first century A.D.

WHAT IT IS: A glass amphora made during the rule of the first Roman emperor, Augustus Caesar. It is one of the most famous artistic glass vessels ever created.

WHAT IT LOOKS LIKE: The vase has a cobalt blue background with opaque white human and imaginative figures and objects cut in a cameo relief. It is almost 10 inches high.

Around the start of the common era, the greatest craftsmen of ancient Rome toiled hard in their workshop to create a magnificent glass vase embodying serene scenes of white figures and objects against a striking dark blue background. It is probably safe to say that these artisans could hardly have imagined that this fragile vessel would survive thousands of years into the future, be owned by a succession of distinguished people, be smashed into hundreds of pieces on more than one occasion and painstakingly restored to almost its original splendor, and be assiduously studied for centuries by scholars trying to determine its original utilitarian purpose and the perplexing meaning of its idyllic scenes. Yet these events are all part of the extraordinary heritage of the so-called Portland Vase, which, for all its beauty and grandeur, remains today an artistic mystery of the ages.

The technology of glassmaking began somewhere in the Near East twenty-five hundred to three thousand years before the start of the common era, advancing from all-glass beads and rods to intricately made decorative vessels by Augustus's time. Early craftsmen discovered a few ways to combine the basic ingredients of sand, soda, lime, silica, and wood fuel into glass, but it wasn't until glassblowing was invented around 50 B.C. that production developed into a fine art.

With glassblowing, glassmakers could shape objects artistically, and production was less expensive. Other techniques such as painting and making clear glass (because of impurities, glass in ancient times was normally colored) enabled artisans to produce many marvelous pieces. Perhaps the most famous of these is the Portland Vase.

The Portland Vase is an example of glass sculpted in cameo style. It was probably made by taking a gather of cobalt blue glass and partially dipping it into a crucible of molten white glass before blowing and fashioning the whole into the desired shape. The outlines of the design were no doubt incised first, before all the background white glass was carved away and the figures and motifs modeled in detail. The result was a design of white figures and objects against a dark blue background.

Around the Portland Vase are pictured two basic scenes, each about half the circumference of the vessel's body. One scene features a foreground of a man and a woman resting on long, flat slabs of stone to the left and a woman sitting upright on a narrow pile of flat stone slabs to the right. The man is naked, although one end of a garment hangs by his left leg and his hands hold different points of the garment. Garments are draped around the lower halves of the two women. The woman in the middle of the scene, sprawled on the long, flat stones next to the man, has her right arm raised and bent at the elbow, with her hand resting on top of her tilted head. The man at the left and the woman at the right have their heads turned and are looking to the woman at the center of the scene. In the background a single column is at the extreme left, and a column with an entablature is at the extreme right. A tree stands behind the long slab of stones upon which rest the man and woman, and at the far right a mask with a mustache and beard, and horns rising out of thick hair that is parted in the middle and flows down to the sides of the face, is suspended in midair.

In the other scene are two men and a woman, a Cupidlike figure in the air, and a mask hanging at the extreme right, with two trees and a structure of two columns and an entablature in the background. One man, at the left foreground, is standing naked, his right foot in front and flat on the ground, his left leg behind him with the ball of his foot on the ground and his heel raised. The man's right arm is holding a garment; his left arm is locked with the arm of a woman, who is sitting on the ground with a

The two scenes of the famous Portland Vase. One of the mysteries of the vase is the meaning of the scenes. Do they signify life? death? a mythical representation? Long studied and debated, they will probably never be definitively understood.

garment draped over her extended legs and a snakelike creature crawling up her left arm. The other man is standing also, with a garment draped around his left arm. His body is turned to the other people, and he is looking at them. His left leg is straight; his right leg is resting on top of a small pile of stones. The man's right arm is bent, with the elbow resting on his right leg and his chin resting on the top of his right hand. The mask is similar to the one in the other scene.

The vase was apparently constructed for a specific purpose, and its scenes were fashioned to tell a particular story or impart some message, but what? Like any great artistic object of antiquity, it raises a hodgepodge of questions: Why was it made? Who made it? For whom was it made? What do the scenes mean? What symbolism is there? Answering these questions as they pertain to the Portland Vase requires a comprehensive knowledge of ancient Rome—its people, culture, and mythology—and even then, at best, one may offer only educated explanations. Since the vase's discovery hundreds of years ago, scholars have diligently studied and analyzed it and attempted to interpret its scenes. These scenes almost undoubtedly reflect the intended use of the vessel, and therefore the variety of their interpretations shed light on why the vase was made.

In their book *Glass of the Caesars*, Donald B. Harden, Hansgerd Hellenkemper, Kenneth Painter, and David Whitehouse examine various interpretations put forth by scholars, dating back to the 1630s. Many of the interpretations consider the figures to be characters of Greek mythology, such as Thetis, Peleus, and Achilles. Other interpretations regard the figures to be real-life Romans of historical importance, perhaps the parents or relatives of Augustus, the first Roman emperor, who ruled from 27 B.C. to A.D. 14. In some scholars' view, the vase was made as a funerary urn; this theory is based on various interpretations of the scenes and figures, such as the identification of one of the figures as the Greek mythological hero Theseus, who in legend was killed by being thrown into the ocean. Other scholars have determined the scenes to celebrate the romance and courtship of Achilles' mother, Thetis, to the king of Phthia, Peleus, and therefore have deemed the vase a wedding gift. Numerous other interpretations of the scenes and figures have been made, and these have included birth and death.

The identity and symbolism of the snakelike creature and the masks have also been a subject of debate. Exactly what are they, and what or whom might they represent? Explanations have included mythological figures and real-life people.

Not much is known about the history of the vase. Scholars cannot determine who owned the vase in ancient Rome, and even its emergence during the Renaissance period is shrouded in mystery. It was said to have been discovered in a sarcophagus outside Rome in the early 1580s, but there seems to be no contemporary documentation of its unearthing at this time. Whatever its Renaissance provenance, by the early seventeenth century it was owned by Cardinal Francesco Maria Borbone del Monte, who died in August 1626 and whose heir, Alessandro, sold it to Cardinal Antonio Barberini. The vase remained in the possession of the Barberini family, distinguished collectors of art in Rome who exhibited majestic paintings and sculptures in their palace, for 150 years.

The vase was next acquired by a Scottish architect living in Italy, James Byres, who in the early 1780s sold it to Sir William Hamilton, an Englishman with a rather interesting background.

The grandson of a duke, Hamilton was an archaeologist who had frequently climbed Vesuvius, wrote about discoveries at Pompeii, and sold ancient Greek artifacts to the British Museum. From 1764 to 1800 he was the British minister in Naples. He served as host to Vice Admiral Horatio Nelson in 1798, after the eminent English naval commander destroyed the French fleet in the Battle of the Nile.

Around 1784 Sir William Hamilton was in England, and Margaret, the duchess of Portland, saw the vase he had brought with him from Naples. She was enthralled with it and sought it for her collection. It was a pastime of wealthy Britishers in the eighteenth and nineteenth centuries to collect and display antiquities, rare books, curios, and paintings by great artists. Indeed, it was a sign of great prestige to own a piece of history: an original such as a Greek sculpture, a Spartan relief, a frieze of a famous structure. In their country homes or city residences, the English collectors would set up galleries of antiquities for friends to visit and marvel over— acquisitions for which the collectors dispensed fantastic sums. Some private collectors, like Henry Blundell (1724–1810) and Charles Towneley (1737–1805), acquired valuable artifacts during their lifetimes (many of these later finding their way into museums). The duchess of Portland purchased the vase along with some other relics Hamilton offered.

This engraving of the "Portland Museum" was in the catalog of Lady Portland's estate that was auctioned after she died in 1785.

Margaret wasn't able to enjoy her new vase for long, since she died on July 17, 1785, about a year after acquiring it. Following her death, her illustrious "Portland Museum" of valuable works of art was auctioned. From April 24 to June 7, 1786, more than three dozen sessions were held to sell the duchess's collection, which had been divided into some four thousand lots.

Margaret's son, the duke of Portland, purchased the ancient Roman vase and in 1810, after a family friend broke off the vase's base, lent it to the British Museum, where it presumably would be safe and could be enjoyed by a wide audience. In 1845, however, William Mulcahy, a young man who had been drinking for several days leading up to his visit to the museum, grabbed an object and shattered the glass display case housing the vase, and then the vase itself. Mulcahy, who falsely gave his name as William Lloyd, was sentenced to a jail term for breaking the case—although not the vase, because, peculiarly, British law did not provide penalties for destroying items of high value—but was soon released after an anonymous person paid his fine. The duke of Portland, meanwhile, received notice from the museum about the smashing and pronounced the culprit "mad." Exactly one century after William Mulcahy smashed the vase, the Portland family sold it to the British Museum.

The Portland Vase has been restored three times. After Mulcahy broke it into some two hundred pieces, it was repaired by the museum's John Doubleday, who was unable to fit in all the chips. Over time the glue's color changed, and in 1949, four years after the British Museum purchased the vase from the Portland family, a conservator named James H. W. Axtell carefully broke it apart and repaired it again, using a transparent glue. In 1986 Nigel Williams, the chief conservator of ceramics at the museum, and a team of assistants broke the vase, then restored it with a modern epoxy and other materials. They were also able to insert more than a dozen of the chips left over after Doubleday's repair.

In a way, the Portland Vase has come full circle in its two-thousand-year history with respect to its creation and preservation, as craftsmen of the nineteenth and twentieth centuries have painstakingly preserved a delicate glass vessel meticulously produced in an ancient workshop. Indeed, after two millennia, this great work of art continues to draw people to contemplate its beauty.

LOCATION: British Museum, London, England.

The Veil of the Virgin

DATE: Circa 6 B.C. to 4 B.C. (by tradition).*

WHAT IT IS: A piece of clothing that Mary supposedly wore at the birth of Jesus.

WHAT IT LOOKS LIKE: The cloth measures approximately 83½ inches long by 18 inches wide. It is beige and made of silk fabric and has some stains caused by humidity.

According to the evangelists Luke and Matthew, the following are the circumstances of the birth of Jesus Christ:

The expansive Roman Empire enjoyed great prosperity for about two centuries beginning in 30 B.C. But in the land of Judea in the early part of this period, Herod was king and under him the Jews suffered. A shrewd ruler who gave unflagging allegiance to the emperor Augustus Caesar, Herod not only imposed cruelty on the Jews but was unduly paranoid about potential successors dethroning him. Indeed, overcome by chronic mood swings, he would frequently order even sons and relatives to be put to death. At this time, grappling with the severity of their lives, some Jews put their full faith in the belief that the Messiah's arrival was imminent.

A priest in the temple at Jerusalem named Zechariah was one day visited by an angel and was told his wife would give birth to a boy who would precede the Messiah and unite broken families, straighten out the

*By tradition, the date of the Veil of the Virgin would coincide with the birth date of Christ. The exact date of Jesus' birth is not known, but many scholars agree that it is most probably between 6 B.C. and 4 B.C., because according to the New Testament, Herod the Great ordered the death of all children in the vicinity of Jesus' birthplace two years or younger (Matthew 2:13–15), and Herod died in 4 B.C.

unrighteous, and prepare the Messiah's people for his arrival. As Zechariah and his wife, Elizabeth, were both of mature years, he expressed incredulity at this prophecy and was consequently rendered mute. Yet Elizabeth did become pregnant.

During Elizabeth's sixth month of pregnancy, the angel Gabriel went to Galilee, where there lived a relative of Elizabeth, a woman named Mary who was engaged to Joseph, a descendant of King David. Gabriel told Mary that she would become pregnant with a boy she would name Jesus, who would be the Son of God and a king as David was. But Mary said she was a virgin and could not imagine how this could come to be. Gabriel explained that the Holy Spirit would come upon her, as he had upon Elizabeth, who was beyond childbearing age.

Mary then went to Judea to visit Elizabeth, whose baby stirred inside her when Mary arrived. Elizabeth told Mary that she was honored that the mother of the Lord should come to visit her. A few months later Elizabeth gave birth to a boy she wanted to name John. Friends pointed out that she had no relatives by that name, and asked her husband what he wanted to name the baby. Zechariah wrote down the name John, and his voice came back to him.

A census for tax purposes had been ordered at this time by Emperor Augustus, and all subjects of Rome were ordered back to their hometowns. Mary and Joseph, who lived in Nazareth, went to Bethlehem, where Joseph's ancestor David had been born. Joseph had been shocked that Mary was pregnant but was told of the circumstances in a dream. He was also told not to be afraid to marry his betrothed, and that her son, Jesus, would be the salvation of his people.

Mary gave birth to an infant boy, whom she covered in cloths and named Jesus, and laid him in a manger in Bethlehem. Some Magi, or "wise men" (who were probably Chaldean astrologers), observed a star rise in the east and associated this with a passage in Hebrew scriptures that predicted a baby was to be born king of the Jews, and set off on a journey to worship him. When they came to Jerusalem, they inquired as to the whereabouts of the baby who would be the Jewish Messiah. Word about the men's arrival to worship the baby reached Herod, and he became distressed. He summoned Jerusalem's religious leaders and asked where the Messiah will be born and they told him in Bethlehem, for the prophet wrote that from Bethlehem will come a leader to guide the people of Israel. Herod then secretly invited the three men to a meeting and asked them when the star had appeared. Then he told them to go to Bethlehem, requesting that when they had found the young child, they bring him word so that he too might worship this future king of the Jews. Guided by the same star they saw before, the men found Mary and her child and offered the infant gifts.

In a dream, the men were warned to avoid Herod and consequently returned home by another route. Herod, infuriated, ordered the killings of all boys up to the age of two in Bethlehem and its surrounding areas. The boy Jesus was saved, however, when an angel told Joseph in a dream to flee. Joseph took Mary and their son and escaped to the land of Egypt.

The first appearance, in a cathedral in Chartres, France, of a cloth believed to have been a fragment of the clothing Mary wore at the birth of Jesus was sometime during the Middle Ages. It is not known precisely when the cloth came to the cathedral; one story holds that it was acquired during the reign of the ninth-century king of France Charles II. At that time Chartres had a bishop named Gislebert, who had for many years been affiliated with the imperial chancery. Because of the king's admiration for the bishop, for the dedication ceremonies of Chartres's cathedral, which began construction in 859, he may have bestowed upon its inhabitants the holy object.

Located in north-central France, Chartres had a long history, dating back to Roman times. The Normans laid waste to the town in 858 and returned again in 911 to destroy it. This time, however, the bishop Gantelme called upon the sacred cloth to offer protection. The city was enclosed by a wall at the time, and Gantelme had the cloth placed on one of the outer sides. So inspired were the city's soldiers that the enemy soon fled. The people of Chartres rejoiced, and the Virgin's dress was placed in a boxlike reliquary in the cathedral's choir.

In 1194 a miracle was reported in Chartres. A raging fire swept the sanctuary of the revered relic of the Virgin Mary, the Notre-Dame Cathedral. The fire was looked upon as a major catastrophe for Chartres since the people deemed it a kind of withdrawal of divine favor. Mary's veil had been an attraction for pilgrims, the centerpiece of religious festivities and fairs that brought prosperity to the area. The people despaired, lamenting all they had done wrong and their consequent fall into disfavor with the Lord.

Three days after the church burned down—three being a symbol of the Resurrection, no doubt—something incredible happened. Clerics emerged from the ashes carrying the tunic of the Blessed Virgin Mary. The priests had been in the crypt of the church when the fire broke out and

The veil in the cathedral.

miraculously were saved, along with the cloth. (Two priests sequestered it in a "hiding place" where precious vases were stored during invasions or fires.) That the cloth survived was taken as a sign that Mary was dissatisfied with the cathedral and wanted a new one built. This new task was taken up with relish, and over the next half century a grand new church was built exactly above the crypt. The western facade of the old church survived the fire and was utilized and enhanced for the new cathedral.

For centuries the cloth was venerated by pilgrims, who could barely see it in its reliquary. But there is a record of the bishop of Mérinville verifying it in 1712. Although the cloth was originally more than sixteen feet long, during the revolution of 1793 it was cut into several fragments to hide it more easily; the pieces were distributed among different families.

The largest piece was recovered in 1819 and restored to the cathedral. The church commissioned a study in 1927, and the "Monsieur le Conservateur" of the Historical Museum of Fabrics in the Chamber of Commerce in Lyon concluded his expert report with the following: "The wrapping around the Chartres relic very likely dates back to the eighth or ninth century. It is far more difficult to determine the time of the relic itself because it is a piece of fabric which is quite plain, and usually the main characteristic of a fabric is essentially its decoration; but there is nothing stopping us from considering this veil as belonging to an earlier antiquity. It is quite allowed to think that the Virgin Mary wore this veil at the time of Jesus' birth, but it is only a hypothesis."

Today the Veil of the Virgin (Le Voile de la Vierge) is presented for the veneration of the faithful on the first Sunday of each month and on important feasts.

LOCATION: Notre-Dame Cathedral, Chartres, France.

The Crown of Thorns

DATE: A.D. 30 (by tradition).

WHAT IT IS: A wreath that has been venerated through the centuries as the crown placed on Christ's head when he was mocked by the Roman soldiers as the "King of the Jews" before the Crucifixion.

WHAT IT LOOKS LIKE: Rush reeds fill the ring, which has a diameter of more than 8 inches. There are no longer any thorns included with the Crown of Thorns, for they were dispensed years ago as relics themselves.

And they platted a crown of thorns and put it upon his head, and a reed in his right hand; and they kneeled down before him, and mocked him, saying, "Hail, King of the Jews!"

—Matthew 27:29

The last days of Jesus Christ are described in the New Testament.

The night before Jesus' crucifixion, Roman soldiers and a large crowd carrying clubs, swords, lanterns, and torches went to the Garden of Gethsemane where Jesus and his disciples were gathered. The religious men had come to the garden after their Passover meal, which would become known as the Last Supper, and now Jesus was praying as his disciples rested. Judas, a disciple of Jesus but a traitor to him, approached and kissed him, revealing to the others that this was the man whom they should arrest. Simon Peter, one of Jesus' disciples, raised his sword and hacked the right ear off a man in the crowd, but Jesus told Peter to put away the sword, and touching the man's ear, healed him. The soldiers seized and bound Jesus and took him to the courtyard of the high priest.

The chief priests and Council, also known as the Sanhedrin, immediately held a trial. A procession of witnesses recited various trumped-up charges against Jesus, ending with two men who testified they had heard Jesus say, "I am able to destroy the temple of God, and build it back up in three days." The high priest asked Jesus to respond to this accusation, but Jesus did not answer. "I adjure thee by the living God," the high priest said, "that thou tell us whether thou art the Christ, the Son of God." Jesus responded that he was what the high priest said. "Nevertheless," Jesus continued, "I say unto you, henceforth ye shall see the Son of Man sitting at the right hand of power, and coming on the clouds of heaven." The high priest became livid and ripped his own garments as he shouted "Blasphemy!" There was no need for further witnesses, the high priest said. "Behold, now ye have heard the blasphemy. What think ye?" The group answered that Jesus was "worthy of death."

The next morning Jesus was taken to Pontius Pilate, the Roman governor, who, inside his palace and removed from the crowd that wanted Jesus killed, asked him some questions. Pilate then returned to the people outside and said he did not find Jesus guilty of the crimes of which he was accused. Now it was a custom that during the Passover the Roman governor would set a prisoner free, and it just so happened there were two men in Pilate's custody: Barabbas, a robber; and Jesus of Nazareth. Pilate assumed the crowd would want the latter released, but the crowd shouted for the freeing of Barabbas. Hoping to pacify the group calling for the death of Jesus of Nazareth, Pilate had him scourged inside the palace. He had his centurions flog Jesus, then spit on him, beat him over the head, and finally strip him and put a scarlet robe on him and a crown of thorns over his head, and ridicule him as the "King of the Jews."

After the scourging and mocking, Pilate again came out before the crowd and said he could still find no crime committed by Jesus worthy of death. He brought out the prisoner before the crowd.

Jesus stood before the crowd with the crown of thorns on his head and the robe draped over him. Pilate told the people to crucify Jesus themselves, for he still could not find him guilty. But the people shouted back that under their law Jesus ought to die because he appointed himself the Son of God. Pilate became fearful now and returned once more inside the palace with Jesus, and asked him where he was from. Jesus would not answer, and when Pilate said he had the authority to release or crucify him, Jesus answered that Pilate's power had been given to him by God and that those who delivered him to Pilate were guilty of a greater sin. Pilate again

sought to release Jesus, but the crowd cried out, "Away with him, away with him, crucify him!" Pilate asked if they wanted their king crucified, and the people responded that their only king was Caesar. And thereupon Pilate turned Jesus over to the will of the people, and the soldiers led him away to be crucified.

The wreath set upon Jesus' head in mockery of a king's crown is of a class of artifacts called liturgical relics—objects or mementos connected with a holy person or a saint, or the body or a body part of such an individual. People have venerated liturgical relics through time—feverishly in the first millennium since Christ, and even to some extent today—as being imbued with healing powers or having particular emanations owing to their association with a holy person.

Because liturgical relics were thought to have mystical powers, possessing them was like having a personal talisman or amulet. It was the practice in centuries past for churches, as well as kings, noblemen, and wealthy families, to acquire divine objects avariciously and display them in magnificent shrines and reliquaries. People would come from afar to visit and touch them, leaving contributions behind in gratitude and reverence.

History contains many stories of celebrated persons possessing putative liturgical relics. For example, the Roman emperor Justin II was supposed to have owned a piece of the cross on which Jesus was crucified; Charlemagne also claimed wooden fragments and nails of the True Cross—relics of the Passion of Christ were especially popular and revered.

Indeed, just about every great event of the Old and New Testaments was resurrected in one sort of physical manifestation

An artist's rendition of Jesus wearing the Crown of Thorns.

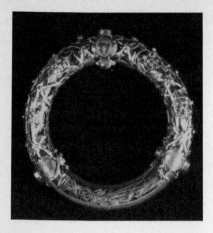

The Crown of Thorns as it exists today, enclosed in a ringlet.

or another during the Middle Ages. There were, for instance, the tablets of the Ten Commandments, the Golden Calf, Moses' staff, fragments of the burning bush, Christ's manger, loaves from the Last Supper. Saints were revered too and were represented by all manner of anatomical parts: ears, legs, arms, fingers, heads, hair, burned flesh, and complete bodies. There was no limit to the kinds and numbers of relics that surfaced. Enterprising individuals even claimed to have discovered relics of fictional legend, such as King Arthur's round table. In an effort to halt the practice of selling bogus objects—indeed, to curb the mania for relics and the abuses in worshiping them—the Roman Catholic Church eventually mandated its approval for introducing new sacred objects.

But what of Jesus' crown of thorns? Did it actually exist? And if so, could it possibly have survived through the ages?

There is a historical record of a crown of thorns dating from 409. At that time it was said to be in Jerusalem among the sacred relics of Mount Zion, where people made pilgrimages to worship it. Occasionally, individual thorns from the crown were presented as gifts and these became venerated relics at the locations they were subsequently taken to.

In 1063, when the safety of the Crown of Thorns in Jerusalem was threatened, it was taken to the royal palace at Constantinople (formerly called Byzantium). Constantinople grew so poor that when Baldwin II became emperor in 1228, he had to travel to other countries to raise money, and eventually realized he would be forced to sell off the city's holy relics to help out. The king of France, Louis IX, was aware of the sanctity of the Constantinople collection and wanted to purchase it. He did, but first he had to pay off the Venetian financiers to whom Baldwin II entrusted his young son as collateral for a loan. When the relics, including the prized Crown of Thorns, arrived in Paris in 1239, they were carried through the streets by the king and others in a grand parade. Around the middle of the thirteenth century Louis IX began construction of the Sainte-Chapelle in

Paris, intended to be a regal and magnificent shrine for the relics of the Passion that he had obtained, especially the Crown of Thorns.

The safety of the sacred relics was jeopardized by the French Revolution—some were melted, others looted—and in 1806 the crown was moved to a nearby cathedral, Notre-Dame de Paris. It has lain here for nearly two centuries along with other relics of the Passion of Christ, and people come from all around the world to venerate it.

Though it has a long documented history, can this be the original crown of thorns, the *very* crown of thorns placed upon the head of Jesus Christ some two thousand years ago? Proving that would be difficult if not impossible, but in a sense the authenticity of the Crown of Thorns and other relics is secondary to their incredible history, to their significance in the medieval context, and to their profound meaning to the faithful of both the past and the present.

LOCATION: Cathedral of Notre-Dame, Paris, France.

The Holy Lance

DATE: A.D. 30 (by tradition), the Nail of the True Cross; eighth or ninth century, the lance.

WHAT IT IS: A lance of the Holy Roman Empire that according to tradition contains a piece of nail driven into a limb of Jesus Christ during the Crucifixion. Middle Ages rulers who possessed the Holy Lance believed it conferred upon them the divine right of monarch or emperor as coming from God and Jesus Christ.

WHAT IT LOOKS LIKE: It is a winged lance made of steel, iron, and brass that lacks a shaft and measures approximately 20 inches long. The lance has an elliptical hole in its middle occupied by a crafted rodlike piece of iron said to be or contain particles of a Nail of the True Cross. An iron band holds together the blade, which is broken in two pieces, and around this are a silver sleeve and gold cuff, each with inscriptions.

But when they came to Jesus, and saw that he was dead already, they broke not his legs; but one of the soldiers with a spear pierced his side, and forthwith came there out blood and water.

—John 19:33–34

Pontius Pilate, the Roman governor, could not appease the crowd before his palace calling for Jesus to be killed, and finally acceded to the pressure. His soldiers led Jesus away and had Simon from Cyrene, a man whom they met on the way out, come with them to carry the cross. When they got to Calvary (in Hebrew, Golgotha), the "place of the skull," they offered Jesus a drink to numb him against the tremendous pain that would be induced by the Crucifixion. He tasted it but declined to drink.

Jesus was crucified from 9:00 A.M. to 3:00 P.M., during the last three hours of which a darkness came over the land. The Roman soldiers drove nails into Jesus' limbs, suspending him from the wooden beams as his weight bore down and the terrible agony set in. Two other men were crucified by his side, and above Jesus' cross the soldiers attached a sign, "This is Jesus the Nazarene, the King of the Jews." People passed by and shouted insults at Christ. "If thou be the Son of God," they cried out, "come down from the cross." Chief priests, scribes, and elders came by and taunted him. "He saved others; himself he cannot save. If he be the King of Israel, let him now come down from the cross, and we will believe in him. He trusted in God; let him deliver him now, if he will have him. For he said, 'I am the Son of God.' "

At the end, Jesus, in agony, shouted, *"Eli, Eli, lama sabachthani?"* which in Aramaic means "My God, my God, why have you forsaken me?" A soldier dipped a sponge into cheap wine and placed it at the end of a stick for Jesus to drink. Then Jesus cried out and gave his last breath. The Gospel according to Matthew says the earth rumbled and rocks cracked into pieces, graves came apart, and many who had died were brought back to life.

The Roman soldiers broke the legs of the two men who were crucified with Jesus, to hasten their deaths as the Sabbath was approaching. But when they came to Jesus, they did not break his legs, seeing that he was already dead. Instead, a Roman centurion whom tradition names as Longinus—the name itself may actually have derived from the Latin word for *lance*—took a spear and thrust it into his side, out of which poured blood and water.

There are two relics of the Passion that have historically been confused: the Spear of Longinus and the Holy Lance. Tradition tells us that the Spear of Longinus was the spear of the Roman centurion that pierced the side of Christ during the Crucifixion. The Holy Lance was a product of the eighth or ninth century in which a Holy Nail was inserted. Both are spears and relics of the Passion, reason enough for confusion, and yet to add to the mix-up, writings up to the tenth century referred to the Spear of Longinus as the Holy Lance.

Organized worships of relics of the Passion began with the legend of Saint Helena, mother of Constantine, the Roman emperor and founder of the Byzantine Empire. During the first half of the fourth century, when Saint Helena was advanced in years, she dedicated herself to performing Christian deeds. A former pagan who was divorced from Constantine's father when he was made ruler of territories of the newly divided Roman Empire and was required to have a noble-born wife, Helena followed Constantine in converting to Christianity after his spiritual awakening. Helena then made a pilgrimage to the Holy Land and sponsored the building of churches. As the foundations were being laid for the Church of the Holy Tomb on Calvary, site of the Crucifixion, a miraculous discovery was made. The cross on which Jesus was crucified and the nails that were driven into his body were reported found.

Helena's True Cross and Nails were conserved at the Church of the Holy Tomb, joined at some point by a Spear of Longinus, whose own provenance is unclear.* All these holy relics remained at Calvary without incident until 614, when the Persian king Khosrau II Parvez attacked Jerusalem and carried off the treasures of the Passion. The Byzantines later seized the spear and placed it in the royal treasury at Constantinople.

The Byzantines began a tradition of claiming to be the bearers of the true Spear of Longinus. Still others claimed to possess the Longinus spear, or Holy Lance, which brings to attention a problem common to all relics of the Passion, the so-called brandeum, or relics by touch: in the Middle Ages people would touch an object to an authentic relic and believe that the power of the authentic relic was transferred to the object that touched it.

When crusaders sacked Constantinople in 1204 (the Fourth Crusade), many of the city's artworks and treasures were taken as booty. The holy relics disappeared too, although in 1492 Sultan Bajazet II presented to Pope Innocent VIII a Spear of Longinus that still exists today at the Vatican (in a small chapel inside the interior of the pillar of Veronica, one of

---

*The Longinus legend goes back at least to the sixth century, as evidenced by the Rabula Gospel, written in Syriac and dated to A.D. 586. One of its miniature paintings depicts Jesus and the two thieves nailed onto crosses, with soldiers and spectators gathered around. To the left of Jesus is a Roman soldier holding a spear up to his side with Greek letters written above the soldier's head giving his identification as Longinus.

four pillars that hold the great cupola of the Vatican Basilica). Whether this was the Constantinople Spear of Longinus is not known with certainty.

Now we cut to the story of a lance made in the eighth or ninth century that was united with a purported Nail of the True Cross and became a venerated weapon believed to confer divine invincibility upon its bearer. With the lance and its Holy Nail, supposedly from Saint Helena's reliquary, rulers entered into battle with supreme confidence. The lance was handed down from one ruler to another, each one convinced that possession of this sacred object guaranteed their right of sovereignty.

An early owner of this Holy Lance, made during the dynasty of Charlemagne, was King Rudolf of Burgundy. Count Samson, adviser to Italy's King Hugo, in the early 920s delivered the Holy Lance to Rudolf in the hope that he would oust Berengar, the emperor of Italy. But the German ruler King Henry I coveted the lance as a treasure that would confer on him the divine right as ruler and ensure victories in all military campaigns. Rudolf bestowed the lance on Henry in exchange for gifts. The lance became a symbol of the German empire and on Henry's death in 936 was passed on to his eldest son, Otto.

Three years later a revolt within his kingdom threatened Otto's power. Otto did not participate in the battle but observed it while clenching the Holy Lance. His forces crushed the rebels, and thereafter the Holy Lance brought comparisons to the *virga Dei*, Moses' staff. Later, Otto's Lombardian kingdom came under siege from foreign invaders. All attacks were staved off by Otto, who was

The Holy Lance

crowned emperor in 962. Victories were attributed to his sacred instrument, the Holy Lance. (Much of the connection between Otto and the Holy Lance was recorded by Liutprand, a tenth-century Italian historian.)

Near the end of the eleventh century, Henry IV, a Roman emperor, had a silver sleeve with an inscription fitted over an iron band which was used to hold together the lance, whose blade had somehow broken into two pieces. Henry's inscription paid tribute to the "Nail of the Lord." About two and a half centuries later, Karl IV, another Roman emperor, ordered an inscribed gold cuff to be placed over the sleeve. This inscription similarly paid tribute to the Holy Nail, but in referring to the lance itself as the lord's lance, it actually was identifying it as the Spear of Longinus. It is not known why such an identification was made, but it is wholly incorrect.

In the thirteenth century Pope Gregory IX designated the Holy Lance "Constantine's Lance" and held that it was the very same weapon used by the Roman centurion Longinus to pierce the body of Christ. The association of the lance with Longinus was decidedly apocryphal, but arose out of the ongoing conflict between Rome and Byzantium (later known as Constantinople), which always prided itself as the city that possessed the True Spear. Gregory wanted to irk the Byzantines.

The Holy Lance, or Heilige Lanze, became an insignia of the Holy Roman Empire, in later centuries combined with the empire's cross (Reichskreuz), crown (Reichskrone), apple (Reichsapfel), and scepter (Szepter). The empire comprised the territories controlled by Frankish and German kings from 800, when Pope Leo III crowned Charlemagne the emperor, to 1806, when Napoleon helped bring about its demise.

In the sixteenth century the lance came to the Habsburgs, a royal family of Austria. The Habsburg dynasty venerated the lance and preserved it with other insignia of the Holy Roman Empire (Reichskleinodien).

In 1938, on the eve of the Second World War, the Reichskleinodien, along with the Austrian Crown Jewels and valuable works of art, were packed in crates and transported to a concrete air-raid shelter in Nuremberg. The treasures remained there during the war and escaped seizure by Adolf Hitler or any of his Nazi minions. The treasures survived the war unscathed, even despite a major Royal Air Force attack on Nuremberg in March 1944. (The RAF suffered its heaviest casualties of the war in this raid, perhaps a strange coincidence with the Holy Lance's being kept in this city.)

At 2:00 P.M. on August 2, 1946, U.S. Army officers in Nuremberg, accompanied by municipal officials, ordered an inspection of crates stored in cell number 3 of the Upper Schmiedgasse. The cell contained twelve crates, and in crate 8 was found the Holy Lance. Shortly after, the Second World War of the twentieth century having ended, the lance and the other sequestered treasures in Nuremberg were returned home to Vienna.

LOCATION: Kunsthistorisches Museum, Vienna, Austria.

The Shroud of Turin

DATE: A.D. 30 by tradition; 1260 to 1390 by carbon dating. Modern scientific analysis is continuing.

WHAT IT IS: The shroud is a linen sheet that for at least six centuries has been reputed to be the one in which the corpse of Jesus Christ was wrapped and entombed after the Crucifixion. Radiocarbon tests of a single sampling of cloth from a worn (and repaired?) and controversial corner of the shroud produced a date from the mid–fourteenth century. Despite this finding, there are many puzzling, inexplicable elements about the cloth and the image on it, and many people continue to believe that it may be the shroud of Christ.

WHAT IT LOOKS LIKE: The shroud measures 14 feet 3 inches long by 3 feet 7 inches wide, and bears faint front and back negative images of a man who has been crucified. The linen cloth has a herringbone weave, is burned in some places, and has yellowed through time.

In the hours after the Crucifixion, Joseph of Arimathea went to the Roman governor, Pontius Pilate, to ask for permission to take away the body of Christ. Pilate, after ascertaining that Jesus was in fact dead, consented, and Joseph went to Calvary with a man named Nicodemus, who brought along a mixture of aloes and myrrh. The two men carried the body to a nearby garden in which there was a new tomb. Precisely how the body was prepared for burial is not known, but Joseph and Nicodemus probably, in accordance with Jewish burial customs for torture victims, spread out a linen cloth on a burial bench in the tomb and laid the unwashed body upon it. (While normal Jewish custom was to wash the body of the deceased, a victim of violence was not washed.) The spices were used in some manner, but it is not clear from the Gospels exactly how; the body could have been "packed" with spices still in their containers, the great share of the spices could have been burned as incense within the tomb, a "wash" of the spice mixture could have been "painted" on the walls and bench of the tomb just prior to the burial, the linen cloth could have been dabbed or sprinkled with the spices, or the mixture could have been directly smeared on the body. Since it was close to the Sabbath, when Jews were prohibited from fully preparing a corpse for burial (including washing, anointing, plugging up all the orifices, tying the jaw shut, tying the hands and feet, and wrapping or dressing the corpse), and because the body of Jesus had been so brutalized from the scourging and Crucifixion, Joseph and Nicodemus did the minimal treatment permitted, left the cloth-enfolded corpse inside the tomb, rolled a rock in front of the entrance, and left.

John's Gospel tells us that on the third day after the Crucifixion, in the darkness of the Easter morning, Mary Magdalene went to the tomb to see the body. She found the stone removed and ran to get two of Jesus' disciples. They entered the tomb and saw that the body was missing. The disciples left, and Mary Magdalene stood outside weeping. Then she crouched down and looked inside and saw two angels where the body of Jesus had lain. They asked her why she was weeping, and she replied that her Lord had been taken away, and she did not know where he was. Then she turned and saw Jesus before her, only she did not recognize him. He asked the same question, but, thinking he was the gardener, she asked where he had placed the body so that she might take it away. Jesus then called her name, and she realized who he was, saying in Hebrew the word *teacher*. Jesus said that she must not touch him, for he had not yet ascended to heaven. He asked her to go to his disciples and tell them she had seen the Lord, and all that he had said to her. This conversation transpired while the linen cloth, from which the dead Jesus had arisen, was left lying in its place—on the burial bench—in the tomb.

Throughout the centuries of the first millennium after his death (approximately April 7 of A.D. 30, according to many New Testament scholars), several shrouds purported to be the burial cloth of Jesus Christ emerged. False claims were commonly made, for the Shroud of Christ would be among the holiest of relics, with potential benefits of immense riches and power. But one of these relics may actually have been what later became known as the Turin Shroud. There is the Veronica Cloth, for instance, which had once been known as the Image of Edessa, or, after it was moved from Edessa (Urfa in modern-day Turkey) to Constantinople in 944, as the Mandylion. Scholars historically described it as a cloth bearing a Christlike image of only a face (as opposed to a full body). Some evidence indicates that the Mandylion, which probably dates at least from the sixth century, was a smaller cloth than the Turin specimen. But many sindonologists, or shroud scholars, attribute this to the cloth having been publicly displayed only in folded form.

Other alleged "True Shrouds" include revered cloths in a monastery near Jerusalem and on a tiny island near the British Isles. Over the years, various stories and legends surfaced, such as the one of Saint Helena, the mother of Constantine, discovering the Holy Shroud in Jerusalem. Saint Helena is said to have established in Constantinople a collection of major holy relics, including the True Cross.

Although the written record reveals no unequivocal mention of the Turin Shroud until late in the Middle Ages, there are early pictorial renderings that support its existence prior to this time. Of the more certain references to the shroud, the oldest is that of a Byzantine *tremissis*. This late seventh-century coin, which bears a frontal bust of Christ, has some twenty-one features with matching representations on the shroud. For example, on the coin there are strange lines connecting the pupils of the eyes to the eyebrows; a defect in the weaving of the linen cloth traverses exactly the same eye areas. The peculiarities on this coin can best be explained as meticulously depicted flaws in the weave of the shroud, which was used as the engraver's model. The multitude of matching features suggests the shroud was in existence at least as early as about A.D. 690, when the coin was engraved, and this in turn implies that the shroud was already, in Byzantine tradition, considered a holy cloth connected with Christ.

Another significant artifact that supports the existence of the shroud prior to the thirteenth century is the Hungarian Pray Manuscript, an illuminated manuscript that dates from 1192 to 1195, some sixty-five to two hundred years earlier than the age of the Turin cloth as determined by modern radiocarbon tests. A picture of the crucified Christ shows a burial cloth with two remarkable features. There is a strange geometric pattern on the cloth (probably the artist's attempt to render the herringbone weave) and a peculiar L-shaped configuration of circles corresponding to a burn pattern seen today on the shroud itself (an apparent attempt to represent the holes from a fire). The Turin Shroud was burned on two occasions. The first fire happened prior to 1516 since these holes appear in a drawing of the shroud dated to that year. But if the Hungarian Pray Manuscript can be entered as evidence, that fire must have happened even before 1192. The second fire occurred in 1532.

Continuing along the trail of evidence for a pre–thirteenth-century shroud, we find a description of a shroud seen in Constantinople by the French knight Robert de Clari during the sack of the city in 1204 by soldiers of the Fourth Crusade. Could this be the Turin Shroud? De Clari described a shroud that strongly resembles it. Could, in fact, the Image of Edessa, or Mandylion, the de Clari shroud, and the Turin Shroud be one and the same? Such a claim would require specific written and pictorial evidence.

Such evidence came to light in the 1980s. Willi K. Müller, a German medical doctor–sindonologist, first made public an important identification of such a picture in a lengthy medieval text known as the Skylizès Manuscript. The significance of this was later explored by the French re-

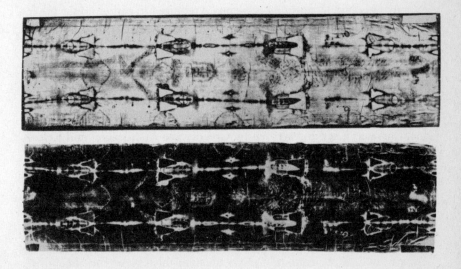

Pictured are positive (top) and negative (bottom) photographic images of the shroud.

Negative and positive images of the face on the Shroud of Turin.

searcher Brother Bruno Bonnet-Eymard. In the text, profusely illustrated by colorful drawings, an artist has depicted a cloth being presented to the East Roman emperor Romanus I (Lecapenus), who ruled in the first half of the tenth century. The cloth is so long that the bearer must drape one end across his shoulder while Lecapenus is required to gather up the other end to keep it from touching the floor. This extraordinarily long cloth had a face in the middle. And since it is labeled "Holy Mandylion," the so-called small cloth that bore the Lord's face, one is forced to ask, "If this cloth were so small, why would the artist have depicted it as very long?"

In 1982 an Italian classical scholar, Dr. Gino Zaninotto, discovered in the archives of the Vatican a revealing document (Codex Vatican Graec. 511). This was a sermon written by Gregory the Archdeacon and Refer-endarius. Gregory, who witnessed the presentation of the shroud or Mandylion to Romanus I as depicted in the Skylizès Manuscript, de-scribed an image on the cloth bearing not only the face but also a wound in the side and possibly even more than this. From the artistic and written evidence, then, a case may be made for a link among the Mandylion, the de Clari shroud, and the Shroud of Turin.

It is now time to examine the documented history of the Shroud of Turin. The written record indirectly implies that around 1354 Geoffrey de Charny, a knight who had recently been in a military campaign, built a church in Lirey, France, for a cloth bearing the image of a tortured Christ. Although it was branded an artist's creation in 1389 by Bishop Pierre d'Arcis with the clear intent that it be dismissed, the de Charny family apparently disagreed, for it remained carefully guarded by them until the mid–fifteenth century. In the second half of the fifteenth century, Margaret de Charny, through an arrangement with Duke Louis of Savoy, turned the shroud over to the protection of the Savoy family. For a long time they kept it sequestered at the Sainte-Chapelle in Chambéry, France. The cloth was almost destroyed when a fire erupted there in 1532, but some quick-thinking priests and civilians rescued it. In 1578, when the dukes of Savoy became the kings of Sardinia and Northern Italy, they brought it with them to the capital city of Turin, where it has been ever since. The shroud remained in the Savoy family until the death, in 1983, of King Umberto II, who willed it to the Vatican.

The shroud was a bona fide religious icon for many people. Its image of a crucified man certainly evoked the Passion of Christ, and its overseers guarded it zealously, as they continue to do today. Its rare public exhibitions only add to its mystery.

An event occurred in May 1898 that swelled public interest into worldwide excitement and controversy. A weeklong exhibition of the cloth was held at the cathedral that housed it, and during that time an amateur Italian photographer named Secondo Pia, having obtained permission, produced the first photographs of the shroud. In his darkroom, as the images emerged on the glass plates, Pia was in awe. In Pia's photographic negative, dark and light representations became reversed, and the subtle image of the shroud became vivid. What could only be perceived faintly on the cloth became startlingly apparent in the negatives!

Pia's work provoked intense debate. Comprehensive scientific experiments were performed, and experts of all kinds joined the argument over the shroud's authenticity.

The experiments had begun in 1900 after Yves Delage, an agnostic, showed his friend Paul Vignon the photos that Pia had taken in 1898. They were soon joined by René Colson (a professor of physics) and Armand Gautier (a professor of biological medicine). These investigators performed tests until 1902—laboratory simulations, because permission had not been granted to use the actual shroud—that might either show the shroud to be a forgery or help substantiate claims supporting its veracity. They tried creating a similar image on a comparable linen cloth by painting and dressing a body with chemicals and pressing the sheet against it, obtaining similar photographic negatives from other linen cloth images; they analyzed the wounds and scourge marks and their arrangements on photographs of the shroud, and compared them to damage that might be inflicted by actual ancient weapons and a crucifixion; they studied simulations of blood staining and clotting on the cloth and made chemical tests. These men approached the shroud legend with great skepticism, but their investigations convinced them they were dealing with an artifact of history and that the shroud was indeed a burial cloth.

Delage presented the Pia photographs and the scientific findings to the French Academy on April 21, 1902, and the story hit the papers on April 23, 1902. Paul Vignon's first publication, *The Shroud of Christ* (first in French, then in English), also appeared that same year. Based on his careful study of the Pia photographs and his painstaking work, Vignon proposed that there was a relationship between the image and cloth-body distance—that is, that there was three-dimensional information coded into the shroud.

Then, in the early 1930s, an eminent French surgeon, Pierre Barbet, performed experiments with cadavers and suggested a solution to a mystery of the shroud that was a point of contention among its doubters: Why were both thumbs missing from the image of the hands on the cloth? Barbet spiked a nail experimentally through the wrist of an amputated arm and found that the thumb moved inward toward the center of the palm, the nail having hit a tendon in the wrist. Barbet's findings increased the shroud fever. New photographs of the shroud taken just prior to that time by a professional named Giuseppe Enrie, using equipment and techniques more modern than Pia's, supported Pia's results and supplied Barbet with a powerful tool for his medical researches.

In 1973 and again in 1978, the head of the Zurich, Switzerland, police lab, Dr. Max Frei, had removed dust samples from the shroud. From his study of the pollen in this material, he identified fifty-eight kinds of plants represented on the cloth, of which forty-four grow in Palestine. Seven of these were desert-derived salt-loving types and could not have come from France or Italy where the shroud is known to have been housed. Frei concluded that the shroud must once have been in the Holy Land.

Tests conducted on samples removed in 1978 by American, Swiss, and Italian teams showed at least 95 percent support for an as yet unidentified image-causing mechanism. Many scientists were inclined to associate that mechanism somehow with a proposed body once enwrapped in the cloth. Only the testing conducted by an American microscopist, Dr. Walter C.

the area in 1973. Evidence for worn corners requiring a medieval repair is inherent in the fact that what appear to be "patches" on each corner of the "side-strip" side of the shroud are, in fact, cutaway portions of the shroud itself that have been stitched down to the Holland backing cloth, added in the spring of 1534. So the sample extracted could have been affected when the cloth was repaired in 1534, and therefore the carbon-14 date might have been altered by the admixture of newer threads. In this latter case the relationship of the sample to the cloth as a whole would not be precisely known until a scientifically controlled date was obtained from another area of the shroud.

All these scenarios would provide a source of more modern carbon that would seriously skew the date of the cloth, making it appear younger than it actually is. When research is finally completed, the truth will probably be a combination of some of these findings.

Despite all the investigations and tests conducted, there still remain some very puzzling questions about this cloth. It clearly bears the image of a man who was crucified, but is that image natural or is it an artist's painting? The preponderance of accumulated evidence supports the natural-causes explanation rather than the artist's painting, but this has not yet been scientifically verified. If it is an artist's image, who made it and why? How could a medieval forger create a negative impression before the science of photography was developed?

Why do a majority of physicians and forensic pathologists around the world who have specialized in the study of the shroud come away deeply impressed with the accuracy of the body stance, the blood flows, the technical medical nuances of crucifixion, and the amazing anatomical precision not yet known to medicine? Does this boldly imply that some fourteenth-century artist experimented by crucifying hapless victims until he got it right?

Some of these mysteries may never be solved, making it difficult for some to reject the Shroud of Turin as a fake, but allowing others to continue to venerate it as an authentic holy object.

Location: Cathedral of St. John the Baptist (Royal Chapel of the Shroud), Turin, Italy.

The Blood of Saint Januarius

DATE: 305 (by tradition).

WHAT IT IS: The liquefying blood of a saint who lived some seventeen hundred years ago.

WHAT IT LOOKS LIKE: The blood is kept in a small glass vial. In its usual state, the blood is dried, solid, and dark. As a liquid, it has a color ranging from purplish to bright red.

The practice of extracting from deceased holy persons body parts or fluids to be venerated for the purpose of inducing miracles was well established in A.D. 305, when an obscure Italian bishop named Januarius died. When the bleeding of corpses began is not known exactly, but this practice would reach its height in certain parts of Europe in the sixteenth, seventeenth, and eighteenth centuries.

Letters, journals, books, and church records chronicle numerous attempts to draw blood from holy people hours, days, even years after they expired, often with successful results. Typically, someone would open a vein or bleed an arm of the cadaver with the hope of obtaining blood. Witnesses sometimes claimed that before blood was drawn, the corpse would yield perspiration from the forehead or exude a pleasant smell. Sometimes the volume of blood that poured forth from a cut on a body from which life had been extinguished several days earlier was so great that witnesses dabbed cloths in the blood and handed them out in the belief that they would afford the recipient protection and good fortune. In one extreme case, the body of a priest was disinterred in Italy in 1750, nearly four years after his death. A witness, Father Joseph Landi, wrote of the astonishment of those present upon seeing a body "as entire, flexible and beautiful as on the day of his death." Just as astonishing must have been what happened shortly after, for when the corpse was bled, Father Landi recorded, the witnesses noticed "bright blood to gush forth from the incision."

Although the liquefaction of saints' blood is a prodigy that has been well documented, some skeptics doubt that the blood actually came from their bodies. Interestingly, exhibitions of the blood relics on the feast days of these saints have regularly been marked by liquefactions. Of all the blood relics, the most famous is that of Saint Januarius (San Gennaro), long celebrated by throngs of people who have come to witness its miracle. Not much is known about this late third-century Italian—not his family background, not his early years, not what he looked like. About all that is known about him is that he was dedicated to the service of God and that he died a martyr a long time ago.

Januarius was a bishop in Beneventum (now Benevento), a town in central Italy, at a time when Christians suffered harsh persecution under the Roman emperor Diocletian. Diocletian was a strong ruler who made sweeping governmental reforms and brought stability to the empire. But during his reign the treatment of Christians, who refused to worship him, was severe.

Among the Christian clerics who fell victim to the religious persecution was the bishop Januarius. Presumably, he declined to renounce his religious faith and was executed, probably by beheading. According to some accounts, as his corpse was being conveyed to Naples, the town that later made him its patron saint, it was bled.

Of course it stretches the imagination not only to believe that preserved today in a glass vial is the blood of a third-century bishop, but further, to accept that this blood, dry and solid in a vessel, liquefies several times each year on the same days. An amazing proposition to be sure, but that is the long and documented history of the "Blood of Saint Januarius."

The Blood of Saint Januarius is said to liquefy at least eighteen times each year. The event occurs on the feast day of Saint Januarius in September and during the next seven days, on the sixteenth of December, on the first Saturday in May, and during each of the next eight days. The blood relic's history has demonstrated that there is not necessarily a direct correlation between liquefaction and heat and light, for the dried blood has liquefied in dim lighting and on December days when the temperature was below freezing, and has remained in a solid state on hot summer days. The "feast of the miracle" is usually carried out in a ceremony where the vial is displayed before shouting worshipers, invoking the Lord to work

The liquefying blood in its vessel.

the miracle. Liquefaction does not always take place in the normal interval, sometimes happening prematurely or protractedly. Indeed, deviant liquefaction, or failure to liquefy at all, has traditionally been regarded as an omen of catastrophe or misfortune. Believers in the blood miracle have attributed various disasters to the unsuccessful exhibitions they followed.

The blood has some curious properties. In its hardened state, its volume and weight may at times vary considerably, and the liquefactions seem to have their own "personalities," sometimes lethargic, other times animated. Sensational phenomena associated with the blood's liquefactions have been reported. The eminent theological scholar Herbert Thurston wrote, "It is stated, though I have as yet met with no quite convincing evidence of the fact, that at the moment when the liquefaction takes place . . . a slab of stone at Pozzuoli, supposed to be connected with the martyrdo of the Saint, is seen to redden and to be covered with moisture."

Three Italian scientists reported in the October 10, 1991, issue of *Nature* magazine that by mixing chalk and iron chloride they produced a gel that liquefied when it was shaken and hardened when it was not disturbed. Medieval apothecaries would have known how to concoct such gels, they claimed, and therefore could have made what became the so-called blood relics. The scientists noted that modern scientific testing would reveal the composition of the blood relic, but that the Roman Catholic Church prohibits this.

At any rate, those who look upon the Saint Januarius blood relic with skepticism should consider that it does have characteristics—observed, confirmed, and documented by dubious observers as well as believers— that seem to defy scientific explanation. Perhaps its mysteries will one day be conclusively solved. But for now, and for hundreds of years already, the inexplicable, perhaps miraculous behavior of the dark substance in the small glass vial has led many to believe that it does indeed have some type of holy connection.

LOCATION: Naples Cathedral, Naples, Italy.

The Rubens Vase

DATE: Circa 350.

WHAT IT IS: A rare Byzantine work of art that through the centuries has often narrowly escaped being shattered and has disappeared on several occasions, only to resurface in another time and place. It has a distinguished list of owners and is named after one of them, the renowned seventeenth-century Flemish painter Peter Paul Rubens.

WHAT IT LOOKS LIKE: The vase is a 9-inch-high cameo sculpted of solid agate. Carved in the relief are sneering horned satyrs and winding vines.

In 1941 an antique vase was brought up for auction in a collection of art objects in New York City. Experts suspected it had belonged to, among other notables, the celebrated English author William Beckford and Peter Paul Rubens. Furthermore, it seemed to have a very dramatic history—it had frequently been pillaged or had disappeared but always, astonishingly, reemerged.

There was no definitive proof for any of these conjectures, however. Such proof of an association with legendary people or events would cause its value to soar, but without it, the object would remain a curiosity. The ideal situation for a perspicacious buyer would be to secure but not publicize the proof until the object was in the collector's possession. How could proof be found?

At the time of the 1941 auction, Marvin Chauncey Ross, a museum curator, had recently examined an illustrated book about William Beckford's residence, Fonthill Giffard. Beckford, famous for his 1780s occult novel published in French, *Vathek*, in 1796 had architect James Wyatt build for him in Wiltshire a Gothic- style home that became England's most sumptuous private residence. An antiquarian of sorts, Beckford collected interesting old artwork and books.

On the frontispiece of the Fonthill Giffard book, Ross observed an object illustrated in the lower right-hand corner. After close examination Ross came to a startling conclusion. It was none other than the vase being auctioned. Further research yielded a revealing letter written by someone to whom Beckford had shown his collection. The writer mentioned "a vase composed of one entire block of Chalcedonian onyx," which Beckford had speculated was "one of the greatest curiosities in existence." Of the vase, the writer noted that Beckford had also said that Peter Paul Rubens "'made a drawing of it, for it was pawned in his time for a very large sum. And I possess an engraving of his drawing.' And opening a portfolio he immediately presented it to my wondering eyes."

Voilà! Not only had Ross found that Beckford had possessed the vase, but he himself had linked it to Rubens. And with that came to light more stories about the vase, because Rubens had written about it in his own letters. From inventories of royal art collections dating back to the fourteenth century, Ross was also able to identify other owners of the vase, and the dramatic story of this remarkable object unfolded.

The vase had been sculpted in the mid–fourth century, probably in a royal workshop of a Byzantine emperor. Little is actually known about it until the Fourth Crusade, in 1204, when Constantinople, the capital of Byzantium, was captured. The vase was probably found in a royal palace and, with other objects, taken clandestinely to France.

Around 1368 the vase came into the possession of the duke of Anjou, who stored it in a medieval fortress. When he died his brother, King Charles V of France, inherited the vase. Charles V, a respected ruler known as "the Wise," supported the arts and established a royal library in the Louvre, which would become

The Rubens Vase

France's national library, the Bibliothèque Nationale. The vase was displayed in the Louvre.

Charles V died in September 1380. Thirty-five years later, his widow-cousin, Jeanne de Bourbon, bestowed much of his royal artwork on the Notre-Dame Cathedral in Paris. Among these works was the Byzantine vase, which the prelates sold for a pittance near the end of the sixteenth century to help the financially troubled church.

In 1619 the vase was inconspicuously offered for sale in a Paris flea market. The painter Peter Paul Rubens recognized its superb craftsmanship and bought it for a rather healthy sum. Less than a decade later he himself became financially strapped, and he was forced to sell the vase. He found a buyer in India, said to be none less than the Mogul emperor himself, Jahāngīr. But the vase never made it to Jahāngīr—or India—because the ship on which it was journeying was wrecked off Australian shores. Legend has it that a handful of the crew went to nearby Java for help and when they returned to the site of the shipwreck they found that more than two hundred passengers had died fighting over the treasures aboard the marooned vessel. The Rubens Vase disappeared at this time.

What happened to the vase or into whose hands it fell next is not known, but Beckford purchased it in 1818.

Beckford added the vase to his collection at Fonthill Giffard, where he lived in virtual seclusion. But when he moved in 1822, he sold it to his son-in-law, the duke of Hamilton. This was fortunate, because shortly afterward the 250-foot central tower of Fonthill Giffard toppled, demolishing most of the building; it is almost certain that the vase would have been destroyed had it still been there.

The duke of Hamilton owned the vase until the 1880s, when it was purchased for almost eighteen hundred pounds (about $8,760) by Sir Francis Cook. Cook displayed it in the early 1900s at the Burlington House in London; four years later a catalog of Cook's collection of art objects was published, and it included the vase. At this time it was called the Hamilton Vase, after its previous owner, and it was strongly conjectured to have been owned by Rubens. But without definitive proof, this was still conjecture.

In 1925 Henry Walters, an art expert whose father, William, established an art museum in Baltimore in 1871, purchased the vase for eighty-five hundred dollars. Walters died six years later; in 1941 his widow put up for auction pieces from their personal collection.

It was at this time that Marvin Chauncey Ross, sitting in the New York

City offices of Parke-Bernet, knew something the other bidders didn't: the vase's sensational history—its ownership by French royalty and Rubens and Beckford, the sale to the Grand Mogul of Delhi, and the shipwreck.

But history aside, Ross, as a scholar and connoisseur of art, also appreciated the vase for what it was: a work of art unlike any other object known from the Byzantine world.

A large, richly carved hard stone vessel, the Rubens Vase showed Byzantine technical audacity at its most sublime level. Its extremely refined and sophisticated craftsmanship and lavish use of materials reflected the splendor of Byzantine court life, which was without equal in the Mediterranean world for about a thousand years. There are other surviving objects from the Byzantine Empire that possess some of the qualities of the Rubens Vase, but its closest relatives are really quite different, and that is very unusual. There are hard stones cut in the shape of vessels but none anywhere near as elaborate as the Rubens. Another surviving vessel from the late Roman world was cut as elaborately as the Rubens Vase, but it was made of glass, not agate. Although undoubtedly other agate cameo vases like the Rubens Vase were made—people ordinarily don't make just one of something—the fragility of these agate vessels made it unlikely that any would endure to the twentieth century. The Rubens Vase apparently is one of a kind.

Ross sat apprehensively in the audience with a trustee of the gallery where he was the curator. With the approval of the gallery's board of directors, they were permitted to bid up to five thousand dollars for the vase, although they didn't expect the bidding to go nearly that high.

To Ross's surprise, the bidding went just that high—and higher. Devastated, he sank his head into his hands and lamented, not bothering to follow the bidding to its conclusion. On the train ride home he sat depressed. When the train arrived at its destination, Ross's companion, the trustee, sent him into shock when he revealed that while Ross had his head buried he had raised their ante card, bidding five hundred dollars of his own money over their official allotment. Ross was euphoric; they had brought the Rubens treasure home after all.

LOCATION: Walters Art Gallery, Baltimore, Maryland.

The Antioch Chalice

DATE: Sixth century or early seventh century.

WHAT IT IS: A plain silver cup embedded in an outer cup that is artistically decorated with images of Christ and the apostles. A worldwide sensation attended the chalice when it was asserted to be the sacred relic believed for nearly two millennia to be one of the greatest of all lost treasures, the Holy Grail.

WHAT IT LOOKS LIKE: The inner cup is ovoid and dented, and its lip is bent over the rim of the outer cup, which is cut through to form human figures, animals, and vines. The outer cup is set on a base. The chalice measures more than 7½ inches high, and the diameter of the outer rim is over 7 inches.

Within a two-year period beginning early in 1908, four silver Byzantine treasures came to light in Syria. The first one surfaced in Stuma and was eventually confiscated by Turkish authorities, who handed it over to an Istanbul museum. In 1909 a British archaeologist discovered a treasure from Riha that was in private hands and held in low profile, since the owner feared it would be impounded by government officials as the first had been. Then in 1910 it was announced that another silver hoard had been unearthed in Hama, and some months later a fourth cache of silver objects was revealed to have been discovered in Antioch.

A bit of mystery shrouded the last treasure, which stood out from the others because it contained the ornate double chalice. According to Gustavus Eisen, in his two-volume publication *The Great Chalice of Antioch*, the treasure was discovered by Arab workers digging a cellar in Antioch.

The workers refused to reveal the cellar's location, but it was believed to have been near the subterranean ruins of an ancient church. This would accord with a tradition that Constantine the Great, founder of the Byzantine Empire, distributed great treasures of silver to the empire's churches sometime early in the fourth century. The workers split the hoard between them.

The Antioch treasure was eventually acquired in its totality by the Kouchakji Brothers, an antiquities firm of Aleppo (in Syria), Paris, and New York. Salim and Constantin Kouchakji spent two years gathering the pieces from their different owners. When the timing was right, they sent the items to their brother George in Paris, who hired a prominent specialist to clean the pieces of oxidation. When World War I erupted, the objects were dispatched to New York, where they could be kept safely and where another Kouchakji brother, Habib, lived with his son, Fahim.

Of the seven objects of the Antioch hoard, Fahim sensed the double cup was an article of extremely special provenance. He sought out the Swedish anthropologist Gustavus Eisen to study and write about it. Dr. Eisen made an exhaustive study of the chalice: the separate vessels, the artwork, the biblical symbolism of the decorations.

The chalice is a double cup, one inside the other. The inner cup is plain and rough, not decorated as is the outer one. It has an ovoid shape typical, Eisen pointed out, of chalices from the time of Christ. Eisen believed that it was made by a different person and at a different time than the outer cup; it was simple and not tampered with by any artisan because, he suggested, it "was a relic of great sanctity."

Apparently, the outer cup was sculpted at a later time. A relief occupying the majority of the exterior depicts twelve seated human figures. Elaborately intertwined around them are twisting vines with hanging clusters of grapes, perched animals, and objects that may be interpreted as symbols. Near the rim, where the inner cup's top is bent over, is a chain of rosettes.

Of the human figures, Eisen identified two as Christ, first as a boy and then after his resurrection. The boyish figure's face is innocent and bright; the resurrected Christ bears a gentle, pensive expression. Above and below his resurrection image are, respectively, a dove and an eagle, the former the symbol of the Holy Ghost, the latter of the Roman Empire.

Seated around Christ at different levels in the postresurrection illustration are several apostles: Peter, John the Divine and his brother James, Mark, Andrew, Jude, James the Lesser, Paul, Matthew, and Luke. Work-

The Antioch Chalice

manship of the highest artistic caliber provided the distinctive character associated with each of the apostles. In his detailed investigation of the human figures, animals, and objects, Eisen refuted earlier interpretations and used the Bible and ancient records to painstakingly identify the characters and the significance of the objects. Eisen concluded the inner cup to be "a precious relic of the earliest years of Christianity."

The Holy Grail? The cup from which Christ and each of the apostles drank at the Last Supper? Although the Last Supper took place in Jerusalem, Antioch would not be an improbable burial site for the Holy Grail, if indeed it ever existed. According to the New Testament (Acts 11:26), Antioch is where believers in Jesus "were first called Christians." Eisen and others claimed that the inner cup was indeed the very sacred relic associated with Christ and arduously sought through the millennia. If this were true, here was a find of profound importance.

The Holy Grail as the Last Supper cup is the central symbol of a tradition that has inspired many myths; some have taken on complex spiritual and philosophical meanings. It is said that Joseph of Arimathea used the cup to catch the blood of Christ during the Crucifixion. There are references to a holy cup in the New Testament: "The cup we use in the Lord's Supper and for which we give thanks to God; when we drink from it, we are sharing in the blood of Christ" (1 Corinthians 10:16). According to other traditions, the Holy Grail is said to be a fountain of inexhaustible nourishment, always replenishing itself with sustenance to cure the ailing who drink from it; those who imbibe from the cup are protected from evil. The New Testament says, "You cannot drink from the Lord's cup and also from the cup of demons" (1 Corinthians 10:21).

After the first millennium, the search for the Holy Grail became the subject of a variety of romances, involving, among the notable characters, King Arthur and the Knights of the Round Table, Sir Galahad, Parsifal, and Gawain. In these romances the grail had many different manifesta-

sought to release Jesus, but the crowd cried out, "Away with him, away with him, crucify him!" Pilate asked if they wanted their king crucified, and the people responded that their only king was Caesar. And thereupon Pilate turned Jesus over to the will of the people, and the soldiers led him away to be crucified.

The wreath set upon Jesus' head in mockery of a king's crown is of a class of artifacts called liturgical relics—objects or mementos connected with a holy person or a saint, or the body or a body part of such an individual. People have venerated liturgical relics through time—feverishly in the first millennium since Christ, and even to some extent today—as being imbued with healing powers or having particular emanations owing to their association with a holy person.

Because liturgical relics were thought to have mystical powers, possessing them was like having a personal talisman or amulet. It was the practice in centuries past for churches, as well as kings, noblemen, and wealthy families, to acquire divine objects avariciously and display them in magnificent shrines and reliquaries. People would come from afar to visit and touch them, leaving contributions behind in gratitude and reverence.

History contains many stories of celebrated persons possessing putative liturgical relics. For example, the Roman emperor Justin II was supposed to have owned a piece of the cross on which Jesus was crucified; Charlemagne also claimed wooden fragments and nails of the True Cross—relics of the Passion of Christ were especially popular and revered.

Indeed, just about every great event of the Old and New Testaments was resurrected in one sort of physical manifestation

An artist's rendition of Jesus wearing the Crown of Thorns.

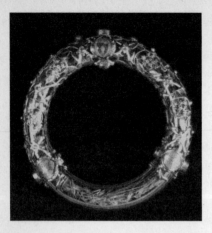

The Crown of Thorns as it exists today, enclosed in a ringlet.

or another during the Middle Ages. There were, for instance, the tablets of the Ten Commandments, the Golden Calf, Moses' staff, fragments of the burning bush, Christ's manger, loaves from the Last Supper. Saints were revered too and were represented by all manner of anatomical parts: ears, legs, arms, fingers, heads, hair, burned flesh, and complete bodies. There was no limit to the kinds and numbers of relics that surfaced. Enterprising individuals even claimed to have discovered relics of fictional legend, such as King Arthur's round table. In an effort to halt the practice of selling bogus objects—indeed, to curb the mania for relics and the abuses in worshiping them—the Roman Catholic Church eventually mandated its approval for introducing new sacred objects.

But what of Jesus' crown of thorns? Did it actually exist? And if so, could it possibly have survived through the ages?

There is a historical record of a crown of thorns dating from 409. At that time it was said to be in Jerusalem among the sacred relics of Mount Zion, where people made pilgrimages to worship it. Occasionally, individual thorns from the crown were presented as gifts and these became venerated relics at the locations they were subsequently taken to.

In 1063, when the safety of the Crown of Thorns in Jerusalem was threatened, it was taken to the royal palace at Constantinople (formerly called Byzantium). Constantinople grew so poor that when Baldwin II became emperor in 1228, he had to travel to other countries to raise money, and eventually realized he would be forced to sell off the city's holy relics to help out. The king of France, Louis IX, was aware of the sanctity of the Constantinople collection and wanted to purchase it. He did, but first he had to pay off the Venetian financiers to whom Baldwin II entrusted his young son as collateral for a loan. When the relics, including the prized Crown of Thorns, arrived in Paris in 1239, they were carried through the streets by the king and others in a grand parade. Around the middle of the thirteenth century Louis IX began construction of the Sainte-Chapelle in

McCrone of McCrone Research Institute in Chicago, argued for the possibility that an artist might have rendered the image on the shroud. However, the preponderance of scientific evidence collected made this conclusion a most controversial one.

The Shroud of Turin Research Project, Inc., or STURP, was formed in 1977 specifically for the purpose of scientifically studying the image mechanism. At the 1978 examination of the shroud, using 6.3×–64× microscopy, the American STURP researchers learned that the image is confined only to the crowns of the threads, that is, the image is found only on the very uppermost portion of each exposed thread in the image area of the fabric. They also learned that the darkness or lightness of the image is not due to darker or lighter fibers, as one might expect in a painting, but instead all image fibers are the same color, straw yellow. Wherever there are more of these fibers, the image is darker. It is this phenomenon that gives the shroud image its three-dimensionality when examined with a space-age machine known as a VP-8 Image Analyzer, explaining and underscoring Vignon's proposal made in 1902.

Shortly after the STURP team returned from Turin, two of their scientists tested the red material in the blood areas with thirteen different chemical tests and determined that it is in fact blood on the cloth and that it probably was there *before* the image was there because there is no evidence of the image beneath the bloodstains.

Simultaneously, an Italian team headed by forensic pathologist Dr. Pierluigi Baima Bollone, conducting independent tests, went even further, stating that their results not only showed it was human blood but proved it was blood type AB!

Since the advent of radiocarbon dating in 1949, experts called for such an analysis to be made which would fairly and accurately date the cloth. For years this idea was rejected because it would require large samples of the cloth to be cut. However, over time the technique became refined so that it required only postage stamp–size samples.*

---

*In 1949 W. F. Libby invented an *indirect* method of counting radiocarbon breakdown (called beta counting) by a means somewhat analogous to a Geiger counter. That method would have required a piece of cloth the size of a handkerchief, obviously too much. The owners of the shroud preferred to wait. In 1977 Dr. Harry E. Gove and his colleagues invented a *direct* method of counting individual C-14 isotopes. This is known today as accelerator mass spectrometry (AMS) and allows the use of considerably smaller samples—in this case postage stamp–size pieces of cloth.

Finally, in 1988 carbon-14 tests were conducted to determine the age of the cloth. If the tests showed the cloth came from the time of Jesus or before, it might be the true Holy Shroud; if they showed it came from a later time, it could be spurious. Investigators cut a single swatch from a corner of the cloth and sent it, along with controls (samples whose dates of origin were definitely known) from the early second century and from the late Middle Ages, to laboratories in the United States, England, and Switzerland. Nuclear accelerators measured the residual radioactive carbon isotopes in the flax from which the linen was made. Such tests can have an accuracy of 95 percent, and the results can be correct within a range of two hundred years or less. The carbon-14 tests rendered a mean date for the shroud sample in the mid–fourteenth century.

Radiocarbon dating has proven over the years to be fairly reliable as an indicator of the age of an object. However, in certain special cases the age determined by the tests does not always match the age expected. Thus archaeologists well know that the radiocarbon test is but one data point that must be evaluated in the light of the spectrum of data collected. The Shroud of Turin may be one of these special cases. Whenever there is a question surrounding the radiocarbon results, one looks at three sources for error: the chemical pretreatment, the equipment used, and the sample itself.

Following the testing of the shroud in 1988, scientists and investigators from around the globe scrutinized the published results. Aside from some statistical problems, there was no evidence that the pretreatment or equipment could be blamed. This meant that if an error had been introduced, the problem had to lie with the sample itself.

Recently two important leads have been uncovered. First, Russian scientists have shown in their Moscow laboratory that the fire of 1532 could have induced a serious error of perhaps some five hundred years by intruding extra carbon into the actual chemical structure of the fibers. Second, an investigator in the United States has discovered the presence of what he calls a "bio-plastic coating" created by a fungal/bacterial symbiotic relationship. This coating actually covers the very fibers from the corner from which the radiocarbon samples were removed. Experiments demonstrated that the pretreatment commonly used in the laboratories for preparing samples for testing might not have removed this serious contaminant.

Moreover, the sample was taken from what is called the "Raes' Corner," named after the Belgian textile expert Dr. Gilbert Raes, who studied

tions—a stone or vase or plate, for instance. This has led some scholars to speculate that the grail is not a physical object but a spiritual force that provides life in whatever form it appears. Thus it may present itself to different groups in different ways, but it is said that as a symbol of religious purity it may appear only to those noble enough in character to perceive it.

Some scholars say it is not the grail itself that is important, but rather the symbolism attached to it, the eternal quest for the highest human potential. Still, the search for the grail—the object—however fantastic, has been and continues to be an active endeavor, one that the searchers believe will bring them eternal life. Some hold that Joseph of Arimathea, who caught Christ's blood from the cross, brought the grail to England, specifically to Glastonbury, where according to legend it still resides at the bottom of the well in which Joseph hid it. No one has ever been able to find it there.

The attachment of the grail legend to the chalice found in Antioch caused its value to rise dramatically. The Kouchakjis, obviously delighted by the controversy, sought a rich collector to purchase the object. One candidate was the banker and philanthropist John Pierpont Morgan. One of Morgan's assistants in New York examined it before its cleansing in Paris, but Morgan died in 1913 before he could even see it. The Kouchakjis' pièce de résistance was then exhibited around Europe, where people flocked to gaze at it; its home base later became a Wall Street bank vault.

Despite scholars' almost unanimous rejection of Eisen's chalice as the Holy Grail—it was generally agreed it could not have been made before the fourth or fifth century—the object eventually priced itself out of the private market. Was the chalice's association with the grail a fabrication for commercial purposes? Had Eisen been a pawn of the Kouchakjis, hired to call attention to, and hence raise the value of, the object?

By this time, the chalice was an object of intrigue. Thomas Costain wrote a novel about it, *The Silver Chalice*, which Warner Brothers turned into a movie starring Paul Newman in his first motion picture role. Clearly, the chalice had captured the public's imagination. In 1950 it found a home when it was purchased by the Cloisters, a museum of Western medieval art in New York City that is a branch of the Metropolitan Museum of Art.

Outrageous claims surrounded the chalice even then. The most remarkable story comes from 1963.

It was Easter Sunday morning. A guard at the museum was making his rounds before the doors opened to the public. He peered through a heavy safety door with a small window into the Cloisters' treasury, where the chalice was kept. Awestruck, he saw the chalice quiver and then suddenly rise three inches off its display block. The guard, frantic, retrieved the head watchman, who also witnessed the chalice levitating. The first guard fell to his knees in prayer. The chalice had levitated at approximately the same time that, according to the Gospels, the Lord Jesus Christ was raised from death almost two thousand years earlier.

The phone rang at the Greenwich Village apartment of Thomas Hoving, the assistant curator of the Cloisters. A hysterical voice told him a phenomenon had taken place at the museum and that he had better rush up there before the premises were besieged by reporters and camera crews.

Arriving at the Cloisters, Hoving found the guards on the verge of religious ecstasy, ready to announce a miracle and summon thousands of pilgrims to the museum that very day. Hoving, ever calm, took a careful look around the treasury and was able to provide a rational explanation for the mystical occurrence.

Between the lights hidden in the pedestal and the interior of the display case was a plastic grid that served to diffuse the beam of the spotlights. A burglar-alarm system had been arranged so that if a thief were to lift the chalice off its display surface, a spring-loaded peg would rise, triggering an alarm in the main office. The plastic grid just happened to collapse at that particular time, making the chalice rise and setting off the alarm. The spring-loaded peg lifted the grid—and the chalice—into the air.

A coincidence? Perhaps. But the guards were never convinced the levitation had anything to do with the alarm system. In any case, the Cloisters kept the story quiet.

Although the Antioch Chalice–Holy Grail identification has been thoroughly discredited—soon after the publication of Gustavus Eisen's books in 1923, scholars began making detailed refutations—the mystery, or at least the obscurity, of the Antioch Chalice's provenance continued to trouble other scholars over the years. It seemed odd in retrospect that the great Stuma, Riha, Hama, and Antioch treasures had been discovered so close together in time. The finds appeared to be linked in other ways as well: by similar workmanship, inscriptions, corrosion, and damage. Could the treasures all have originated in the same place? Could the different treasures in fact have all been part of one large treasure, buried together?

In her book *Silver from Early Byzantium*, Dr. Marlia Mundell Mango offers compelling evidence that there was in fact only one treasure—the "Kaper Koraon Treasure," unearthed in the same place and at the same time: Stuma, 1908—and that the four different "discoveries" were actually a clever ruse devised by antiquities dealers, the Kouchakjis in particular, to avoid confiscation of the valuable objects by the Turkish authorities. (According to Mango, Kaper Koraon was a village whose church received dozens of silver objects between A.D. 540 and 640.)

Some controversy still remains about the chalice itself: scholars disagree over whether it is indeed a liturgical chalice or a goblet or a hanging lamp. But whatever doubts and controversies remain, what cannot be denied and what is universally agreed upon is that the Antioch Chalice is incontrovertibly a most magnificent work of art from early Christian civilization.

LOCATION: Metropolitan Museum of Art, New York, New York. (On loan from the Cloisters.)

The Book of Kells

DATE: Circa 780 to 830.

WHAT IT IS: One of the greatest illuminated manuscripts ever made.

WHAT IT LOOKS LIKE: It contains 340 leaves (680 pages) bound in four volumes. The pages measure 13½ inches by 9½ inches.

We are fortunate that some marauder of the early eleventh century saw fit to discard—and not destroy—an elaborately decorated parchment manuscript after stealing it and purloining its gold cover. Thankfully, serendipity stepped in to rescue the leavings from obscurity so that they would be available for future generations to savor, and from which to learn about the medieval artisans who created them.

The Book of Kells is a masterpiece among illuminated manuscripts—the term applied to texts ornamented with lavishly designed letters and color pictures—ranking with Les Très Riches Heures du Duc de Berry (Condé Museum, Chantilly, France) as the best ever created. Indeed, the Book of Kells has sometimes been called "the most beautiful book in the world."

Illuminated manuscripts were a product primarily of medieval times and followed other forms of written communication set down on materials such as stone tablets, clay tablets, wood boards, bamboo strips, papyrus, leather, vellum, and parchment. Book production began thousands of years earlier, in such ancient places as Egypt, Sumeria, and Babylonia, and continued over the centuries in other cultures throughout the Roman Empire, which began about 27 B.C. and endured until about A.D. 400.

On various mediums, people set down everything from law codes and religious codes to philosophies and mythologies, and in the first millennium prior to the birth of Christ the Greeks and Romans especially achieved a high level of literary accomplishment. Several epic poems were written, including the *Iliad*, attributed to the Greek poet Homer (ninth to eighth century B.C.), and the *Aeneid*, by the Roman poet Virgil (70 to 19 B.C.). Accompanying texts with colored drawings existed prior to the first millennium A.D.—the *Papyrus Book of the Dead* (British Museum, London), created about 1250 B.C., is an example—but the actual practice of producing manuscripts with meticulously written letters and copious illustrations executed in painstaking detail did not realize its potential as an art form until the Middle Ages, which began about A.D. 500 and continued until about 1450.

Unlike previous eras, where libraries flourished and learning was held in high esteem, during the Middle Ages' early centuries—the Dark Ages, as they came to be called—it was survival, not books, that occupied most people's attention. Barbarians swept through Europe destroying the Roman Empire, seizing land, razing libraries, devastating trade and industry, and uprooting social systems. Eventually a feudal system arose in western Europe; the farmers, who gave their land over for protection to noblemen and toiled long, hard hours, were basically ignorant, unable to read or write. Over time the church rose in prominence and power, collecting taxes and asserting political influence. The church also became the center of learning, albeit primarily for its prelacy, but it was here that high culture was preserved.

In the monasteries monks would work in rooms called scriptoria and labor painstakingly to copy and illuminate old Latin and Greek texts. Great care was given to producing books that were actually works of art in themselves. Many illuminated manuscripts were produced throughout Europe during the Middle Ages—for the church or for the wealthy nobility—and they have traditionally been categorized by the place of origin, such as Celtic or Byzantine or Anglo-Saxon or Dutch, each category being known for particular artistic styles and embellishments. the Book of Kells, with its exquisite ornamentation, is an outstanding example of Celtic art produced by the Irish monasteries.

An elaborate reproduction of the Four Gospels with pictures, the Book of Kells contains handsome cursive lettering, imaginative designs, skillful portraits, and masterful coloring. The Latin text of the Gospels is written in majuscule script. The paragraphs begin with unique decorative capital letters that take on different shapes picturing creatures and plants and geometric forms, and that stand out from the rest of the text. The inter-

The chi-rho page from the Book of Kells. Brilliantly drawn animals, human figures, letters, and objects in this ninth-century work, also known as the Gospel of Columcille, celebrate the four Gospels.

laced designs of various objects suggest a variety of interpretations, including life and death, immortality, etherealness, and mystery.

The text of the manuscript is brought to life with pictures of various events in the life of Jesus Christ. Whether it is the scene of Jesus' birth or his arrest before the Crucifixion, the illustrations reflect the warmth or despair of the event. Numerous exotically drawn animals adorn the pages, including cats, birds, mice, fish, lizards, scorpions, and horses, and are often depicted in funny ways. In their decorations the monks exhibit a range of emotions, from humor to religious devotion, from a love of life to an appreciation for nature, and provide through their illustrations an extraordinary view of medieval culture and civilization.

Many mysteries surround the provenance of this masterpiece. Who were its scribes and painters, and how many were there? Where was it created? How long did it take to produce? There is scholarly conjecture, but no definitive answers exist.

The anonymous Book of Kells is believed to have been created by monks working in a scriptorium on the island of Iona, part of the Inner Hebrides, off the northwest coast of Scotland. Here a monastery was founded by Saint Columba (Columcille) in the early 560s. Probably sometime in the late eighth century—almost two centuries after the death of Columba in 597—a group of monks set themselves to the painstaking task of creating this ornamental manuscript for religious services. Analysis of the style of the letters and of the painting seems to indicate several monks were actually engaged in its production.

If the book had been created by the end of the eighth century, it fortuitously survived the rapaciousness and barbarism of invaders. In 795 Norsemen began a series of attacks on Iona in search of booty. They came again in 802, and four years after that, and again two decades later. In their raids they not only took various relics but destroyed certain objects and slaughtered monks. By 880 all the monks' relics had been removed from Iona, mostly to Ireland.

The Great Gospel of Columcille was taken to the village of Kells, in the central eastern part of Ireland. It was kept in the cathedral there, and the worshipers made pilgrimages to the village to see this relic. Its reputation spread, and of course it was an object of temptation to plunderers. In 1007 a robber stole the one-volume manuscript and its case from the cathedral at Kells. He extracted its gold cover festooned with valuable gems (never since found) and discarded the pages. Many of the leaves were found eleven weeks later submerged in sod, a discovery recorded in the Annals of Ulster. The manuscript remained at Kells until the 1650s, when it was taken to Dublin. (This was at a time of political instability because of the civil war in England and the rise to power of the Puritans and Oliver Cromwell.) After 1661 the manuscript was taken for safe-keeping to Trinity College, where only once did it suffer a casualty—the result of ineptness rather than deliberate mutilation. In 1821 a binder cropped the manuscript in various places, cutting off sections of the design. In 1953 the Book of Kells was separated into its individual Gospels and bound into four volumes.

Within a hundred years after the invention of printing around the mid-1400s, the golden age of illuminated manuscripts came to an end. Over the centuries many superb artifacts were lost in Europe in such conflicts and calamities as the Crusades, the Black Death, the Hundred Years' War, the Wars of the Roses, the Napoleonic Wars, and much more. But as turmoil ravaged much of the outside world, the Book of Kells was kept sequestered in quiet rooms, perhaps not unlike the scriptoria in which it was created. The pages of this majestic work show the artistic genius of the medieval monks who, as much as they brilliantly illuminated the pages, created a work for the ages, one that owing to the good graces of serendipity and careful preservation will shine on for posterity.

LOCATION: Trinity College Library, Dublin, Ireland.

The Bayeux Tapestry and the Domesday Book

DATE: Circa 1070s, Bayeux Tapestry; 1086, Domesday Book.

WHAT THEY ARE: The Bayeux Tapestry is an embroidery that pictorially depicts the conquest of England by William, the duke of Normandy. The Domesday Book is William's exhaustive survey of landholdings and livestock in England, made twenty years after he became the ruler of the country.

WHAT THEY LOOK LIKE: The Bayeux Tapestry measures almost 20 inches wide and 230 feet long. It is embroidered on linen with dyed wools of different colors. Latin inscriptions accompany the various scenes.

The Domesday Book is in two parts: Great Domesday (split into two volumes in 1986), a survey of thirty-one counties, containing nearly 400 folios written in two columns; and Little Domesday, a survey of three counties, containing 450 folios written in a single column, and only slightly smaller. Both are written on parchment made from sheepskin, and the text is in Latin.

The lack of a clear successor to a childless king set the stage for a momentous medieval drama. Inevitably, the denouement was bloody, but it was also surprisingly swift; in the measure of a fleeting moment, the social fabric of a nation and the course it would take through the currents of history were altered dramatically. The story of the last conquest of England by an outsider and the conqueror's vivid accounting of his new kingdom, both unique records that are intertwined historically, are remarkably preserved in two separate artifacts of the day.

The future of England lay in darkness in January 1066, when King Edward the Confessor died and left no child to inherit his coveted realm. When the very next day the earl of Wessex, Harold Godwineson, hastily installed himself on the royal seat, thoughts of conquest began fomenting in the minds of powerful men in surrounding lands. Tostig, Harold's exiled brother in Flanders, wanted to return to his homeland and take the throne for himself. King Harold Hardraade of Norway, ever on the lookout to expand his empire, also coveted England. And William, duke of Normandy, believed himself the rightful heir of Edward, claiming the king had promised him the crown and that Harold had sworn a sacred oath to support William as Edward's successor after William obtained his release when he was taken prisoner in France and held for ransom.

While Harold Godwineson tended to the tasks facing the new royal administration, what was really on his mind were the hostile fleets he knew would press through the seas and land on the shores of England. Anticipating a major assault by Duke William, he mobilized his forces on England's southern coast. Tostig was the first to launch an attack, however, and he was repelled by Harold's superior troops.

By August the English army grew tired of waiting for William—who was delayed by unfavorable winds—and with its provisions nearly exhausted, it disbanded. Then the Norwegians attacked at Stamford Bridge—joined by Tostig, who had taken refuge in Scotland—and defeated the men serving the earls of that area. Harold summoned his available forces north, and they crushed the aggressors.

By now William was anxiously awaiting the right winds to launch his ambitious campaign. Realizing the formidable task of taking on the English militia on their own grounds, he assembled the most potent army he could. He appealed to Norman aristocrats and prelates for financial support. He denounced Harold's violation of his sacred oath and received the blessing of the papacy in Rome. Professional warriors throughout Europe were attracted to his mission for the booty that the conquest promised.

Sometime after dark on September 27, William and an army of approximately eight thousand warriors and a large number of horses on hundreds of vessels set sail from St.-Valéry-sur-Somme, arriving the next morning at the English coastal town of Pevensey. The troops immediately proceeded to Hastings, a more strategic location; from there they pillaged the surrounding countryside, baiting Harold to expedite orders to march his troops south. Several days later an army of English soldiers, exhausted and hungry, arrived from Stamford Bridge near York and made camp. The following morning, the fourteenth of October, 1066, William launched an attack at Hastings. The encounter was a brutal affair, fought with metal maces, battle-axes, lances, swords, spears, clubs, and arrows, and William defeated Harold. He continued his campaign north and finally gained recognition of his claim to the English throne.

Probably within a decade of the Battle of Hastings, work began on a wall hanging recording the events that caused William to invade England and the conquest itself. It is not known for certain who made or commissioned the work. Traditionally, it was held that King William's wife, Matilda, stitched it as a tribute to her husband, with the help of her attendants. This theory was discounted by nineteenth-century investigators, however, who believed the work was commissioned by William's half-brother, Odon de Conteville, a bishop in the French town of Bayeux. The evidence does indeed point to the bishop, given William's largesse to Odon; the tapestry's premise being skewed in favor of William, justifying his attack on England; the featuring of Odon in the work; the home of the tapestry being the same town as Odon's; and other factors. If this is true, it is also quite ironic for two reasons: the tapestry was probably made in England, whose people were conquered by the leader it glorifies, and Odon eventually fell out of favor with William and by his orders was imprisoned.

The Bayeux Tapestry is on eight pieces of cloth and in the eighteenth century was divided into fifty-eight scenes. Its extended length and narrow width give it the appearance of an enlarged ribbon, and what a colorful one it is. People, animals, boats, weapons, trees, buildings, and other objects are stitched in action scenes in brightly colored wools against a light background; the Latin inscriptions appear above the action near the top. The craftsmanship is of extremely high quality: the artwork is detailed (facial expressions are apparent, for example, and costumes are decorative), the stitching brings out contrast and depth, and the text is woven clearly.

The story illustrated and narrated in the Bayeux Tapestry begins with

A panel scene from the Bayeux Tapestry: Duke William of Normandy issuing commands to his soldiers after Harold, the emissary of the king of England, is captured in France.

King Edward in conversation. By some accounts, he is ordering Harold to go to Normandy to announce to William that he has chosen him as his successor. The English duke, Harold, and his soldiers set off on their journey on horseback, with a pack of hounds in front of them. At Bosham church (which can still be found in Sussex) Harold prays for divine blessing in his mission. Later, Harold and his men are dining when word comes that the wind is favorable. Harold and his crew board their ships.

A storm blows Harold's fleet off course. Instead of landing on the coast of Normandy, the ships land on the coast of Ponthieu. The crew disembarks, and Harold is taken prisoner by the owner of the land, Count Guy de Ponthieu. Harold is taken to the count's palace and held for ransom. Representatives of Duke William, who heard about Harold's abduction, come to Guy's palace. Failing to obtain Harold's release, they report back to the duke, who dispatches a couple of knights to effect Harold's emancipation. Count Guy delivers his prisoner to William, who brings the Englishman to his castle, where they talk. William is said to promise one of his daughters to be betrothed to Harold. Then William leads an army of Normans, with Harold joining them, in a mission to expel the duke of Brittany, Conan, a disloyal subject. Along the route horses fall in the

Arrival at the English port of Pevensey by Duke William's ship.

quicksands of Mont-St.-Michel bay. The Norman soldiers attack the enemy. In defeat, Conan turns over the city keys to William. William knights Harold, then brings him to Bayeux, where the English duke takes a sacred oath to support William as Edward's successor.

Harold returns to England and reports to King Edward, who dies shortly thereafter. Saxon nobles offer Harold the crown of England, and Harold becomes king. People sight a comet, commonly believed to be a harbinger of disaster; astrologers say the comet portends bad luck for Harold.

Messengers leave by ship to tell Duke William of Harold's ascension. By William's orders, men chop down trees to build a fleet. Weapons are gathered and carried to the ships. By horse and by foot, William's massive army travels to the vessels. They cross the Channel and arrive at Pevensey. The horses are let off the ships, and the army rushes to Hastings, where the men prepare a meal, blessed by Bishop Odon.

William receives a message that Harold's troops are coming. William's soldiers leave Hastings and ready for war. Scouts inform both William and Harold about the opposing army's position, and William urges his men to fight bravely and intelligently.

The battle begins. Many Englishmen are cut down, including Harold's brothers Lewine and Gyrd. The casualties mount on both sides. William raises his helmet to let his men know he is still alive, and his troops are spurred on. Saxon soldiers are killed, and then Harold, king of England, is himself mortally wounded. The remaining Saxon soldiers flee, and William, duke of Normandy, has conquered England.

The Bayeux Tapestry took about ten years to make. By the time it was finished, William was firmly implanted as the king of England, and many of his soldiers had become permanent residents of a new land.

As mighty as William the Conqueror was, much of his reign was spent quelling rebellions and warding off invasions by foreigners. To the English, William himself was a foreigner, a Norman. The rewards he gave to his soldiers and Norman supporters came at the expense of staunch Anglo-Saxons. Resentful old English nobility, regarded as a threat to the new king's power, were killed or compelled to flee the country.

William performed quite competently in defending his realm, as Normans and Anglo-Saxons melded under one feudal system. But on Christmas 1085, almost twenty years after he was crowned, at a meeting convened at the royal court in Gloucester, William held "very deep speech" with his witan (counselors) about English land and its ownership. For complex reasons, including the need to assess geld (land tax) liability (particularly in view of William's need to buttress his army in the face of more likely foreign invasions) and the king's desire for a written record of his feudal kingdom and its wealth, he decided to conduct a survey of his realm.

The survey commenced in 1086. Commissioners, or *legati*, were dispatched to hold inquests in the country's shires. It was the task of the king's representatives to compile detailed accounts of how much land and livestock everyone had and what their values were; what land William had in the country; and what taxes he should collect annually from each shire.

According to a later medieval document, the commissioners requested much information:

> The name of the estate; who held it in the time of King Edward; who holds it now; how many hides [units of land ownership]; how many ploughs on the demesne [the lord's land]; how many among the men; how many villeins [free peasants in between cot-

The Domesday Book actually consists of two books, Great Domesday (in back) and Little Domesday.

tars and sokemen in status]; how many cottars [lowest subordinate peasants]; how many slaves; how many freemen; how many sokemen [free peasants]; how much wood; how much meadow; how much pasture; how many mills; how many fishponds; how much has been added or taken away; how much, taken altogether, it used to be worth and how much now; how much each freeman or sokeman had or has. All this [to be given] three times, that is, in the time of King Edward, as it was when King William first gave the estate, and as it is now; also whether it is possible that more [revenue] could be taken from the estate than is being taken now.*

The survey was referred to by various names over the next century. But *Domesday*, meaning judgment day, dominated popular usage. This was no doubt because of tales of woe passed on about the inquests, which were conclusive and dreaded affairs that consumed the lives of Englishmen for the better part of a year.

*From *Domesday: A Search for the Roots of England* by Michael Wood (New York: Facts on File Publications, 1986).

Information obtained by the king's authorities was turned over to the royal treasury at Winchester, where it is believed a single scribe transferred the information into a single volume, Great Domesday. Little Domesday was written in the hand of several men during the period of the inquests and probably not transferred to Great Domesday because of the death of William in 1087.

Domesday is not a perfect document. There are errors, inconsistencies, and omissions; northern counties and large towns such as London and Winchester were not included in the survey. No doubt its imperfections are due, in part, to William's desire to accomplish the survey quickly.

On the surface, the Domesday volumes appear as simple inventories of properties. Yet between the lines they contain a wealth of data to which scholars have devoted lifetimes of study. They are an invaluable treasury of information on medieval life, cryptic in part, with new jewels constantly being brought to the surface.

Both the Bayeux Tapestry and the Domesday Book are remarkable eleventh-century historical works. The tapestry presents a fascinating chronicle of the last conquest of England, and the Domesday Book offers a vivid portrait of feudal England that sheds light on every layer of English society, from slaves and shepherds to knights and barons and King William himself. That such massive undertakings were executed and carried out so methodically is as astonishing as their preservation through the centuries.

LOCATIONS: Bayeux Tapestry: William the Conqueror Center, Bayeux, France.
Domesday Book: Public Record Office, London, England.

The Holy Child of Aracoeli

DATE: Circa 1490s.

WHAT IT IS: A small statue of a child, venerated for working miracles.

WHAT IT LOOKS LIKE: The statue is 20½ inches high and made of wood, and has a 4-inch-high crown. It is dressed in a gown bedecked with golden chains, pins, lockets, and other jewels given by people as expressions of gratitude.

The letters pour in daily: supplications from the sick and needy, confessions from the contrite, appeals for solace from the bereaved. From around the world, the faithful send missives to a little statue known as the Holy Child. The correspondents expect no earthly acknowledgment of their prayers and entreaties but devoutly believe their letters will be answered in a more ethereal way.

The story of the Holy Child of Aracoeli is part fact and part legend, the latter an unavoidable consequence of time and reverence becoming intertwined with the subject. The saga begins in Jerusalem at the close of the fifteenth century, when a Franciscan friar fashioned a wooden statue in the image of a young Jesus Christ, the wood allegedly from an olive tree in Gethsemane, the garden tended by the Franciscans. The Garden of Gethsemane, the New Testament tells us, was where Jesus went after the Last Supper, entered into an intense time of prayer, was strengthened by an angel, and then arrested prior to the Crucifixion.

The friar ran into trouble when it came time to paint the carved figure, because he lacked the desired coloring materials. Having commenced this project with great enthusiasm, the friar was deeply distressed and prayed

The Holy Child of Aracoeli, venerated for its miraculous healing powers and charitable favors.

fervently for help. Then, as legend has it, he fell asleep, during which time an angel appeared and painted the statue. Word of the miracle spread, and people came from all over to see Il Santa Bambino, the Holy Child.

Soon the friar was summoned to Rome, and he brought the figure with him with the intention of placing it in the Nativity Scene at the Church of Santa Maria in Aracoeli, located on the top of the Campidoglio hill. He traveled to Italy by boat, but during the voyage a violent storm forced the passengers to throw their cargo overboard, and the friar despairingly dropped the Holy Child into the sea. Incredibly, however, the encased statue floated into the port of Livorno not long after the boat from which it was dropped arrived. The Holy Child's reputation became even more widespread, and people flocked to admire it. Eventually, the custom arose of petitioning the divine infant for miracles.

Deemed a miracle worker, the Bambino had its own share of close calls. During the sacking of Rome in 1527, the statue was stolen, but it was later recovered; in 1798, after Napoleon had swept through Italy, some of his soldiers in Rome started a fire and began throwing valuables into it. A local citizen urgently offered money for the statue and saved the Bambino from being incinerated.

The reforms and liberal goals of Pope Pius IX, who was elected in 1846, were opposed by the common people and sparked revolts throughout Italy in what became known as the War of 1848 and 1849. Hostilities abounded, and in one episode Romans stormed the pontiff's stable to seize his coaches and burn them in the People's Square. But even the wrath of the people at this incendiary moment was no match for their love of the Holy Child. A local public official named Sturbinetti suggested the rioters spare Pius's finest carriage and let it be used to transport the statue to the homes of the sick. The Holy Child was frequently taken to the very ill to give benediction. Indeed, many stories were told about the miraculous recovery of terminally ill people after the Bambino was brought before them. So revered was the Holy Child that formal recognition was accorded on May 2, 1897, when Pope Leo XIII crowned the statue in a solemn rite.

Veneration of the Bambino continues today, primarily by mail. The envelopes are inspected to see whether they contain money, offerings of gratitude for the benign favors asked of the statue. Any money found in the letters goes to help the poor. The letters are placed around the Holy Child for a period of time, after which they are destroyed to make room for new ones.

Every Christmas, thousands of letters from children around the world arrive at the cathedral on the Campidoglio. Often whimsical but always sincere, the notes express special hopes and desires. By tradition, the Bambino's benediction and miracles reach everywhere and to anyone who believes in its workings—young and old alike.

With its glowing boyish face and fine physical condition, it sometimes is difficult to appreciate that the Holy Child is half a millennium old. That in itself is a small miracle.

LOCATION: Church of Santa Maria in Aracoeli, Rome, Italy.

Columbus's Books of Privileges

DATE: 1498 and 1502.

WHAT THEY ARE: Compilations of documents setting forth titles, honors, prerogatives, and financial benefits granted to Christopher Columbus between 1492 (before his first voyage to the New World) and 1502 (prior to his fourth and last voyage) by King Ferdinand and Queen Isabella of Spain.

WHAT THEY LOOK LIKE: The so-called Genoa, Paris, and Washington codices are written on vellum, the Veragua codex on paper. The Genoa and Paris codices contain forty documents, the Washington codex has thirty-six documents (on forty-seven leaves). The Veragua codex contains twenty-nine documents (on thirty-six leaves); it is encased in a dark brown leather binder with pieces of iron, and painted on the back cover is the shield, or coat of arms, of Columbus. The other codices are bound also, and the Genoa and Paris codices also bear Columbus's coat of arms.

The world at the dawn of the sixteenth century was on the brink of remarkable change. Just fifty years earlier Johannes Gutenberg of Germany had invented movable type, opening the gateway for mass dissemination of the printed word. Leonardo da Vinci of Italy was performing ingenious scientific and engineering experiments, foreshadowing the spirit, imagination, and brilliance with which people would one day make great discoveries and usher in technological eras. Nicolaus Copernicus of Poland was peering into the firmament and making observations that would lead him to disprove the long-held Ptolemaic theory of an Earth-centered universe in favor of a solar system composed of planets revolving around the sun. But perhaps the most extraordinary change for Europeans was the discovery of the other half of the planet by Christopher Columbus for Spain, opening extraordinary new vistas for trade and colonization. Leading men westward in three caravels across an expansive, dangerous, and unknown ocean in his maiden voyage in 1492, Columbus chased a wild dream and changed the world forever.

Now, in the year 1500, the admiral of the Indies stood in the royal court of King Ferdinand and Queen Isabella of Spain. The once-mighty mariner was weeping, proclaiming his allegiance, importuning for benign consideration from the sovereigns, with an abject humbleness previously inconceivable. Less than two months before, he had been arrested in the New World, shackled, and put on a caravel to be returned to Spain. It was a prodigious fall from grace for Don Cristóbal Colón, who just a handful of years earlier had been exalted as the world's most renowned navigator.

Inspired by Marco Polo's grand and romantic tales of the exotic mineral- and spice-opulent Indies, Christopher Columbus in the 1480s longed for a seagoing mission west to Asia. He sought financial backing from various royal patrons, but his plan was rejected as too costly and impractical. Interest later came from the rulers of Spain, King Ferdinand and Queen Isabella, although they too thought the cost of the mission prohibitive— supplying vessels, fitting out the crew, and financing other aspects of it— especially at a time when their soldiers were trying to expel the Moors from Spain. There was also the matter of *mercedes*, or rewards. It was the practice of the day for explorers to negotiate concessions for their discoveries: rights, property, benefits, honorary titles, and so forth. Columbus demanded such extensive privileges that even Ferdinand and Isabella were taken aback.

The sovereigns ordered a study of the planned mission, but because they were preoccupied with more pressing matters they were in no rush for its completion. Columbus waited patiently for six years, hoping the king and queen would finance his mission and grant him his requested privileges, only to be eventually turned down. Disappointed, he left the court in Santa Fé. Shortly afterward, however, a friend of Columbus's, a

royal treasurer named Luis de Santángel, convinced Isabella that the risks of financing the expedition would be small in comparison to the potential gains, and that if Columbus sought out another ruler to sponsor him he could go on to make discoveries that would be disadvantageous to Spain. Negotiations resumed between the explorer and the sovereigns, and finally Columbus received the royal backing he wanted.

Among the concessions granted Columbus in April 1492 were the title of admiral, his appointment as governor over all the lands he might discover, and a tax-free income of 10 percent of all revenues—gold, silver, and spices—obtained in these lands. Through the years Columbus would collect more rights, or privileges, and the documents conferring these privileges were in various instances signed by Ferdinand and Isabella and royal officials.

Columbus's 1492 expedition resulted, of course, in the discovery of the New World.* The small Spanish fleet landed in the Bahamas and went on to discover Hispaniola, an island of the West Indies, now the site of Haiti and the Dominican Republic. On December 25, 1492, one of Columbus's ships, the *Santa Maria*, was wrecked in Hispaniola. Columbus had to leave forty crew members behind, but he returned to Spain with gold trinkets bartered from the natives, slaves, and the monumental news of the world across the ocean. Columbus was honored on his return, and granted the titles Admiral of the Ocean Sea, and Viceroy and Governor of the Indies.

El almirante's exultation was short-lived, however. Sent by Ferdinand and Isabella back to the New World in 1493, Columbus found to his dismay that the men left in Hispaniola had been killed in clashes with the natives. Columbus, who brought approximately one thousand men to the New World on his second voyage, discovered more islands but returned to Spain three years later with little of value for Ferdinand and Isabella.

---

*Other Europeans and Asians may have preceded Columbus into the New World, parts of which were clearly inhabited by the time he arrived, but by "discovery" it is meant that with his 1492 voyage Columbus initiated a Renaissance exploration of the New World by Europeans, which led to colonization and settlement, and the cultural, economic, and sociological development of the Western Hemisphere. It should be noted that much criticism has been directed at Columbus, particularly during the period of the 1992 Columbus quincentenary, when the explorer was accused of committing numerous atrocities, but historians have traditionally credited Columbus with "discovering" America and have cited his navigational skills, bravery, and indomitable spirit.

After he arrived in Spain, Columbus began to compile the privileges that he had collected in the New World. His reputation diminished, he believed that the Spanish monarchs now favored other navigators over him, and he wanted to safeguard what had been conferred on him, which was so immensely important to him. The admiral had some of the original documents granted to him through the years, but others were missing. Columbus requested authorized copies of what he did not have and compiled them in a set. As a wayfarer, he needed to deposit them with someone he could trust. This quality he found in his friend Fray Gaspar Gorricio, who resided in the Monastery de las Cuevas in Seville.

A third opportunity to travel to the New World came in 1498, after Ferdinand and Isabella decided to back Columbus once again. He sailed to new places and returned to Hispaniola, finding turmoil on the island. From inedible food to a lack of gold, the colonists were restless and unhappy. Many returned to Spain denouncing Columbus, and it wasn't long before their criticism reached the ears of the king and queen.

The sovereigns grew concerned about reports that Columbus was performing incompetently, as well as about other reports they heard about sickness and rebellion, lack of conversions to Christianity among the native population, and meager profits. Action had to be taken.

In the summer of 1500 a fleet of Spanish ships arrived at Hispaniola, and a man named Francisco de Bobadilla presented to Columbus a royal letter of commission confirming his appointment as governor of the island. Incredulous that the king and queen would usurp his position, Columbus would not recognize Bobadilla's claim, even with the letter. Bobadilla had him arrested and chained and put on a vessel to return to Spain. He also seized all of Columbus's possessions, including the documents of privileges he had in his possession on the island.

Several weeks after he arrived in Spain, Columbus was ordered released by Ferdinand and Isabella, who dispatched funds to enable him to come to court at Granada. When he appeared in court, Columbus, now forty-nine years of age and somewhat infirm, wept before them and apologized. The sovereigns, in consideration of his fantastic accomplishments, reinstated all his privileges and revenues that had been halted when he was arrested. (They did not grant, however, Columbus's request that Bobadilla be punished.)

Eventually the king and queen approved a fourth voyage for Colum-

bus. By 1502 Columbus was in Seville, and preparations were well under way for the expedition, which would return him one final time to the New World. Before he was to embark on this voyage, however, there was one thing he wanted to accomplish.

Afraid that the transcripts of the coveted privileges bestowed upon him by King Ferdinand and Queen Isabella could be lost, damaged, stolen, or confiscated, he wanted to have multiple copies of the original documents conferring these privileges made and disseminated to different locations and stored for safekeeping. Columbus's position in Spain was certainly tenuous now, and he intended to ensure as best he could that he and his descendants would be entitled to those rights and privileges he was accorded and which he felt he had rightfully earned.

Columbus obtained official authorization from the king and queen to have authenticated copies of his privileges transcribed, and on January 5, 1502, magistrates and public notaries of Seville gathered at Columbus's house. The magistrates examined Columbus's original titles and privileges and then authorized the notaries to make copies.

The tenor of the privileges may be appreciated from a scribe's introduction:

> In the most noble and most loyal city of Seville, Wednesday the fifth day of the month of January, in the year of the nativity of our Saviour Jesus Christ one thousand five hundred and two. On this said day, at the hour when Vespers are said, or a little before or after, being in the dwelling house of the Lord Admiral of the Indies which is in this said city in the parish of St. Mary, before Stephen de la Roca and Peter Ruys Montero, ordinary Alcaldes in this said city of Seville for the King and Queen our Lords, and in the presence of me Martin Rodrigues, public scrivener of this said city of Seville, and of the undermentioned witnesses, did appear there present the very magnificent Lord Don Christopher Columbus, High Admiral of the Ocean, Viceroy and Governor of the Islands and Main Land, and laid before the said Alcaldes certain patents and privileges and warrants of the said King and Queen our Lords, written on paper and parchment, and signed with their royal names, and sealed with their seals of lead hanging by threads of coloured silk, and with coloured wax on the back, and countersigned by certain officers of their royal household, as ap-

The first vellum page of Columbus's Books of Privileges, now at the Library of Congress. It is the only copy that begins with the May 4, 1493, proclamation of Pope Alexander VI, specifically acknowledging Columbus's discoveries.

peared in all and each of them. The tenor whereof, one after the other, is as follows.*

Copies were made on vellum and paper. Not each copy was derived in total from the original set; a comparison of the codices has revealed variations that would be consistent with successive generations of copying. (Columbus scholar Frances G. Davenport reported in a 1909 study that the so-called Genoa codex was made from the original book, and, at least partially, the Paris copy was based on the Genoa codex, and the Washington copy was based on the Paris version.)

Columbus made provisions for his Books of Privileges to be disbursed as follows: One vellum copy (ultimately known as the Genoa codex) was to be delivered to Nicolò Oderigo in Genoa via Francisco de Rivarola; another vellum copy (the Paris codex) was to be delivered to Oderigo via Francisco Catano. The paper copy was to be delivered by Alonso Sanchez de Carvajal, an agent of Columbus, to Hispaniola. The remaining vellum, or file copy, was to be dispatched with the original set to the Monastery de las Cuevas, where the admiral's close friend Fray Gaspar Gorricio resided.

In May 1502 Columbus departed from Cadiz on his last voyage to the New World. As Columbus embarked westward across the ocean, his "privilege codes" began their own circuitous journeys.

The two vellum copies that were sent to Oderigo were retained by him for safekeeping and passed on to his descendants, one of whom presented them to the republic of Genoa in 1670. These copies were later to take different routes.

*Translated by Henry Harrisse in his introduction to *Christopher Columbus: His Own Book of Privileges, 1502,* published in London in 1893.

Around 1805 one of the Genoa copies was seized and taken to Paris, one of the many cultural and artistic appropriations of Napoleon in his zealous attempt to enrich France with the antiquities of foreign lands. Envoys of the French Institute traveled to major cities of Europe to take inventories of their museums and archives and submitted reports of what they found. Crates of treasures poured into Paris, which was gradually fulfilling Napoleon's vision as a central repository for the continent.

That status was transient, however. Within about ten years, after Napoleon abdicated and France signed treaties providing for the restitution of property to the countries it had ransacked, most of the treasures were returned. One that was not, however, was the Columbus codex, which subsequently lay unrecognized for years.

The other Genoa copy ended up in the patrician family of Count Michelangelo Cambiaso. Cambiaso's descendants had planned to sell his historic collection of documents, but the city's governing body appealed to the king of Sardinia, Vittorio Emanuele I, who in 1816 ordered the papers, including Columbus's *Libro dei privilegi*, to be returned to Genoa. This set of privileges today resides in the same Genoa archives as three letters written by Columbus between 1502 and 1504, including one in which he discusses his codices of privileges.

It is not known what happened to the paper copy taken to Hispaniola by Alonso Sanchez de Carvajal, for it was never seen again.

The fates of the original Book of Privileges and the vellum file copy that were sent to the Monastery de las Cuevas in Seville are also shrouded in mystery. They were used in a lawsuit in 1511, and what remained of the family archives in the monastery was removed by a Columbus descendant in 1609. After that, what happened to these two volumes is not precisely known, except that at some point they were separated.

But more than two hundred years later, in 1818, there was a curious development. Edward Everett, a Harvard professor of Greek literature who would become a prominent statesman in America (most remembered for the speech he delivered at Gettysburg prior to President Lincoln's address), purchased in Florence, Italy, a set of vellum documents containing various privileges conferred upon Christopher Columbus by King Ferdinand and Queen Isabella of Spain. Could this be the missing vellum file copy that was the partner of the original set in the Seville monastery?

One of the documents contained the notation that it was made under the authorization of King Ferdinand and Queen Isabella, copied from the originals by Martin Rodrigues. Everett read the Genoa codex when it was published in Italy in 1823, and the next year he described his Columbus documents in a published speech. The historical value of the transcripts went largely unnoticed, however, and Everett kept them filed away.

For the 1892 quatercentenary celebration of Columbus's arrival in the New World, the city of Genoa produced a facsimile of its vellum copy, and Henry Harrisse and Benjamin F. Stevens published an elaborate facsimile edition of a copy that Harrisse had found in 1880 in the archives of the Department of French Foreign Affairs in Paris—the copy confiscated in Genoa during Napoleon's military sweep. While researching his introductory essay, Harrisse had read Everett's 1824 description of his Columbus documents. Intrigued by the possibility that Everett's copy was the missing vellum file copy, Harrisse wanted to compare it with the Paris and Genoa codices.

In 1892 Harrisse contacted Everett's son, William, who said he did not know the whereabouts of the documents his father had written about. Everett, in fact, had previously been queried about them by the nineteenth-century historian Justin Winsor. In the introduction to his book *Christopher Columbus: His Own Book of Privileges, 1502,* Harrisse wrote that to his knowledge the Paris and Genoa codices were the only known vellum copies to exist, although he suspected the documents Everett described might indeed be the missing third vellum copy. (Harrisse conjectured that the paper copy taken to Hispaniola was consumed by "worms and ants.")

Subsequently, William Everett was going through some papers in an old desk of his father's and found what seemed to be the missing Columbus documents. He took them to England, where an authority asserted they were of little value. So he returned to Massachusetts, placed the documents in a desk drawer, and essentially dismissed any notion that they might be significant. A few years later a fire broke out, but fortunately the Columbus documents were not damaged. Everett decided he should make another attempt to find out what they were.

This time he brought the transcripts to Wilberforce Eames, a librarian for James Lenox, the great American bibliophile whose collection of books in part formed the New York Public Library. Eames immediately recognized the compilation as having tremendous historical significance, and he contacted Herbert Putnam, the librarian of Congress. Some months later, in 1901, the library purchased this compilation (the Washington or Florentine codex).

Christopher Columbus (standing and pointing) has an audience with King Ferdinand and Queen Isabella at the Royal Court of Spain. (This lithograph was made in 1892 by Mast, Crowell & Kirkpatrick.)

How this Book of Privileges surfaced in Italy is not known, but historians have offered speculations. One possibility is that Columbus's grandson, Luis, sold the documents to someone in Italy around 1520. Another is that the documents left Spain in the seventeenth century following a court case in which Baldassare Colombo, an Italian claiming to be a descendant of Columbus, exhibited to the Council of the Indies a compilation of privileges notarized by Martin Rodrigues in 1502 as proof that he should be the next heir to the title. He may have legally or illegally brought back the documents with him to Italy in 1605.

Because of the Washington codex's undocumented history, there remains the possibility that it is not one of the original copies made in Christopher Columbus's home in Seville in 1502, although none of its transcripts bear a date later than 1502 and no evidence has surfaced that contradicts this being the original's partner at the monastery. Although this copy lacks some of the documents contained in the Genoa and Paris codices, the fact that it also lacks an elaborate rubricated title page and colored coat of arms supports the possibility that this was the file copy retained with the originals. Still, the Washington codex awaits a thorough, scholarly investigation before it can irrefutably be affirmed as the missing file copy.

And what of the original Book of Privileges? The historical record is also basically silent on this set, but there is a possibility that some of the original documents are today in the Veragua codex acquired with the Veragua papers by the Spanish government in 1927.

Containing documents written through 1497 and in 1498 (there is also a 1501 transcript, but this does not seem to have been an original part of the book), the Veragua codex is the oldest known compilation of Columbus's privileges to exist. Most of its transcripts were written before Columbus's third voyage to the New World in May 1498, with one document written while he was in Santo Domingo (dated December 4, 1498). The Genoa, Paris, and Washington codices appear to be based, at least partially, on the Veragua codex.

Little is known about the history of the Veragua codex except that it once was part of the archive of the duke of Veragua in Madrid. (A descendant of Columbus, the duke was named after a region in the New World, later part of Panama, that the admiral had explored.) In 1927 the codex was acquired by the Spanish state and placed with other Columbus documents in the General Archives of the Indies in Seville. The Veragua codex is written in Castilian Spanish, as are the copies made in 1502.

The Veragua codex is not a complete set of Columbus's privileges. For that reason the historical importance of the 1502 codices becomes greater. As the only complete or nearly complete compilation of Columbus's documents, they present a better record and perspective of his life and the nature of his voyages.

In the wake of Columbus's monumental 1492 achievement, numerous other explorers including Cabot, Cabral, Balboa, Ponce de León, Verrazano, Pizarro, Cartier, Drake, Champlain, and Hudson sailed to the Americas in search of riches, land, fulfillment of political and religious objectives, and adventure. This new wave of exploration was inevitable. Realizing the competitive aspects of his profession, Columbus undoubtedly had a greater appreciation for his privileges.

What is astonishing about the books of privileges is not only that they have survived through the centuries and not only that the codices are a few of the small number of Columbus artifacts to exist today, but that they are in essence the contracts accorded for opening up the western half of the world to Europeans.

In a romantic sense what we have today is a written representation of the dreams and hopes, of the ambitions and purpose, that motivated one man to embark half a millennium ago on a dangerous mission that became a turning point in history. And were it not for the "Admiral of the

Ocean Sea" possessing enough business savvy to negotiate these privileges in the first place, and to protect himself with multiple copies in the second, we wouldn't have a record today of his objectives and rewards, of what are known as Columbus's Books of Privileges.

LOCATIONS: Genoa codex: Municipality of Genoa, Genoa, Italy.
Paris codex: Ministry of Foreign Affairs, Paris, France.
Veragua codex: General Archives of the Indies, Seville, Spain.
Washington codex: Library of Congress, Washington, D.C.

The Cantino Map

DATE: 1502.

WHAT IT IS: A highly decorative planisphere that showed the course of the New World to Europeans of the Renaissance period. It was considered a treasure in its day and is today the oldest Portuguese handmade nautical map in Italy showing the coast of America.

WHAT IT LOOKS LIKE: The planisphere is designed on parchment consisting of six sheets of different sizes glued together to form a chart 85.53 inches by 40.16 inches. It is mounted on a canvas backing.

The d'Este dynasty was one of the most powerful families of Italy of the fifteenth and sixteenth centuries. Like other ruling clans such as the Gonzaga and the Medici, they collected notable artifacts and relics of the day and displayed them prominently in their homes. This not only showed off their wealth but demonstrated their passion for knowledge and culture.

The duke of Ferrara, Ercole I d'Este, was devoted to intellectual pursuits and had a pipeline to the exciting voyages the Portuguese were making through Alberto Cantino, who may have been his emissary or secret agent. Stationed in Lisbon, Cantino was directed by the duke to report discoveries in the New World and to furnish him with any maps he could acquire of new lands and routes. The world was expanding as European explorers made their first forays to exotic places, purportedly full of riches and strange peoples.

Cantino finally found for his master an elaborate map of the Old and New Worlds. Called La Charta del navicare, it was probably the most up-to-date geographical chart of the world. This chart showed the world as it

The Cantino Map, once perhaps the greatest contemporary nautical map of the New World, was rediscovered in 1870 in an Italian grocery shop hanging as a partition.

---

was known in 1502, with the newly discovered territories up to Columbus's second voyage. It also indicated ownership of the various areas, mainly Spanish and Portuguese, with captions and flags placed about the map. It was especially important for its inclusion of the boundary lines (*raja*) laid down by Pope Alexander VI in the Tordesillas Treaty of June 7, 1494, to end the quarrel between Ferdinand V of Spain and John II of Portugal.

Mapmaking was a specialized and highly regarded profession at the time. It is not known who in Lisbon made the map, and the circumstances under which Cantino obtained it are vague and slightly suspicious, but in a letter written in November 1502 from Rome, Cantino was pleased to advise Ercole d'Este that for twelve ducats he had purchased a map that would be of interest to him.

The duke received the map, and it stayed in the possession of his family until 1598, when Pope Clement VIII stripped away all royal authority from Cesare d'Este. The deposed duke moved to Modena, a city near Ferrara in northern Italy, and brought with him the collection of treasures accumulated over the years by his family. The map that Alberto Cantino had secured almost one hundred years earlier came too, finding a home in Cesare's new residence, in a red leather case bearing the gold seals of the duke, where it remained for more than two and a half centuries. In 1859 the people of Modena rebelled, and in the turmoil the Cantino Map was pilfered, after which it vanished and was thought to have been destroyed.

After the 1859 uprising, when the rebels wanted Modena to join the kingdom of Vittorio Emanuele di Savoia (the future Kingdom of Italy), Francesco V d'Austria Este sought refuge in Vienna, bringing with him some of the most important manuscripts from his library. Nine years later, in 1868, the Treaty of Florence mandated that the duke, who was still living in Vienna, must return to the Italian Kingdom and the Regia Biblioteca Estense all the manuscripts he took with him, with the exception of a few that Italian authorities recognized to be family properties.

In 1870, Giuseppi Boni, a collector living in Modena, was walking down the Via Farini when he happened to peer into a grocery store. Unbelievably, the Cantino Map, the old map that had been in the Este palace, was there in the store, hanging on a board used as a room divider. Boni persuaded the store owner to sell it to him. On April 25, 1870, Boni donated the Cantino Map along with several other maps to the Regia Biblioteca Estense, the deed of the gift reading, "Tutte queste carte io le dono alla R. Biblioteca Estense, perchè in essa siano custodite e conservate ("I donate all these maps to the Royal Estense Library because I want them to be kept and preserved there.")

The Cantino Map has remained at the library ever since.

LOCATION: Estense Library, Modena, Italy.

The Hope Diamond

DATE: 1642 (inconclusive).

WHAT IT IS: A diamond noted for its remarkable color, size, clarity, beauty, and history.

WHAT IT LOOKS LIKE: It is a very brilliant deep blue faceted ovoid diamond that measures 25.60 millimeters by 21.78 millimeters by 12.00 millimeters (length, width, depth) and weighs 45.52 carats. The diamond is set in a pendant in which it is encircled by sixteen white diamonds.

The Hope's color is a combination of blue, caused by boron, as in all blue diamonds, and gray. The depth and intensity of its color and the occasional highlights that flash from its facets are unique. Vivid reds, yellows, and greens can be seen from different angles.

It was owned by three, maybe four kings. It disappeared from the public eye for twenty years before probably surfacing in an altered form, then returned to obscurity for twenty-seven more years. Its alteration is said to have produced other magnificent stones that may or may not exist today. And it is most famous for bringing great misfortune upon whoever owns or wears it. What is fact, what is legend, and what is speculation about the Hope Diamond—one of the largest blue diamonds in the world and one of the most famous gems ever to have existed—and what are its mysteries still waiting to be solved?

The story of the "blue" begins in the seventeenth century in India, with Jean-Baptiste Tavernier, a French jewel trader. Tavernier made a half-dozen journeys to the Orient during his lifetime, marvelously adventurous excursions lasting four, five, or six years, and in 1642, at the end of his second trip to India, he probably acquired a 112³/₁₆-carat, rough-cut deep blue diamond that may have come from the nearby Kollur mine in the great diamond market of Golconda.

What Tavernier paid or exchanged for the diamond or from whom he purchased it is not known. In his memoirs he wrote of his visits to the diamond mines but never mentioned his commercial transactions. It was the law of the mines that all gems belonged to the Grand Mogul, so Tavernier may have dealt with the ruler himself in acquiring the large stone.

Tavernier's blue diamond became part of the magnificent French crown jewels in 1668 when King Louis XIV, the Sun King, purchased it along with fourteen others shown to him by the trader. Louis XIV was a man of extravagant tastes—just eight years earlier he began building a palace at Versailles whose cost would eventually run to $100 million—and he had a passion for fine jewels. In 1673, to enhance the brilliance in the stone, the king had the royal jeweler recut it (actually it was sawn), and the result was a sparkling sixty-seven-and-one-eighth-carat gem almost in the shape of a triangle. This diamond, which became known as the French Blue, was set later by Louis XV's court jeweler in another of the French crown jewels, the Golden Fleece. During the one hundred twenty years it remained a crown jewel, it passed from Louis XIV to Louis XV, and to Louis XV's grandson, Louis XVI, who was crowned in 1774 and continued the extravagant ways of his forebears.

During the eighteenth century in France, the peasantry and working class grew increasingly restless under the oppressive rule of the monarchy. By 1789 the country—under King Louis XVI and his profligate wife, Marie Antoinette—was bankrupt, and revolution finally erupted. Mobs stormed the Bastille prison in Paris; poor people around the country invaded the homes of the upper class; men and women attacked the Versailles palace.

Under a new constitution in 1791, the king was granted limited powers. The indignant Louis XVI sought assistance from other European leaders to quash the uprising. In June 1791 the king and Marie Antoinette attempted to flee to Austria where the queen's brother, Joseph II, was emperor, but they were stopped and returned to Paris. Shortly after, custody of the French crown jewels was returned to the National Assembly. They were stored in Paris in a repository called the Garde Meuble and put on public display.

The Garde Meuble then became the scene of a bizarre spree of burglaries. The repository was not usually well guarded or sealed tightly, and on a few evenings in September 1792, when bands of men came to steal its valuable contents, one of the metal bars that were supposed to keep the windows shut was unsecured, granting the men easy access. The looting of the crown jewels was a prelude to the fatal blows that would be dealt to the royal family. In January 1793 the guillotine's blade fell on Louis XVI, and nine months later on his wife, Marie Antoinette.

Ostensibly, the French Blue disappeared from history because no blue diamond of its weight and appearance was ever recovered. But could the same diamond have emerged later under a new "identity," in a new shape?

There is documentation that a large blue diamond of almost forty-five carats was owned in 1812 by one Daniel Eliason, a London diamond merchant who died in 1824. The diamond was described and sketched in color by an English jeweler, John Francillon, in a legal memorandum that he signed and dated London, September 19, 1812.

This blue diamond was in fact what came to be called the Hope Diamond by 1839. The description and measurements of the traced stone matched with the Hope; Francillon's writing and illustrations are the first recorded evidence of the Hope Diamond. And though there is virtually no definitive way of proving this is the recut French Blue—the only way would be to compare it with the original or by chemical analysis, which wasn't performed on the French Blue—the likelihood that it is is very strong.

The French Blue was stolen before the South African diamond fields had been discovered (in the 1860s) and had begun producing blue diamonds. There were few, if any, other large blue diamonds known in Europe through the eighteenth century, which is why, along with its extremely brilliant and dark blue color, it was simply called the French Blue. For the Hope suddenly to emerge in 1812 without any prior history is so unlikely that one may safely assume it began its public existence as the well-known earlier stone.

Claims have been made that certain other blue diamonds of European vintage are the issue of the recutting of the French Blue. These diamonds have ranged in weight from one to fourteen carats and most prominently include the so-called Brunswick Blue. But scholars who have compared the dimensions and shape of the sixty-seven-carat French Blue in illustrations with those of the forty-five-carat Hope gem have concluded that the cutting could have resulted in no other stone.

Because of an amnesty law passed in France in 1804 forgiving all crimes committed in time of war after the passage of twenty years, Francillon's documentation of the stone owned by Daniel Eliason in 1812 signaled its appearance on the gem market. At that date it was legally marketable because twenty years and one day had elapsed since the last possible date of the disappearance of the French Blue from the Garde Meuble in Paris in 1792. However, the history of the blue diamond from its 1812 documentation through 1839, when another record of it was made, is mostly obscure. But there is published evidence and a portrait to suggest that for a period during this interval, in the 1820s, the diamond was owned by the king of England, George IV.

In August 1839 a lavish catalog of the private collection of pearls and precious stones owned by Henry Philip Hope was printed in England. Hope, for whom the alluring blue stone had been named, was a gem and art collector. He came from a prominent Amsterdam banking family that had emigrated to London during the Napoleonic Wars and earned a vast fortune. Hope's brother Thomas, an author, was notable, apart from his books, for being parodied with his wife in French artist Antoine Dubost's 1810 portrait of *Beauty and the Beast*.

How did Hope acquire the blue diamond? Perhaps in a private sale from the estate of King George IV after his death, through his connections with the court—the king died leaving enormous gambling debts. Henry Philip Hope himself died very shortly after the printing of the catalog, which offered a vivid description of the blue gem.

The diamond stayed with the Hope family through the end of the nineteenth century. After Hope's death, it passed to his nephew, Henry Thomas Hope, and then to his nephew's grandson, Lord Francis Pelham Clinton Hope (Hope's great-niece required him to use the Hope name to obtain the inheritance). A spendthrift, Lord Francis repeatedly petitioned the court for permission to sell it but was blocked by his siblings. The court finally granted approval, and Lord Francis sold the diamond in 1902 to a New York jewelry firm, Joseph Frankel and Sons.

In 1908 Frankel let it be known that the gem was for sale, and a Syrian dealer named Selim Habib, of whom very little is known, purchased it for a tremendous price. Habib took the Hope back to Paris with him unset, and soon after, in June 1909, mounted an auction, in which the Hope was offered as part of a group of very opulent, famous diamonds.

The auction was a complete failure since none of the bids reached any of the reserve prices. Habib immediately canceled the entire proceedings

Many people believed the Hope Diamond brought a curse upon whoever owned or wore it.

and very quickly sold the Hope to an associate of Pierre Cartier, the jeweler. Habib himself was ruined by the auction and was never able to recover from the loss.

The firm of Pierre Cartier acquired the stone, and set it in what is believed to have been a pearl necklace, and Cartier showed it in 1910 to Edward and Evalyn Walsh McLean of Washington, D.C., when they were on a visit to Paris. The couple were from fabulously wealthy families, Edward the son of a newspaper magnate and Evalyn the daughter of a gold miner who had "struck it rich" out west.

Over breakfast at the McLeans' hotel, Cartier tried to dazzle the couple with tales about the stone's curse. In her autobiography, *Father Struck It Rich*, Evalyn Walsh McLean says Cartier ran through a litany of stories—from the French trader Tavernier having stolen the diamond and later being devoured by rabid dogs to Selim Habib drowning shortly after he sold it. There is no documentation for any such stories, and it was (and maybe still is) not uncommon for dealers to play up myths attached to jewels to enhance the jewels' image and their salability. In any case, Mrs. McLean wasn't scared off by the stone's reputation—"Bad luck objects for me are lucky," she told Cartier—but she said she didn't like the setting, and that was the end of that.

Cartier then had the stone reset in the setting in which it is presently seen and brought it to Washington, D.C., in 1911. He asked the McLeans if they would keep it over the weekend. This time Mrs. McLean decided she wanted it, and negotiations were commenced. It is difficult to give the exact purchase price since the contract states $180,000 (excluding interest), while in her autobiography Mrs. McLean gives the price as $154,000, less some jewelry she was returning to Cartier.

Because she knew her mother-in-law would object to her purchasing the diamond with the renowned curse—it is not known exactly when the McLeans took possession of the Hope, but the contract is dated February 1912—Evalyn took the precaution of having Cartier make the sale final. But not long after she called her mother-in-law about the purchase, the mother-in-law died, as well as the woman she was with when Evalyn called. It was only at this point that Evalyn decided it might be prudent to have a priest bless the gem. In her autobiography she writes about the experience.

> We were in a small side room of the church, and Monsignor Russell donned his robes and put my bauble on a velvet cushion. As he continued his preparations, a storm broke. Lightning flashed. Thunder shook the church. . . . Across the street a tree was struck and splintered. . . . Monsignor Russell's Latin words gave me strange comfort. Ever since that day, I've worn my diamond as a charm.

Yet it was with Mrs. McLean that the Hope's legend of bad luck grew. After she acquired the stone, her father became an alcoholic and died; her father-in-law lost his wits; her son, Vinson, died in 1918 at the age of nine in a car accident; she separated from her husband, Edward, who suffered a nervous breakdown and was committed in 1933 to a mental institution where he later died; her daughter, a senator's wife, died while still in her twenties.

Was this stone cursed? Certainly, Evalyn Walsh McLean knew tragedy before acquiring the diamond. Her younger brother, Vinson (for whom her son was named), died in an automobile accident in which she was also injured; a subsequent operation took an inch off one of her legs and left her addicted to drugs for a time.

But the tragedies that befell the McLean family while the Hope was in their possession were not so unusual; misfortune can plague any family. During the time that the Hope family possessed the diamond, other than the spendthrift Lord Francis running through money and being desperate for more, having his wife leave him, and incurring sundry other, more minor misfortunes—all not so unordinary occurrences in life—the family suffered no real bad luck or tragedy.

Evalyn Walsh McLean had a fondness for gems and enjoyed the spotlight, and the Hope Diamond satisfied and promoted both interests. A social lioness, she gave splashy dinner parties and visited wounded servicemen in the hospital. And what better way to provide thrills and amusement than by offering a glimpse of the famous cursed blue diamond suspended around her neck? She even let the volunteers at the hospital wear the gem.

Mrs. McLean wore the Hope Diamond almost every day after acquiring it. She died of pneumonia in 1947 at the age of sixty-one. Two years after her death, the jewels of Evalyn Walsh McLean were purchased by the diamond merchant Harry Winston. During the time he owned it, Winston sent the Hope to numerous shows and benefits as a part of his showcase of exquisite jewels, which hired models would wear; this was essentially an advertising and public relations effort. In 1958, nine years after acquiring it, Winston donated the Hope Diamond to the Smithsonian Institution. The famous diamond dealer mailed the Hope to the Smithsonian (the postage came to $2.44), insuring the package privately for $1 million. For insurance reasons he couldn't be photographed, but there later was a presentation ceremony, which his wife attended.

Throughout its history the Hope Diamond has been described as a perfect gem. Using modern analytical technology, the Gemological Institute of America in 1988 graded the Hope Diamond a VS_1 in clarity because of several small blemishes and whitish graining in the body of the stone. (VS_1 stands for "very slightly included" and is characterized by minor blemishes or minute crystals that can be found in the diamond under 10× magnification.) Nevertheless, the Hope Diamond is visually exquisite and exhibits the rare property of phosphorescing a strong red after being exposed to shortwave ultraviolet light.

The legend of the Hope Diamond's curse is so embedded in the lore of the stone that it has virtually displaced the gem's real, marvelous history. And it is a history in which some mysteries still persist: The night the diamond was stolen from the Garde Meuble in 1792, why was the metal bar not fastened in the window? What happened to the diamond for the twenty years it disappeared, from 1792 to 1812, and who cut it to its present shape? Was it John Francillon? In the remote possibility that the

Hope is not the French Blue, what happened to the French Blue and where did the Hope come from? These questions may never be answered, but the imagination is stirred by the gallant, ice-blue Hope Diamond, which belonged to three French kings and was stolen at the end of the French Revolution. It was never recovered but was almost certainly taken to England, recut in secrecy, and probably belonged to a fourth king while in England. Eventually, this fabulous stone found its way to America, where it rests quietly today, as radiant as ever.

While the mysteries of the diamond may never be solved, one thing is known for sure: it is a magnificent jewel whose fame and beauty and true history are surpassed by few other gems.

LOCATION: National Museum of Natural History, Washington, D.C.

Edmond Halley's Astronomical Observation Notebooks

DATE: 1682.

WHAT IT IS: The two notebooks in which the great English astronomer and natural philosopher recorded his observations of the comet that was named for him.

WHAT IT LOOKS LIKE: The primary notebook contains about two hundred folios and measures approximately 9 inches high by 8 inches wide by 2 inches thick. The other notebook has some ninety folios of linen rag paper and measures $7\frac{5}{8}$ inches high by $6\frac{1}{10}$ inches wide by $\frac{3}{4}$ inch thick. Both notebooks were restored in 1986, their decaying bindings each replaced with a cream-colored vellum binding.

> Dear God: Save us from the devil, the Turk, and the Comet.
> —Pope Calixtus III, 1456

As Edmond Halley peered into the heavens through his telescope in 1682, he could hardly have dreamed that the spectacular comet he was following would one day be his ticket to immortality. Although he would eventually come to suspect that the moving body was a regular visitor to our part of the solar system and had been for centuries, science at the time was not yet advanced enough to provide a clear explanation, much less a mathematical proof.

Europe in the sixteenth and seventeenth centuries was in the throes of scientific revolution. Polish astronomer Nicolaus Copernicus fired an early salvo in this revolution by offering an alternative to the long-held

Aristotelian theory that the Earth was the center of the universe. Galileo agitated the papacy in Rome by offering observational evidence for the Copernican view of a sun-centered universe gathered by the first astronomical use of a telescope. (Ultimately the Inquisition found Galileo guilty of promulgating sacrilegious beliefs and forced him to make a retraction.) Kepler's laws of planetary motion and Newton's law of gravitation further supplanted old beliefs, creating a new science from traditional astronomy and eroding ecclesiastical dogmas.

Up to that time, humankind's fascination with the cosmos was characterized by a belief that the positions of planets and stars were augurs of good or bad fortune on Earth. The appearance of a comet was an evil omen: disastrous events such as wars or assassinations seemed always to be accompanied by the recent or impending arrival of a comet. When the Turkish army was marching across Europe in the fifteenth century, for example, Pope Calixtus III interpreted the appearance of a comet in the night sky as a sign of defeat for the enemy and was able to rally his forces to repel the invaders at Belgrade. Earlier, in 1066, as Duke William of Normandy was mounting a fleet to cross the English Channel and seize England from King Harold, a comet graced the heavens. A scene from the Bayeux Tapestry (see page 104) shows the comet blazing over King Harold as his vassals point to the sky in fright. (It bears the Latin caption ISTI MIRANT STELLA, which may be translated as, "these people gaze in wonder at the star.") Harold was defeated by the Normans in the brutal and bloody Battle of Hastings. (The comet of 1066 depicted in the Bayeux Tapestry is Halley's Comet during its return to the vicinity of the sun in that year.) As a general point about the astrological significance of comets, what was considered bad news for one side—Harold or the Turks in these cases—is good news for the other—Duke William or Calixtus.

With the publication in 1543 of Nicolaus Copernicus's *De Revolutionibus*, or *On the Revolutions*, scientific reasoning began to usurp astrologically based beliefs. That the Earth was a ball rolling around in space must have been a bit difficult to digest in those days, but the theory eventually gained support and laid the foundation for modern astronomy. It was in this climate of scientific investigation that astronomers began the more careful study of comets. Previously, comets in the solar system were believed to travel in a straight line toward the sun, where they would either burn up or move away. Could they instead be making orbiting journeys in the solar system? Scientists worked long hours to answer this question; it was not until Edmond Halley put his mind to the problem that the answer was found.

Edmond Halley was born in London in 1656. He displayed a penchant for science early in life and attended the Queen's College of Oxford University. At nineteen he published a treatise on the movement of planets, and then he traveled to the south Atlantic Ocean island of Saint Helena off Africa to catalog the uncharted skies of the Southern Hemisphere. He became a member of the Royal Society and was made England's second Astronomer Royal in 1720. In addition to being a distinguished astronomer, Halley was noted for his accomplishments in geology and cartography. But what Halley would most be remembered for is identifying a single comet seen repeatedly by human beings since at least 240 B.C.

Renowned scientists of the day believed that celestial motion was based on immutable physical laws, but they could not come up with the mathematical proof. Scientists such as Edmond Halley, Christopher Wren, and Robert Hooke were stumped. Halley sought out Cambridge mathematician Isaac Newton to engage his help with this apparently insoluble riddle and was stunned to find out that Newton had already worked it out— several years earlier!

Halley was so impressed with Newton's brilliance that he provided the money to publish Newton's work *Philosophiae Naturalis Principia Mathematica*, or *Mathematical Principles of Natural Philosophy*, in which Newton quantified the gravitational force between two bodies, and which is now considered one of the great scientific works of all time.

Using this conclusive proof of gravitational attraction, Halley was able to draw a remarkable conclusion. With the force of gravity, comets in the solar system traveled in elliptical paths around the sun, returning to it as they completed each orbit. Halley was able to determine that the comets of 1531, 1607, and 1682 were one and the same, and that this faithful space traveler had probably been illuminating the sky throughout the ages, striking fear in the observers below.

Some of Halley's early work was set down in notebooks of linen rag paper, a durable but expensive writing surface made, as its name suggests, by pulping rags of linen. As a writing medium Halley favored iron-gall ink, a type of ink that had been in use for a thousand years. It was made by steeping oak galls, the galls formed on the roots of oak trees as a result

A page from Edmond Halley's notebook in which he recorded his observations of the comet of 1682.

of the infestation of wasp larvae, in a solution of ferrous sulfate. Ink thus made could vary in color from sepia to deep black, depending on the amount of tannin introduced into the mixture from the oak galls.

Halley's principal observation record of the comet named for him, sometimes referred to as the Islington notebook after the small village north of London where Halley was living at the time (Islington today is a borough of Greater London), contains a miscellany of writing, including tabulated lists of the astronomer's observations of the 1682 comet in his own hand, historical observations of the comet, and a set of rules of elementary arithmetic. In the other notebook, which mostly contains mathematical calculations, Halley put down some observations of the 1682 comet, but this notebook does not have the tabulated observations of the primary record. In each notebook, Halley wrote in both Latin and English.

Halley's observations of the 1682 comet, along with those of the first Astronomer Royal, John Flamsteed, enabled him to determine that the comet returns to the vicinity of the sun and passes Earth's orbit every seventy-five or seventy-six years. He predicted the comet would be visible again in 1758.

Edmond Halley died sixteen years before that landmark date. Had he lived, he would not have been disappointed. Sometime after sundown on Christmas Day of that year, an amateur German astronomer named Johann Palitsch observed a faint glow in the sky. Over the next few months, this dot grew to splendid luminescence, as people everywhere looked to the heavens and witnessed the return of Halley's Comet.

LOCATION: Department of Manuscripts and University Archives, Cambridge University Library, Cambridge, England.

The Declaration of Independence

DATE: 1776.

WHAT IT IS: The manifesto in which the congressional representatives of the thirteen original American colonies avowed the need to dissolve their bands of alliance with Great Britain and declared their right to be free and independent states.

WHAT IT LOOKS LIKE: The engrossed document (as opposed to the draft) that contains the signatures of the members of the Continental Congress is a single sheet of parchment measuring 29¾ inches long by 24¼ inches wide.

If there is one sublime symbol of the principles of liberty and equality, it is that most venerable of American democratic instruments, the Declaration of Independence. But while the grand principles of the Declaration have inspired generations of citizens to stake their lives on the doctrine of liberty, the document's own history has been blighted by homelessness, itinerancy, and a desperate struggle for its very own survival.

By the spring of 1776, after numerous injustices had been imposed by England upon those under its rule in the New World, the colonies had come to the conclusion that independence from the British Empire was imperative. The colonists had repeatedly petitioned their British brethren for fair treatment, but their pleas were arrogantly ignored. The question had been debated in Congress on June 7, when Virginia's senior delegate, Richard Henry Lee, moved that the united colonies become "free and independent states," with any political connection to Great Britain "totally dissolved." Three days later a committee was formed to express Lee's resolution in a formal declaration.

The bulk of the draft, written in Philadelphia between June 11 and June 28, was the work of Thomas Jefferson, a scholarly lawyer also from Virginia, with some input from the other committee members: John Adams, Benjamin Franklin, Robert R. Livingston, and Roger Sherman. The most profound influences on Jefferson probably came from the writings of the English philosopher John Locke, who, some ninety years earlier, had vigorously supported the right of Englishmen to rebel against the monarchy, and from George Mason's Virginia Declaration of Rights (some of the phraseology in Jefferson's Declaration of Independence is strikingly similar to that of Mason's doctrine). On June 28 the draft was presented to Congress, and three days later debate began on the resolution.* But except for a handful of men, the colonists were determined to break their political ties to the British immediately. On July 2 the Second Continental Congress voted to approve the committee's resolution, effectively declaring independence on this day. (July fourth is traditionally celebrated as Independence Day possibly because the fourth is the date on which the Declaration was adopted and given to the printer to have official copies sent out.)

For two days the Congress worked on the draft, cutting out hundreds of words and adding some of their own. On the second day, July 4, the Congress in the Pennsylvania State House adopted the final draft of the Declaration. The draft was given to a Philadelphia newspaper editor named John Dunlap, who rushed to his press and printed paper broadsides, or sheets, of the colonies' Declaration of Independence. These

---

*Jefferson's draft submitted on June 28 is not known to exist anymore, but at the Library of Congress is a fragment (one page) of the earliest known draft of the Declaration, and a "Rough Draught," as Jefferson called it, with emendations he made prior and subsequent to the delivery of the submitted copy (it includes changes made in Congress). After June 28 Jefferson wrote out other copies, five of which still exist today. One was for Richard Henry Lee, which is now at the American Philosophical Society in Philadelphia; another was for George Wythe, a lawyer from Williamsburg and professor at the College of William and Mary under whom Jefferson had studied law, which is at the New York Public Library; a copy now called the Washburn copy, named after the manuscript collector Alexander C. Washburn, which exists as a fragment, is at the Massachusetts Historical Society in Boston; another copy he retained is at the Library of Congress; and a copy he made in 1783 for James Madison is also at the Library of Congress.

Philadelphia, 1776: the Second Continental Congress shortly after the signing of the Declaration of Independence.

broadsides were then distributed to public officials so they could inform local citizens about it.* Fighting with the British had been going on for over a year now, and on July 9 the Declaration was read to General Washington's army in New York City.

Several days later the representatives from New York approved the resolution—they had not voted on July 2—and Congress commissioned an engrossed (formal and stylized) copy of the thirteen states' "unanimous declaration."

Between July 19 and August 2, a penman, possibly Timothy Matlack of Philadelphia, inscribed Jefferson's immortal words on the prepared skin of a young animal (either a sheep or a calf), in a style of calligraphy called copperplate hand, or English hand.

With the engrossed copy completed, the Continental Congress met again on August 2, 1776, so its members could sign it. John Hancock, the president of the Congress, was the first to sign the Declaration of Inde-

---

*About two dozen copies of Dunlap's first printing of the Declaration are known to exist today. In 1991 a Dunlap copy found in the back of a picture frame that a Philadelphia man paid four dollars for at a flea market was sold at auction for $2.2 million. Several days after Dunlap printed the Declaration on paper broadsides, he printed it on parchment, but almost all these copies became lost over time and today there is only one known Dunlap parchment broadside (American Philosophical Society).

pendence (his was the largest signature); other signers included Benjamin Franklin, John Adams, Samuel Adams, Richard Henry Lee, and Thomas Jefferson. Not all the representatives were present at this meeting, however, and some signatures were added to the fifty recorded ones over the next several months. Then the parchment was rolled up and tucked away in an office of the Pennsylvania State House.

From here on, the Declaration was to lead a nomadic existence.

The first of some twenty-five excursions to various resting places over 176 years commenced around December 12, 1776, when the document was dispatched on a carriage with other official papers to Baltimore, where Congress was meeting. Although it had been only a very short time since the Declaration was adopted and signed, it was already revered. In fact, the young American Congress recognized the importance of all its official documents and had them transported to whatever city in which it reconvened. Consequently, the Declaration was rolled up again and again and transported to Philadelphia, Lancaster, York, Annapolis, Trenton, and New York City, where it stayed for five years before being returned to Philadelphia in 1790. Then real trouble began.

In 1800 the Declaration made a circuitous journey over water to bring it to the District of Columbia, the new seat of the federal government. In its first dozen years there, it went to no fewer than three sites: the Treasury Building, the "Seven Buildings," and the War Office Building. When the War of 1812 broke out, the Declaration was seriously threatened. What satisfaction the British would get out of incinerating the Declaration of Independence! But action was taken before the British seized the capital and began torching government buildings. With the eruption of war, the document was whisked away—the first of two removals under such circumstances—to protect the original scroll bequeathed by the Revolutionary delegates, now almost all dead, as if it were a holy relic. Virginia seemed to be safe ground. First the document was sequestered in a gristmill on the Virginia side of the Potomac near Great Falls; then, with danger of a British raid in the area mounting, it found refuge in the basement of a private home in Leesburg.

When the war ended, the Declaration was returned to the nation's capital. But its troubles were not over. As early as 1817 it had begun to deteriorate physically. Richard Rush, the secretary of state, observed the signatures fading due to what he called "the hand of time." Despite this, government officials were still somewhat reckless with the precious document. In the early 1820s Congress ordered facsimile copies made from the original Declaration for distribution to the surviving signers, the president and vice president, to governors of the country and of U.S. territories, to other officials and government buildings, and to various colleges selected by the president. Copies may have been made by a pantographic (tracing) process, or as one theory holds, by a "wet transfer" method that would have taken off some of the Declaration's ink.

Conditions at subsequent locations helped further the Declaration's decline. In 1841 the parchment document went to the gaslit Patent Office of the Department of the Interior (now the National Portrait Gallery of the Smithsonian). Exhibited in the Hall of Models (in the same frame as George Washington's Commission as Commander-in-Chief of the American Revolutionary Army [Library of Congress, Washington, D.C.]) for more than thirty years, across from a sunlit window, the words of Jefferson were bleached away little by little, day after day. A reporter for the October 1870 issue of *Historical Magazine* called attention to the writing, deeming it so far gone "that in a few years only the naked parchments will remain." In 1876 the Declaration was conferred to its old home in Philadelphia, the State House, now called Independence Hall, for the nation's centennial. James McCabe, the author of a centennial souvenir book, noted that the document was "faded and crumbling."

The Patent Office requested to be the custodian of the Declaration once again, but instead—luckily—it was exhibited in the library of the State, War, and Navy Building in March 1877. Shortly after, the Patent Office was beset by fire.

Government officials grew increasingly distressed about the document's deteriorated condition. A committee of the National Academy of Sciences was summoned to determine whether the document could be restored, but concluded that chemical treatment might cause even more damage. They recommended that officials either "cover the present receptacle of the manuscript with an opaque lid or remove the manuscript from its frame and place it in a portfolio." In 1894 the Declaration was deposited in a steel safe of the State Department.

In 1921 President Warren G. Harding decided that American documents of importance, including the Declaration and Constitution, should be made available for the public to see, and he issued an executive order to this effect on September 29. The librarian of Congress received a phone call the next day from the State Department informing him of the president's decision, and that a transfer of the documents could be made when he was ready. Naturally, a celebration of some sort would be expected to mark the conveyance of America's cherished documents from the State Department (which had had physical custody of the records of the U.S. government since 1789, when Thomas Jefferson was the first secretary of state) to the Library of Congress, 132 years later. But so excited was the librarian that he immediately appropriated a mail truck and collected the documents himself. A simple but spirited ceremony finally took place a couple of years later when a shrine for the documents was unveiled. With the president and several dignitaries present, Herbert Putnam, the librarian of Congress, adjusted the Declaration and the Constitution in their holders and locked their display cases; shortly afterward, the guests moved to another room and sang "America."

These original documents continued to be exhibited at the Library of Congress until December 1941, when the Japanese bombed Pearl Harbor. Again, government officials took heed of the potential danger and dispatched the Declaration and the Constitution (and other records) to the Bullion Depository at Fort Knox, Kentucky, where they were safeguarded. In April 1943 the Declaration was brought back to Washington, D.C., where it was exhibited at the Jefferson Memorial for the bicentennial of Thomas Jefferson's birthday, then was returned to the Library of Congress, where it was displayed.

Although it was presumed by many that the Declaration and Constitution would reside at the Library of Congress, there was a movement, begun several years earlier, to bring these documents to the National Archives. Arguments were proferred as to why the National Archives would better be able to safeguard, preserve, and display the documents than the Library of Congress, and that the documents in fact legally belonged in the National Archives, which was established in 1934 to preserve America's historical records. Perceived legal obstacles and the competition for custody of America's revered documents—President Franklin Delano Roosevelt wouldn't take action until Herbert Putnam retired as librarian of Congress—delayed any transfer.

Finally, after a long and protracted effort, the documents were moved to the National Archives in 1952. On December 13 the documents were conveyed along a parade route, and two days later, they were installed in their shrines, accompanied by an official ceremony, with a speech by President Harry Truman. This brought the three Charters of Freedom—the Declaration, the Constitution, and the Bill of Rights—together under one roof, and exhibited for the first time ever together.

In their new—and presumably permanent—home, the Charters of

The symbol of a free and independent nation, the Declaration of Independence was placed in pouches and moved around Virginia in 1814 as British soldiers set fire to Washington.

Freedom emerge each morning from a fifty-ton steel vault. The vault's two-part lid opens, gears engage, and the mechanism holding the containers in which the documents are encased comes out of the vault and raises the containers (and documents) up into the mezzanine-level Rotunda Shrine and into their bulletproof glass cases, where they are held in place for viewing. In their containers, the documents are conserved according to the latest preservation technology. At the end of the day the precious documents are returned to their steel vault for the night.

The signatures of the Declaration are now nearly invisible, but the text is still readable, especially under the special green filters that protect it from light. Indeed, conservators report that when the document is viewed out of its vault under regular examination light, the text is clear.

The vision of Jefferson and his colleagues thus lives on in a literal, as well as a figurative, sense. Those eloquent words learned by every young student in America—"We hold these truths to be self-evident, that all men are created equal, that they are endowed by their Creator with certain unalienable Rights, that among these are Life, Liberty, and the pursuit of Happiness"—can be visually and emotionally savored in their original form. Protected by the devoted wardens of America's heritage, the hallowed Declaration has survived a multitude of hazards so that all future generations may bear witness to the noble ideals set out by the country's founders in 1776.

LOCATION: National Archives Building, Washington, D.C.

George Washington's False Teeth

DATE: 1789.

WHAT IT IS: The lower, or mandibular, denture worn by the great American statesman when he served as first president of the United States. It was made by John Greenwood of New York.

WHAT IT LOOKS LIKE: The plate, made of hippopotamus ivory, has accommodations for eight natural human teeth, six of which survive and are connected to the base by gold pins. Inscriptions appear on the surfaces of the denture.

To clarify a popular misconception from the start, let it be said that George Washington never owned and never wore wooden teeth. He did wear false teeth—when he was inaugurated he had only two natural teeth left—but in their various incarnations these were fashioned out of ivory, the teeth of other animals, and human teeth, including his own.

The provenance of the spurious wooden tooth tale is not known, but various explanations have been offered: an artist painting Washington's portrait gave the toothless president a wooden set to hold his cheeks to a normal facial contour; the ivory bases of Washington's dentures somewhat resembled wood; wooden dowels used to repair Washington's appliances were mistaken for wooden teeth; nineteenth-century viewers of the late president's dentures mistook them for wooden teeth. But not only has no evidence of Washington wearing wooden teeth ever turned up, such dental prosthetic restorations were not known in the United States in his day (they have never been a part of the American dental profession). However, wooden teeth were known in the Orient—they were fashioned

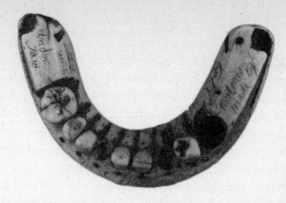

The bottom of a denture worn by George Washington when he was president. Washington's false teeth were carved from the teeth of sheep, deer, elephants, and other animals; contrary to popular belief, they were not made of wood.

from hardwood in nineteenth-century Japan, a practice probably imported from China.

George Washington was born in Virginia on February 22, 1732. His dental problems began in his youth and worsened over time. Why were Washington's teeth so bad?

It was a combination of the stressful conditions of the time—of anxiety, responsibility, and frustration, lack of needed medical and dental care, and diet; it is unlikely that heredity was a factor. Washington was prodigiously fond of nuts; John Adams noted that as a young man Washington was in the habit of cracking walnuts with his teeth.

Washington's adult life was one of constant struggle. From the time he served in the Virginia militia as a young man until his leadership of the American forces in the Revolutionary War, his life seemed a perpetual battle against exigencies of the frontier wilderness, the natural elements, and human foes. Ironically for such a rugged and triumphant leader of men, Washington was defeated by tooth decay and periodontal disease: one by one his teeth fell out or had to be removed.

When exactly Washington started wearing false teeth is not known, but he undoubtedly had a combination of false and natural teeth in 1783, when he was fifty-one and commander-in-chief of the Continental Army. In that year, while stationed in Newburgh, New York, he wrote a letter to Major Andrew Billings asking for sealing wax and making a fervent request: "I pray you to send me a small file or two, one of which to be very thin, so much so as to pass between the teeth if occasion should require it." Washington was known to apply to fellow officers for pincers for fastening dental wires, scrapers for cleaning his teeth, and other dental paraphernalia, and he had already visited a number of colonial dentists.

In colonial America, dentistry was entirely unregulated. Some physicians practiced it, as did others trained as dentists by knowledgeable and skilled preceptors, but virtually anyone could call himself a dentist. Many who did were primarily silver- or goldsmiths, ivory turners, or manually dexterous artists. The practice grew more sophisticated over time, as indicated in one dentist's January 9, 1772, advertisement in the *Virginia Gazette*:

> Mr. Baker, Surgeon Dentist, Begs Leave to inform the Gentry that he is now at Mr. *Maupin's*, in *Williamsburg*, and will wait on them on receiving their Commands. He cures the SCURVY in the GUMS, be it ever so bad; first cleans and scales the Teeth from that corrosive, tartarous, gritty Substance which hinders the Gums from growing, infects the Breath, and is one of principal Causes of the Scurvy, which, if not timely prevented, eats away the Gums, so that Peoples Teeth fall out fresh. He prevents Teeth from growing rotten . . . fills up, with Lead or Gold, those that are hollow . . . transplants natural Teeth from one person to another . . . makes and fixes artificial Teeth with the greatest Exactness and Nicety, without Pain or the least Inconvenience, so that they may eat, drink, or sleep, with them in their Mouths as Natural Ones, from which they cannot be discovered by the sharpest Eye.

Washington was acclaimed as a hero in his own time for leading the colonial army to victory over the better-equipped and better-trained British forces, ultimately winning independence for the new nation. After serving his country so patriotically, he settled into well-deserved retirement at Mount Vernon near the end of 1783. At Mount Vernon Washington personally made adjustments and repairs to his dentures, and made specific suggestions for their improvement to his dentist. With most of his teeth gone by now, he was obliged to eat soft foods. His breakfast staple, according to his granddaughter Nelly Custis was hoecake with butter and honey.

In the spring of 1789 Washington was notified at Mount Vernon that he had been elected president. Although tired after years of serving his country in strenuous endeavors and hesitant to take on the political leadership of the new republic, he selflessly agreed to serve once more. By then there were only two natural teeth in his mouth: a molar and a bicuspid in his lower jaw. Soon to take office, he desperately needed a set of wearable dentures that would give him an acceptably pleasing appearance. He had already consulted several dentists in Philadelphia, Maryland, and Virginia, including Baker, but his favorite was John Greenwood of New York.

Greenwood, a former furniture apprentice and Revolutionary War scout, was descended from a line of dental practitioners and was a skilled ivory turner. He was only twenty-nine at the time he embraced the prestigious assignment of making the first president a set of false teeth.

Greenwood constructed a dental prosthetic appliance for Washington out of hippopotamus ivory. He carved a mandibular base to hold eight human teeth, affixed with gold pins that held each of the teeth at a right angle to its axis. One of them was Washington's penultimate tooth, the right molar, which was removed shortly after he was inaugurated. An aperture was made in the fitting to accommodate the president's last tooth, his lower second bicuspid. The upper and lower plates were connected posteriorly by gold spiral springs, and pink sealing wax was applied to the bases of the dentures to make them look like gums.

Wearing the mechanism was a challenge. Unless the lip and facial muscles were continually exerted to keep it in place, the dentures would shift around. Such a device not only caused discomfort but could result in a strained or unnatural countenance. "The Father of America" was not known as a great orator—there isn't any record of his making any long speeches—and this may have been due, in part, to his ill-fitting dental appliances (he wore other ill-fitting appliances while president). Despite the shortcomings of Greenwood's mechanism, however, Washington apparently used it for eight years.

After the president's death, inscriptions were carved by Greenwood on the lower plate. He wrote "the tooth" and "under jaw" in appropriate places and added, "This was Great Washington's teeth."

Similar dentures were made for Washington that now exist either as a set, a single plate, or a fragment. These include a mandibular fragment in ivory at the London Hospital Medical College (it was taken to England during the Civil War by a daughter of Chapin A. Harris, one of the founders of the first dental school, the Baltimore College of Dental Surgery; the maxillary appliance was apparently taken to South America and lost); a full set with bases of lead alloy and ivory and cow teeth weighing four ounces that is stored at Mount Vernon (this set has traditionally been attributed to the artist Charles Willson Peale, but there is no documentary evidence contemporary with Peale to support this claim); and a 1795 lower prosthesis made of hippopotamus ivory by Greenwood at the National Museum of Dentistry in Baltimore (while on loan to the Smithsonian in 1981, the upper was pilfered for its gold).

Wooden dowels were used by Greenwood to repair the 1795 appliance, but never were the appliance's teeth fashioned of wood. The wooden dowels were used to refasten the teeth to the lower plate after Greenwood had sawed them off to achieve a different inclination and make Washington's lips appear less pouty and swollen.

Even in Washington's time, health-care services were expensive. To repair his dentures, Greenwood once billed the president fifteen dollars. The 1795 set Greenwood made cost Washington sixty dollars. Both were hefty sums in early American times.

Washington was self-conscious about his dental ailments and felt they were a matter of private concern. In 1755, when he was twenty-three, he covered up in his ledger book a payment of almost fifteen pounds to his dentist to settle what he referred to as a "hat bill." And he couldn't have been very pleased when a letter he wrote to a dentist in 1778 was captured by the British. General Washington's missive: "A day or two ago I requested Colonel Harrison to apply to you for a pair of pincers to fasten the wire of my teeth. I hope you furnished him with them. I now wish you would send me one of your scrapers, as my teeth stand in need of cleaning and I have little prospect of getting to Philadelphia."

Whereas Washington was embarrassed about his dental problems, John Greenwood apparently enjoyed the notoriety and prestige he gained from serving as the first president's dentist and unabashedly capitalized on it. Before Washington died in 1799, Greenwood, in a public notice, quoted a compliment Washington paid him earlier that year in a letter: "I shall always prefer your services to that of any other in the line of your present profession." After the chief executive's death, Greenwood continually promoted himself as "Dentist to his Excellency, Geo. Washington, late President of the United States of America," "Dentist to the Immortal Washington, the Father of his Country," or some such statement.

Washington's rough-fitting false teeth were uncomfortable to wear. In Gilbert Stuart's portrait of Washington, the mouth is puffy and the lips are tight, creating a pouting expression.

Greenwood may even have had another claim of distinction: making the dentures with which Washington was laid to eternal rest. Although there seems to be no evidence from Washington's time to support this claim, Greenwood's son, Isaac John Greenwood, wrote in a letter dated November 3, 1860, "There is a pair of false jaws with human teeth on *now* in the head of President Washington, 'in the tomb at Mt. Vernon,' made by my father, John Greenwood, in 1799, and they are made with the bone gums—I think of the *elephant's tooth* 'ivory,' and made from molds of beeswax."

A legend in his own time, Washington was a favorite subject of artists. Portraits of him consistently reflect the consequences of tooth loss and inadequate prosthodontic restoration, evident in a stern and tight-lipped expression. Cotton was sometimes used to fill out his lower face, but this actually made his lips look puffy. Gilbert Stuart is said to have commissioned a dentist to make a set of dentures for Washington; one of his Washington portraits appears on the U.S. one-dollar bill (as a mirror image).

George Washington is such a revered figure of American history that the display of his dental prostheses has been controversial. When Greenwood's 1789 plate was exhibited at a New York City museum in the 1920s, it was swiftly removed after the Daughters of the American Revolution complained that his dentures were "indelicate, personal and sacred." Mount Vernon, which acquired its set from a descendant of Martha Washington, has never exhibited it on the estate.

In the fall of 1796, as Washington was nearing the end of his second administration, his remaining tooth, alas, had to be removed. Greenwood kept it, and eighteen years later had a jeweler set it in a gold-and-glass locket, which he linked to his gold watch chain and carried until the day he died. Today, Washington's last natural tooth reposes under the same roof as the lower denture that Greenwood created for him in 1789.

LOCATION: New York Academy of Medicine, New York, New York.

The Crypt of John Paul Jones

DATE: 1792.

WHAT IT IS: The coffins containing the remains of John Paul Jones.

WHAT IT LOOKS LIKE: John Paul Jones's corpse is in its original leaden coffin, which is inside a 1905 oak coffin with silver handles and a lid secured with silver screws, and the two coffins themselves are enclosed in a 1913 black-and-white Royal Pyrenees marble sarcophagus. The sarcophagus is supported by sculpted bronze dolphins and decorated with bronze seaweed on top. It measures 94 inches high by 69 inches wide by 108 inches long.

The saga of the search for John Paul Jones's coffin might be appropriately titled, in modern-day pop parlance, "Raiders of the Lost Crypt," because it is a tale fraught with suspense, archaeological mystery, and even eerie special effects, so to speak. But this is a true tale, with the buried treasure being the "Father of the American Navy,"* a heroic figure in his own time who fought brilliantly and indomitably in the name of freedom but whose remains became lost somewhere in a foreign land. An American went to the rescue, and like any worthy cinematic adventure, this one has a happy ending, not to mention an astonishing, hair-raising finale.

---

*Some license is taken in referring to John Paul Jones as the "Father of the American Navy." At least two other early naval officers, Commodores John Barry and Thomas Truxtun, have been referred to in this way by biographers.

. . .

Paris, 1899. Horace Porter was troubled, unable to contain his sense of shame any longer. For the two years he had been the U.S. ambassador to France he had been haunted by the memory of John Paul Jones, one of the greatest American naval commanders, who, he suspected, had lain forgotten for the last century under Paris, an abandoned corpse in a deserted cemetery. To Porter, it was a disgrace that no real effort had ever been made to recover Jones's body and return him to the country he had served so heroically when it was just a fledgling republic fighting for its freedom and survival. General Porter, the son of a former governor of Pennsylvania and a Civil War veteran—he was on the staff of General Grant—could tolerate the ignominious neglect no longer. He was going to go after the commodore.

> *John Paul Jones looked out across the North Sea from the deck of the* Bonhomme Richard. *It was the twenty-third of September, 1779, a clear, bright day. Jones beheld forty-one British merchant vessels coming from the Baltic, carrying cargo for Her Majesty's fleet. They were less than a dozen miles away, off Flamborough Head, traveling north-northeast. A magnificent quarry, a chance to strike back at the British who were raiding America's shores, a chance to show the might of the young republic's navy. Jones was going to go after the convoy.* *

Horace Porter's mission to find a single corpse somewhere, anywhere, in or under an entire city was a long shot. Did Jones's corpse in fact still exist? If so, where was it and how could it be located? If it was suspected to be under a certain location in Paris, how would the massive excavation be carried out? And if a body suspected to be Jones's was indeed found, how could it be positively identified? Any lesser man might have cast off the idea of finding Jones's body as an admirable but fanciful and impossible quest, but Porter was tenacious, resolute, and dedicated to public service, not unlike the man whose remains he sought.

---

*This account of John Paul Jones's most famous naval battle, which continues throughout this entry, is based mostly on his own report of the engagement. See "The Crypt of John Paul Jones" in the Sources and Bibliography section of this book for further information.

Ambassador Horace Porter's search for the body of John Paul Jones spanned six years and had workers burrowing under the streets of Paris.

Porter knew a good deal more about John Paul Jones's life than about his afterlife. In 1790, after serving in the Russian navy, Jones went to Paris, where he lived for two years until his death from pneumonia and nephritis (kidney disease) at the age of forty-five. It was known that Jones was interred in the French capital, but it could have been in any number of locations. Porter hoped that locating Jones's death certificate might yield the name of the cemetery where he was buried.

Sadly, the death certificate no longer existed, Porter learned. It had been incinerated in a fire twenty-eight years earlier. Porter found a reproduction in a Protestant historical journal, but unbeknownst to him some key words had been omitted. Ambassador Porter was off to a bad start.

A shot was fired from the Bonhomme Richard, *a signal for its armed pilot boat to stop chasing the brigantine and come in. A flag was hoisted, a call for its companion ships to get ready for a general chase.*

It wasn't until Porter, in his search for as much information as he could get on John Paul Jones, came across an 1859 publication that he was set straight—or at least had a substantial clue. An antiquarian named Charles Read included the text of Jones's death certificate in an article he had written. The certificate stated that John Paul Jones was buried at eight o'clock in the evening of July 20, 1792, "in the cemetery for foreign Protestants." Aha! These key words had been omitted from the other document Porter had read, and he realized he had been led astray. In his article Read seemed to think the cemetery for foreign Protestants was the old St. Louis Cemetery, which was later abandoned and ultimately covered by urban development.

Various leads turned up in other publications. The *Boston Journal* printed the letter of Samuel Blackden, a close friend of the late admiral. Blackden announced in his letter the death of Jones and reported, "The American minister has ordered the person at whose house the Admiral lodged to cause him to be interred in the most private manner and at the least possible expense!!!" Because of formalities relating to the burial of Protestants, the landlord went to the appropriate public official, a man by the name of Simonneau, who was not only amazed but angered, asserting, "A man who has rendered such signal services to France and America ought to have a public burial." If America would not pay the expense, he added, he would pay it himself.

> *As the afternoon wore on, the American warships* Bonhomme Richard, Alliance, *and* Pallas *were heading for the British at top speed. The sailors were a fighting crew, eager for action. By this time the convoy was retreating for the coast. Their two escort ships,* Serapis *and* Countess of Scarborough, *were waiting to intercept the enemy.*

As it turned out, young America let Jones down in death. No money was forthcoming, and Simonneau paid the total cost of the funeral himself, 462 francs. As Horace Porter wrote in his thorough and endearing report of his search for John Paul Jones, "This brought to light for the first time the mortifying fact that the hero who had once been the idol of the American people had been buried by charity, and that the payment of his funeral expenses was the timely and generous act of a foreign admirer." Porter himself was so upset by this that he sought out any living relatives of Simonneau to reimburse them with accrued interest, but no one could prove him- or herself to be a legitimate descendant.

The 462 francs paid by the French commissary Simonneau was considerably more than an interment of this nature usually cost. The higher price indicated a special coffin might have been used. Jones's body, Porter learned from a letter written by Blackden to the admiral's sister, "was put into a leaden coffin on the 20th, that, in case the United States, which he has so essentially served and with so much honor, should claim his remains they might be more easily removed."

> *It was seven o'clock. Darkness was creeping in. The Americans were closing in on the British. Jones's ship was flying the colors of the Royal Navy. From the* Serapis *came a demand for identification. The British flag came down, the Stars and Stripes rose. Then the* Richard *responded with a cannon blast.*

While Charles Read in his article had opined that John Paul Jones was buried in the St. Louis Cemetery, before any excavation could commence Porter had to be absolutely sure, or as sure as possible, that this was the place of burial. Other writers had made suggestions to the contrary. Although it seemed improbable that Jones could have been buried in other cemeteries mentioned—one wasn't in existence at the time of Jones's burial; another did not permit interment of Protestants—Porter duly checked the records of these cemeteries and found no indication of John Paul Jones being buried in any. Porter even pursued a tip that Jones was buried in his native Scotland, but was informed by a local pastor that the grave in question was that of the admiral's father, John Paul, Sr., who had died in 1767. Still, there were additional possibilities, and each was pursued by the thorough Porter until he was convinced beyond the shadow of a doubt that John Paul Jones was buried in the St. Louis Cemetery.

> *The battle had begun! Eighteen-pounders, nine-pounders, six-pounders—a barrage of fire was furiously exchanged between the two ships. The* Serapis *had fifty guns and was a superior frigate. The British captain, Richard Pearson, knew it, and so did John Paul Jones. Already there had been several deaths and injuries on the* Richard. *Jones knew his only chance was to come in close to the* Serapis, *board her, and engage her crew in hand combat.*

It now became necessary to examine the ground of the old cemetery, which had become buried beneath the streets. The once-sacrosanct burial ground was located beneath an undesirable area of Paris, a section known as "le Combat." Porter wrote, "This name was not chosen, however, on account of the burial there of the most combative of men, but history attributes the term to the fact that this section of Paris was long ago the scene of all the fights in which animals figured—bulls, cocks, dogs, asses, etc."

As his investigation of Jones's interment and what happened to the cemetery in which Jones was buried continued, Porter became more disheartened. In his report he wrote:

> After having studied the manner and place of his burial and contemplated the circumstances connected with the strange neglect of his grave, one could not help feeling pained beyond expression and overcome by a sense of profound mortification. Here was presented the spectacle of a hero whose fame once covered two continents, and whose name is still an inspiration to a world-famed navy, lying for more than a century in a forgotten grave, like an obscure outcast, relegated to oblivion in a squalid quarter of a distant foreign city, buried in ground once consecrated, but since desecrated by having been used at times as a garden, with the moldering bodies of the dead fertilizing its market vegetables, by having been covered later by a common dump pile, where dogs and horses had been buried, and the soil was still soaked with polluted waters from undrained laundries, and, as a culmination of degradation, by having been occupied by a contractor for removing night soil.

The old St. Louis Cemetery—measuring 120 feet by 130 feet, now under an area off the Rue Grange aux Belles that consisted of a garden, a grain merchants' courtyard, a building, sheds, a laundry, a wagon-house, a cesspool, and a well—had come into existence in 1724 and was officially closed in 1793. Burials continued there for more than a decade until it was finally abandoned altogether. But what of the dead? Porter was concerned that corpses might have been moved, and he investigated the records of the old catacombs, where remains would have been buried, but found no evidence of Jones's body being transferred to any.

Finally, Porter considered the possibility that John Paul Jones's lead casket had been melted down to make bullets during the French Revolution. No, he was told. Even in revolt the French would not disturb the holy resting places of the dead.

Porter's investigation had been thorough. He was convinced that if the remains of John Paul Jones still existed, they were right there in Paris in the old cemetery of Saint Louis. An excavation was the next step, but Porter could not foresee what would happen next.

> *The* Serapis *sailed broadside of the* Richard. *Her cannons were roaring. The* Richard *was firing back, but her damage was more serious. There were fires on both ships.*

The success of Ambassador Porter's preliminary investigation became publicly known, and those in the area of the old St. Louis Cemetery, needy people no doubt, thought they stood to gain substantial sums in exchange for the rights to dig on their properties. As Porter wrote, "Self-constituted agents immediately began to busy themselves with circulating fantastic stories regarding the fabulous prices that were to be paid for the property, the whole of which it was said was going to be bought by a rich government, at any cost, as the only means of getting access to the cemetery and making the excavations necessary to find the body of its great Admiral." In fact, the entire investigation and excavation to follow were being paid for by Porter from his own personal funds. Unable to meet these additional financial demands, Porter had to hold up his search for John Paul Jones's body for two years.

> *Jones's vessel took the wind to the* Serapis's *bowsprit. The ships smacked into each other, Pearson's stern to Jones's bow. Their yards became tangled, one enemy's cannons rubbing the other.*

Porter maintained a low profile, and the commotion attending the sale of excavation rights finally died down; those demanding payment gave up. On February 3, 1905, digging began with the sinking of a shaft under a laundry. Here's Porter on the challenges:

> The project presented serious difficulties from the fact that the filling of the earth above the cemetery was composed of the dumpings of loose soil not compact enough to stand alone, and the shafts and galleries had to be solidly lined and shored up with

heavy timbers as the excavations proceeded. The drainage was bad in places and there was trouble from the water. The walls of one of the buildings were considerably damaged. Slime, mud, and mephitic odors were encountered, and long red worms appeared in abundance.

Workmen sunk shafts and shoveled long underground tunnels, galleries, through the submerged cemetery. They knew they were looking for leaden coffins, so they made "soundings" between the galleries with iron bars.

Burrowing through the sunken graveyard was an unpleasant, if not revolting, task. The laborers continuously dug into bones and skeletons and skulls. Piled every which way, they were a horrific sight. In the darkness underneath the earth, remnants of the dead popped out to greet the workmen.

> The Richard *was leaking badly. Her twelve-pounders were decimated; their firing crews had abandoned them. The eighteen-pounders on the lower gun deck were also disabled. Virtually all the men who operated them had been killed when the* Serapis *first fired on the guns. Some seamen on the poop were also killed, and the French officer in charge abandoned the station. Only Jones's nine-pounders on the quarterdeck remained intact, but some of the men there were seriously wounded.*

Nineteen days after excavation began, the first leaden coffin was found. It bore an inscription plate revealing a name and date of death. The remains were not those of John Paul Jones. Not until after another month of constant burrowing in the subterranean trenches did the workmen turn up a second leaden coffin. This one, too, had an inscription plate, and it also revealed that the remains were not Jones's.

The laborers, the supervisors, the engineer of mines of the Department of the Seine, Porter—all participating in the search were disappointed but went on with their work. It was more than a century earlier that Jones was supposedly interred in the cemetery, and anything could have happened to the coffin and its remains in the interval. At times the search seemed futile, ridiculous.

On March 31 another leaden coffin was found. This lacked identifica-

Stone, who went on to become a captain in the U.S. Navy, held the right hand of the dead admiral and found it soft and pliable. In a letter he wrote sixty years later, Stone noted, "There was a feeling of awe in the room. Here were the almost lifelike remains of a man who died in July 1792." It might be said that the last person to see John Paul Jones, to gaze into and study his face, to hold the hand and feel the soft flesh of the Revolutionary War hero, lived until 1983, the year Captain Stone died.

> *The battle off Flamborough Head in the North Sea raged on under the light of the moon. Flames were out of control in several areas of both the Serapis and the Richard. Smoke funneled off to the leaden sky. On the Richard, crimson blood was flowing across the deck.*

A complete medical examination of the corpse was made by the most eminent physicians, pathologists, anthropologists, and scientists of the

day, and the results correlated with the extensive reports made on Jones when he was alive. From these alone there was no doubt that the body was Jones's. In the room during the examinations were busts made of the admiral by the renowned sculptor Jean-Antoine Houdon, and the resemblance was uncanny. There was an ornament sewn into Jones's hair, which measured two and one-half feet long. It was the letter *J* in one direction, and *P* when turned over. No, there was not the slightest uncertainty whatsoever that this was the body of the great John Paul Jones.

Bust of John Paul Jones by Jean-Antoine Houdon.

> *At 9:30 p.m. the Alliance came into close range. But instead of assisting the Richard, she fired into her stern. The crew of the Richard shouted out to stop, but the Alliance continued to fire, and her volleys killed several men. The full moon pro-*

John Paul Jones's head, more than a century after his death. (The photograph was taken on April 11, 1905, after an autopsy was performed on Jones.)

vided sufficient light, and the design of the Richard was markedly different from that of the Serapis. Jones was being attacked by his own men!*

The corpse of John Paul Jones had been in excellent condition when unearthed, but after exposure for a few days it started to deteriorate rapidly. After the autopsy, the sections cut away were placed back in the body. Jones's body was chemically treated and the shirt he had been found in put back on. The corpse was then wrapped in its winding sheet and placed back in its coffin, which was itself then encased in a wooden coffin.

Jones's master-at-arms freed all the prisoners below deck. They were directed to operate the pumps, but some cut down their captors. Although both ships were sustaining serious damage and injuries, up to this point it appeared the Richard *would defeat her opponent. Now her situation, as Jones later wrote, was "deplorable."*

With the spectacular discovery of the corpse of John Paul Jones, after a search that consumed six years of Ambassador Porter's life, it was

---

* The captain of the *Alliance*, Pierre Landais, was mentally unstable, not to mention professionally incompetent for his rank. Jones was infuriated that the French ship was shelling his while he was engaged with the enemy, and later, in his report to the U.S. minister to France, Benjamin Franklin, he wrote that he "must complain loudly" of Landais's conduct, and was advised by his men to arrest the captain. It is ironic that Landais was assigned to the *Alliance*, named to symbolize the friendship between the United States and France and the support France pledged to give to America during the war.

now time for the ceremonies. The United States sent a fleet of warships to France to bring back the body of its old hero. On July 6, 1905, after a service in the American Church of the Holy Trinity, Jones's coffin was carried through the streets of Paris and over the Seine, as thousands of spectators watched the grand parade of French and American soldiers and sailors. It was a spectacular send-off. The coffin was to be put on a train to Cherbourg, where the American Naval Squadron awaited.

A shout from Captain Pearson aboard the Serapis: *Would the Americans like to strike her colors? Would the Commodore like quarters? John Paul Jones became livid. He responded, "I have not yet begun to fight!"*

Jones wouldn't give up. His men who hadn't been killed or injured continued fighting fiercely. The main mast of the Serapis *began to quiver.*

On the morning of July 23, 1905, the American Naval Squadron, in double column formation, cruised into Annapolis and anchored. The next day, John Paul Jones's casket was transferred to another vessel that steamed to shore between the two columns as the ships fired a salute. There wasn't much fanfare at this point, as preparations were under way for a proper ceremony.

Officials of cities throughout the United States had written to President Theodore Roosevelt, asking if Jones's body could be brought to their cities, but Roosevelt thought the proper resting place for Jones could only be at the U.S. Naval Academy, where the nation's future naval officers are edu-

This photo of John Paul Jones's body was taken after doctors autopsied it.

cated. A newly planned chapel was under construction at the time, so the casket was placed in a temporary vault across the street. On April 24, 1906, Jones's casket was carried into the armory, and an elaborate ceremony was held. Addresses were given by President Roosevelt, the French ambassador to the United States, and Ambassador Porter to an overflowing crowd of U.S. senators, congressmen, sailors, and citizens, as well as a number of French naval officers, as France had dispatched a fleet to America for the occasion. After the ceremony the casket was carried to Bancroft Hall, which at the time was a brand-new midshipmen's dormitory. It was put on biers under the grand staircase.

> *There was less firing coming from the* Serapis. *The British could be near defeat. The crew of the* Richard *stepped up their firing.*

For seven years Jones's body remained in the dorm until Congress decided to appropriate additional funds to finish the crypt in the Naval Academy chapel. (Congress also reimbursed Porter for the monies he had personally laid out to find Jones, and Porter donated the sum to a memorial for Jones.) Finally, on January 26, 1913, Jones's body was moved in. His double casket was placed inside a handsome marble sarcophagus, built at the academy by the French sculptor Sylvain Salières (1865–1920), with marble donated by the French government. Embedded into the marble floor around the sarcophagus, in metal letters, are the names of the ships Jones commanded during the American Revolution, and nearby is a gold-hilted sword given to Jones by King Louis XVI.

> *At 10:30 P.M. the British flag was struck. John Paul Jones had prevailed. Jones took his prize, the* Serapis, *as his own conflagrant vessel would soon sink in the murky ocean. Jones won an important victory for America, one that would enter the history books and immortalize him.*

In July 1787, the itinerant Jones traveled to New York from Europe to take care of some personal and professional interests. A few months later, in the autumn, he returned to the Continent, never knowing he was saying good-bye for the last time to the country he served so well and loved so much.

With the Revolutionary War over, Jones needed work that would befit his heroic status and leadership ability. But because the navy was discontinued, there were no ships to command, and he was disappointed that he had not been given a rank and assignment appropriate for his status. So the following year, while in Copenhagen, Denmark, to try to settle accounts over ships he had captured during the Revolutionary War—it was the custom of the time that if a ship was captured it would be sent to a friendly port for an agent to sell it, with the prize money to be divided among the navy crew after the government was paid its majority share— he decided that Empress Catherine's offer of a naval commission to help the Russians fight the Turks was serious and too alluring to pass up.

But Jones was worried that accepting the offer might jeopardize his American citizenship. The Scottish-born sailor considered himself an American citizen since the time he visited his brother in Fredericksburg, Virginia, at age thirteen—there were no naturalization procedures in those days—and always took great pride in his adopted country. On March 27, 1788, he wrote to the U.S. minister at Paris, Thomas Jefferson, who assured him that an appointment to the Russian navy would not alter the status of his American citizenship.

Health problems plagued Jones during his venture with the Russians. He became ill during the rough trip to St. Petersburg in April to pick up his commission as a Rear Admiral of the Russian navy signed by Empress Catherine. On May 26, 1788, Jones hoisted his flag aboard the *Wolodimir*, at the mouth of the Dnieper River, but became ill again six months later, in November, while he was engaged in the Liman campaign in the Black Sea, and the following month returned to St. Petersburg. With his relationship with the Russian authorities having also steadily declined from the beginning, Jones, after obtaining a two-year leave of absence, left Russia in July 1789 and headed for Paris.

In France Jones was something of a hero; during the war sumptuous banquets and speeches were given in his honor, and the French people held a deep affection for him. Although his health continued to be problematic, the spirited naval commander continually beseeched the new American minister to Paris, Gouverneur Morris, for work. This finally came on June 1, 1792, when President George Washington and Secretary of State Thomas Jefferson appointed Jones a U.S. commissioner to treat with the Dey of Algiers for the release of captured American merchants (Algiers was one of the Barbary states that was stopping American and other countries' merchant shipping and seizing the cargoes and ships and holding the crews for ransom). But sadly, Jones's health had deteriorated badly, and his symptoms included signs of jaundice. The forty-five-year-old Jones died in the French capital on July 18, probably before he even received his appointment. The great war hero was buried in a Paris cemetery, paid for not by the United States but by a Frenchman as an act of homage. John Paul Jones was seemingly abandoned at his end by his country, until Horace Porter embarked on his relentless search to bring him back to America.

A remarkable 113 years after his death, John Paul Jones was home again.

LOCATION: United States Naval Academy Chapel, Annapolis, Maryland.

HMS *Victory*

DATE: 1805.

WHAT IT IS: Vice Admiral Horatio Nelson's flagship at the Battle of Trafalgar.

WHAT IT LOOKS LIKE: The first-rate ship of the line* is 226 feet long and more than 51 feet wide. It has 104 guns and three decks.

Napoleon was on a militaristic rampage bent on devouring every country in sight. England set out to stop him or at least maintain its supremacy on the seas, lest Napoleon storm its shores with an enormous and confident invading army. The British were determined to oust Napoleon from power as a grave threat to its—and other European countries'—sovereignty. By 1802, after several French victories, a temporary calm had settled on Europe, but beneath the surface the situation remained tense and volatile. These circumstances set the stage for what is considered the greatest naval battle in history.

By 1803 war was imminent. The English blockaded the French fleet at Toulon, keeping England safe, but in 1805 Napoleon devised a plan for the French fleet to unite with the Spanish fleet in the West Indies, from where the combined naval forces could storm across the Atlantic, defeat the English navy, and conquer England.

The commander of the French fleet at Toulon, Admiral Pierre de Villeneuve, managed to elude the British blockading fleet, escape into the Atlantic, and head for Martinique. This ruse was intended to shake off the

---

*A ship of the line was the largest of the warships in existence at that time.

British and disguise his real intentions. The English fleet commander, Vice Admiral Lord Nelson, however, followed Villeneuve across the Atlantic and hounded him back to Cádiz. Here the French sought safety in the harbor with the Spanish fleet, which was then ready to join forces for the invasion. The English fleet assembled off Cádiz, determined to prevent the combined enemy forces' escape, and so after two years it seemed there would finally be a showdown.

The combined French and Spanish fleet did indeed leave Cádiz, heading south for the Mediterranean, with Nelson a dozen miles west. During the hours of darkness, Nelson ordered his vessels to make a southward approach; by daybreak the enemies—some nine miles apart—were able to spot each other. The engagement was now inevitable.

The location: off the coast of Cape Trafalgar in southwestern Spain. The date: the twenty-first of October, 1805. With thirty-three ships of the line, the French and Spanish fleet's sturdy double- and triple-deckers were filled with dozens of cannons and thousands of soldiers ready to destroy the British, with twenty-seven ships of the line.

About noon the British navy began to make its battle approach. In the morning the French fleet had changed its formation from a basically straight line to a crescent and was now heading north. Instead of closing in parallel—ship-to-ship—formation, Nelson, having previously decided his battle tactics, ordered his men-of-war to approach in two columns and cut the enemy fleet at the center and at the rear. In this way, he could wreak much destruction before the van could come around to join the fighting.

As the wind carried the Royal Navy closer and closer to the French and Spanish fleet, the situation was tense. Both fleets were strong and well armed, and there would be great losses on each side. Leading the northerly British column was the one-armed, half-blind Lord Nelson in the flagship, HMS *Victory*; the southerly squadron, headed by Admiral Sir Cuthbert Collingwood in the *Royal Sovereign*, charged in first.

Behind the *Victory* were the *Téméraire*, *Neptune*, *Leviathan*, *Conqueror*, *Britannia*, *Ajax*, *Agamemnon*, *Orion*, *Prince*, *Minotaur*, and *Spartiate*. They broke through the line at the center, Collingwood's squadron at the rear. Ships pulled up broadside to one another, and the raging combat commenced.

After firing upon and killing or wounding approximately half of the 800 seamen on board the *Bucentaure*, and incapacitating 20 of its 80 guns, the *Victory*, carrying more than 850 men and 100 guns, was en-

The Battle of Trafalgar *by Wyllie. Some sixty warships fought in this epic battle, in which Horatio Nelson's vessel the* Victory *engaged in combat with the* Redoubtable.

gaged by the 74-gun *Redoubtable*. Fighting between the two ships, which now lay alongside each other, was furious. The *Victory* suffered heavy casualties and Nelson, while commanding the fleet from the quarterdeck, was shot by an enemy sniper and died three hours later in the cockpit of the *Victory*.

The *Téméraire* cut through to aid the *Victory* but was fired on by a French ship also called *Neptune*. Another French ship came up to finish her off, but the *Victory*'s starboard guns were now manned again to repel her attack. Then the *Téméraire*, whose crew did not yet know their admiral was dying, came broadside on the *Redoubtable* and assaulted her with gunfire, killing almost half her crew of over 630.

Meanwhile, other British ships were pulverizing other enemy vessels, even where they were outnumbered in guns. Villeneuve's flagship, the *Bucentaure*, was once again ravaged, first by the British *Neptune*, then by the *Conqueror*, and the French commander surrendered. By late afternoon almost half the French and Spanish fleet were captured. Their casualties were in the thousands.

The Royal Navy was victorious but lamented the death of its esteemed admiral. Collingwood did not bother to chase the fleeing enemy vessels but brought the fleet in with the captured warships in tow.

After Trafalgar, the *Victory*, which had been launched in 1765, was refitted at Chatham where she had been built. In 1808 she became involved in maneuvers in the Baltic under Rear Admiral James Saumarez, then continued to see action in other operations until her combat service was ended in 1812. Beginning in 1813, she underwent a major refit, during which time a plaque was placed on the quarterdeck where Nelson had fallen. During her career the *Victory* served as a flagship for several British admirals, including Augustus Keppel, Francis Geary, Richard Howe, Hyde Parker, Samuel Hood, and Joseph Yorke.

Today the *Victory* sits in dry dock, the only remaining ship of the line and now a shrine for the English. For it was on board this vessel that the country's most masterful, loved, and enduring naval hero executed his brilliant plan of attack against the combined French and Spanish fleet. It was here that Lord Nelson and his men fought so valiantly to save England. It was on the *Victory* that the Royal Navy's commander in chief charged into battle in a contest that probably decided, for a time, the fate of Europe.

LOCATION: H.M. Naval Base, Portsmouth, Hampshire, England.

Vice Admiral Lord Nelson's Uniform Coat

DATE: 1805.

WHAT IT IS: The undress coat* worn by Horatio Nelson when he was shot during the Battle of Trafalgar.

WHAT IT LOOKS LIKE: About 45 inches in length, the coat is made of dark blue wool cloth and has epaulets of gold lace with gold wire bullion. In the left shoulder is a hole made by the musket ball that penetrated Nelson's body and killed him.

It was at once a day of exalted joy and overwhelming grief for England. With the defeat of the enemy naval forces at Trafalgar, a nation was saved, but its most beloved war hero, fervently adored by both his countrymen and -women and the sailors who served under him, was lost. Indeed the national outpouring of grief was so tremendous that "it seemed as if no man," as Samuel Taylor Coleridge aptly put it, "was a stranger to another—for all were made acquaintances in the rights of a common anguish." But despite a poignant funeral and ample state rewards for his immediate family, Nelson's repeated dying wish—that his country provide for his beloved Lady Hamilton and their daughter, Horatia—was ignored. Lady Hamilton eventually became destitute and was forced to sell the very coat her cherished Nelson had been wearing when he was shot as he led the British navy to its most important victory ever.

As the British men-of-war sailed into battle against the combined French and Spanish fleet on the afternoon of October 21, 1805, Nelson,

*An undress coat was meant for everyday wear, as opposed to a full dress uniform which was worn only for ceremonial occasions.

forty-seven years old, was aware of a fighter's vulnerability in war. Just hours before the first carronades roared, Nelson, wearing his undress coat, wrote a bequest, which he had witnessed later by the ship's captain, Thomas Masterman Hardy, in which he hoped that should he die, his homeland would give Emma Hamilton "an ample provision to maintain her rank in life. . . . These are the only favours I ask of my King and country at this moment when I am going to fight their battle."

Lady Emma Hamilton was the woman with whom Nelson had carried on a torrid—and sensational—love affair. It began while she was married to Sir William Hamilton, the British envoy at Naples, and he to Frances Nelson. The two never married. Although both publicly denied their intimacy, it was common knowledge. Many, including the king, disapproved. There was even an offspring of their illicit liaison, Horatia, in whom Nelson rejoiced. But Horatia never knew Nelson was her biological father, for this was not proved until after both of their deaths.

As the *Victory* was about to enter battle, there was deep concern that Nelson would draw the enemy's fire. "He was dressed as usual in his Admiral's frock coat," the ship's surgeon, Dr. William Beatty, later remembered. The long blue coat had nine gilt buttons on each side of the front, three buttons and two stripes of gold lace on each cuff, and four resplendent stars of Nelson's four orders of chivalry emblazoned across the left breast. But the men would not speak of their fears before battle. As Dr. Beatty wrote:

> Several officers of the ship now communicated to each other their fears and anxiety for His Lordship's personal safety, to which every other consideration seemed to give way. Indeed all were confident of gaining a glorious victory, but the apprehensions for His Lordship were great and general; and the Surgeon made known to Doctor Scott his fears that His Lordship would be made the object of the Enemy's marksmen, and his desire that he might be entreated by somebody to cover the stars on his coat with a handkerchief. Doctor Scott and Mr. Scott (Public Secretary) both observed, however, that such a request would have no effect; and that they also knew His Lordship's feelings on that subject so well, that they were sure he would be greatly displeased with whoever should take the liberty of recommending any change in his dress on this account: and when the Surgeon declared to Mr. Scott that he would avail himself of the opportunity

Horatio Nelson lies wounded on the deck of HMS Victory.

of making his sick-report for the day, to submit his sentiments to the Admiral, Mr. Scott observed, "Take care, Doctor, what you are about; I would not be the man to mention such a matter to him." The Surgeon notwithstanding persisted in his design, and remained on deck to find a proper opportunity for addressing His Lordship; but this never occurred.

In the Trafalgar battle, the *Victory* engaged the French warship *Redoubtable*. After fighting broke out, Captain Hardy did point out to Nelson that his stars might make him a conspicuous target, but the vice admiral curtly responded that it was too late to be changing a coat.

Just before 1:30 P.M., Nelson was standing on the quarterdeck with Captain Hardy. A sharpshooter perched on the mizzenmast of the *Redoubtable* took aim at Nelson and discharged a bullet that ripped through his upper left chest.

The one-armed Nelson—he had lost his right arm in 1797 in an attack on Santa Cruz de Tenerife—fell on his fingertips and knees, then crumpled onto the deck. Captain Hardy summoned some seamen, who carried Nelson below. Nelson covered his face with a handkerchief so the sailors wouldn't lose their spirit by seeing their commander in chief seriously wounded. He was taken to the cockpit, where dozens of men who had been struck and mutilated in the battle lay fighting for their lives. The vice admiral was put on a bed, and his clothes were removed. He told the ship's surgeon, William Beatty, to tend to the others since his condition was hopeless. "I am a dead man," he told Hardy. "It will all be over with me soon." Then he besought his close friend Hardy to look after his dear Emma.

Hardy returned to the deck while the ship's chaplain tended to Nelson. As the battle raged above, Nelson's thoughts dwelled on Emma and Horatia, now four years old. While the chaplain massaged his chest to alleviate the sharp pain and the ship's purser held up the bed to support Nelson's shoulders, the admiral repeated his legacy to Lady Hamilton and Horatia. Later, Hardy returned below and told Nelson that more than a dozen enemy ships had been captured, and when Nelson expired at 4:30 P.M. on the *Victory*, he knew his troops had defeated the French and Spanish and that England was safe from invasion.

After the battle the *Victory*'s casualties were buried in a cemetery at Cape Trafalgar, but Nelson's corpse, embalmed in a cask of spirits, was kept on the ship for return to England and a state funeral. The country mourned its fallen leader, especially the devoted sailors who served with Nelson. One man who took part in the Trafalgar battle noted, "Chaps that fought like the devil sit down and cry like a wench." Hardy brought to Emma the admiral's last letter, his sword, pigtail, and the coat he was wearing when he was pierced by the fatal bullet. About a month after Nelson died, Lady Hamilton wrote, "My heart is broken. Life to me now is not worth having. I lived but for him . . . I am very, very ill."

With inheritances from both her late husband, Sir William Hamilton, who died in 1803, and Nelson, Emma Hamilton had enough money to live comfortably. But inconsolable at her lover's death, she embarked on a downward course, spending recklessly, gambling heavily, and landing in jail. Pensions, annuities, titles, and cash stipends had been awarded to Nelson's siblings and widow for his heroic contributions to England, but the admiral's request that the country provide for his lover and daughter was ignored.

In 1813 Lady Hamilton, now indigent, sold Nelson's Battle of Trafalgar undress coat to Alderman Joshua Smith, who helped her flee to Calais to escape a prison sentence. Smith died in 1844, and his widow sold the uniform to Sir Nicholas Harris Nicolas, who in turn sold it to Queen Victoria's husband, Prince Albert. In 1845 the prince presented Nelson's coat to the Greenwich Royal Hospital for Naval Pensioners, the buildings of which later housed the Royal Naval College. In 1937 the trustees of Greenwich Hospital moved the coat—whose date of manufacture is not known; it could have been anytime after Nelson became a vice admiral in

1801 to just before he died—to a museum on loan, where it continues to be exhibited today.

Lady Hamilton became an alcoholic and died in 1815. Unable to recover from the emotional trauma she suffered as a result of Nelson's death, she must have been truly heartbroken to sell the uniform Nelson had refused to shed on board the *Victory*. Nelson risked his life wearing the coat but donned it in the belief that it would inspire his men in one of England's most decisive naval battles—one that the nation so gloriously won.

LOCATION: National Maritime Museum, Greenwich, London, England.

The Star-Spangled Banner

DATE: 1814.

WHAT IT IS: The flag that inspired Francis Scott Key to compose the words to the tune that in 1931 became the official national anthem of the United States.

WHAT IT LOOKS LIKE: It survives as a 34-by-30-foot flag (it was originally 42 feet by 30 feet), with fifteen red and white stripes and fifteen stars of five points arranged in five rows of three stars each. The stars and stripes were handsewn with English bunting, and an Irish linen backing was later applied for support. The original flag weighed approximately 85 pounds, but after the linen backing was applied in 1914 by Smithsonian textile workers, the flag's weight increased to almost 300 pounds.

The night sky lit up with the fiery glow of rockets. The sounds of bombs exploding filled the air. Thick clouds of smoke billowed high. With great apprehension the three Americans aboard a small flag-of-truce vessel on the Patapsco River strained to see through the darkness and mist what havoc the fleet of British warships up ahead were wreaking upon Fort McHenry.

It was the early morning hours of September 14, 1814. Francis Scott Key, John S. Skinner, and Dr. William Beanes were being detained by the British until the attack ceased. The British, having recently torched Washington, were on a path of destruction. Their assault on Fort McHenry had begun almost a day before, and if they could neutralize this barrier to Baltimore, they just might be able to take the city.

British troops were spread all over North America. They were defending their country's frontier fortifications in Canada and attacking important American cities and tidewater towns. England was at war with the United States.

It was a war that the United States had entered gradually and reluctantly. The country had a policy of neutrality, begun in the days of President John Adams. But as England and France struck at each other's commerce, the United States got sucked up in the imbroglio. The two European powers had imposed upon each other—and countries doing business with them or their territories—blockades, trade prohibitions, and unfair cargo duties. Sanction after sanction hurt the United States, which had enjoyed healthy trade relations with Europe. England, with its omnipotent navy, even seized U.S. ships and impressed their crew members into service aboard British ships.

Outrage among Americans was growing. Under President Jefferson, the United States had made efforts to fight back without going to war, but the 1807 Embargo Act halting all foreign trade hurt too many merchants and the less austere Non-Intercourse Act in 1809 reinstating foreign trade to all countries but France and England simply wasn't enough to mitigate the surging anger. John Calhoun, Henry Clay, and other expansion-minded congressmen who became known as the War Hawks resented the mercantile damage England had caused and pressed for war. President James Madison, inaugurated in 1809 and ever hopeful to continue a policy of neutrality, finally asked Congress on June 1, 1812, to declare war against Great Britain. It did so seventeen days later, on June 18, and Madison signed the declaration; thus began the War of 1812, which lasted for three years.

Now, in the summer of 1814, the British, after having ravaged the American capital, set their sights on the city of Baltimore. The soldiers at Fort McHenry were prepared and even had two new flags with which to greet their invaders. Anticipating the British invasion, the fort's commander petitioned superiors for a large banner—he said he wanted a flag so large the British would have no difficulty seeing it from a distance—and a local resident, Mary Pickersgill, was commissioned in the summer of 1813 to make two: a forty-two-by-thirty-foot flag (a normal garrison flag was forty by twenty feet) and a smaller, twenty-five-by-seventeen-foot flag.

On August 16, 1814, the British fleet arrived in Chesapeake Bay. On September 12 five thousand troops disembarked ten miles downriver from Baltimore to commence a land assault on the city. At the same time, other ships prepared to attack Fort McHenry from the Patapsco River.

When the naval bombardment was launched the next morning, September 13, the British had some foreign company among them. A few days earlier, Francis Scott Key, a thirty-five-year-old Georgetown lawyer, and John S. Skinner, the U.S. commissioner of prisoners, sailed from Baltimore to seek the release of Key's friend, Dr. William Beanes, a Maryland physician who was being held prisoner aboard a British warship on a misconduct charge. They were successful in obtaining Beanes's release, but now that they were aware of the planned assault on Baltimore and could therefore inform the city residents about it, they were held behind the bombardment squadron with the rest of the fleet until the British completed their attack. The three Americans were anchored on the Patapsco near North Point, about eight miles south of the fort.

The British naval bombardment continued throughout the day and into the next. When sunlight finally penetrated the early morning darkness of

As the British bombarded Fort McHenry in 1814, Francis Scott Key watched from a flag-of-truce vessel behind the action.

September 14, visibility was still poor in the Baltimore harbor because it was raining. Some hours later, when the mist cleared, Francis Scott Key peered out from his vessel toward land. Throughout the night, ships of the British navy assaulted Fort McHenry with rockets and bombs—about fifteen hundred of them—and Key and his compatriots wondered if the fort had surrendered. So Key was surprised and elated when he beheld the shore through a telescope. Standing tall over the ramparts of the fort was the U.S. flag, its prominent stripes and glimmering white stars streaming ever so gallantly. Key set down several stanzas of verse expressing his exaltation and patriotic pride.

Key may have thought the flag he saw flew defiantly through the perilous fight, but documents indicate that the forty-two-by-thirty-foot ensign was not hoisted until 9:00 A.M. on September 14 when the British, unable to penetrate the fort, broke off their attack. As they began to sail away, the defenders of Fort McHenry raised the flag to show their resoluteness, strength, and unbridled spirit. During the bombardment the smaller of the two flags was flying over the fort but probably would not have been readily seen by Key from his distant position.

The Americans on the truce ship were restrained from leaving the vessel for two days until British forces sailed down the Chesapeake Bay. On the evening of September 16, 1814, Francis Scott Key returned to Baltimore. He stopped at the Indian Queen Hotel and revised the draft notes of the poem he had written on the morning of September 14. (He probably discarded the paper on which he set down his inspired words while on the vessel, but the paper onto which he copied his lyrics survives and is at the Maryland Historical Society, Baltimore, Maryland.) The next day, September 17, Key took the poem to Judge Joseph H. Nicholson, his brother-in-law and a captain of artillery in the fort during the battle, who liked it and urged that it be published. That day, "Defense of Fort M'Henry" was printed on a handbill and distributed. The first newspaper publication of the poem was on September 20 in the *Baltimore Patriot*.

The first public singing of Key's poem, given a new title in a theater advertisement, took place at the Baltimore Theatre on the evening of October 19, 1814. The advertisement, published earlier that day, proclaimed, "After the play, Mr. Hardinge will sing a much admired NEW SONG, written by a gentleman of Maryland, in commemoration of the GALLANT DEFENCE OF FORT M'HENRY called THE STAR-SPANGLED BANNER." Indeed, Mr. Hardinge did sing the song after the play.

The melody to which Key fit his spirited verses was the British tavern

This is the earliest existing copy of "The Star-Spangled Banner" in Francis Scott Key's hand. It is believed that the paper on which Key originally wrote the lyrics was either lost or destroyed, and that he rewrote them on this sheet of paper after reaching Baltimore so his printer would have a legible copy.

Horace Porter, seated on the far left, appears with members of his team in this photo taken in 1905 at the site of discovery of Jones's coffin. The man kneeling at the far right holds his pickax over the spot where Jones's coffin was found and unearthed.

ably well-preserved body of someone they could not mistake. They held medals bearing the admiral's portrait near the face and looked back and forth from the flesh to the inscribed image. Let Porter tell you the reactions of the witnesses at this incredible moment:

> We instinctively claimed, "Paul Jones!" and all those who were gathered about the coffin removed their hats, feeling that they were standing in the presence of the illustrious dead—the object of the long search.

The corpse was removed to the Paris School of Medicine where it was scientifically examined. In fact, the organs were so well preserved that physicians performed an autopsy.

During this time Ambassador Porter's eleven-year-old nephew, John Gilbert M. Stone, was in Paris. The lad received a message to come to the medical school to catch a glimpse of the legendary seaman.

tion and had such a pungent alcoholic smell about it that opening it in the gallery was impossible until air could be directed in through another tunnel.

It was curious that an old coffin such as this would have such an emanation. Workers dug and dug, and a week later there was proper ventilation so the coffin could be opened.

Down in the gallery, Porter and the engineers and many of the laborers gathered around the leaden coffin. The light was dim. The top of the coffin had been fused tightly and was removed with some effort. The coffin had apparently been filled with alcohol at the time of burial. The liquid had evaporated through a small opening in the lid, but the odor was still strong.

> *The* Serapis *and the* Richard *were locked together. French sharpshooters atop the* Richard *caused the British seamen to abandon the deck. Guns were fired from the* Serapis *from the below deck. The casualties aboard the* Richard *were heavy, and the ship sustained serious damage.*

Inside the coffin was a body wrapped in a winding sheet and packed snugly in straw. The sheet was slowly unwrapped in the dark, stuffy gallery. Excitement ran high at the possibility that this was the body of one of the greatest naval commanders ever to have lived. But given that John Paul Jones had been dead for more than a century, a positive identification would undoubtedly require extensive investigation.

> *The last sniper atop the* Serapis's *masts was shot by a contingent of Jones's men. This set the stage for a crushing setback for the British. A seaman on the* Richard *crawled out on a yard with a supply of grenades. One hit a powder magazine on the* Serapis, *causing a major explosion.*

As the sheet was removed, the witnesses huddled around the coffin with flickering candles, breathing the musty thin air below the city of Paris, anticipating the viewing. And what they saw shocked them, gave them chills, for before them was something they could not even have dreamed. Lying in a coffin with soft skin and hair intact—only the tip of the nose was damaged, obviously from the coffin lid—was the remark-

tune "To Anacreon in Heaven." This wasn't the first time the melody had been borrowed. It had been used in 1798 for "Adams and Liberty" by Robert Treat Paine,* a Massachusetts poet, and again in 1813 for the song "When Death's Gloomy Angel Was Bending His Bow" by the Washington Benevolent Society. Even Key had used the tune in an earlier poem.

When the commander of Fort McHenry, Major George Armistead, died in 1818, the larger garrison flag was presented to his widow, Louisa, as a keepsake. The flag was to stay in the Armistead family for the next nine decades. As it turned out, the flag had a better chance of surviving the British mortar bombs than of remaining unscathed in the hands of the Armisteads.

The family's biggest weakness in preserving the flag was its willing compliance with requests for pieces of it. The pruning began shortly after the war when, it is believed, a soldier who had been among the defenders of Fort McHenry died, and his widow asked for a swatch of the flag to bury with him. Initially, requests came from Fort McHenry veterans, but eventually others also desired a memento of the celebrated American victory.

Louisa Armistead's largesse with the flag was continued by her daughter Georgianna, who was born at Fort McHenry in 1817; eight feet of stripes in the fly (or unattached) end of the garrison flag were ultimately trimmed off.

Perhaps the Armisteads felt no compunction in paring the Star-Spangled Banner because they could not appreciate the national treasure it would become. Nineteenth-century Americans prior to the Mexican War were not sentimentalists and did not take to deifying ordinary objects. Furthermore, whereas the song that emanated from the battle achieved immediate local popularity, it would be decades before its significance as a patriotic gem was realized. So it is logical to assume that the Armisteads, or anyone of the day for that matter, could not help but regard the flag as nothing more than a glorified souvenir.

Prior to the twentieth century, the Armisteads permitted the flag to be displayed for public view on only two occasions. The first was in 1824 when the marquis de Lafayette, who had served as a major general in the

---

*The Massachusetts poet Robert Treat Paine (1773–1811) is not to be confused with the Massachusetts judge (1731–1814) of the same name who signed the Declaration of Independence.

When dawn broke on September 14, 1814, Francis Scott Key beheld this flag flying at Fort McHenry after a British bombardment of the fort through the night, and was duly inspired to write the words to "The Star-Spangled Banner."

Continental Army during the Revolutionary War, came to the United States for the last time. Lafayette had asked to see the flag, and it was returned to Fort McHenry, where full honors were given to the venerable French statesman. When he alighted his barge at Fort McHenry, he found the roadway to the fort lined on both sides with veteran defenders of the 1814 assault on Baltimore. To Lafayette's delight, the flag was displayed inside George Washington's Revolutionary War marquee (field tent) and was flanked by French and American cannons used at Yorktown during the siege of 1781. Half a century later, the flag was exhibited in Boston.

By the time of the Civil War, Georgianna Armistead had married William Appleton, a Boston shipowner and entrepreneur, and took the flag north with her. In 1874 the Boston navy yard was loaned the flag subsequent to a request by George Preble, the captain and commander of the naval rendezvous (recruiting office) in Boston and one of the earliest historians of the flag. It was at the Boston navy yard, probably, that the very first known photos of the Star-Spangled Banner were taken.

Toward the end of the nineteenth century, interest in the flag was surpassing the ability to keep it safe in a private home. The Armistead-Appletons deposited the Star-Spangled Banner in a bank vault in New York, where the family had relocated.

In 1912 the family donated the flag to the Smithsonian Institution. To maintain and maximize the condition of the tattered and faded flag, the Smithsonian commissioned a team of expert needlewomen in Boston to remove the worn-out canvas backing and replace it with Irish linen. First given as a loan, in 1907, and then as a gift, in 1912, from the Armisteads, the flag came to the Smithsonian with the stipulation that it never be removed. During World War II, however, the flag was removed from display, and it was stored in the Luray Caverns, an underground cave system in Virginia.

One bona fide mystery of the Star-Spangled Banner that remains is the presence of a piece of red cloth in the shape of a V on a white stripe in the center of the flag. The emblem is seen in the Boston navy yard photographs of 1874 but is not believed to have been on the flag originally, since there is no reference to it in the historical literature. One possible explanation is that it is a returned souvenir that was sewn back on to help preserve the flag.

Nearly one-fifth of the flag has been cut away. It is remarkable that it did not disintegrate altogether, considering its early treatment and the perishability of its materials. Almost two centuries after the flag was hoisted following the relentless bombardment of invaders, it continues to be a symbolic reminder that freedom is a fundamental and inalienable right, to be safeguarded and defended at all costs, as it continues gallantly to stand

> *O'er the land of the free*
> *and the home of the brave!*

LOCATION: National Museum of American History, Washington, D.C.

Napoleon's Penis

DATE: 1821.

WHAT IT IS: Allegedly, the penis of the infamous French emperor, excised on the day after he died.

WHAT IT LOOKS LIKE: A shriveled finger.

It was late afternoon, May 5, 1821. After nearly six wretched years in banishment on Saint Helena, a remote south Atlantic island, Napoleon, once the dreaded despot whose empire dominated central and western Europe, lay like a waxen doll, a pathetic semblance of his former vigorous self. A stomach ulcer and disease—what doctors at the time thought was cancer—had drained his vitality. Although his ailments occasionally sent him into delirium, his mind had for the most part been sharp, and he had prepared for death by dictating communications, reminiscences, and a last will and testament. In his will he disbursed his property and estate in an apparently fair and equitable manner, providing for his companions in exile, his valet, former and present servants and secretaries, soldiers who had served in campaigns with him, widows and children of soldiers who had died in battle under him, villages that had suffered his attacks, aides, old acquaintances from Corsica, his mother, brothers and sisters, nieces and nephews, his wife, and, most of all, his son. Napoleon estimated his personal inventory to be substantial, and his specific bequests included everything from cash, silver, gold, diamonds, homes, and land, down to his shirts, waistcoat, breeches, handkerchiefs, saddles, traveling boxes, books, chalice cloths, pillowcases, gold chains, a saber, a cloak, and a bandanna.

In his last days, as the pain became severe—like a knife plunged into his gut that kept turning slowly and forcefully, as Napoleon described it—he anticipated death, even dictating the official announcement (with the date

Some say that Napoleon was poisoned at Saint Helena. Others attribute his death to cancer or a liver abscess. Perhaps future testing will solve the mystery—or fuel the debate.

to be filled in) of his passing and requesting the transport of his body to France. He was also quite concerned about guiding his son, the duke of Reichstadt, to a judicious career of power based on the wisdom of his experience. On April 13 and 14, 1821, he had summoned a friend, General Charles-Tristande Montholon, so that he could dictate a testament for the boy. And dictate he did, eloquently filling a dozen pages, imploring his son not to avenge his death but to learn by it, not to imitate his conquests without necessity but to rule in peace, to continue his work diplomatically, to be a progressive thinker, and to reward fine service. He closed by telling his son he hoped the youth was worthy of his destiny.

That his beloved boy might know what illness beset his father, Napoleon had requested an autopsy of his corpse. It was a totally selfless and loving gesture: whatever information could be gained from this, he felt, might help doctors treat his son if he developed this cursed Bonaparte legacy or even prevent its onset. Napoleon had continually blamed the English for exacerbating his pitiful condition by condemning him to an unhealthy climate and through the despicable treatment accorded him by the austere governor of the island, Sir Hudson Lowe.

Soldiers and doctors went in and out of Napoleon's dwelling, called Longwood, all day, waiting for him to succumb. Last rites had already been administered by Father Ange Paul Vignali, an abbé who had been sent to the island by Napoleon's uncle, Joseph Cardinal Fesch. Now Napoleon was completely debilitated, unable even to drink water. After 5:30 P.M. Napoleon was hanging on to life by the barest thread. Minutes later, the former French emperor, age fifty-one, expired.

An artist's depiction of blessings on the remains of the former French emperor. Later, British soldiers exhumed Napoleon's remains from their cement vault. The emperor had been buried in four coffins: tin, mahogany, lead, and mahogany, one within the other.

The next day Napoleon's corpse was stretched out before more than fifteen people, and an autopsy was performed. The once most powerful and feared man in the world now lay humbly exposed in death. Francesco Antommarchi, a physician-pathologist from Corsica, opened him up, with Napoleon's close associates and several English doctors observing. A gastric ulcer had perforated the wall of Napoleon's stomach and was adhered to the left lobe of the liver. The internal surface of the stomach, as the autopsy report was to state, was a mass of cancerous disease or portions advancing to cancer, and the perforation was large enough to admit a finger. A debate ensued over whether liver disease or the island's climate had catalyzed Napoleon's demise. (Later diagnoses and tests of specimens from Napoleon's body indicate that Napoleon did not have cancer but another disease; credence is given to the diagnosis that Napoleon suffered from a liver abscess.)

During his exile, Napoleon sometimes displayed great bitterness. Such resentment would be understandable, of course, from a man who had tasted such power and glory and was now banished to a remote tropical

was hopeless. "I am a dead man," he told Hardy. "It will all be over with me soon." Then he besought his close friend Hardy to look after his dear Emma.

Hardy returned to the deck while the ship's chaplain tended to Nelson. As the battle raged above, Nelson's thoughts dwelled on Emma and Horatia, now four years old. While the chaplain massaged his chest to alleviate the sharp pain and the ship's purser held up the bed to support Nelson's shoulders, the admiral repeated his legacy to Lady Hamilton and Horatia. Later, Hardy returned below and told Nelson that more than a dozen enemy ships had been captured, and when Nelson expired at 4:30 P.M. on the *Victory*, he knew his troops had defeated the French and Spanish and that England was safe from invasion.

After the battle the *Victory*'s casualties were buried in a cemetery at Cape Trafalgar, but Nelson's corpse, embalmed in a cask of spirits, was kept on the ship for return to England and a state funeral. The country mourned its fallen leader, especially the devoted sailors who served with Nelson. One man who took part in the Trafalgar battle noted, "Chaps that fought like the devil sit down and cry like a wench." Hardy brought to Emma the admiral's last letter, his sword, pigtail, and the coat he was wearing when he was pierced by the fatal bullet. About a month after Nelson died, Lady Hamilton wrote, "My heart is broken. Life to me now is not worth having. I lived but for him . . . I am very, very ill."

With inheritances from both her late husband, Sir William Hamilton, who died in 1803, and Nelson, Emma Hamilton had enough money to live comfortably. But inconsolable at her lover's death, she embarked on a downward course, spending recklessly, gambling heavily, and landing in jail. Pensions, annuities, titles, and cash stipends had been awarded to Nelson's siblings and widow for his heroic contributions to England, but the admiral's request that the country provide for his lover and daughter was ignored.

In 1813 Lady Hamilton, now indigent, sold Nelson's Battle of Trafalgar undress coat to Alderman Joshua Smith, who helped her flee to Calais to escape a prison sentence. Smith died in 1844, and his widow sold the uniform to Sir Nicholas Harris Nicolas, who in turn sold it to Queen Victoria's husband, Prince Albert. In 1845 the prince presented Nelson's coat to the Greenwich Royal Hospital for Naval Pensioners, the buildings of which later housed the Royal Naval College. In 1937 the trustees of Greenwich Hospital moved the coat—whose date of manufacture is not known; it could have been anytime after Nelson became a vice admiral in

Horatio Nelson lies wounded on the deck of HMS Victory.

of making his sick-report for the day, to submit his sentiments to the Admiral, Mr. Scott observed, "Take care, Doctor, what you are about; I would not be the man to mention such a matter to him." The Surgeon notwithstanding persisted in his design, and remained on deck to find a proper opportunity for addressing His Lordship; but this never occurred.

In the Trafalgar battle, the *Victory* engaged the French warship *Redoubtable*. After fighting broke out, Captain Hardy did point out to Nelson that his stars might make him a conspicuous target, but the vice admiral curtly responded that it was too late to be changing a coat.

Just before 1:30 P.M., Nelson was standing on the quarterdeck with Captain Hardy. A sharpshooter perched on the mizzenmast of the *Redoubtable* took aim at Nelson and discharged a bullet that ripped through his upper left chest.

The one-armed Nelson—he had lost his right arm in 1797 in an attack on Santa Cruz de Tenerife—fell on his fingertips and knees, then crumpled onto the deck. Captain Hardy summoned some seamen, who carried Nelson below. Nelson covered his face with a handkerchief so the sailors wouldn't lose their spirit by seeing their commander in chief seriously wounded. He was taken to the cockpit, where dozens of men who had been struck and mutilated in the battle lay fighting for their lives. The vice admiral was put on a bed, and his clothes were removed. He told the ship's surgeon, William Beatty, to tend to the others since his condition

The Star-Spangled Banner

DATE: 1814.

WHAT IT IS: The flag that inspired Francis Scott Key to compose the words to the tune that in 1931 became the official national anthem of the United States.

WHAT IT LOOKS LIKE: It survives as a 34-by-30-foot flag (it was originally 42 feet by 30 feet), with fifteen red and white stripes and fifteen stars of five points arranged in five rows of three stars each. The stars and stripes were handsewn with English bunting, and an Irish linen backing was later applied for support. The original flag weighed approximately 85 pounds, but after the linen backing was applied in 1914 by Smithsonian textile workers, the flag's weight increased to almost 300 pounds.

The night sky lit up with the fiery glow of rockets. The sounds of bombs exploding filled the air. Thick clouds of smoke billowed high. With great apprehension the three Americans aboard a small flag-of-truce vessel on the Patapsco River strained to see through the darkness and mist what havoc the fleet of British warships up ahead were wreaking upon Fort McHenry.

It was the early morning hours of September 14, 1814. Francis Scott Key, John S. Skinner, and Dr. William Beanes were being detained by the British until the attack ceased. The British, having recently torched Washington, were on a path of destruction. Their assault on Fort McHenry

1801 to just before he died—to a museum on loan, where it continues to be exhibited today.

Lady Hamilton became an alcoholic and died in 1815. Unable to recover from the emotional trauma she suffered as a result of Nelson's death, she must have been truly heartbroken to sell the uniform Nelson had refused to shed on board the *Victory*. Nelson risked his life wearing the coat but donned it in the belief that it would inspire his men in one of England's most decisive naval battles—one that the nation so gloriously won.

LOCATION: National Maritime Museum, Greenwich, London, England.

forty-seven years old, was aware of a fighter's vulnerability in war. Just hours before the first carronades roared, Nelson, wearing his undress coat, wrote a bequest, which he had witnessed later by the ship's captain, Thomas Masterman Hardy, in which he hoped that should he die, his homeland would give Emma Hamilton "an ample provision to maintain her rank in life. . . . These are the only favours I ask of my King and country at this moment when I am going to fight their battle."

Lady Emma Hamilton was the woman with whom Nelson had carried on a torrid—and sensational—love affair. It began while she was married to Sir William Hamilton, the British envoy at Naples, and he to Frances Nelson. The two never married. Although both publicly denied their intimacy, it was common knowledge. Many, including the king, disapproved. There was even an offspring of their illicit liaison, Horatia, in whom Nelson rejoiced. But Horatia never knew Nelson was her biological father, for this was not proved until after both of their deaths.

As the *Victory* was about to enter battle, there was deep concern that Nelson would draw the enemy's fire. "He was dressed as usual in his Admiral's frock coat," the ship's surgeon, Dr. William Beatty, later remembered. The long blue coat had nine gilt buttons on each side of the front, three buttons and two stripes of gold lace on each cuff, and four resplendent stars of Nelson's four orders of chivalry emblazoned across the left breast. But the men would not speak of their fears before battle. As Dr. Beatty wrote:

> Several officers of the ship now communicated to each other their fears and anxiety for His Lordship's personal safety, to which every other consideration seemed to give way. Indeed all were confident of gaining a glorious victory, but the apprehensions for His Lordship were great and general; and the Surgeon made known to Doctor Scott his fears that His Lordship would be made the object of the Enemy's marksmen, and his desire that he might be entreated by somebody to cover the stars on his coat with a handkerchief. Doctor Scott and Mr. Scott (Public Secretary) both observed, however, that such a request would have no effect; and that they also knew His Lordship's feelings on that subject so well, that they were sure he would be greatly displeased with whoever should take the liberty of recommending any change in his dress on this account: and when the Surgeon declared to Mr. Scott that he would avail himself of the opportunity

Vice Admiral Lord Nelson's Uniform Coat

DATE: 1805.

WHAT IT IS: The undress coat* worn by Horatio Nelson when he was shot during the Battle of Trafalgar.

WHAT IT LOOKS LIKE: About 45 inches in length, the coat is made of dark blue wool cloth and has epaulets of gold lace with gold wire bullion. In the left shoulder is a hole made by the musket ball that penetrated Nelson's body and killed him.

It was at once a day of exalted joy and overwhelming grief for England. With the defeat of the enemy naval forces at Trafalgar, a nation was saved, but its most beloved war hero, fervently adored by both his countrymen and -women and the sailors who served under him, was lost. Indeed the national outpouring of grief was so tremendous that "it seemed as if no man," as Samuel Taylor Coleridge aptly put it, "was a stranger to another—for all were made acquaintances in the rights of a common anguish." But despite a poignant funeral and ample state rewards for his immediate family, Nelson's repeated dying wish—that his country provide for his beloved Lady Hamilton and their daughter, Horatia—was ignored. Lady Hamilton eventually became destitute and was forced to sell the very coat her cherished Nelson had been wearing when he was shot as he led the British navy to its most important victory ever.

As the British men-of-war sailed into battle against the combined French and Spanish fleet on the afternoon of October 21, 1805, Nelson,

*An undress coat was meant for everyday wear, as opposed to a full dress uniform which was worn only for ceremonial occasions.

rock where he was, at least in his mind, acutely maltreated. But some people who had attended Napoleon on Saint Helena also harbored a great resentment against him. Antommarchi and the Abbé Vignali, like others there, had endured the difficult and miserable isolation of the island and the abuse showered upon them by Napoleon himself because of the promise of riches at the end of his life. They were impatient by the time of his drawn-out death and in the end doubted whether they would be bequeathed an equitable portion of Napoleon's estate for their time of service on Saint Helena.

During the autopsy Antommarchi cut out Napoleon's heart and stomach, and these organs were sealed in separate silver vases that would be placed in the coffin with Napoleon's corpse. It has been alleged by some that at the end of the autopsy, Antommarchi also excised Napoleon's penis. While there is no definite confirmation of this, causing some historians to express doubt, there is also no written refutation. Only the circumstances surrounding such a claim can be examined.

Many British physicians were present during the postmortem. It is improbable that Antommarchi would have been allowed by the British to cut off Napoleon's noble organ, or if he was given consent, to keep it. Still, Napoleon's second valet, Louis Etienne Saint-Denis, claimed in his posthumously published memoirs, "Before sewing up the body, Antommarchi, taking advantage of a moment when the eyes of the English were not fixed on the body, had taken two little pieces from a rib which he had given to M. Vignaly and Coursot." With so many Englishmen present, some people doubt that Antommarchi could even have made such extractions. On the other hand, the stench from a corpse with peritonitis, after twenty-four hours with no refrigeration, perhaps would have been enough to drive away the sentinels, as they saw Antommarchi completing the sewing up of the lower end of his long midline incision.

The governor of Saint Helena, Sir Hudson Lowe, was concerned that companions of Napoleon might try to acquire a piece of his remains after the autopsy. Lowe ordered Dr. Archibald Arnott to guard the corpse and make sure no one would try to extract any portion of it while it lay in state.

The provenance of Napoleon's excised personal member begins with the Abbé Vignali. When he returned to Corsica after Napoleon died, he claimed to have with him the penis and a share of Napoleon's effects that had been divided among the emperor's aides at Saint Helena.

In 1828 the Abbé Vignali was killed as a result of a personal feud. His sister, Roxanne Vignali Gianettini, inherited as part of his estate, in addition to the Abbé Vignali's green silk vestments and diary and University of Rome diploma (citing him as a doctor of medicine), the collection of Napoleon pieces, which included the alleged penis; the emperor's silver cup from his traveling dressing case; a pair of his white breeches; hair from the emperor's body, face, and head; a bandanna Napoleon frequently wore during his exile; a copy of Napoleon's will in the hand of the priest (one of only three known copies); and Napoleon's waistcoat.

When Roxanne died, her estate passed to her son, Charles-Marie Gianettini, who later testified that the Abbé Vignali's Napoleonic possessions were painstakingly and honorably safeguarded at the family home, and in 1916 he gave a complete list of the relics in a notarized affidavit. The Abbé Vignali's collection was later sold to Maggs Brothers, a book dealer in London. The penis, which the French gracefully referred to as "a mummified tendon," went along with it.

In 1924 the A. S. W. Rosenbach Company, a reputable book dealer in Philadelphia, purchased the Vignali collection from Maggs Brothers for the sum of four hundred pounds. (Vignali's nephew, Charles-Marie Gianettini, was alive and ninety-six years old at the time.) The penis wasn't the type of item normally associated with the venerable firm, but owing to both its historical interest and its whimsicality, such a relic was probably hard to resist.

In their biography of Abraham Simon Wolf Rosenbach, Edwin Wolf II and John F. Fleming wrote about Rosenbach's ownership of the Vignalis' Napoleonic relics: "But what gave spice to the collection . . . was an unpleasant looking piece of desiccated tissue, politely described as a 'mummified tendon taken from Napoleon's body during the post-mortem.' The authenticity of the remarkable object had been confirmed by the publication in the *Revue des Deux Mondes* of a memoir by Saint-Denis in which he expressly stated that he and Vignali took away small pieces of Napoleon's corpse during the autopsy." And of Dr. Rosenbach's willingness to share with others this piece of Napoleon, his biographers added, "Few so intimate portions of a man's anatomy have ever been displayed to so many."

In 1927 Napoleon's penis was exhibited at the Museum of French Arts in New York City. One newspaper described it as a "shriveled eel."

In November 1944 the Abbé Vignali collection was sold by Rosenbach to Donald Hyde of Somerville, New Jersey. The collection was sold by Hyde's widow, Mary, in 1969 through Rosenbach's successor and biogra-

pher, John F. Fleming, to Bruce Gimelson, a private dealer in Philadelphia.
Gimelson put the Abbé Vignali collection (including the penis) up for auction by Christie, Manson & Woods in London on October 29, 1969. For
the auction Christie printed a "Catalogue of Printed Books, Manuscripts
and the Celebrated Vignali Collection of Napoleon Relics removed from
Saint Helena." After a discussion of property left by Napoleon in his will,
the catalog states, "There remained a number of objects not dealt with
under the will which were divided between Vignali and his companions.
It is Vignali's share of these objects which forms the celebrated Vignali
Collection." There followed descriptions of many of the objects in the Vignali collection. Here is how the catalog described the penis: "a small
dried-up object, genteelly described as a mummified tendon, taken
from his body during the post-mortem. (The authenticity of the macabre
relic has been confirmed by the publication in the *Revue des [Deux]
Mondes . . .*)"

The Christie, Manson & Woods auction never took place. It was halted
when Gimelson objected to the collection being broken up; the Abbé Vignali collection, having been intact for so many years, had a charming
history to it, Gimelson maintained, and he wanted to preserve it. Gimelson tried to market the collection himself, but his price could not be met.
(Gimelson had hoped the French government would take an interest, but
it didn't turn out that way.) Coming to the realization that it made financial sense to break up the collection, Gimelson auctioned it off in
1977 at the Hotel Drouot in Paris. The majority of it went to the Musée
des Invalides, and the sale brought approximately one hundred thousand
dollars.

Napoleon's penis was purchased by Dr. John K. Lattimer, a leading
American urologist and medical school professor (he served as president
of both the American Urological Association and Societé International
d'Urologie) whose interest in unusual artifacts had led him to acquire
such relics as Hermann Goering's suicide capsule container, Adolf Hitler's
hair, and the nooses used to hang two of the conspirators for the murder
of President Lincoln, Mary Surratt and Lewis Powell. One of Lattimer's
reasons for purchasing the penis was to cut off small pieces of it to ana-
lyze and thus settle the debate about whether Napoleon was poisoned by
arsenic or mercury. He has yet to do this but has plans to conduct these
toxological tests, as well as make a DNA profile so there will be a reference point against which to compare other Napoleon specimens.

Another reason why John Lattimer purchased Napoleon's penis was to keep it out of unscrupulous hands. He felt it should be afforded both privacy and dignity.

It is doubtful the penis was ever preserved in chemicals; it was most probably air-dried. Today Napoleon's penis is stored in its original glass casket in a morocco leather box bearing his crest.

During his exile on Saint Helena, when the world seemed to have forgotten him and those who had risen to elevated stations because of their previous association with him didn't even so much as inquire about his welfare, Napoleon reflected upon his many accomplishments. He believed he had rid France of anarchy and stabilized its government, enacted his nation's most effective code of laws, and always acted with the noblest ambition. His achievements were undeniable, and he hoped they would be recognized, aware that history might cast him off as a tyrannical dictator. "For all the attempts at curtailment, suppression and mutilation," he wrote, "it will be hard to make me disappear completely."

With his penis putatively surviving the ages, one imagines he could hardly have appreciated how prophetic that statement was.

LOCATION   College of Physicians and Surgeons of Columbia University, New York, New York.*

---

*This has not been designated the permanent repository of Napoleon's penis by its owner, Dr. John K. Lattimer, who may place it at any location he wishes at any time.

London Bridge

DATE: 1831.

WHAT IT IS: The bridge that spanned the Thames River in London, England, for nearly 140 years.

WHAT IT LOOKS LIKE: The bridge has five elliptical arches and is made of granite. It is 952 feet long and 35 feet wide.

When the fourth London Bridge opened in 1831, it continued the heritage of a structure that had provided a vital transportation route throughout much of England's past. But it seemed unlikely that the new bridge would ever be able to match the notoriety of its predecessors. Armies had defended kingdoms from hostile invaders by hurling stones and shooting arrows from atop their towers; knights had jousted on their spans. Shakespeare even wrote verses about the famous London Bridge that presided during his lifetime, the same bridge upon which the severed heads of traitors to the English crown had been prominently displayed, impaled on pikes planted in its stones.

Yet this latest monument would eventually attain a genuine distinction of its own: it is the only major bridge ever to be dismantled, transported across the ocean to another continent, and reconstructed block by block exactly as it was in its original setting.

London Bridge has a long history, much of it marked by strife and misfortune. No one knows for sure when the first bridge was built over the Thames. Legend has it that the Romans erected one about A.D. 43, but among the many treasure heaps of Roman artifacts found near the Thames, no evidence of any kind of bridge from that period has ever been found.

A timber bridge was in existence about A.D. 944, and although this is not thought to be the first such structure over the Thames—earlier bridges having been destroyed by flood, fire, and other natural disasters—it is generally regarded as the first London Bridge.

In A.D. 994, the people of London successfully defended the city from an attack launched by King Sweyn of Denmark. One reason the Londoners triumphed, according to historian John Stow's 1598 *Survey of London*, was that the enemy soldiers "were drowned in the river Thames because in their hasty rage they took no heed of the bridge." Ten years earlier, angry citizens had thrown a woman from the bridge to drown in the Thames for allegedly performing black magic by inserting pins into a nobleman's image.

Around the end of the first millennium, London Bridge was sacrificed to help England's King Ethelred the Unready, who had been exiled to France, regain his realm. England at the time was held primarily by Danes. When Ethelred secretly entered his homeland to form a militia, he encountered another old enemy, King Olaf of Norway. But Olaf was now eager to help fellow Christians, having recently converted to the faith. The two kings put together a fleet; its ships had scaffoldings specially designed to enable the warriors to reach up with their swords and strike the Danes fighting on top of London Bridge. The canny Danes outwitted this ingenious tactic by deluging the attackers with a stream of stones hurled from the bridge, and defeat for Ethelred's troops seemed inevitable. But in a brilliant strategic stroke, the remaining men, waiting until the tide was strong, approached the timber structure, tied ropes from their vessels around the bridge's beams, and with all their power rowed on, tearing down the bridge and emptying the Danes into the river. The timber bridge was eventually reconstructed, but it was ravaged by fire in 1136, and yet another was thrown up to replace it.

Soon thereafter, Londoners recognized the need for a bridge of greater durability and wider carriageway. In 1176, while the latest timber bridge was still intact, work begun close by on a stone bridge. A priest named Peter Colechurch designed it, but he did not live to see his vision become reality; it took more than three decades to finish. It was a magnificent structure, more than twenty feet wide and nine hundred feet long, sixty feet above the river at the center, supported by twenty arches. This third London Bridge was so sturdy that buildings and homes were erected on it. It was to endure for almost six and a half centuries.

London's medieval bridge was the scene of many royal occasions, but it was also beset by disaster. Fires at both ends in July 1212 caused thousands of people on the bridge to die. No sooner was it repaired than ice blocks floating down the Thames destroyed five arches, putting it temporarily out of commission.

Beginning around 1305, a brutal practice was instituted by Edward I, the king of England, and continued by his successors, for which London Bridge was the main showcase: the display of the severed heads of those who refused to recognize the king as head of both the country and the church. These so-called traitors were executed and decapitated; often more than a dozen decaying heads glared down balefully from the tops of pikes mounted on the roof of the arched Stone Gate House at the Southwark end of the bridge.

The English kings of this period had sunken into a state of savagery. At one point Sir William Wallace, a Scottish nationalist, was in the habit of leading vicious raids against the English. An assault against a count at Scone drew the wrath of King Edward, who gathered a massive army and crushed the Scots. Sir Wallace fled but was later betrayed by a countryman, Sir John Menteith, who captured him and delivered him in shackles to London. He was tried, pronounced guilty, and hanged, and his head set upon a pole on London Bridge. But Edward also ordered his body cut into quarters and the sections displayed throughout the country as an example of what punishment to expect for treacherous behavior. The crowns of numerous other "traitors" through the years were exhibited on the stone bridge, including that of the great statesman Sir Thomas More.

In 1437 a stone gate with a tower on it at the Southwark end fell, bringing down with it several arches. London's Great Fire of 1666, which ravaged most of the city, spread to the bridge and destroyed many of the houses on it.

For nearly 650 years, the stone bridge over the Thames linked London to the district of Southwark. Near the end of its existence, London Bridge was in a continual state of disrepair, sometimes said to be falling down (although the famous children's ditty actually referred to one of the previous London Bridges). Two temporary timber bridges were built, the second after the first was destroyed by fire, while repairs were being made to the stone bridge. But in the early nineteenth century, the stone structure, which also needed arches of a wider span, was finally deemed too dangerous.

A number of engineers presented plans for a new bridge; the plan proposed by architect John Rennie was selected. On June 15, 1825, some one hundred feet west of the decrepit stone monument, work began on Rennie's bridge. It was built of granite quarried in Devon, Scotland, and Cornwall, in addition to stones cannibalized from its predecessor. Six years later, in August 1831, the new bridge was completed and dedicated in a festive ceremony. Boats lined the Thames as King William IV and Queen Adelaide arrived in a royal barge to commence the proceedings. Later, thousands gathered on top of the bridge for a sumptuous feast.

As London's growth continued to explode into the twentieth century, the new bridge also proved insufficient. In the late 1960s, city planners realized a new one had to be built. Not only was the structure sorely inadequate for the vastly increased amount of traffic, but the bridge was gradually sinking into the Thames at a rate of about an inch every seven years.

By a quirk of fate, the needs of two different parties came into play: one needing to get rid of the old to make way for the new, and the other to make way for the new by way of the old. To help finance the costs of building the new bridge without raising taxes, the city of London decided to sell the old bridge. For an American real estate developer who wanted

When the fourth London Bridge opened on August 1, 1831, the king of England led a cavalcade of celebrants across the bridge as boats filled the Thames River below. Here, in a later photo, strollers and people in horse-drawn carriages cross the bridge.

The London Bridge today in Lake Havasu City, Arizona.

to build a new town on a tract of land in the western United States, this was pure serendipity.

The entrepreneur was Robert P. McCulloch, Sr., an oil magnate who in 1963 had successfully bid on the largest parcel of federal property ever sold to a private individual. For seventy-five dollars an acre, he purchased 16,630 acres of barren Arizona desert. Then he heard that the London Bridge was for sale, and he had a brainstorm: What better way to attract people to a desert town and develop a thriving tourist industry than by importing none other than the celebrated London Bridge?

McCulloch's engineer, C. V. Woods, thought McCulloch had rocks in his head. He couldn't be serious about bringing the London Bridge to the American West! But McCulloch was in dead earnest, tendering an offer to the city of London of $2.46 million. McCulloch wasn't the highest bidder, but the city fathers, perhaps in a fit of sentimentality or preservationist fervor, awarded the bridge to him. Whereas the other bidders simply wanted to dismantle the bridge for its granite, McCulloch wanted to reconstruct the bridge as it originally was, over water.

John Rennie's London Bridge was carefully dismantled, the stones numbered to enable the bridge to be precisely reconstructed. The pieces were shipped by way of the Panama Canal to Long Beach, California. Trucks brought the stones to McCulloch's tract of desert in Arizona, and in September 1968, after all five arches had arrived, reconstruction began. It was like building the world's largest jigsaw puzzle. Bulldozers piled sand from the surrounding desert under the arches to support them while the concrete was drying. Under the bridge a channel was dredged, into which water was diverted from a nearby lake.

It took just over two years to build the bridge, which opened on October 10, 1971. With shipping, labor, and other fees, the total cost to reconstruct the London Bridge eventually came to $7.5 million. But McCulloch's gamble paid off; land buyers flocked to obtain lots.

In one respect, McCulloch saved a bundle. Because the ten thousand tons of granite blocks were more than one hundred years old, the savvy developer imported them as antiques, paying not one cent in tariffs.

LOCATION: Lake Havasu City, Arizona.

Jeremy Bentham:
A Philosopher for the Ages

DATE: 1832.

WHAT IT IS: An effigy of the famous Englishman.

WHAT IT LOOKS LIKE: The figure is stuffed and dressed, and sitting composedly on a chair in its original booth, which is made of wood with a glass front. (This booth is enclosed in another case.)

Jeremy Bentham, renowned nineteenth-century English philosopher, had this rather, well, unusual philosophy. It called for people to put their bodies to good use after they died and indeed, Bentham made clear, what good uses they could put them to! Corpses—or "Auto-Icons," as he called them—could replace stone or marble monuments in churches, or, with copal varnish used to weatherproof them, they could alternate with trees leading to country estates. Of course it would be the decision of their owners whether to use full-body Auto-Icons or Auto-Icons of just the head, but, hey, those who were to become Auto-Icons had no need to fret. At least they'd be getting out there!

Now it would probably be safe to say that for most people, the thought of having their body on public display after they died—for the viewing pleasure of others—would be depressing, if not outright repugnant. Did Bentham mean to follow his own philosophy?

In his will Jeremy Bentham directed that when it appeared his life had come to an end, his physician—who should first ascertain "by appropriate experiment" that no life remained in his body—should dress the deceased's skeleton in one of his black suits, place it on a chair in the manner he was accustomed to sit in life, place his staff in his hand, and have the whole configuration installed in a glass case with an engraved

With a wax head adorning his body (and his real head on the floor between his feet), Jeremy Bentham lives on today as an "Auto-Icon."

plate for both scientific illustration and public view. A celebrated figure in his time, Bentham probably realized his Auto-Icon would draw attention.

Bentham achieved fame because of his application of utilitarian philosophy (the idea of promoting the greatest happiness of the greatest number) to questions of ethics, jurisprudence, politics, and prison reform. A wide-ranging thinker, he extended his imagination to uses of the dead and with great zealousness set forth his ideas in an unpublished treatise entitled "Auto-Icon; or, farther uses of the dead to the living." This embraced the ideas that dead bodies could be used in certain ways for the edification and enjoyment of living people, and that for the benefit of future generations, corpses should be preserved in their own likeness.

Bentham listed eleven categories of uses of the dead: "moral, political, honorific, dehonorific, money-saving, money-getting, commemorative, genealogical, architectural, theatrical, and phrenological." He envisioned people becoming comfortable with the sight of Auto-Icons and consequently becoming better able to deal with their own mortality; the exchanges of ideas based on mock debates between celebrated Auto-Icons; a more beautiful world with Auto-Icons adorning properties, homes, and buildings.

To fulfill his vision Bentham suggested a multitude of ways in which Auto-Icons could be used: as collateral for loans; as stage props for dramatic purposes; for aesthetic purposes such as the wealthy maintaining in their mansions a room of Auto-Icons as they would statues; as subjects for instructive public lectures on the human anatomy. Bentham suggested churches exhibit Auto-Icons on religious holidays with sacred music playing in the background to arouse spiritual awakening. He proposed a temple in which corpses would be shifted for display in a Hall of Fame or a Hall of Infamy, depending on how their reputation fared. So thorough was Bentham in his plan that he expanded on everything down to the sartorial and gender aspects of displaying Auto-Icons and suggested a litany of display possibilities. Why use barber poles, he wondered, when "a pair of fashionably-dressed ladies" would do?

Bentham wanted his own body used in anatomical demonstrations and hoped that it would not only communicate to scientists "curious, interesting and highly important knowledge" but also "show that the primitive horror at dissection originates in ignorance and is kept up by misconception and that the human body is as much more beautiful than any other piece of mechanism as it is more curious and wonderful."

Bentham's postmortem directions were carried out but seemed to get off to a shaky start. On June 9, 1832, three days after his death, Bentham's trusted friend Dr. Thomas Southwood Smith delivered an anatomical lecture at the Webb Street School of Anatomy and Medicine with Bentham's corpse by his side. In the audience were friends and supporters of Bentham who received invitations for "an illustration of the structure and functions of the human frame." But the 3:00 P.M. session was interrupted by a thunderstorm so violent that it disconcerted even the iron-nerved Smith.

Soon afterward Smith undertook the making of Bentham's effigy. He extracted Bentham's fleshy parts and deftly hinged the bones together into a skeleton. Unfortunately, the preservation of Bentham's head didn't go as well. Smith extracted the fluids of the head "by placing it under an air pump over sulphuric acid," as he later wrote. But "by this means the head was rendered as hard as the skulls of New Zealanders . . . all expression was of course gone."

Would the spirited Bentham be condemned to eternal life with a stony face? No, that certainly wouldn't do him justice. Smith had a well-known French medical model maker, Jacques Talrich, make a wax head. Some people claimed that Talrich's model, which even used some of Bentham's own hair, bore an astonishing likeness to the original.

Bentham was indeed on his way to becoming an Auto-Icon. Smith stuffed the skeleton with straw, hay, and wool, dressed the figure in the actual garments of the philosopher, seated it in a chair with Bentham's cane in one hand, and deposited the whole icon in a mahogany-and-glass case.

Many people paid calls upon Jeremy Bentham in his posthumous repose at Smith's Finsbury Square offices, until the physician moved to new quarters some seventeen years later. Not having room for the Bentham assemblage in his new quarters, Smith donated it to the Anatomical Museum at University College London.

It was expected that in his new home, in an institution frequented by the public, Jeremy Bentham would enjoy widespread attention and the greetings of his former colleagues and the curious. But that was not the case in the beginning. Dr. Smith expressed his disappointment that "no publicity is given to the fact that Bentham reposes there in some back room."

Over the years, the body—whose padding has been replaced at least twice—was moved from one location in the college to another, being consigned to a museum, a library, and a faculty office. Even Bentham's real head suffered an indignity. It had been stored on a ledge above a door until students from a rival school, King's College, stole it in the 1960s as a prank for Rag Day, when students organized events to raise money for charity, and demanded a twenty-five-pound ransom for its return. College officials got it back after they promised not to contact the police if the head was returned. The students did return the head, and today it is kept locked safely away.

Some legends have grown about Bentham. For example, his ghost is supposed to haunt the building where he now resides. At night, it is said, one may hear Bentham tapping "Dapple," his walking stick (named after the donkey of Cervantes' Sancho Panza), along the corridors.

Perhaps the most famous story attached to the effigy of Jeremy Bentham is that he would be wheeled into meetings of the college council, to sit alongside distinguished staff members. The secretary would record in the minutes, "Mr. Bentham present but not voting." It is certainly a whimsical and amusing yarn but simply untrue.

Still, Jeremy Bentham is very much "alive" today as an Auto-Icon, and from time to time he even attends special functions. In 1986 he helped kick off the International Bentham Society by honoring his fans with a corporeal appearance. And the Auto-Icon made its first international trip, when, from June through October 1992, it was displayed at a major exhibition on London at Essen, Germany. Today the college beadles where he resides even unlock the outer case doors of his glass booth to afford a better view.

In 1831, the year before he died, Jeremy Bentham wrote "Farther uses of the dead to the living," in which he made his case for preserving corpses as Auto-Icons for people's benefit. When the unpublished pamphlet was eventually discovered, the question in people's minds was: Is Bentham putting us on?

With Bentham's Auto-Icon continuing its bizarre heritage after more than 150 years, the same question may be asked today.

LOCATION: University College London, London, England.

The One-Cent Magenta

DATE: 1856.

WHAT IT IS: Arguably the world's most valuable stamp.

WHAT IT LOOKS LIKE: It is octagonal, magenta, and bears the design of a ship and the Latin motto *Damus Petimus Que Vicissim* (To give and seek in return). This design is similar to the British Guiana colony seal. The stamp measures 2⅕ inches horizontally and 1⅗ inches vertically. It is signed with the assistant postmaster's initials, "E. D. W."

It is only a small piece of paper, with its corners clipped off, but for its weight and size, it is perhaps the single most valuable object in the world.

Indeed, most stamps appreciate in value over time, some dramatically. But why has this magenta stamp, issued for only a penny in a remote British colony, soared in price higher than any other?

The story of the One-Cent Magenta begins in April 1856 in British Guiana (later called Guyana), in the northern part of South America, off the Atlantic. The colony's post office exhausted its inventory of stamps from its normal supplier, the British concern Waterlow and Sons, and unable to wait for a new shipment to arrive, engaged a local company in Georgetown to run off a new supply.

The company, being primarily a printer of newspapers, was not in the business of making stamps, and the resulting issues were not particularly attractive. The stamps bore ordinary black type on magenta, or dark purple, paper and a simple picture of a ship to imitate the colony's seal. In separating the printed stamps the postmaster probably clipped the edges. The reason for this is unclear, except perhaps to form an octagon, but

British Guiana 1 cent Magenta of 1856

In 1873 a twelve-year-old boy found this bright magenta-colored stamp, saving from extinction an issue of stamps made in British Guiana. The boy sold it for less than $2.50, and just over a century later the stamp brought in nearly $1 million.

since the stamps could easily be counterfeited postal officials were ordered to initial them.

The stamps from this series—both one-cent and four-cent stamps—were purchased and used over the years but apparently few people were saving them. Some four-cent stamps would survive, but although no one at the time realized it, the one-cent was on the verge of extinction.

But then, in 1873, a twelve-year-old local schoolboy with an avid interest in stamp collecting came across either a wrapper or envelope with the "black on magenta" and soaked off the stamp, which had on it a canceled mark of Demerara (the name sometimes used for the colony) and bore the initials "E. D. W.," after the assistant Demerara postmaster, E. D. Wight. L. Vernon Vaughan could hardly have imagined that he was saving what would one day become the world's most valuable stamp, and when he soon received on approval some handsome new stamps from England, he was delighted that a local dealer by the name of N. R. McKinnon was willing to take off his hands the uncommon but unattractive "black on magenta" for a handful of shillings (reported over the years as anywhere from fifty cents to $2.50) so he could purchase the new shipment he received.

Eventually McKinnon came to realize that the One-Cent Magenta was indeed rare and a few years later sold it to a Scottish dealer, who in turn sold it to an English collector, who in turn sold it for over $800 to a Parisian collector. Although this was believed to be a record, its value would soar with the next owner. The value of stamps, like antiquities, depends upon their rarity and history of ownership. Because this last gentleman went on to build perhaps the greatest stamp collection in the world and was becoming a legend in philatelic circles for his all-consuming passion for stamps, the One-Cent Magenta would later bring in an astronomically higher price when it would be offered for sale—after its owner's death.

The collector was Philippe la Rénotière von Ferrari, the son of a wealthy family; his mother was an Austrian duchess. Philippe developed an interest in stamps at a young age, and with money not an obstacle, went around to stamp shops buying whatever he wanted. Later, with a full-blown passion for stamps, he went around purchasing whatever collections he desired. He acquired numerous fabulous collections, eventually building his into the world's greatest and most valuable. Unlike collectors of later generations who would specialize in certain kinds of stamps, Ferrari collected stamps from all over and of all kinds, including numerous rare stamps.

Count Philippe von Ferrari died in 1917 at the age of sixty-nine and left his million-dollar-plus collection to a Berlin museum. However, after World War I, in claiming war reparations from Germany, France obtained the magnificent Ferrari stamp collection. France sold off the Ferrari collection in a series of fourteen auctions beginning in 1920 and ending five years later. The auctions drew international attention but the stamp that caused the most sensation was the One-Cent Magenta, considered the rarest in the world. Among the parties said to be interested in bidding on the stamp were three kings.

In the end, the winning bidder was Arthur Hind, a wealthy American textile manufacturer and well-known stamp collector. Hind (through his representative) bid approximately $36,000 and brought the "black on magenta" home with him to Utica, New York.

Some colorful anecdotes attend Hind's possession of the stamp. For example, one day someone came to his office claiming to possess another One-Cent Magenta. He showed it to Hind, who asked him how much he wanted for it. They settled on a substantial amount, and the next day Hind took possession of the stamp. Upon receiving it he burned it with a match and declared, "Now there's still only one!"

After Hind died in the mid-1930s, the British Guiana one-cent stamp was exhibited at the 1939–40 New York World's Fair and around the world. Hind's widow, who had to go to court to take ownership of the stamp since there was a dispute, then sold it for more than $40,000 to an anonymous man from Florida (it was Frederick Small, an Australian engineer) who kept it until 1970. Throughout this time, Small never publicly displayed the stamp, although he sometimes showed a facsimile. The stamp was then purchased for $280,000 by a syndicate of Pennsylvania investors headed by Irwin Weinberg, a Wilkes-Barre, Pennsylvania, stamp dealer who first saw the One-Cent Magenta exhibited in 1940 at the New York World's Fair. Traveling with bodyguards and the stamp locked in a suitcase handcuffed to his wrist during the 1970s, Weinberg exhibited the magenta stamp in Tokyo, Prague, Hamburg, Paris, London, New York, and other cities. Tens of thousands of avid collectors queued up all over the world to see this icon of philately. When the stamp wasn't on the display circuit, it was stored in a bank vault. Purchased as a hedge against inflation, the One-Cent Magenta reaped rewards for its owners ten years later when it brought in the sum of $935,000. At the moment of delivery, Weinberg printed his initials on its back, continuing a modern tradition associated with the stamp.

The one-cent British Guiana stamp was purchased by a member of a prominent industrial family, the Du Ponts. Although the owner probably keeps the stamp in a bank vault, legend has it that from time to time he sleeps with it under his pillow. Wealthy stamp collectors from all around the world would love to acquire it.

It has been claimed that the One-Cent Magenta is not authentic; some have said that the Four-Cent Magenta, which looks identical to it except for the denomination, was altered. To date, no evidence at all has surfaced to substantiate this claim, and the stamp was once studied by philatelic experts and pronounced to be authentic.

Although market conditions make valuing an object speculative, the million-dollar Four-Cent Magenta is an extraordinary item considering its weight and that it is made only of paper. It weighs 120 milligrams, or less than two grains. Considering that there are 480 grains to a troy ounce, two grains is virtually weightless. Yet this "weightless" paper could probably command more money than any other substance of its weight and size. Rare stamps on envelopes have been sold for fantastic sums, but there is the added element here of the envelope. At an auction held in March 1991 in Europe, an exotic envelope with the mid–nineteenth-century British Penny Black was auctioned for $2.4 million. In November 1993, again in Europe, the "Mauritius cover," an envelope bearing two stamps that was mailed in 1847, was sold at auction for $3.3 million. Some experts believe the One-Cent Magenta would fetch an even higher price on the open market.

The One-Cent Magenta was created in a printer's shop in northeast South America in mid–nineteenth-century British Guiana. Were it not for a schoolboy's astuteness, this stamp would be extinct. It is the last of its kind, at once a sole survivor and superstar in the world of philately.

LOCATION: In the vicinity of Newtown Square, Pennsylvania.

John Brown's Bible

DATE: 1859.

WHAT IT IS: The Bible that abolitionist John Brown read ardently after his failed raid on the Harpers Ferry armory, while awaiting his execution in prison. In a way, Brown himself comes alive in the text—that is to say, the book evokes his personality—since the radical antislavery proponent marked off numerous hellfire-and-brimstone passages condemning violence and oppression.

WHAT IT LOOKS LIKE: The Bible measures 6 inches by 4 inches and has a light brown leather cover. It was printed by the American Bible Society in 1854 and has 767 numbered pages.

The verdict was in. For leading the insurrection at Harpers Ferry, for usurping property of the federal government, for murder, for treason to Virginia, the antislavery activist was guilty. The defendant having rejected an insanity plea, the trial moved swiftly, and the sentence was set. John Brown was to be hanged on the gallows.

The trial ended on November 2, 1859, six days after it commenced. Brown and his men had been taken prisoner by soldiers after they seized the federal arsenal at Harpers Ferry, Virginia, on October 16. Even before this time, there were many people who wanted to put him on trial. For the past few years the abolitionist had been leading raids to free slaves and had been involved in the killings of proslavery people.

In Kansas, which had not yet decided the slavery question for itself, he conducted guerrilla operations and was viewed as radical by proslavery people. Brown moved around a lot to carry out what he saw as a divinely ordained mission to abolish slavery. By taking over Harpers Ferry at a time when the country was moving toward civil war, he had hoped to rouse the black population to action and subsequent freedom. That did not happen, and the raid was an immediate failure—with injuries and fatal casualties on both sides. Now the trial was over, and with the sentence to be carried out in a month and lawmen fearing a lynching scene, Brown and his associates would remain under heavy guard in jail.

John Brown whiled away the last days of his life behind bars, convinced that his actions were justified and that his purpose was noble. While the proslavery faction despised him and eagerly awaited his execution, his reputation in other quarters as a martyr grew during his trial and incarceration.

Hundreds of people came to visit Brown in prison, and he eventually even gained the sympathy of his jailers. One attendant, John Frederick Blessing, was a baker and confectioner who dutifully brought Brown and his men cakes, oysters, and various other delicacies. The abolitionist appreciated Blessing's kindness, and a warm friendship developed.

In the days before his execution, Brown received comfort not only from strangers but from his beloved Bible as well. In sworn, notarized affidavits made in January 1893, George W. Engle and Charles C. Conklyn, assistant guards who escorted Brown from prison to the courthouse and guarded him there each day of the trial, noted "the devoted attention and religious fervor shown by John Brown in the study of his Bible and in marking certain verses therein." Jail guard John E. Hilbert recorded Brown's "constant perusal and study of the Bible." Indeed, Brown marked passages that mirrored his personality, temperament, and beliefs, such as the following:

> Destruction cometh; and they shall seek peace, and *there shall be none*. Mischief shall come upon mischief, and rumour shall be upon rumour; then shall they seek a vision of the prophet; but the law shall perish from the priest, and counsel from the ancients. The king shall mourn, and the prince shall be clothed with desolation, and the hands of the people of the land shall be troubled: I will do unto them after their way, and according to their deserts will I judge them; and they shall know that I *am* the Lord.
>
> —Ezekiel 7:25–27

Before he was hanged, John Brown gave John Frederick Blessing, one of his jailers, the Bible he read and marked in prison. "With the best wishes of the <u>undersigned and his sincere thanks</u> for many acts of kindness," wrote the abolitionist on the flyleaf. "There is no commentary in the world so good in order to a right understanding of this blessed book as an honest Childlike and teachable spirit."

To mark passages, Brown usually either drew ink lines running down the margins or folded page corners.

So earnestly devoted was Brown to his Bible, which he always kept by his side, that "sometimes [he] did not even lay aside the book when his physician entered," recalled Dr. G. F. Mason, who treated the wounded prisoner in the jail at what was then Charlestown, Virginia (now Charlestown, West Virginia).

Brown did pay attention to some of the visitors he had a fondness for. He spoke kindly and serenely with a judge's wife who came from Boston to see him, causing her to weep when she left. He spoke calmly with reporters and clergymen and soldiers.

On the day before he died, John Brown was allowed to see his wife, Mary, one more time. Mary had made a fervent but unsuccessful appeal on behalf of her husband to the governor of Virginia, and she was in an emotional whirlwind. The couple spoke about their children, the family's future, his burial, and the burials of those who were killed in raids with him. They hugged emotionally as Mary, prohibited from being with him his final night, departed.

Before John Brown was led away to die, he extended his appreciation to John Frederick Blessing, the jail guard who showed kindness to him and his fellow prisoners, and to whom he had become deeply attached. He gave to Blessing his cherished Bible, with an inscription (dated November 29, 1859) on the flyleaf.

On the morning of December 2, 1859, John Brown was led out of his cell by some prison guards. He passed his fellow raiders and blessed them, saying he hoped to meet them again in heaven.

With the area filled with militiamen and spectators, the abolitionist rode to the place of execution. It was on a hill in rolling countryside. There were a thousand U.S. soldiers present and a score of citizens. Many were happy to see him finally get his comeuppance and wanted to witness this long-awaited event. Brown was escorted up the scaffold, a hood was placed over his head, and his feet were bound. The swift thrust of an ax cut a rope, dropping the false floor on which Brown stood. His body fell, suspended only by the noose around his neck. After a few moments, life passed from the man who had been obsessed with liberating the black slaves, the abolitionist whose actions would reverberate throughout the turbulent years ahead.

Abolitionist John Brown

John Brown's Bible was to be a sacred relic in the Blessing home for over thirty years. The family protected and preserved it, and they never permitted any leaves to be taken out or any additions or changes to be made. With the hundreds of visitors—friends and curiosity seekers—to the Blessing home, intrigued by the legendary martyr's Bible and eager to touch it, about the only effect on the book through the years was the soiling and tearing of the flyleaf.

John Frederick Blessing died in 1869, and his widow, Emily Jane, requiring money for some badly needed repairs on her home, was forced to sell the Bible in 1893. She was very old and would have preferred to pass along this family treasure to her children, but economic hardship prevailed. Although she had received offers as high as $250, she wanted to sell it to Frank G. Logan, a Chicago banker who she believed would diligently guard and conserve it. Logan (1851–1937) was also a collector of art, historical manuscripts, and letters; his collection of John Brown items included cotton from Brown's coffin and Brown's pistol from his Kansas campaign. Logan had offered only $150 for the Bible. A Charlestown, West Virginia, notary public, B. D. Gibson, acted as an intermediary to facilitate the sale.

In a letter dated December 21, 1892, Gibson urged Logan to pay Mrs. Blessing the $200 she wanted, telling him this was still an excellent deal because "there are no precedents by which to rate the value of the John Brown relics, because he was a martyr whose principles succeeded ultimately and speedily too." Gibson, who indicated that his letter was not written "in any spirit of barter or dicker" but because he wanted to see the book "in the proper hands," even went so far as to offer to advance the extra $50 himself, payable up to a year after a date Logan would elect. He proposed that Logan exhibit the Bible at the World's Fair to make up the $50. And to sweeten the deal, Gibson noted that he had induced the Blessings to include along with the Bible a picture of John Brown sitting down and holding a copy of the *New York Tribune* and a copy of *Made-Up Stories* (part of *Mrs. Follen's Twilight Series*), autographed for John Frederick Blessing by one of Brown's raiders, John E. Cook. A deal was struck, and less than three weeks later a pasteboard box containing the items was placed in a wooden crate that was nailed shut and shipped by U.S. mail to Logan in Chicago. In the 1920s the Bible, along with other articles in Logan's collection, was obtained by a private nonprofit organization.

A song about the controversial emancipator-martyr grew popular in the Union as the war between the states raged on. While his "body lies amould'ring in the grave," goes the lyric, "his soul goes marching on." It still does today, in John Brown's Bible.

LOCATION:　Chicago Historical Society, Chicago, Illinois.

Captain Danjou's Wooden Hand

DATE: 1863.

WHAT IT IS: The artificial left hand of a French foreign legion commander who was killed in battle. In this battle, a small company of legionnaires gallantly and heroically fought a large army that attacked them. The commander's artificial hand was recovered from the battlefield and became a revered relic among the French foreign legion.

WHAT IT LOOKS LIKE: The hand is wooden, and the fingers are slightly curled.

The scene was intense. Southern Mexico, near the eastern coast, mid–nineteenth century. Swampy lowlands infested with malaria-carrying mosquitoes, an oppressive tropical climate. This poor country was politically unstable, its civilization was backward, and sovereignty was a function of military supremacy.

The French were trying to seize control of the nation. Napoleon III sensed an opportunity to wrest control of a huge parcel of land from the current Mexican leader, an Indian named Benito Juárez, and used the excuse of the country's unresolved financial debts to send in troops. But the Mexicans, like their forefathers who had fought hard for independence from Spain just decades earlier, were determined to be free of foreign domination.

Assisting the army of France in Mexico was the French foreign legion, an elite band of professional fighters that was created in 1831 by Louis Philippe, then king of France. The legion was composed mostly of rogues, fugitives, and rebels—it was a volunteer force with a "no questions asked" enlistment policy—who endured severe training and who prided themselves on being brave and highly skilled. Friction with the French army caused the thousands of legionnaires dispatched to Mexico to be as-

Captain Jean Danjou became a legend in the French foreign legion after the battle in Camerone.

signed to patrol and work in rough and unhealthy areas.

On the morning of April 30, 1863, Captain Jean Danjou of the French foreign legion was leading a company of sixty-two men and two officers on a reconnaissance mission on a trail between Veracruz and Puebla. A huge shipment of gold—remuneration for the French forces in Mexico—was to be sent to Mexico City by carts. A company of the French foreign legion drew the assignment to guard it along this part of the route.

The company's regular officers and half its regular men were ill from dysentery and malaria, so volunteers were recruited from other companies. Captain Danjou was among the volunteers. Danjou was a veteran of several legion campaigns, and his left hand had been ripped off during an engagement in the southern Crimea. The thirty-five-year-old officer used a prosthetic wooden hand, over which he always wore a white glove.

Around 8:00 A.M., after his troops had been marching for hours without eating, and the sun was beginning to beat down mercilessly, Captain Danjou decided to give his men a respite: coffee, a short rest, then back on their feet. But just as the men were settling down, a sentinel shouted. Materializing out of the countryside was an incredible sight: an army, a huge army of Mexican nationalists, both on horse and on foot.

Quick-minded, Captain Danjou issued an order. A few thousand feet back the company had passed through the village of Camerone. It had been partially destroyed, but a hacienda was still standing. This would be a good defensive fortification from which the men could fight the Mexicans until backups arrived. The legionnaires disappeared into the brush as the Mexicans swooped down, capturing a number of them.

Forty-nine of the legionnaires made it back to the hacienda. There they engaged in a battle with their attackers. Less than an hour after fighting began, a Mexican soldier approached the hacienda under a flag of truce. His message was simple: the Mexican army was two thousand strong, and the French company could not possibly prevail. If the legionnaires surrendered, they would not be mistreated.

Surrendering was not part of the code of the French foreign legion. That would be cowardly and disgraceful. Danjou responded to the insulting offer with animation: the Mexicans would have them only when they had killed every last one of them.

So the fighting raged on. Despite being vastly outnumbered, the French troops fought valiantly and caused many Mexican casualties. But in the end there were simply too many soldiers and guerrillas. One by one the legionnaires, dehydrated now, were picked off. In the late morning Captain Danjou was struck by a round and died.

The French mercenaries' numbers dwindled until there were only about a half-dozen left. After nearly ten hours of fighting, the Mexican nationalist commander, Colonel Milan, decided to put an end to the skirmish, lest the foreigners' perseverance be an embarrassment to him. When the Mexicans stormed the hacienda, the legionnaires put up a last effort and charged them with their bayonets. The Mexican forces engulfed them and moved in for the final kill. However, a Mexican officer decided to spare the few remaining warriors, so these men were captured and the other still-living but wounded legionnaires were carried by stretcher to a hospital, where many succumbed despite medical treatment.

Colonel Milan did not pursue the cargo of gold—perhaps because he forgot about it—which was on its way back to the French base after its carriers heard the gunfire.

The backups that the legionnaires hoped would soon arrive did not come until early the next day, at which point the Mexicans had taken the wounded men as hostages, and only the residue remained—corpses. Strangely, the body of Captain Danjou, the gallant commander, was nowhere to be found. However, a legionnaire officer spotted Danjou's wooden hand in the rubble, scooped it up, and carried it with him for the duration of his service in Mexico and then back to legionnaire headquarters in Algeria.

Camerone. Danjou. The battle and its commander became legends in the French foreign legion. In the twentieth century, April 30, the day of the historic battle, was established as an annual ceremony in France, commemorated with a parade and a recounting of Danjou and the legionnaires' heroic stand.

The prosthesis used by the French commander to gesture, to direct his men, to carry out actions as if it were his real hand, is an intimate rem-

The wooden hand of Captain Danjou. Found in the rubble after an 1860s battle in Mexico, the prosthesis became a symbol to legionnaires of courage and fortitude.

nant of that historic battle. This object bears witness to the bravery of all those who fought the battle at Camerone, and indeed to that of the French foreign legion itself. New generations of this elite organization see the wooden hand of Captain Jean Danjou as an emblem of what they stand for, of the quintessential esprit of *la légion étrangère*.

LOCATION: French Foreign Legion Museum, Aubagne, France.

Major General Daniel E. Sickles's Leg

DATE: 1863.

WHAT IT IS: The fractured right tibia and fibula of a forty-three-year-old Civil War general.

WHAT IT LOOKS LIKE: A shattered lower leg bone.

One of the great pieces of folklore of the Civil War involves one Daniel Edgar Sickles, a general who was wounded at Gettysburg. After a doctor amputated his leg, Sickles proudly dispatched it with his compliments in a coffinlike box to the Army Medical Museum in Washington, D.C., where he regularly brought his friends to join him in admiring this gruesome battle souvenir.

If Sickles's bequest seems a bit eccentric, it was only one of a series of audacious acts that characterized this controversial and colorful fellow. Born in New York City on October 20, 1819, to George Sickles, a patent lawyer, and his wife, Susan, Daniel grew into an unruly youth, at times running away from home or dropping out of school. He was blessed, however, with a charming personality and loving parents, who, in an attempt to mature him, sent him off to private school. This effort proved fruitless, for young Daniel quit that school, too, in response to a teacher's admonishment. Attracted to journalism, Daniel became an apprentice for a newspaper, but he was eventually coaxed home by his father after the lawyer's business investments finally hit pay dirt.

More conflict between father and son resulted in more itinerancy for Daniel, until George Sickles finally arranged for his son to stay with some friends prior to entering college. Daniel found happiness in the home of Lorenzo Da Ponte, an old Italian with an eclectic background that included serving as Mozart's librettist. The household, comprising Lorenzo's scholarly children and a young couple (the wife had been adopted by Lorenzo) and their infant daughter, Teresa, offered quite a Bohemian atmosphere.

Daniel entered college but dropped out soon after, devastated when Lorenzo and one of his sons suddenly died within a short period of each other. He went to work for an attorney and learned quickly, demonstrating an aptitude for law. He was admitted to the bar and followed in his father's footsteps by becoming a patent lawyer. But over the next few years, he developed an unsavory reputation for frequenting bordellos and misappropriating clients' funds. He also joined the corrupt world of New York politics, this being the heyday of Tammany Hall, and with the aid of influential friends he was elected to the legislature. While in the public eye, Sickles boldly continued his questionable antics, which included bringing a favorite lady of the evening to a meeting of the august New York State Assembly. Despite his relentless womanizing, he eventually decided to settle down. The object of his affection was a girl half his age, Teresa, the seventeen-year-old daughter of the couple he lived with at the Da Pontes' (whose mother Sickles was said to have seduced).

All the hot water Sickles got into as a result of his undignified peccadilloes while an assemblyman was a minor nuisance compared to the scandal that was to afflict him as a New York congressman living in Washington, D.C. In the late 1850s the nation's capital was feverish with political activity as the debate over the slavery issue reached a crisis level. Sickles wasted no time ingratiating himself with the resident bigwigs, men such as Washington district attorney Philip Barton Key, the son of Francis Scott Key, and President James Buchanan.

Harboring presidential ambitions himself, Sickles plunged into the turbulent political waters. With equal gusto but much greater discretion now, he resumed his philandering.

His work frequently took him out of town, leaving his beautiful young wife alone and vulnerable to the flirtatious men of Washington society. One who was attracted to her was Philip Barton Key, a widower and father of four children. At first, the time they spent together—horseback riding, strolling, and other leisurely pastimes—was surely innocent; the fortyish Key professed no more than fatherly affection for Teresa, now twenty-three. But soon their admiration took on a physical aspect.

So torrid was this love affair that the prominent Key, a strikingly attractive man with a reputation as a charmer, rented a house nearby. Rendezvous were frequent. The lovers devised an elaborate set of signals, including mounting a red ribbon from a second-story window to indicate that Key was inside and waiting. Neighbors in front and back couldn't help but notice the frequent coming and going of Key and the mysterious woman dressed in a black raglan cloak.

Rumors cycled through the Washington gossip mill until everyone of consequence, it seemed, knew about the affair—everyone, that is, except Daniel Sickles. Finally, Sickles received a note, signed only with initials, that revealed to the incredulous congressman that Key had rented the house "for no other reason than to meet your wife, Mrs. Sickles." The note continued, "He hangs a string out the window to signal her that he is in, and leaves the door unfastened and she walks in and . . . with these few hints I leave the rest to your imagination." Wanting to be unequivocally certain of his wife's purported indiscretions, Sickles had a close associate, George Woolridge, spy on Teresa and interview his servants. Woolridge confirmed the contents of the note. In a rage, Sickles confronted his wife and demanded that she write a lengthy confession. "I did what is usual for a wicked woman to do," she stated, and provided details of when and where she and Key met and how the two undressed and went to bed together.

Sickles summoned his friend Samuel Butterworth for counsel on how to deal with the situation without harming his chances of becoming president. During this Sunday-morning conference, as Sickles paced the floor, he looked out the window only to spy Key standing in a park across the street shaking a white handkerchief in another brazen signal to Teresa. Butterworth ran out to engage Key in conversation while Sickles went to his gun chest.

Sickles soon caught up with Key. "You villain, you have defiled my bed and must die!" Key took cover but was defenseless as Sickles, a marksman, plugged several bullets into him. Sickles was arrested and charged with murder. After a wrenching and sensational trial in which he pleaded temporary insanity (the first use of such a defense), he was acquitted, enabling him to sustain his career in politics, for he had recently been elected to another term in Congress.

Teresa was banished in ignominy to the seclusion of her parents' home in New York. After all this, Sickles began to feel remorseful about his own sexual transgressions. Realizing he was still in love with his wife, he attempted to reunite with her, but in a supremely ironic twist of public capriciousness, his constituents were so offended by his desire to reconcile with a disgraced woman that his political career was destroyed. His former wife was left to herself in shame.

Major General Daniel Edgar Sickles and his leg bone, which he sent in a makeshift coffin to the Army Medical Museum with his compliments and frequently visited.

No longer a congressman, Sickles returned to his law practice in the spring of 1861. By this time the conflict between the North and South had grown explosive, and a man like Sickles was not content to vegetate in an office while history was being made. He recruited a volunteer brigade in New York and was made a brigadier general. After successfully commanding his brigade in its maiden engagement, he was provisionally promoted to a major general and given responsibility for the Union army's Third Corps. He led this group through a campaign at Chancellorsville, Virginia, and on to Gettysburg.

On the morning of July 2, 1863, the second day of a fierce three-day battle at the site, General George Meade ordered Sickles to position his men near troops already posted at the Round Tops, two hills in the south of the Gettysburg battlefield that made for a strategic position for the Union army. Later in the day Sickles, without permission, advanced his men beyond this position, a costly move. The Confederates, led by Lieutenant General James Longstreet, wiped out about half the division. Early in the evening, as Sickles sat on his horse observing the action, a twelve-pound cannonball ripped his right leg open. His horse panicked, but Sickles was able to calm it and dismount alone. Some soldiers rushed him off in an ambulance wagon to a nearby ravine, where Dr. Thomas Sim, a surgeon and medical director of the Third Army Corps, severed the leg low in the thigh. Dosed with opium and clutching his amputated shinbone, which Dr. Sim returned to Sickles because a general's leg was deemed a special war memento, he was carried by stretcher for miles to a train and taken to Washington. While he was recuperating, President Lincoln paid him regular visits. At one point a nurse showed the wounded man a flyer urging doctors to "collect and forward to the office

Daniel E. Sickles wearing the regulation dress uniform of a U.S. army general around the turn of the century. Sickles was the last major general of the two armies that fought at Gettysburg to attend the fiftieth anniversary Gettysburg reunion, held from June 30 to July 4, 1913, and attended by 54,000 veterans of the north and south. The following year, 1914, Sickles died at the age of ninety-four.

of the Surgeon General all specimens of morbid anatomy, surgical or medical, which may be regarded as valuable." So, deeming his shinbone a worthy contribution to medical science, Sickles forwarded it to the Army Medical Museum, where it was put on display.

Having only one leg didn't lessen Sickles's passion for life. He was only forty-three and had many more accomplishments ahead of him. Within two months his stump was healed, and he was up and about, even riding a horse again. He became military governor of the Carolinas, minister to Spain, a New York City sheriff, and again a U.S. congressman. As a representative, he spearheaded a drive to make the site of battle at Gettysburg a national military park. He even became intimate friends with James Longstreet, the former Confederate general who had commanded the bloody attack that took off his leg. Longstreet graciously absolved Sickles of blame for taking his advanced position at Gettysburg by composing a document avowing that Sickles's initiative "saved the battlefield to the Union" and expressing the hope that "the nation, reunited, may always enjoy the honor and glory brought to it by that grand work."

LOCATION: National Museum of Health and Medicine,* Washington, D.C.

*Known as the Army Medical Museum during the Civil War.

The Gettysburg Address

DATE: 1863.

WHAT IT IS: The handwritten manuscript of the speech read by President Abraham Lincoln at the dedication of the national cemetery at Gettysburg, Pennsylvania.

WHAT IT LOOKS LIKE: The following is a description of what is called the Nicolay copy of Lincoln's Gettysburg Address: It is on two pages. Page 1 is $9\frac{7}{8}$ inches long and $7\frac{7}{8}$ inches wide, is written in brown ink, and has "Executive Mansion" printed at the top in bold letters, and "Washington, ..., 186 ." below it. It is lined horizontally in blue ink and has a tannish color (perhaps from the effects of time). Page 2 measures $12\frac{5}{8}$ inches by $7\frac{11}{16}$ inches, is written in pencil, is also ruled in blue ink, has an irregular tear on the lower right corner (the missing portion of the sheet is about $1\frac{1}{8}$ inches by $4\frac{1}{4}$ inches), and is lighter in tone than page 1 (it may have been off-white in 1863). Page 2 has sometimes been referred to as a sheet of foolscap, but the term does not quite apply. It is too small and would not qualify as drawing paper. Both pages have fold marks—two on page one and three on page two.

One of the great mysteries of American historical documents concerns Abraham Lincoln's Gettysburg Address. Lincoln wrote the address in his hand at least five times—that is to say, five copies of the Gettysburg Address in Lincoln's hand exist today. But the reading copy, the one that the beleaguered president held on that autumn day of November 1863 as he looked out at more than ten thousand spectators gathered on the ravaged Pennsylvania battlefield, would be a priceless manuscript, a supreme national treasure. Does the reading copy survive, and if it does, which one of the five known copies is it?

The five copies are each known by their former owners. Accordingly, they are the Nicolay copy, named after John George Nicolay, Lincoln's principal personal secretary; the Hay copy, named after John Hay, an assistant to Nicolay; the Everett copy, for Edward Everett, the famed orator; the Bancroft copy, for George Bancroft, a diplomat and historian; and the Bliss copy, for Alexander Bliss, a colonel in the U.S. Quartermaster's Department. The Everett, Bancroft, and Bliss copies can be ruled out immediately as the reading copy. It is well documented that they were written by Lincoln after his Gettysburg Address at the request of others so that copies of his speech could be sold at "sanitary fairs"—fund-raising events sponsored by local organizations of the U.S. Sanitary Commission for the benefit of injured soldiers.

That leaves the Nicolay and Hay copies as the contenders for the reading copy. Or perhaps Lincoln wrote another copy, the *real* Gettysburg Address, and it has been lost or destroyed.

To understand the provenance of the speech, one must have a sense of the historical context. Here are the circumstances of the Gettysburg battlefield commemoration and of Lincoln's invitation to speak.

From the first to the third of July 1863, Union and Confederate soldiers fought one another in one of the most vicious battles of the Civil War. Seventy-five hundred soldiers lay dead in the fields; more than twenty-six thousand were wounded, many requiring the amputation of one or more limbs; and more than ten thousand were missing or captured. The magnitude of the Union victory and the need to honor the fallen soldiers at Gettysburg brought together the political leaders of the North in commemorating the enormous casualties of their army. Less than five months after the last cannons resounded, statesmen, soldiers, and citizens gathered to consecrate the battleground.

The idea to set aside a portion of the twenty-two-thousand-acre Gettysburg battle site to bury its dead came from David Wills, an attorney in the small Pennsylvania town. Charged with overseeing the medical attention given to those ravaged by the battle, Wills was so overwhelmed by the spectacle of temporary graves and exposed remains on the fields that he recommended to Pennsylvania's Governor Andrew Curtin that the dead be reinterred with proper burial rites in an area that would be designated a cemetery. Curtin approved the idea, and eighteen states of the North that had lost men in the battle participated in the venture. Wills became the superintendent of the Gettysburg Cemetery Commission.

From the start of this enterprise the commissioners wanted to have America's most acclaimed living orator as the principal speaker for the dedication ceremony. They succeeded in procuring the orator: Edward Everett, a former president of Harvard, congressman, governor, minister to Britain, U.S. senator, and U.S. secretary of state, accepted an invitation sent to him in September. So the commission went ahead with its plans, postponing the ceremonies from October 23 to November 19 to accommodate Everett, who requested more time to craft his speech for so solemn an occasion. On the second of November, Wills extended an invitation to President Lincoln to deliver "a few appropriate remarks."

Lincoln accepted the invitation, which surprised those around him. Usually, his hectic schedule forced him to decline public appearances, even at important functions. In this instance the enormity of the battle and the opportunity to define the war as one against human injustice certainly influenced Lincoln's decision to attend.

Unfortunately, the circumstances attending Lincoln's actual writing of his address are vague. Did he write it in Washington before his departure for Gettysburg? On the train to Gettysburg? At Gettysburg, after his arrival and before the ceremonies commenced? Or a combination of these?

These questions were investigated by two of the foremost Lincoln scholars, David C. Mearns and Lloyd A. Dunlap, in their 1963 book *Long Remembered*. The authors gathered recollections and testimonies of eyewitnesses, evaluated their credibility and the evidence at hand, and arrived at a conclusion.

According to Mearns and Dunlap, the evidence strongly indicates that Lincoln began writing the speech while at the White House—exactly when is open to question. Noah Brooks, a reporter who knew Lincoln well, declared in 1878 that he had been with the president on November 15, four days before the ceremonies, and that the president had mentioned receiving a copy of Everett's speech. Lincoln quipped that Everett sent the speech out of fear that he might say something similar, but that Everett need not worry; Lincoln's remarks would be brief. In response to Brooks's question as to whether he had written his own speech, Brooks quoted Lincoln as saying, "Well, I have written it over two or three times, and I shall have to give it another lick before I am satisfied. But it is short, short, short." A year later, former U.S. attorney general James Speed noted that Lincoln had once spoken to him about the preparation of his speech and claimed to have written "about half a speech" the day before he left for Gettysburg.

Around noon, on Wednesday, the eighteenth of November, Lincoln boarded a special train of four cars. Lincoln's family didn't travel with him. The younger Lincoln boy, Tad, was seriously ill, and his wife, Mary Todd, was distressed; their third son, Willie, had died just a year earlier, and their second son, Eddie, several years previously. But during the trip Lincoln was composed, and at times he even displayed his keen sense of humor.

It was on this train, legend has it, that Lincoln wrote his speech. But did he really? Many historians believe Lincoln did no writing during the journey, but there are conflicting accounts, some from people who claimed to have been eyewitnesses and to have actually seen him scribbling on a piece of paper or an envelope braced on his knee.

Lincoln's train arrived in Gettysburg at 5:00 P.M. The president was led to David Wills's house (which still stands on the southeast quadrant of the square in the center of town), where he was to spend the night in a second-floor bedroom. Dinner was served for Lincoln and other guests. Late in the evening, Lincoln begged to be excused to work on his speech and retired to his room. Here again, the accounts of his work on the speech differ.

Historians agree that the president had already written at least part of the speech and had brought it with him to Gettysburg. Lincoln finished the speech at Wills's house sometime between when he arrived that evening and before the ceremonies the next morning, but except for the governor, Andrew Curtin, no one witnessed firsthand the president writing that evening.

As Mearns and Dunlap report, Curtin said in 1885 that he had observed the president writing his address "on a long yellow envelope." Such envelopes were of the kind officially used in the Lincoln White House. Curtin recalled the president leaving the social gathering that evening to show what he had written to his secretary of state, William Seward, who was a guest in the next house, then returning and copying his address "on a foolscap sheet." Some claimed that this foolscap was the same from which he read the address at the ceremony. James Rebert, a sergeant in a Pennsylvania cavalry, assigned to Lincoln on the morning of the Gettysburg procession, later said that he met Lincoln in his room and was asked to wait a few minutes until the president finished writing. Rebert noted that Lincoln had several pieces of pencil-inscribed notes before him, which, after completing his writing, he folded and put in his pocket.

That Lincoln finished his draft in pencil has been disputed by some historians. They contend that on the night before the ceremony, Lincoln did not like the way his speech ended and destroyed his second sheet; the next morning he copied in ink his first draft onto two new pages and used them when he delivered the address.

However, most evidence suggests that a two-page ink draft was not written before the speech. Both Nicolay and his assistant, John Hay, report that Lincoln finished his address in pencil on the page he read from at the ceremony. This pencil-written page would be the companion to an ink page with the words "Executive Mansion" written at the top, which Wills asserted he saw in the copy Lincoln read from during the speech. (No ink copy later made by Lincoln has these words printed on any of the sheets.)

The Gettysburg ceremonies began with a procession to the battlefield, at about eleven o'clock on the morning of November 19, 1863. It was a cool, clear autumn day, and a large crowd was present—probably ten thousand to thirteen thousand, although estimates range from as few as five thousand to as many as twenty thousand. Lincoln rode in the procession on a horse and presumably reached the speaker's platform at eleven-fifteen. The military salute and introductions probably occupied another twenty-five minutes, with a military band performing just before Edward Everett began a two-hour speech on the battle.

At about 2:00 P.M., Lincoln arose from his seat and took the podium. From his pocket he withdrew two folded pages, which he held in his hands and referred to while speaking. As he looked out at the audience, his heart was torn. His only desire was for the country to reunite. He felt no bitterness toward the South, but rather he agonized for it; he felt the loss of the Confederate states. He spoke the words that would soon be immortalized: "Four score and seven years ago . . ." The speech was short, only two minutes, yet applause interrupted Lincoln's address a few times and sustained clapping followed at the conclusion. The reception in the press, however, was by no means wildly enthusiastic, and many of the newspaper accounts were unfavorable. "Ludicrous," said the *London Times*; "Silly, flat," lamented the *Chicago Times*, "an offensive

A rare photograph of President Abraham Lincoln (pointed out by arrow) on the speaker's platform before he delivered his speech at the dedication ceremonies of the Gettysburg National Cemetery. Lincoln's speech was so brief that camera crews were still setting up when the president finished.

exhibition of boorishness and vulgarity." But there were also many positive descriptions, and the next day Everett sent a note to the president in which he declared, "I should be glad if I could flatter myself that I came as near to the central idea of the occasion in two hours as you did in two minutes."

On November 23 Wills wrote the president asking for the original manuscript of his speech for archival purposes. Nicolay later wrote that Lincoln made a copy but changed some of the words to match the newspaper versions of his speech, which differed from his manuscript. Relying on his memory of exactly what he said at Gettysburg, his original draft, and the newspaper accounts, the president wrote out a new draft. It is possible that Wills never received an original or copy of the speech. John Page Nicholson, a soldier and later chairman of the Gettysburg National

These pages of the Gettysburg Address, known as the Nicolay copy, or first draft, are believed by some scholars to have been the copy that Lincoln read from at Gettysburg.

Park Commission, noted that four days after the Gettysburg procession Lincoln wrote out a copy of his speech and presented it to John Hay. Interestingly, few people knew about this copy of the address until its existence was made public in 1901. Further support for the Hay copy not being the reading copy arises from the fact that the copy does not contain any folds.

As mentioned, the Nicolay copy, which is assumed to have been given to Nicolay by Lincoln, unlike the Hay manuscript, contains fold marks. That it was written before the speech is almost a certainty, just as all the other surviving copies being written after the address is almost a certainty. But is it the reading copy?

Mearns and Dunlap conclude in *Long Remembered* that the pages Lincoln held in his hand when delivering his Gettysburg speech are the Nicolay copy. Plausible, perhaps, but there are some problems with that conclusion.

First, the last line on the first page of Nicolay makes little sense. It reads, "It is rather for us, the living, we here be dedica" ("we here be dedica" is penciled in above the crossed-out phrase "to stand here"; the next page picks up with "ted to the great task remaining before us"). The words do not fit together; it would not be characteristic of Lincoln to deliver a speech from a manuscript with such sloppily edited prose.

Another important point weighing against the Nicolay copy is that it lacks the words *under God*. The several contemporary published newspaper accounts of Lincoln's Gettysburg Address include the words *under God*. How is it that reporters picked up these words, yet they do not appear in the Nicolay or Hay copies?

It is possible that Lincoln ad-libbed, but that, too, would have been out of character. Rather, it was typical of Lincoln to perfect a speech before delivery. That he did not complete the speech until the morning he gave it would make it more likely that he improvised the phrase, but it would still be improbable, for he clearly took considerable pains in composing the speech.

Indeed, there are unresolved problems with the conclusion that the Nicolay copy was Lincoln's reading copy. That it was written before Lincoln went to Gettysburg, or when he was there, is quite probable. Lincoln was still working on his speech at David Wills's home both the evening before and the morning of his address. The second page of Nicolay has the appearance of being drafted in Wills's home. It was written in pencil (page 1 is in ink) and is on different paper. It's almost as if Lincoln lost page 2 and tried to remember what he had written. That supposition can't be verified, however, and there are arguments against it, but the Nicolay copy should at least be considered contemporary to the event. Perhaps it was one of Lincoln's last working drafts, or perhaps he read from one or the other of its pages, so at least one page of the reading copy survives. Yet why one and not the other?

Alternatively, it might be judicious to conclude that the reading copy is lost in its entirety. After the speech some reporters, surprised by its brevity, asked to see the manuscript. It's possible that Lincoln may have handed it to a journalist and that it was never returned. In the end, of course, all the arguments both for and against the Nicolay copy or a lost copy as the real Gettysburg Address come down to pure speculation.

There are three explanations for the reading copy: it is the Nicolay copy; it was lost or destroyed sometime after the event; or it lies hidden somewhere. Some of the theories are tantalizing, but the mystery of the Gettysburg Address may never be solved.

LOCATIONS: Nicolay copy: Library of Congress, Washington, D.C.*
Hay copy: Library of Congress, Washington, D.C.
Everett copy: Illinois State Historical Library, Springfield,
Illinois.
Bancroft copy: Cornell University, Ithaca, New York.
Bliss copy: The White House, Washington, D.C.

*The Nicolay copy at the Library of Congress is permanently sealed in a special filtered case with an argon gas environment.

The Appomattox Surrender Tables

DATE: 1865.

WHAT THEY ARE: Two tables that were part of a momentous event in American history. On one, Lieutenant General Ulysses S. Grant wrote the terms of surrender for the Confederate Army of Northern Virginia and signed it. On the other, General Robert E. Lee signed a letter stating he agreed to accept the terms of surrender. These transactions essentially brought an end to the Civil War.

WHAT THEY LOOK LIKE: Grant sat at a wooden trestle table with an oval top and two spool legs at each side, connected to bases that are joined by another spool. Lee sat at a wooden table with a pedestal base and a square white sculptured marble top.

A divided nation had long dreamed of this moment. For four difficult years, American society was torn apart by the all-consuming war between North and South. More than half a million lives had already been lost; whole cities had been torched; brothers and sons and fathers were pitted against one another on opposite sides of the firing lines. A sense of hopelessness and futility pervaded the land. As the conflict dragged on, people prayed for the day when it would come to an end.

On the morning of April 9, 1865, General Robert E. Lee made a final attempt to break through Union forces that were preventing the Confederate Army of Northern Virginia from moving south. The effort failed and resulted in assaults by Union troops.

The McLean family sitting outside their house in August 1865, where General Lee surrendered to Ulysses S. Grant four months earlier.

Deeming his situation, and that of the South, hopeless—just five months earlier General William Sherman had burned Atlanta and torn through Georgia—Lee directed Lieutenant General James Longstreet and Major General John Brown Gordon to send out flags of truce across the battle lines, which were about a mile long. (Portions of one flag of truce do exist today. A Captain Robert Mooreman Sims of the Confederate army fastened his white linen towel to his saber and rode into General George Armstrong Custer's camp. The towel came into the hands of Lieutenant Colonel Charles Whittaker, who shared portions of it with Custer. One portion is now at the Appomattox Court House National Historical Park, Appomattox, Virginia; another is at the National Museum of American History, Washington, D.C.)

Union commanders accepted this offer of surrender and set a meeting for that very same day. Lieutenant General Ulysses S. Grant allowed Lee to select the site of the meeting, and that turned out to be the home of Wilmer McLean in Appomattox Court House, a village that held the county seat.

McLean traded in sugar during the war and was a private resident of Appomattox Court House. He lived there with his wife and five children,

A divided nation is united. This painting shows Union general Ulysses S. Grant sitting on the right at an oval table, on which he wrote the terms of surrender of the Confederate army, and Confederate general Robert E. Lee sitting at the square white marble-topped table with a pedestal base, on which he signed a letter accepting Grant's terms of surrender.

and the family owned several slaves. General Lee ordered his military secretary, Lieutenant Colonel Charles Marshall, to ride into Appomattox Court House to select a site for the meeting. In his memoirs Marshall wrote that the first person of property he met was Wilmer McLean. He asked McLean to suggest a site, and McLean pointed out a home. Marshall rejected it because it was unoccupied and poorly furnished. McLean then volunteered his own home.

At about 1:00 P.M., General Lee arrived at the three-story redbrick McLean residence, accompanied by Lieutenant Colonel Charles Marshall, who entered the house with him, and Private Joshua O. Johns, who remained outside with the horses. Shortly afterward, General Grant and several Union generals and staff officers arrived. They held their meeting in the first-floor parlor room, a typical mid–nineteenth-century middle-class parlor, soon to become known as the "surrender room." Lee was dressed in a fresh uniform and carried his sword; Grant was wearing a soiled private's uniform with a lieutenant general's stars, and he didn't have his sword.

There were two tables (some accounts say three) in the parlor. General Lee sat at a marble-topped table placed to the left of a spool-legged oval table, where Grant sat.

Grant allowed Lee to surrender with dignity. There was no humiliation, not even a demand that Lee turn over his sword. They carried on a discussion in a gentlemanly fashion, as they had in their correspondence to each other over the past few days.

On April 7 Grant had written to Lee that "the result of the last week must convince you of the hopelessness of further resistance" and asked him to prevent any further bloodshed by surrendering. That night Lee wrote back asking the terms under which Grant would accept the surrender of the Army of Northern Virginia, and Grant replied the next day, April 8, with the condition "that the men and officers surrendered shall be disqualified for taking up arms again, against the Government of the United States, until properly exchanged." Grant was confident Lee would surrender and communicated this in a letter to Secretary of War Edwin M. Stanton.

Lee did surrender—on April 9 he requested in two communications an "interview" to discuss the terms—and now Grant, seated across from Lee, was ready to write out the terms of surrender. Before Grant at his table was a manifold writer, a kind of ledger book in which the user placed carbons between its sheets to make duplicate copies. Using a mother-of-pearl-tipped stylus to write, Grant wrote out the words that would end the Civil War (the letter would be on two pages):

> Appomattox C. H. Va.
> Apl. 9th 1865

> GEN R. E. LEE,
> COMD. G C.S.A.,

> GEN.

> In accordance with the substance of my letter to you of the 8th inst. I propose to receive the surrender of the Army of N. Va. on the following terms: towit;
> Rolls of all the officers and men to be made in duplicate. One copy to be given to an officer designated by me, the other to be retained by such officer or officers as you may designate. The officers to give their individual paroles not to take up arms against

the Government of the United States until properly exchanged and each company or regimental commander sign a like parole for the men of their commands.

The Arms, Artillery and public property to be parked and stacked and turned over to the officer appointed by me to receive them. This will not embrace the side Arms of the officers nor their private horses or baggage. This done each officer and man will be allowed to return to their homes not to be disturbed by United States Authority so long as they observe their parole and the laws in force where they may reside.

Very respectfully
U. S. Grant Lt. Gn

After writing out the surrender terms, Grant reviewed it quickly with Lieutenant Colonel Ely S. Parker, then handed the letter (manifold copies at Scheide Library, Princeton, New Jersey, and the New-York Historical Society, New York City) over to Lee to review and discuss. Lee read it and acknowledged the terms were generous and "would have a very happy effect upon my army," and requested some minor changes, which he made in pencil (the letter above contains Lee's changes). After some other discussion, Grant told Lieutenant Colonel T. S. Bowers, a senior adjutant, to write the letter over in ink so the military surrender could be formalized, but Bowers was too nervous and gave the job over to Colonel Parker. The Union officers had not brought ink with them, and General Lee's secretary, Lieutenant Colonel Charles Marshall, offered his inkwell. After writing out a copy at the oval table, Parker handed the letter over to Grant, who signed the document (Marshall retained the ink copy of the letter, and his descendants passed it on October 12, 1955, to Robert E. Lee's birthplace, Stratford Hall in Stratford, Virginia). At the marble-topped table Lee signed in ink a letter to Grant dated April 9, prepared by his military secretary, Colonel Marshall: "I received your letter of this date containing the terms of the surrender of the Army of Northern Virginia as proposed by you. As they are substantially the same as those expressed in your letter of the 8th inst., they are accepted. I will proceed to designate the proper officers to carry the stipulations into effect." Although some Confederate armies would continue fighting and the last would not surrender until June 23, the War Between the States had essentially been ended.

Lee, who spoke little during the meeting, left McLean's house in midafternoon, followed by Grant. Lee returned to the Confederate camp and told his troops to go home and "become as good citizens as you were soldiers." News of Lee's signing of the surrender agreement was greeted with frenzied cheers by the Union soldiers. They began to celebrate but were immediately ordered to halt by General Grant, who felt the defeat of the opposing army, brethren in nationality, needn't be celebrated.

The momentousness of the parley did not go unappreciated by its eye-witnesses, who yearned for some trophy of the room for posterity. Even McLean recognized that the furnishings of his surrender room were no longer ordinary objects but wonderful historical mementos, and by some accounts he was not inclined to give them up. Before we concern ourselves with the oval and marble-topped tables, perhaps the two most prized pieces of the room, let's consider the disposition of the other parlor furnishings that were removed from McLean's house the day of the surrender and which have survived. There are four such items: The cane-back chair in which General Lee sat was obtained by Charles Whittaker, the chief of staff on General Custer's command. The swivel chair on which General Grant sat—it tilted back, had wooden arms and a black horsehair back—was obtained by General Henry Capehart, a brigadier general in General Custer's cavalry division. Both chairs are now at the National Museum of American History.

On the marble-topped table where Lee signed the letter was a pair of candlesticks. These were obtained by Brigadier General George Sharpe, the assistant provost marshal of the military police for the federal army. Sharpe purchased them from McLean for ten dollars, and they were eventually donated by Sharpe's children to the Senate House Museum, Kingston, New York. There was also a small rag doll in the parlor that belonged to eight-year-old Lucretia McLean. Later dubbed "the silent witness," the rag doll was obtained by Captain Robert Moore, who was on General Philip Sheridan's staff. The doll was donated to the Appomattox Court House National Historic Park on December 17, 1992.

The only other McLean parlor furnishings from the surrender day known to exist are a secretary-bookcase, which in 1904 was donated to the National Museum of American History by Caroline P. Stokes, who purchased it from Wilmer McLean's daughter, Mrs. Nannie Spilman, and two vases that were on the mantle and a sofa, which are all at the Appomattox Court House National Historic Park. Now back to the prized pieces of the room, the surrender tables.

The spool-legged oval table on which Grant wrote the terms of surrender went to Major General Philip H. Sheridan. One story behind this transaction is that when McLean refused the twenty-dollar gold piece Sheridan offered him for it, Sheridan dropped the money and left, later sending a squad of troops to collect the table. There is also a published account of 1866 that says Custer was seen riding off from the Appomattox surrender with the table over his shoulder.

Whichever account is true, the oval table did become the property of General Custer. The Sheridan account holds that Sheridan, who revered Custer and considered him an important factor in the Union's victory, gave the table to Custer on the day of surrender as a present for his wife, Elizabeth. Indeed, the following day Sheridan wrote a letter to Mrs. Custer stating he had given the table to her husband. Years after General Custer's death at the Little Bighorn River, Elizabeth Bacon Custer went to Paris to teach art and left most of her possessions in storage in the United States. In May 1912 she loaned the oval table to the Smithsonian Institution in Washington, D.C., and in 1936 bequeathed it to the museum along with some other relics of American history, including a portion of Captain Sims's white linen towel, his flag of truce.

General Edward O. C. Ord of the Union army, who had received Lee's white "flag" (one of several white "flags") earlier that day, wanted the marble-topped table on which Lee signed the letter stating he agreed to accept the terms of surrender. By one account, McLean did not want to give it up, and Ord just seized it. In a more credible account, McLean accepted forty dollars from Ord for the table. (Since McLean didn't leave any writing of the events that took place in his parlor on the day of surrender, one has to weigh the different accounts with the reliability of those who rendered them.)

Ord's marble-topped table stayed in his family, first at the Confederate White House at Richmond where the Ords resided following the war, and then in San Diego, where they later moved. After Ord's death his widow was in desperate financial straits, and she thought selling the Lee table might alleviate her situation.

In 1887 Mary Ord corresponded with the prosperous Chicago candy maker and Americana collector Charles Frederick Gunther, for the purpose of selling the table. One of her sixteen children, a daughter, was ill, and Mrs. Ord needed money. Gunther requested proof of the authenticity of the table, and in a letter dated January 12, 1887, Mrs. Ord stated that General Grant's letter identifying the table was left with her papers at

Fort Monroe in Virginia, and "there is no one there I could call upon to look through them in order to get it." She said she would have General Grant's widow, Julia, testify in a letter that hers was the actual table, and that if Gunther purchased the table, she would on her return to Fort Monroe find the letter and turn it over to him. "In the meantime," wrote Mrs. Ord, "I am in great need of money. If you could conclude the bargain at once, and send me the thousand dollars by any safe way, you would greatly oblige."

Julia Grant, at Mrs. Ord's request, confirmed the authenticity of the table. In a letter dated January 26, 1887, Julia Grant wrote "this is to certify that Mrs. General Ord is the possessor of the table which General E. O. C. Ord presented to me in 1865 as the identical one General Grant used to write and sign the articles of the Appomatox [sic] surrender upon." Mrs. Grant actually had the surrender tables confused, incorrectly identifying the Lee table as the Grant table. In March 1887 Mrs. Ord agreed to accept Gunther's offer of one thousand dollars for the table (she had wanted three thousand dollars for it) and asked if he would remit to her a first installment of four hundred dollars. The table was shipped from California to Chicago in three boxes; its condition was so poor (the marble slab was broken) that it could not be sent fully assembled.

The marble-topped table and the oval table, one symbolic of the Confederacy and the other of the Union, were taken away after the surrender by officers of the Union who appreciated their great historical value. It is ironic that the table of the Confederacy went to relieve the financial hardships of the widow of a Union general, and the table of the Union went to the wife of a Union general who led a regiment into one of the most disastrous engagements of nineteenth-century American military history.

LOCATIONS: Lee table: Chicago Historical Society, Chicago, Illinois. Grant table: National Museum of American History, Washington, D.C.

The Bed Lincoln Died In

DATE: 1865.

WHAT IT IS: The bed President Abraham Lincoln was placed on after he was shot, on which he slowly bled for nearly nine hours before he expired.

WHAT IT LOOKS LIKE: The bed is 78½ inches long. It has a peaked headboard measuring 46⅛ inches high and 53¾ inches wide; and a footboard with spool-turned posts and spindles that is 44½ inches high and 53¾ inches wide.

The scene was William Petersen's boardinghouse at 453 Tenth Street N.W., in Washington, D.C. The event was the desperate, hopeless struggle to save the life of Abraham Lincoln, who had been shot a short while earlier at Ford's Theatre. News of the shooting was spreading through the streets of the nation's capital like wildfire, sparking fears and tears that would billow into a national hysteria once the president's fate played itself out. For now, however, the drama was focused in the somber theater of an infantry private's room where an unwilling protagonist was lying on a walnut bed, center stage in this most dramatic episode of American history.

The details of this larger-than-life tragedy are well known. President Lincoln, his wife, Mary, and invited guests, Major Henry Rathbone and his fiancée, Clara Harris, were attending a performance of *Our American Cousin* at Ford's Theatre, having arrived from the Executive Mansion by carriage (Studebaker National Museum, South Bend, Indiana).* The Civil

---

*The Executive Mansion, once known as the President's Palace, was officially named the White House on October 17, 1901, by President Theodore Roosevelt.

War had essentially ended just five days before when Lee signed the terms of surrender at Appomattox Court House. Lincoln was still on the eve of great victory and his legend was spiraling higher, even if sentiment against the Union and against Lincoln continued to run high in the South.

The Lincoln party arrived sometime after the play began at 7:45 P.M. on Good Friday, April 14, 1865, the president having been detained at the White House by discussions with some members of Congress, including the speaker of the House of Representatives, Schuyler Colfax. Different accounts have been given as to exactly when the party arrived—during the first or second act—but it was probably about 8:30 P.M., forty-five minutes after the curtain rose. Lincoln's presence in the theater did not escape notice. There have been various accounts of who signaled the audience's attention and when, but that of Harry Hawk, the actor who played the lead role of Asa Trenchard, the "American Cousin," is given the most credence. According to Hawk, the others on stage performed the following lines:

> FLORENCE: What's the matter?
> DUNDREARY: That wath a joke, that wath.
> FLORENCE: Where's the joke?
> MRS. MOUNT: No.
> DUNDREARY: She don't see it—*

Then the star of the show, Laura Keene, seeing the president and his party being ushered to their box, quickly raised her hand to the balcony and interjected her own improvised line, "Anybody can see *that!*" All heads turned—there were about seventeen hundred people present on three levels of the theater—and the play came to a stop. Laura Keene gestured to the orchestra director, Professor William Withers, who summoned the musicians to play "Hail to the Chief." There were enthusiastic cheers and applause from the audience, and many people rose to their feet. Mrs. Lincoln smiled and curtsied a few times. The president, a forlorn look on his face, modestly bowed.

The state box had been prepared earlier that day by Harry Clay Ford, the treasurer of Ford's Theatre and one of the three brothers of the owner,

---

*From *Our American Cousin: The Play That Changed History*, with an introduction by Welford D. Taylor, 1990. Published by Beacham Publishing, Washington, D.C.

John Thompson Ford. The box normally was divided into two parts, accessed by doorways seven and eight, but that night the partition was removed and Lincoln and his party probably entered through doorway eight. The box was decorated with five flags: two American flags on flagstaffs hanging at either end and the blue Treasury Guard flag (Ford's Theatre National Historic Site, Washington, D.C.) hanging above an engraving of George Washington (Ford's Theatre) at the center, as well as two more American flags Harry Clay Ford added, draping them over the balcony.

In the presidential box at one corner was a red upholstered chair (lost or destroyed over time) on which Miss Harris sat, next to which was a walnut-framed sofa with a tufted back, upholstered in red silk (Ford's Theatre), that Rathbone sat on; continuing across, in box seven, there was a cane-bottom straight-back chair (lost or destroyed over time) on which Mrs. Lincoln sat, and a walnut-framed high-back rocking chair padded with red silk fabric in which the president sat (Henry Ford Museum, Dearborn, Michigan).

A door from the dress circle, or mezzanine, opened into a hallway that led to doorways seven and eight of the presidential box. Unbeknownst to the presidential party, there was a small hole in box seven's door (Ford's Theatre). There are two stories about who put it there. One is that it was done previous to April 14 on the orders of Harry Clay Ford, who was in charge of decorating the box for the president's attendance at the theater; Ford wanted a hole bored so the president's aides could look through it to see who was inside without having to bother the guests. The other story is that the actor who headed the conspiracy to kill the president and others, John Wilkes Booth, made it earlier that day when he came to the theater during a dress rehearsal of the play. In the conspiracy trial that followed Lincoln's murder, Harry Clay Ford did not claim to have ordered the hole made in the door, but long after his death his son, Frank Ford, stated "the hole was bored by my father, Harry Clay Ford, or rather on his orders, and was bored for the very simple reason it would allow the guard, one Parker, easy opportunity whenever he so desired to look into the box rather than to open the inner door to check the Presidential party. As we know Parker left his post to view the performance from the dress circle." Also at the trial a Ford's Theatre clerk by the name of Thomas J. Raybold testified that he saw Booth at the theater box office on the morning of April 14, establishing his presence at the theater before the performance attended by Lincoln. (Raybold also noted that about two weeks earlier,

Booth reserved box four at the theater, then returned in the afternoon to exchange the box for box seven or eight—Raybold wasn't sure which one it was, but thought it was box seven, the one whose door had the hole bored in it.)

During the evening, John Wilkes Booth presented his calling card to a man sitting by the passageway (by most accounts it was Charles Forbes, Lincoln's valet). Presumably Booth told the man he would like to see the president.

While Lincoln was enjoying the play, John Wilkes Booth lurked in the passageway behind him, waiting to seize the most opportune moment to strike at the man whose politics he detested. As the unsuspecting Lincoln leaned forward in his rocking chair toward the railing, Booth probably peered at him through the hole in the door. Booth was familiar with the play and planned his execution to occur during act three, scene two, when only one actor was on stage.

This was a droll scene when Asa Trenchard confessed to Augusta, the girl he loved, and her mother, Mrs. Mountchessington, that he wasn't an heir to a fortune. Asa didn't think that would be a problem since moments earlier Augusta had said all she craved was affection.

"Now I've no fortune," Asa admitted to Augusta, "but I'm boiling over with affections, which I'm ready to pour out all over you like apple sass over roast pork." Mrs. Mountchessington responded, "Mr. Trenchard, you will please recollect you are addressing my daughter, and in my presence." "Yes," answered Asa. "I'm offering her my heart and hand just as she wants them, with nothing in 'em." Mrs. Mountchessington ordered her daughter to her room, and Augusta left in a huff saying, "Yes, ma, the nasty beast." Mrs. Mountchessington then told Asa that because he was not used to the manners of good society, he would be excused of his impertinence, and then she walked away. Now alone on stage, Harry Hawk, the actor playing Asa, said:

> Don't know the manners of good society, eh? Well, I guess I know enough to turn you inside out, old gal—you sockdologizing old man-trap.

Those were the last words Lincoln heard before he was mortally attacked. They were spoken about 10:15, when Booth surreptitiously opened one of the doors to the president's box. As laughter filled the theater, Booth strode a few paces, held a .44-caliber single-shot Derringer

This interior photograph of Ford's Theatre was taken by Mathew Brady's staff photographers in 1865, shortly after the Lincoln assassination. American flags drape the box where the president and his party sat the night the president was shot.

(Ford's Theatre) up to the back of Lincoln's head, and pulled the trigger. The sharp crack of a pistol reverberated through the theater. At once, all those who heard the shot through the laughter looked to the state box as Mrs. Lincoln let out a loud scream. Rathbone rushed over and struggled briefly with Booth, who dropped his pistol and thrust a knife into the upper left arm of Rathbone.*

Everyone's attention was drawn to the commotion in the state box, and an indescribable panic set in among the audience. People began to rise from their seats when Booth, an athletic actor who performed on the stage with deliberate and grandiose moves, leaped from the box onto the stage. But he caught his boot spur on a flag and broke a small bone above his left ankle. (According to the best evidence, it was the Treasury Guard's flag; by some accounts, it was one of the American flags draped at the front of the box. Some witnesses reported that Rathbone lunged at Booth and apparently forced him to catch his boot in the flag.) Waving his knife, Booth shouted Virginia's state motto, *Sic semper tyrannis!* (Thus always to tyrants!), and made his way offstage. In heading to the back doorway, he encountered Laura Keene and the orchestra leader, William Withers, whom he slashed twice—on his neck and his coat—before escaping on horseback. Meanwhile, people were racing to the exits, and the lights were now dimmed. There were cries of "The president is shot!" and frantic calls for a surgeon.

*Based on Rathbone's testimony and a 1914 newspaper article listing the items of the Lincoln assassination conspirators held by the U.S. government, this knife (Ford's Theatre) has been identified as a bone-handled knife with a blade about five inches long and an inscription that reads, "Land of the free, home of the brave."

Moments later, someone pounded on the door at the end of the passageway, but Rathbone had difficulty opening it because Booth had wedged it shut with a wooden bar (Ford's Theatre) so no one could interfere with his assassination as he waited in the passageway to carry it out.*

Dr. Charles Leale, an assistant surgeon with the U.S. Volunteers, was the first to enter the box. Rathbone immediately importuned the surgeon to attend to his arm wound, but Leale, after momentarily looking at Rathbone and determining that his injury was not life-threatening, heeded the cries of Mary Lincoln and Clara Harris.†

Mrs. Lincoln, wailing loudly, was holding her husband, his eyes closed, head slumped forward on the chair. Leale lowered the president to the floor and placed him in a recumbent position. Someone quickly cut open the president's coat and vest. Lincoln was bleeding copiously, his respiration was barely perceptible, and he had no pulse. Leale separated the blood-drenched hair on Lincoln's head, and, upon finding where the bullet had entered, removed a blood clot from it. Leale knew that victims of such injuries never survived long. But he had to attempt to save the president or at least prevent him from immediately succumbing.

As hysteria filled the theater, Leale straddled the president's body. He opened Lincoln's mouth, pulled out his tongue to clear the passageway, and then put his mouth over Lincoln's face and forcefully blew into his mouth and nose, administering artificial respiration. At the same time three other doctors were hitting Lincoln's chest with the palms of their hands in an effort to get the heart beating again and to restore normal

---

*Going from the balcony to the passageway, the door opened by pushing it in. Booth put one end of the bar behind the doorknob and jammed the other end into a hole he chiseled out of the plaster of the wall, probably earlier that day. Pushing on the door from the mezzanine just wedged the bar in farther. The bar was from a wooden music stand that Booth apparently had found in the theater that afternoon and left in the passageway.

†Another point of interest here is that in 1867 Rathbone married Clara Harris, his stepsister, then on Christmas Day 1883 shot and stabbed her to death in bed in Hanover, Germany. German authorities arrested Rathbone, and he was subsequently committed to an insane asylum, where he lived a rather plush life and died in relative obscurity in 1911. Both he and his wife were buried in Hanover, and, according to some accounts, the cemetery where they were interred was bombed into oblivion during Allied air raids of World War II, although their remains could have been removed prior to the war to make room for new remains, as was the custom in Europe. The murder of Clara Harris Rathbone by Henry Rathbone is yet another tragedy that may be associated with those who occupied the state box that night.

It was on this bed that Abraham Lincoln expired after being shot. Ironically, Lincoln's as-sassin earlier lay on the same bed, which was in the boardinghouse to which the president was carried from Ford's Theatre.

breathing. The president's heart did start beating, and Leale determined that death would be forestalled. But he also knew the consequence of the wound, for he turned to his colleagues and grimly announced: "His wound is mortal. It is impossible for him to recover."

It was a wildly emotional scene. Lincoln was lying on the floor with the doctors working on him, futilely trying to restore life. Standing over the president were several men who ran in from the dress circle. Mrs. Lincoln was hysterical. The star of the show, Laura Keene, had also rushed to the box and begged Leale to let her hold the president. He consented, and she put his head on her lap. (Pieces of her dress are at Ford's Theatre and the Illinois State Historical Society Library, Springfield, Illinois; a blood-stained cuff from the dress is at the National Museum of American His-tory.)

Some people in the box called for the president to be taken back to the White House; it might still be dangerous in the theater, and Lincoln could be made more comfortable and receive better attention in bed. But Leale knew the president could not survive a trip to the White House, ten blocks away. He would have to be moved to the nearest house. Several men lifted the president, clutching his body from his head to his feet, and carried him out of the theater and across the street to the three-story brick house of William Petersen, a tailor. Soldiers armed with revolvers and sabers cleared a path as a large crowd watched the procession bearing the dying chief magistrate. Lincoln was carried through the hallway to a back room (ironically, about the same size, nine feet by seventeen feet, as the Kentucky log cabin in which Lincoln was born in 1809) rented by William T. Clark, a private in a Massachusetts infantry. There was now chaos in the streets, and word was spreading that the president had been shot. Soon the Petersen house would fill with executives of the federal government, medical men, Mrs. Lincoln, and the Lincolns' son Robert Todd Lincoln, a twenty-one-year-old captain in the Union army who had been sleeping at the White House.*

Meanwhile, the most relentless manhunt in the republic's history was starting to take shape. Some people had recognized Booth as the president's assailant, but the search expanded as news poured in that Secretary of State William Seward had been stabbed at home and multiple perpetrators were at large. Soldiers, detectives, policemen, and others began a dogged search for the conspirators.

Within a half hour after he was shot, the president was placed on the bed in Clark's room. Ironically, as a friend of Petersen's son would later recall, John Wilkes Booth had earlier sprawled on that very bed and smoked a pipe while visiting a previous boarder, John Matthews, an actor. (Matthews was on stage the night Lincoln was shot, playing an attorney named Mr. Coyle.) But now the urgent mission was to make the president comfortable. The bed was too small to accommodate Lincoln's large frame, and Leale asked that the footboard be taken off. He was told it didn't detach and then suggested cutting it off, but this wasn't practical. On his back, Lincoln was then shifted to a diagonal position with his

---

*Having slept on the ground or on cots over the last few months while serving on Grant's staff, Robert Todd told his parents he didn't want to go to Ford's Theatre that night so he could catch up on his sleep on a bed. He visited his father at the Petersen house, but it was decided that Lincoln's other surviving son, twelve-year-old Thomas (nicknamed Tad), should stay at home and be spared the grief of watching his father die.

head and shoulders reclining on some pillows. His overcoat, pants, frock coat, vest, bow tie, and boots were removed (Ford's Theatre).

Also removed were several of Lincoln's pocket items: a pair of folding spectacles in a case, a pair of gold-rimmed spectacles with sliding "temples," a single sleeve-button with a gold *L* on dark blue enamel, a linen handkerchief, a watch fob of gold-bearing quartz, a pocketknife, a wallet containing a five-dollar Confederate note, and nine newspaper clippings, each one praising Lincoln for some achievement during his presidency (Library of Congress, Washington, D.C.).*

The scene around the president was one of great hopelessness and despair. Lincoln was lying on the bed, covered with blankets. Hot water bottles were applied to his feet, to warm them, and mud plasters were applied to his chest to try to reduce the shock to his body. He received medical attention. As Dr. Charles S. Taft wrote a week later:

> The wound was there examined, the finger being used as a probe, and the ball found to have passed beyond the reach of the finger into the brain. I put a teaspoon of diluted brandy between the lips, which was swallowed with much difficulty; a half-teaspoonful administered ten minutes afterward, was retained in the throat, without any effort being made to swallow it. The respiration now became labored; pulse 44, feeble, eyes entirely closed, the left pupil much contracted, the right widely dilated; total insensibility to light in both.
>
> Surgeon-General [Joseph K.] Barnes and Robert K. Stone, M.D., the family physician, arrived and took charge of the case. At their suggestion, I administered a few drops of brandy, to determine whether it could be swallowed, but as it was not, no further attempt was made. The left upper eyelid was swollen and dark from effused blood; this was observed a few minutes after his removal from the theatre. About thirty minutes after he was

*The president's black ebony walking stick that he carried to Ford's Theatre and stood in a corner of his box is at the Abraham Lincoln Museum, Lincoln Memorial University, Harrogate, Tennessee. The beaver-fur top hat Lincoln wore that night is at the National Museum of American History, which also has the suit he wore the last day of his life before he changed into his evening wear, and the cup, part of the State China, he last sipped from at the Executive Mansion before going to Ford's Theatre.

placed upon the bed, discoloration from effusion began in the internal canthus of the right eye, which became rapidly discolored and swollen with great protrusion of the eye.

All the doctors who saw the president agreed that nothing could be done to save his life. The lead bullet (National Museum of Health and Medicine, Washington, D.C.) had entered the president's head behind his left ear, pierced his brain, and lodged just behind and above the right eyeball (it cracked his skull and destroyed his brain immediately). Lincoln intermittently gasped deep convulsive breaths. His wife and eldest son Robert wept, as did many of the men gathered around. But the brain-dead president clung to life, fighting an injury the doctors said would have killed almost any other person within a couple of hours. "They were gathered around the bed watching," said William Crook, one of Lincoln's aides, "while, long after the great spirit was quenched, life little by little loosened its hold on the long gaunt body."

About ninety people came in and out of the room throughout the night, and four doctors sat by Lincoln's bed throughout the ordeal. Among those standing or sitting around the bed during the dark hours—really just waiting for the president to die—were Secretary of War Edwin M. Stanton; Robert Todd Lincoln; the president's private secretary, John Hay; Secretary of the Navy Gideon Welles; Secretary of the Interior John Usher; Senator Charles Sumner; Surgeon General Joseph K. Barnes; Secretary of the Treasury Hugh McCulloch; the Lincoln family physician, Dr. Robert King Stone; and Assistant Surgeon General Colonel Charles H. Crane.

In the early morning hours another probe was made. As Dr. Taft wrote:

About 2 A.M., an ordinary silver probe was introduced into the wound by the Surgeon-General. It met an obstruction about three inches from the external orifice, which was decided to be the plug of bone driven in from the skull and lodged in the track of the ball. The probe passed by this obstruction, but was too short to follow the track the whole length. A long Nélaton probe was then procured and passed into the track of the wound for a distance of two inches beyond the plug of bone, when the ball was distinctly felt; passing beyond this, the fragments of the orbital plate of the left orbit were felt. The ball made no mark upon the porcelain tip, and was afterwards found to be of exceedingly hard lead.

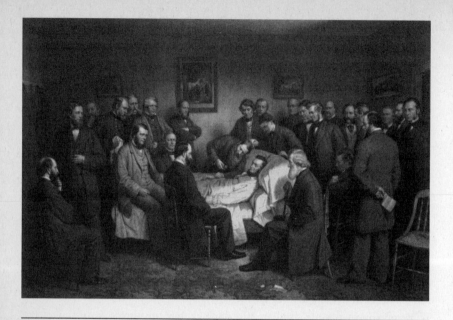

This engraving by Alexander Hay Ritchie (1822–1895) shows the grim deathbed scene when Abraham Lincoln died at 7:22 A.M. on April 15, 1865. Gathered around the president are cabinet members, governors, generals, physicians, his son Robert, and others.

Some difference of opinion existed as to the exact position of the ball, but . . . no further attempt was made to explore the wound.

At 7:22 A.M. on Saturday, April 15, 1865, almost nine hours after he was shot, President Lincoln passed away.

An autopsy was performed on Lincoln in a room on the second floor at the Executive Mansion at noon that same day. Two locks of his hair and six bone fragments from the fatal wound in his skull were taken. These specimens, along with the probes used in attempts to locate the bullet and the bloodstained cuffs of Major Edward Curtis—who, with another pathologist, Lieutenant Colonel Joseph Janvier Woodward, performed the autopsy—still exist today (National Museum of Health and Medicine). The medical kit used in the autopsy also still exists (National Museum of American History).

No death masks were made of Lincoln, but two life masks had been made: one in 1860, when he became a candidate for president of the

United States, by Leonard Volk; the other in Washington, D.C., sixty days before his death, by Clark Mills. (The original castings of both are at the National Museum of American History.)

After the autopsy, Lincoln's body was embalmed. The procedure was performed by two Washington, D.C., practitioners who "sacredly preserved" his blood. According to an article in the April 20, 1865, edition of the *New York World*:

> Three years ago, when little Willie Lincoln died, Doctors [Charles DeCosta] Brown and [Joseph B.] Alexander, the embalmers or injectors, prepared his body so handsomely that the President had it twice disinterred to look upon it. The same men, in the same way, have made perpetual these beloved lineaments. There is now no blood in the body; it was drained by the jugular vein and sacredly preserved, and through a cutting on the inside of the thigh the empty blood-vessels were charged with a chemical preparation which soon hardened to the consistence of stone. The long and bony body is now hard and stiff, so that beyond its present position it cannot be moved any more than the arms or legs of a statue. It has undergone many changes. The scalp has been removed, the brain scooped out, the chest opened and the blood emptied. All this we see of Abraham Lincoln, so cunningly contemplated in this splendid coffin, is a mere shell, an effigy, a sculpture. He lies in sleep, but it is the sleep of marble. All that made this flesh vital, sentient, and affectionate is gone forever.

As for the presidential blood preserved by Brown and Alexander, one imagines they put it in some sort of chalice and sequestered it so that it might remain safe and unsullied, a consecrated liquid in a treasured container. But where did Brown and Alexander keep it, and what did they do with it? There seems to be no record of whatever happened to Lincoln's blood.

Lincoln's body was to be returned to his hometown, Springfield, Illinois, for burial (Lincoln lived there from April 1837 to February 1861). His body was placed in a car of the funeral train along with the remains of his son, Willie, who had died in the Executive Mansion and had been placed in a vault in a cemetery in Georgetown, a section of Washington, D.C. During the journey to Illinois, more than a million people looked at Abraham Lincoln in his open casket. Lincoln's face turned dark during the trip, and the embalmer, Brown—he called himself "Dr. Brown"—rode on the funeral train and touched up the president's face in the major cities where the train stopped: Baltimore, Harrisburg, Philadelphia, New York City, Albany, Buffalo, Cleveland, Columbus, Indianapolis, Chicago. On May 3, 1865, when the train pulled into Springfield, Illinois, where Lincoln's body was received, there was still chalk on his face.

From May through December 1865, Lincoln's body was placed in a public receiving vault, which still exists, at Oak Ridge Cemetery. In December the body was transferred to a temporary tomb of stone and brick, where it remained until September 19, 1871. On that date Lincoln's body was moved into the main tomb and placed in a crypt in a wall next to his sons Willie and Tad (who had died earlier that year). Abraham Lincoln stayed in that crypt until October 1874, when he was moved into an aboveground marble sarcophagus in the burial chamber.

In 1876 an attempt was made to steal the body. A group of counterfeiters wanted to hold it for ransom to obtain the release of one of their friends and two hundred thousand dollars. They were captured during their attempt, however, and served time in prison. Lincoln's body was again moved, this time to the northeast wall of the burial chamber. In 1901, at Robert Lincoln's request, the slain president was buried beneath the floor of the tomb.

The nation mourned the president as no American leader had previously ever been mourned, and the co-conspirators were punished. On the twenty-sixth of April, twelve days after he shot Lincoln, Booth was killed in a shoot-out on the Richard Garrett farm near Port Royal, Virginia, where soldiers from the Sixteenth New York Cavalry Unit hunted him down.* Just before sunrise, sometime between 3:00 A.M. and 4:00 A.M., the soldiers torched a tobacco shed, where Booth was hiding with co-conspirator David Herold. While the shed was burning, gunfire was exchanged, and a bullet ripped into Booth's upper spine, paralyzing him immediately. The soldiers dragged him out feet first and then, because he

---

*The fatal bullet that struck Booth was claimed to have been fired by Sergeant Thomas "Boston" Corbett, who became a soldier after an austere religious awakening. Upon hearing a church sermon in Boston in 1859, he realized how sinful he was because of his trysts with some ladies of the night, changed his first name from Thomas to Boston, and castrated himself before enlisting.

was bleeding and unconscious, splashed water on his face. Booth softly told them to tell his mother, "I did it for my country," before passing out. By this time Herold had already surrendered to the soldiers, who tied him to a tree. A few minutes later Booth came to again and said, "I want to see my hands." The soldiers held both arms in front of his face so he could see them. "Useless, useless," he said, then died.

Objects associated with Lincoln's assassination soon became famous. Mrs. Lincoln's hat was cut up, and the pieces were sold as souvenirs. That is also what happened to strips of sheets stained with the blood of the president and the rug in William Clark's room, as well as other items there. "Everybody has a great desire to obtain some memento from my room," the private wrote to his sister, "so that whoever comes in has to be closely watched for fear that they will steal something. I have a lock of Mr. Lincoln's hair, which I have had neatly framed; also a piece of linen with a portion of his brain. The same mattress is on my bed, and the same coverlet covers me nightly, that covered him while dying."

Clark's bed was seized a few days later by his landlord, William Petersen, whose home was drawing mourners and sightseers from all over. After Petersen and his wife both died in 1871, their children held an auction for the house and its furniture, and the infamous bed was purchased for eighty dollars by a local resident, William Boyd, who in turn gave the bed to his brother, Andrew, in Syracuse, New York. Money difficulties later forced Andrew Boyd to sell the bed, and he found a buyer in 1889 in Charles Frederick Gunther, a thirty-four-year-old German-born Chicago candy maker who would become a great collector of Americana;* the purchase price was approximately fifteen hundred dollars. Gunther moved the Civil War's Libby Prison of Richmond, Virginia, near his establishment and placed his collection inside but returned his treasures to his offices when another building was to be constructed on the site of the museum. Near the turn of the century, a fire wiped out much of his collection, and after Charles Gunther died in February 1920, the Gunther family sold his relics, including the bed, to a private nonprofit Chicago organization.

The bed Lincoln died in, like so many other historical artifacts, was an ordinary object that would have surely been lost to oblivion had it not been plucked by the hand of fate. That this small wooden bed in a pri-

---

*Gunther also purchased one of the Appomattox Surrender Tables (see page 236).

vate's rented room, in a tailor's boardinghouse, should have been Abraham Lincoln's final resting place would have been all but inconceivable only a split second before the fatal shooting.

As the president breathed his last, those present were overcome with grief, still stunned by the circumstances that led them to gaze down upon their moribund leader. Soon after, the late president's body was taken away, leaving the bed a witness for the ages to this tragic event.

LOCATION: Chicago Historical Society, Chicago, Illinois.

Little Sorrel, Stonewall Jackson's Charger

DATE: 1886.

WHAT IT IS: The mounted hide of Stonewall Jackson's battle horse, Little Sorrel. Thomas Jonathan Jackson, nicknamed "Stonewall" by his troops, was a revered Confederate general in the Civil War.

WHAT IT LOOKS LIKE: The hide is sorrel, or rust colored, and is mounted over a plaster of Paris frame. Its height is fourteen hands. (The height of a horse is measured from the ground up to the withers, in units called hands, one hand equal to four inches.) The mane is short and scruffy, having fallen prey to souvenir hunters, and many of the hairs on the tail are replacements, because people also plucked its hairs for souvenirs.

It was the night of May 2, 1863. Chancellorsville, Virginia. The Civil War had been raging for two years now, and fierce combat had taken place here over the past couple of days. More than sixty thousand Confederate soldiers, under Generals Robert E. Lee and Stonewall Jackson, engaged the Federal Army of the Potomac, which was advancing along the Rappahannock. Lee fought the Union army from the front, while Jackson moved to the rear to launch a surprise attack. The Confederates pushed back the 130,000 Union troops, led by General Joseph Hooker, to Chancellorsville, but at a tremendous cost to both sides. The land was now strewn with corpses, the air thick with their stench. There were maimed soldiers crying in agony and raging brush fires and the smell of gunpowder all around. The scene was one of great devastation.

At about 9:00 P.M. General Jackson and a party of his men were riding down the Orange turnpike on the battlefield at Chancellorsville, returning to camp after having examined the troop positions of the enemy. It was a moment of victory for the Confederates, with Hooker's army repelled.

A skillful and successful military leader, Stonewall was revered by the Confederate troops. (Stonewall was a nickname that stuck to him after the Battle of the First Manassas, when Confederate general Barnard Bee, who was being driven by the Union, looked behind him and saw Jackson and his troops on a hill and shouted, "There stands Jackson like a stone wall, rally behind Virginians.") His parents died when he was a child and he had little formal education; nevertheless, he was accepted into the United States Military Academy at West Point, where he graduated number seventeen in his class. Then the young army officer went off to Mexico, which was at war with the United States, and distinguished himself as a soldier in battle there.

With few opportunities for advancement after the Mexican War ended in 1848, Jackson became disillusioned with the army. In 1851 he left the army and went to teach at the Virginia Military Institute (VMI), a school established in 1839 to provide military training and secular education to young men who in times of crisis desired to come to the aid of their country.

At VMI Jackson taught by rote and wasn't a particularly inspiring professor, probably because he had not chosen education as his career. In 1861, after ten years at VMI, Thomas J. Jackson was recruited to fight for the Confederate cause in the War Between the States.

Jackson fought valiantly at Winchester, Cross Keys, Port Republic, and Kernstown, all in the Shenandoah Valley in Virginia, as well as at Antietam in Sharpsburg, Maryland, and Fredericksburg, Virginia. Though he used several different chargers in battle, his favorite was Little Sorrel.

Two years earlier, in 1861, the horse was on board a Union supply train headed for Washington. But Confederates captured the train outside of Harpers Ferry, Virginia (later West Virginia), and one of Jackson's men, surveying the horse stock, selected a pair of sorrel horses and presented them to Jackson as trophies. The smaller of the two horses was intended for Jackson's wife, but the venerable soldier actually preferred it for himself. The big sorrel he was to ride had more spirit than he desired as well as the curious habit of lying down to rest with its legs folded under him, whereas the smaller horse was gentle. Jackson adopted the little sorrel as his warhorse. To some it may have seemed ironic that Jackson chose to

The India-rubber raincoat Stonewall Jackson wore the night he was shot at Chancellorsville, May 2, 1863.

ride a gentle warhorse into battle, but with its calm nature it was easy to control and did not frighten too easily.

And so it was on Little Sorrel that Jackson was returning to camp on the evening of May 2. Ahead were the Confederate pickets, who were under orders to fire at anything that moved in front of the line.

The Eighteenth North Carolina Regiment, hearing the clip-clopping of horses and seeing figures in the dim moonlight, let out a volley of rounds. They picked off a couple of the returning men, and there was shouting by Jackson's party to stop firing, that they were Confederates. But the pickets kept shooting, despite the screams. Suddenly, Stonewall Jackson was hit, and Little Sorrel bolted. The firing continued, so if the horse hadn't retreated, Jackson would probably have been killed on the spot.

Having been Stonewall's mount in his numerous campaigns, Little Sorrel was certainly no novice on the battlefield. But the shooting so disoriented him that he ran, driving Stonewall straight into a branch. Blood poured down Jackson's head, and although he was weak, he managed to hold on to Little Sorrel.

Captain R. E. Wilbourne, a signal officer on Jackson's staff who was riding in with him, grabbed hold of the reins, stopped Little Sorrel, and took the general down. Soon a group of soldiers came to the scene and examined Jackson's wounds. The general had taken one bullet in the right hand and one each in the left wrist and shoulder. With a penknife a soldier cut open Jackson's black, bone-buttoned, India-rubber raincoat and uniform, and then the men took him away.

Surgeon Hunter McGuire amputated Jackson's left arm, which soldiers buried at the Chancellorsville battlefield (the spot was later marked), but little else could be done to save the war hero. On May 10, eight days after he was shot, the thirty-nine-year-old Confederate general died of respiratory complications, having contracted pneumonia. Jackson's death came to be regarded by some as a turning point of the war, what with the Union and Confederate armies fighting the crucial battle at Gettysburg just two months later. Some historians believe that if the Confederacy had the superb military leadership of Jackson at Gettysburg, it might have fared better and the war might have turned out differently.

After Stonewall was taken down from his mount, Little Sorrel ran off and happened into a Union camp. Jackson's charger was widely recognizable, but luckily for him, no one in this particular camp recognized him. He was later recaptured by Confederate cavalry general Jeb Stuart.

After Jackson's death, his thirty-two-year-old widow, Anna, took Little Sorrel to North Carolina, where she went back to live with her father, a minister. Anna later displayed the horse around the country. But by the 1880s this venture no longer produced enough income to feed and maintain the horse, and she gave him to the Virginia Military Institute, where Stonewall had taught before the war. A short time later a dispute developed between Anna Jackson and VMI over the distribution of revenue from exhibiting Little Sorrel at the 1885 New Orleans World's Fair—the school wanted to use it to erect a Jackson monument, and she wanted it to go to a veterans' group and others she selected. The Confederate veterans entered into the dispute by not allowing Little Sorrel to be advertised in any of their publications, feeling that it was inappropriate to use the old charger to raise funds for any cause. As a result the widow directed the horse to be sent to the new Confederate Soldiers' Home near Richmond.

Little Sorrel was a popular attraction at the home—children especially loved to come see him—and he was devotedly cared for by Civil War veterans who marched alongside him, for by this time he was old and feeble. The veterans looked upon Little Sorrel with great affection, considering the charger upon whom Stonewall Jackson rode in many battles a war veteran just like themselves. Many visitors came in his last days, when he couldn't rise without the veterans using a hoist and girdle to lift him onto his legs, but the end was surely imminent when one day the girdle slipped forward and Little Sorrel's vertebral column was broken. The veterans, particularly Tom O'Connell, stayed close by Jackson's old charger in his last days to help comfort him.

At 6:00 A.M. on March 16, 1886, Little Sorrel died at the Confederate Soldiers' Home. There was some discrepancy as to his age; many put it at thirty-six, but according to a Huntington, West Virginia, newspaper obituary, he was thirty-two. His date of birth was not known, and his age was estimated based on the length and wear of his teeth.

Arrangements had been made for Little Sorrel to be mounted after his death. It was prestigious for taxidermists to prepare and mount the skins of famous animals, and in a letter dated July 15, 1939, Frederick S. Webster wrote about how he came to be the horse's immortalizer:

> It was by the sweat of my brow—literally—and the kindly commission from a well known southern gentleman, Colonel E. V. Randolph of Richmond, Va. He came to my studio on Pennsylvania Ave., Washington, D.C., when the horse was still living and made all arrangements for me to go to Richmond when the horse should surrender. A telegram was to advise me of the event. There were no telephones at that time—in 1886, if memory serves me correctly. Shortly thereafter, the expected event happened, and I arrived in Richmond the night before the thirty-six year old champion of years, died.

Frederick Webster was a prominent taxidermist of the time. In the 1870s he had worked for Professor Henry A. Ward's Natural Science Establishment, a museum supply and services outfit based in Rochester, New York. (The skull and leg bones of the famous horses of Robert E. Lee and General Philip Henry Sheridan, Traveller and Winchester, were mounted there.) One of Ward's staff, Carl Ethan Akeley, had recently developed a taxidermic procedure that gave a more lifelike appearance to mounted animals.

Akeley's procedure involved taking precise measurements of the specimen and then using them to make a meticulous clay model of the animal. This model was then used to make a plaster of Paris mold over which the animal's tanned skin would be fitted. With this technique not only was a realistic appearance achieved, but the mount had a long life. Previously, horsehides were mounted on wood, which swelled and shrank and tore the hide.

By May 1886, two months after Little Sorrel died, Webster had the animal's skin immersed in a tanning bath. During this time, he made the mannequin. After the hide was properly conditioned, he cut excess skin from the underside of it to a precise thinness that increased its pliability, then wrapped it around the framework. Because souvenir hunters had re-

Little Sorrel, one of many horses seized by Stonewall Jackson's troops when they raided a railway train carrying provisions for Union cavalry soldiers, was presented to the general by his chief of transportation, Major John Harmon. Jackson came to favor the horse for its easygoing temperament and made it his charger of choice in battle.

moved virtually all of Little Sorrel's tail, Webster had to graft other horses' hairs onto the tail.

As partial payment for his taxidermy work, Webster was given the bones of Little Sorrel. Later he expressed resentment at those who criticized him for not placing the bones in the mounted skin, saying that although it was the practice of taxidermists at the time to use the bones with the ligament when mounting a large animal, such use caused the skin to deteriorate. He noted that it took a great deal of time to mount the horse as he did—it was the first time it was done—but he did this because of the horse's historical importance. "I resent with much feeling," Webster wrote, "the lack of appreciation of my efforts to preserve as *much* of Old Sorrel as was possible, for posterity to see the faithful animal of Civil War days, and the laudable desire to do so without any reward but that of decent respect for unsolicited effort to perpetuate as long as possible, what might prove to tell a dramatic story of a conflict between brother and brother."

Webster finished his taxidermy in time for him to display the hide in his Washington studio during a Grand Army Veterans' convention. Many veterans stopped by his studio and recounted, as Webster noted, "many soul-stirring incidents of their fighting days, facing Old Sorrel."

After it was mounted, the hide of Little Sorrel was sent to the Confederate Soldiers' Home, also called the Robert E. Lee Camp, where it was exhibited until after World War II, when the home shut down. For much of the time that Little Sorrel's hide was on display in Richmond, his articulated skeleton was exhibited in Pittsburgh at the Carnegie Museum. Webster, a member of Carnegie's staff, donated it to the museum in 1903.

In April 1949 Little Sorrel's hide went to another of the horse's old real-life homes, the Virginia Military Institute. Here it was reunited four months later, in August, with Little Sorrel's bones, which the Carnegie Museum loaned to VMI. Carnegie later presented the bones to VMI as a gift.

Little Sorrel's articulated bones were put on display in the biology building at VMI, while his hide was on exhibit in the school museum. When the biology department moved to a new building in 1989 and it wasn't feasible to display the skeleton in the new location, school officials decided to retire the bones. (Officials are waiting for the proper occasion to bury the bones on the parade ground of the campus.)

Little Sorrel is a source of pride and inspiration to the students and faculty of VMI. Because he was both a witness to the Civil War and a participant in it, his remains are a dramatic and touching reminder of the school and region's heritage, of a most crucial conflict in U.S. history. All on campus know Little Sorrel was the steed of one of the school's most famous, if not most militarily gifted, professors. Each year some fifty thousand visitors from around the world come to see the hide of the fighting horse that Stonewall Jackson rode the fateful night he was shot. Little Sorrel stands in a full-scale diorama of a battlefield setting.

There's an interesting story about the India-rubber raincoat Stonewall was wearing the night he was shot. The raincoat was left behind, and a vagrant picked it up and exchanged it for a meal with the foreman of an estate on the battlefield. The foreman didn't believe the vagrant's claim that it could be the general's raincoat, but perhaps took pity on him by agreeing to the exchange.

The raincoat was all cut up and had a bullet hole in it, but the foreman's wife mended it, and he occasionally wore it around the farm. A young ranger later saw the raincoat and noticed Jackson's name written in ink on the inside of the yoke, just below the neck. He offered a handsome sum for the raincoat, and the foreman, figuring he could buy a whole team of horses for what he'd get, agreed to let him have it.

At the end of 1867 the ranger's father sent the coat to Robert E. Lee, who then shipped it to Mrs. Jackson. It upset her to see the raincoat and remember how her husband died, so when a Scotsman came along and begged her to let him show off the coat in an American Civil War museum he'd created in Scotland, she gave it to him. Later she changed her mind and wanted the raincoat back. The Scot sympathized with Mrs. Jackson's wish for this last battlefield relic of the general and sent it off to her from Scotland.

The raincoat passed to Anna Jackson's grandchild, who later gave it to the same institution where the hide of Little Sorrel resides today.

LOCATION: Virginia Military Institute, Lexington, Virginia.

Robert Browning's Reliquary

DATE: Circa 1889.

WHAT IT IS: A container that had once belonged to the English poet Robert Browning, containing strands of hair of John Milton and Elizabeth Barrett Browning.

WHAT IT LOOKS LIKE: The reliquary is scallop shaped and made of silver. Between the covers is a movable panel separating the two locks of hair. The inside covers bear engraved inscriptions, and the reliquary is hinged on its left side. On one side of the panel are a few strands of Milton's light brown hair, held by a knotted black cord. On the other panel is Browning's lock, which is more plentiful and dark brown. Attached to the handle of the reliquary is a silk embroidered ribbon.

> For many years my offerings must be hush'd;
>   When I do speak, I'll think upon this hour,
> Because I feel my forehead hot and flush'd,
>   Even at the simplest vassal of thy power,—
>   A lock of thy bright hair,—
>   Sudden it came,
> And I was startled, when I caught thy name
>   Coupled so unaware;
> Yet, at the moment, temperate was my blood.
> I thought I had beheld it from the flood.
>   —John Keats, "On Seeing a Lock of Milton's Hair"

The seventeenth-century English poet John Milton.

It would seem that the writer of *Paradise Lost* and other great poems left a legacy to civilization other than his literature: his hair. His locks served as inspiration for later poets of England, those of the age of romanticism, whose ranks included William Wordsworth, Samuel Taylor Coleridge, Lord Byron, John Keats, Percy Bysshe Shelley, and Charles Lamb. Milton's hair, in fact, was immortalized by the romantic poets. On January 21, 1818, Keats wrote the poem "On Seeing a Lock of Milton's Hair," and Leigh Hunt, another British poet of the romantic period, composed three sonnets after seeing it.

Milton's hair itself has a long and distinguished list of owners. Its proprietors included poet and essayist Joseph Addison (1672–1719), lexicographer Samuel Johnson (1709–1784), John Hoole (1727–1803, who translated Ludovico Ariosto's *Orlando Furioso* and other acclaimed Renaissance poems), and James Henry Leigh Hunt (1784– 1859).

That Milton's hair has endured for posterity is not unusual. The practice of cutting off locks of one's hair and giving them to others was common in centuries past. In fact, before the age of photography, it was the customary way for people to have a remembrance of friends or loved ones during separations. Many people could not afford to have their portrait painted even in miniature to pass around to their friends or lovers; a lock of hair was not only intimate but readily available and free.

The use of hair was largely replaced in the nineteenth century by autographs. There would be albums in people's homes for visitors to sign. If the visitors happened to be from literary circles, they might write little poems. A number of these manuscript albums exist today with lines by great poets such as Wordsworth, as well as unknown people of the past.

Those who didn't have literary friends would often want a piece of writing in the hand of these people. Individuals would send letters to famous writers asking for a signature or were even cunning and brazen enough to ask some inane question to get a full, handwritten response. (In earlier days it was considered socially improper to write a stranger or for one to acknowledge a letter from a stranger.) This practice was parodied in Muriel Spark's novel *The Girls of Slender Means*. One of the characters writes fawning letters to famous authors so she may sell the autographed letters sent in response.

Making life and death masks to have some keepsake of a person (or for study or some other purpose) was another common practice of the nineteenth century and earlier. Plaster casts of the faces of many famous people exist today, including those of Keats, Washington, Lincoln, and Napoleon. Indeed, there are several death masks of Napoleon in private collections and museums, the casts having been made at Saint Helena and afterward in Europe.

Locks of hair were cut off not only during a person's lifetime but also at death. There was even a fad in the past for people to make wreaths of hair of the deceased. Although these wreaths were actually quite awful looking, they were cherished by their owners. Napoleon himself requested that on his death his hair be preserved and made into bracelets for his wife, mother, son, and relatives.

Hair collecting by men of the past sometimes went beyond the bounds of decency. For example, a watch fob owned by Charles II, the king of England from 1660 to 1685, was reputedly made out of the pubic hairs of his mistresses.

The cutting off and giving away of hair was popular in the United States as well as in Europe. At the Library Company of Philadelphia, for instance, is a lock of George Washington's hair cut off by his barber, Martin Pierie, in 1781. It was presented to the library in 1829 by a descendant of Pierie, in a frame made from a piece of Washington's house at Mount Vernon, a piece of the chestnut tree that Washington planted at Mount Vernon, part of a tree that Lafayette planted, a piece of Independence Hall, a piece of Carpenter's Hall, part of General Anthony Wayne's house, parts of the frigates *Constitution* and *Alliance*, and part of the pew where Washington worshiped at Christ's Church.

The silver, shell-shaped reliquary that contains Milton's and Elizabeth Barrett Browning's hair also has an interesting provenance, having once been owned by Pope Pius V, the sixteenth-century pontiff who alienated much of Europe. It was given to Robert Browning by Katharine de Kay Bronson, a wealthy American who had moved to Italy. Exactly when

Bronson gave the reliquary to Browning is not known, but it likely would have been sometime during the period of their friendship, which began in 1881 and ended when the poet died eight years later. Robert probably could not have imagined that one day the reliquary would be a shrine of sorts to his great love, Elizabeth Barrett Moulton-Barrett.

It was through their poetry that Robert Browning and Elizabeth Barrett, two well-known poets in England at the time, met. A correspondence commenced in early 1845 after Robert read Elizabeth's flattering admiration for him in "Lady Geraldine's Courtship," one of the poems in her fifth book, *Poems*, published the previous autumn. Reading the poem, Robert found himself among the modern poets Geraldine's lover read to her:

> . . . at times a modern volume,—Wordsworth's solemn-thoughted idyl, Howitt's ballad-dew, or Tennyson's enchanted reverie,—Or from Browning some "Pomegrant," which, if cut deep down the middle, Shows a heart within blood-tinctured, of a veined humanity!—

Robert wrote to Elizabeth, proclaiming a love for her verses—and for her as well. Elizabeth responded immediately—her letter is dated January 11, the day after Robert's letter was postmarked—and in gratitude to Browning for his gushing praise of her poetry, wrote, "Such a letter from such a hand! Sympathy is dear—very dear to me; but the sympathy of a poet, and of such a poet, is the quintessence of sympathy to me!" They met several months later, and in November a correspondence began in which Robert beseeched Elizabeth for a lock of her hair. "I will live and die with it," Robert wrote in a letter postmarked the 23rd, "and with the memory of you. If you give me what I beg . . . say next Tuesday . . . when I leave you, I will not speak a word: . . . If you do not, I will not think you unjust."

The next day Elizabeth wrote back, "I never gave away what you ask me to give *you*, to a human being, except my nearest relatives & once or twice or thrice to female friends . . ."

On November 25, Robert met Elizabeth at her family residence at 50 Wimpole Street, where she lived. It was their thirty-first meeting and Elizabeth apparently said something that made Robert think she wanted a lock of his hair, for three days later, on November 28, he sent her one, writing "Take it, dearest,—what I am forced to think you mean—and

Nineteenth-century English poet Elizabeth Barrett Browning, in a portrait by Field Talfourd.

take *no more* with it—for I gave all to give long ago. I am all yours—and now, *mine,*—give me mine to be happy with."

After she received Robert's lock that night—mail was delivered in London up to several times a day in the mid-1800s—Elizabeth finally sent him a ring with a strand of hair and a larger lock of her hair wrapped in paper along with a letter.

Robert proclaimed his joy at receiving Elizabeth's hair in a letter to her postmarked December 2. "I was happy, so happy before!" he wrote. "But I am happier and richer now."

The poetess memorialized this exchange in one of her forty-four love poems published collectively a few years later as *Sonnets from the Portuguese*:

> *I never gave a lock of hair away*
> *To a man, Dearest, except this to thee,*
> *Which now upon my fingers thoughtfully*
> *I ring out to the full brown length and say*
> *"Take it." My day of youth went yesterday.*

Robert and Elizabeth's love affair continued, and in September 1846 they married. Soon the Brownings moved to Italy and settled in Florence, then moved around over the years to other cities in Italy, and to London and Paris.

As for Elizabeth's hair, the strand in the ring she had sent him before they married was destroyed when Robert had the ring resized. From the larger lock she sent him, Robert placed a small portion of it in the ring (The British Library, London), and preserved the balance with the letter in which it was sent. Robert stored Elizabeth's love letters in a marquetry box; Elizabeth kept Robert's in a collapsible morocco case. They took

LEFT: *The locks of two great poets who lived hundreds of years apart are displayed together in this silver scallop-shell reliquary that was owned by Robert Browning. Elizabeth Barrett Browning's hair is shown here.*

RIGHT: *Locks of hair from John Milton.*

these letters to Italy with them, where they remained until Elizabeth died fifteen years later and Robert returned to England with them. (The letters and cases are owned by Wellesley College, Wellesley, Massachusetts.)

The Brownings' friend Leigh Hunt owned a lock of the hair of the great seventeenth-century poet John Milton, whose works included *Comus*, "Lycidas," and *Samson Agonistes*. Hunt had obtained the hair from a Dr. Batty, along with locks from Jonathan Swift (1667–1745), the author of *Gulliver's Travels*, and Samuel Johnson, who wrote one of the earliest collections of words and their meanings, the *English Dictionary*. Hunt had shown Milton's hair to the poet John Keats (1795–1821), who wrote about it in a letter and also composed some verses about seeing it. In the January 1833 issue of *Tait's Edinburgh Magazine*, Hunt traced the lineage of the lock—and wrote that it "must have been cut when the poet was in the vigour of life, before he wrote 'Paradise Lost.'"

On July 13, 1856, about ten years after they were married, Robert and Elizabeth Browning received from their friend Leigh Hunt a portion of the lock of Milton's hair that he owned. It was given in an envelope on which Hunt wrote, "A bit of a lock of the hair of Milton. To Robert & E. B. Browning from Leigh Hunt. God bless them." (The remainder of the lock was sold at Sotheby's on April 29, 1913, for £2.15.)

There is no evidence that Robert Browning placed the locks of either Milton or Elizabeth, who died in Florence in June 1861, in the reliquary when he was alive. More likely, the locks were placed there after the poet died in 1889, either by his son, Robert Wiedeman Barrett Browning, or by his daughter-in-law, Fannie Browning. One or the other probably had the two inscriptions engraved that appear in the reliquary: "E. B. B. to R. B. Nov 29 1845" on one side, and "Milton's Hair, the gift of Leigh Hunt, in a Reliquary given by K. de K. Bronson, to Robert Browning" on the other side.

Little is known about the history of the reliquary except that it was owned by Pope Pius V (this is known from a faint inscription on the rim) but it is conceivable that it was once used in a church. When new Roman Catholic churches were built, a relic of a saint—a body part such as a fingernail or bone or even the saint's entire body—was traditionally placed in a reliquary under the altar. The reliquary could be a large chest or casket or a small container. Milton and Elizabeth Browning may not have been holy persons, per se, but preserving their hair in the reliquary was in keeping with its function as a repository for human relics. The reliquary was in the possession of Robert Weideman Barrett Browning at the time of his death in 1912 and was included in a sale of Browning pictures, autograph letters, manscripts, and other items at Sotheby's the following year.

The reliquary and locks of Milton and Elizabeth Barrett Browning were later acquired in 1933 at the National Auction Gallery in New York by American collector Dallas Pratt, who was actively collecting material related to Keats and his circle. In 1971, as a gift to commemorate the 150th anniversary of the death of John Keats, Dr. Pratt presented the reliquary to a small museum in Italy, the country where Robert and Elizabeth Barrett Browning lived for most of their married life.

Though they lived two centuries apart and led very different lives, both John Milton and Elizabeth Barrett Browning had a number of things in common. Both married relatively late in life—Milton at the age of thirty-six, Elizabeth when she was forty. Both suffered physical handicaps; Milton was blind, and Elizabeth was an invalid, a condition resulting from a back injury. Both studied Latin and displayed literary talents in their childhood. That they share a place side by side today, tangibly and metaphorically, befits two of England's greatest poets—Milton, known for his epics, Elizabeth Barrett Browning, for her sonnets—and the works they have left for posterity.

LOCATION: Keats-Shelley Memorial House, Rome, Italy.

The Elephant Man

DATE: 1890.

WHAT IT IS: The skeleton of Joseph Carey Merrick, dubbed, because of his physical appearance, the Elephant Man.

WHAT IT LOOKS LIKE: The skeleton is mounted in the standing position in a glass case. Merrick was 5 feet 1 inch tall.

An insidious disease dealt a cruel fate to one Joseph Carey Merrick, gradually and painfully imposing upon him horrible deformities, yet not ravaging his mental and physical capacities. Joseph Merrick had to face an unkind nineteenth-century society as a grotesque creature, and while his was a despairing, lonely, pathetic life, his story is also one of courage and survival.

Merrick was born on August 5, 1862, in Leicester, England, to Joseph and Mary Merrick. When he was about twenty-one months old, tumors began to appear on his lip and right cheek—the first obvious symptoms of his disease. He developed deformities that he would later attribute to his mother having been trampled by an elephant in an animal procession while she was pregnant with him, a story that is probably untrue.

Later in his life Joseph Merrick would recall with fondness his mother, Mary, but it is not known whether he remembered her as she actually was or created in his mind an idealized version of her. He would say Mary Merrick was the most considerate and beautiful of mothers and that he loved her deeply, but a surgeon who later cared for him described Mary Merrick as "worthless and inhuman" and claimed she deserted her son at a very young age. In any case, Joseph always spoke of his mother with great pride.

Mary Merrick died when Joseph was eleven or twelve years old—"the greatest misfortune of my life," he called her death in an autobiographical pamphlet—and his father remarried to the landlady of the dwelling where he moved his family. The landlady was terribly insensitive to her stepson's worsening physical anomalies. She demanded that he gain employment, chastising the lad to the point where he found it less onerous to remain on the streets and endure the pangs of hunger and the harsh ridicule of strangers.

Eventually he found a more genial home life with a benevolent paternal uncle. But Merrick's own sense of guilt over not contributing to the financial well-being of the household drove him to seek refuge in the Leicester Union Workhouse, which was run on strict utilitarian principles. The arduous work required of its inmates was difficult for Merrick, since he limped and was so misshapen.

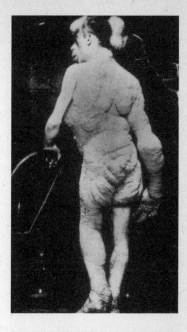

Joseph Carey Merrick in 1886.

Merrick eventually embarked on a peripatetic life, trying to make a go of it himself before having to return to another workhouse. During this time he had an eight-inch-long outgrowth of skin on his upper lip resembling a snout (which in 1882 was cut away at the Leicester infirmary). Realizing his best bet for earning a living was to exhibit himself as a freak, he contacted a local impresario, Tom Norman. Norman found him promisingly grotesque and formed a small conglomerate to manage the attraction he dubbed the Elephant Man. With his misshapen head, enlarged limbs, craggy skin, lumps on his face and body, and lumbering walk, Merrick surely cut the animal-like image that Norman deemed promotable and profitable. Although in Merrick's lifetime displays of human monsters were not publicly accepted in England, as they once had been, they were still a popular underground attraction, bringing in sufficient profit to provide the subject with a better living than that of the average laborer.

In a sordid store in the East End of London in 1884, Merrick made his debut as a freak. Standing before the staring audience, he would slowly undrape the cloth covering his body. The growths on his skin emitted a vile odor, but even this did not daunt the onlookers, who were all too eager to be transfixed by shock and horror. Narration was provided by Tom Norman, who may occasionally have cracked a whip to further the idea that Merrick was half-man, half-elephant.

Frederick Treves, a surgeon from the London Hospital, was informed about the human oddity on display and dispatched his assistant to visit the shop and invite Merrick to be examined. As Treves, who had viewed many disfigured souls, later wrote in *The Elephant Man and Other Reminiscences*, Merrick was "the most disgusting specimen of humanity that I have ever seen." He brought Merrick to his hospital and presented him before a group of pathologists. The Pathological Society of London (now the Pathological Section of the Royal Society of Medicine) drew membership from biologists, related scientists, and interested medical men, as well as pathologists.

Although being put on display as a freak for paying customers would seem to be a depressing affair, Merrick was actually quite content in the shop where he worked for Tom Norman, and said he never wanted to return to the Leicester Workhouse. And through his whole experience of being a freak exhibit, Joseph Merrick managed to maintain an astonishing and sublime sense of pride and self-respect. Once, for example, when a friend of Tom Norman suggested that a hat be passed to patrons to help the poor creature, Joseph looked at his boss and exclaimed, "We are not beggars, are we, Thomas?"

It wasn't long before the police closed down the exhibition shop, and for a time Merrick became an itinerant freak, collecting audiences and quick shillings, always a step ahead of the police. Eventually it became impossible for Merrick to continue to exhibit himself in England, and he decided to leave Tom Norman and try his luck with a touring circus on the European mainland. But there too the exhibition of Merrick was in conflict with the law, and he was eventually abandoned by the circus master, who absconded with all the money Merrick had managed to accumulate, between sixty and two hundred pounds, not a small amount for the times.

Penniless, Merrick had no choice but to return to England, but the journey was a veritable nightmare. His speech was unintelligible. The trip involved a combination of water, railway, and foot passage, which was

This cut-out card model of a Gothic church, made by Joseph Carey Merrick, was possibly given to Merrick by Margaret (Madge) Kendal, a famous English stage actress who enjoyed an epistolary friendship with the Elephant Man; he wrote to her and she bestowed many gifts upon him, although they probably never met.

always a slow and tedious process for Merrick, who could not walk without a staff. Unconcealed, Merrick would be set upon in the street as if he were a wild animal, so he would cover his bloated head with a large black Victorian velvet cap with a potato sack attached (London Hospital Medical College Museum, London) and drape his body with a cape. His peregrinations were marked by startled countenances, shrieks of horror, obscene utterances, and pokes and jabs. As he limped along, each pace was a strenuous exercise, each street an interminable excursion of agony.

Upon reaching the Liverpool Street Railway Station in London, the indigent Merrick was mobbed by a crowd and was soon picked up by the police. Finding a calling card on his person, they promptly summoned the doctor whose name was printed on it. Although London Hospital, where Treves practiced, did not admit patients suffering from incurable diseases, Treves gained permission from the hospital's House Committee to rescue Merrick from the streets and sequester him in a remote room of the hospital. A subsequent letter to the *Times* by the hospital chairman, Francis

Henry Carr Gomm, yielded an outpouring of funds sufficient to pay Merrick's hospital costs for years and provoked widespread attention that was to improve his life even more.

In the hospital, shielded from public humiliation and contempt, Joseph Carey Merrick at last found peace. The change was slow at first, with some volunteer workers obviously uncomfortable about caring for him. But a pivotal moment, Dr. Treves pointed out in the essay he later wrote on Merrick, was when a young woman came to Joseph's room one morning to shake his hand. Merrick wept uncontrollably, in happiness. Word about Joseph Merrick spread, and he soon had many women visitors. He read voraciously, and he even enjoyed assembling model objects from cutout books.

In his new residence Joseph Merrick was even able to live out some dreams. The royal and the rich paid homage, giving him great pleasure; his most esteemed visitor was the princess of Wales. His patrons made arrangements for him to clandestinely go to the theater or make visits to a country estate. Perhaps his greatest satisfaction was that, at last, people would talk to him, shake his hand, smile warmly—courtesies he had never before experienced.

In April 1890, at the age of twenty-seven, slightly more than three years after being admitted to London Hospital, Merrick went to sleep and never awakened.* Following an autopsy, an obituary in the *Times* stated, "Witness believed that the exact cause of death was asphyxia; the back of his head being greatly deformed, and while the patient was taking a natural sleep, the weight of his head overcame him and so suffocated him."

Joseph Merrick's skeleton was cleaned and articulated by the curator of the museum in which his bones were deposited, a Mr. Openshaw. These processes were time-consuming, and the skeleton could not have been ready for display until 1891.

Any ordinary human being subjected to a mere fraction of the hardship and contempt Merrick suffered would turn bitter and cynical. But Mer-

---

*Merrick's disease was unknown during his lifetime. It was at one time mistakenly thought to have been elephantiasis, and then later it was said to be neurofibromatosis, a not uncommon disorder of the nervous system. But there seemed to be differences in Merrick's deformities as described by medical doctors and the symptoms normally suffered by neurofibromatosis victims. In 1979 a rare disease called Proteus syndrome was identified, and by the mid-1980s some medical experts concluded that Merrick had actually suffered from this disease.

rick embraced life and loved people. The *Times* obituary said, "The man had great overgrowth of the skin and bone, but he did not complain of anything."

Of Merrick, Sir Frederick Treves wrote, "Here was a man in the heyday of youth who was so vilely deformed, that everyone he met confronted him with a look of horror and disgust. He was taken about the country to be exhibited as a monstrosity and as an object of loathing. He was shunned like a leper, housed like a wild beast and got his only view of the world from a peephole in a showman's cart."

When Treves first met Merrick, his deformity made him almost unable to move his mouth, and he could only babble and grunt. Treves assumed he was feebleminded—for the better, he thought: "That he could appreciate his position was unthinkable." But this so-called human monstrosity was, in fact, intelligent, and very much aware of his position. In time, Merrick came to be regarded as an exemplary human being for his warmth, understanding, patience, inner strength, and hope.

Despite the hardships he faced in nineteenth-century England, Joseph Carey Merrick embraced life, and his story is one of courage and survival.

LOCATION: London Hospital Medical College Museum, London, England. (This museum is not open to the general public.)

Owney, the Canine Traveler

DATE: 1897.

WHAT IT IS: The stuffed and mounted remains of a famous late-nineteenth-century dog.

WHAT IT LOOKS LIKE: A large, dirty-brown-and-gray mongrel terrier. It is dressed in a gray-brown cloth jacket with burgundy pipings and has approximately 150 tags around its neck and on its jacket.

Meet Owney. Owney was a dog who lived in the late nineteenth century in America. Like other dogs, Owney savored affection, good food, and a warm place to cozy up for the night. But Owney was a particularly adventurous dog—he loved traveling on trains and visiting different places—who also had a strong instinct to protect the mail. He became the beloved mascot of the Railway Mail Service of the United States.

The story of Owney begins in 1888 in Albany, New York, where one nippy fall evening a stray dog wandered into the post office to seek refuge from the cold. A cordial mutual attachment soon grew between the anonymous animal and the postal workers, who eventually gave the dog a home (in the post office, of course) and a name: Owney (after a mailman named Owen who took the dog on his rounds, or deriving from the postal workers' repetitive query to the dog, "Who owns you?").

The workers soon discovered that the postal pet had a penchant for riding in the mail wagon, the horse-driven vehicle that carried letters and packages to and from the Albany post office and local train station. Owney appropriated the seat next to the driver in the wagon, guarding the mail with his life. One day, the story goes, a sack fell out of the wagon on its way to a local post office. Having discovered it was missing, the

Owney, canine comrade of U.S. postal workers and international traveler extraordinaire, with one of his coworkers.

driver returned to find Owney hunkered over it, waiting defiantly for anyone but the driver to try and claim it.

Owney's passion for postal pursuits was realized when the open-minded mail clerks of Albany decided to expand their quadruped's horizons. They put him on a train, the mail coach, of course, bound for the city of New York. Owney was unfettered by chain or leash, with only a collar bearing his name and home (the Albany post office) should he get lost. But the trip was successful, and it opened up new vistas for the budding sentinel.

Soon Owney was zipping around the country as the railway mail dog. He'd sniff the mailbags and lodge in the mail car behind the engine. His unofficial mission, of course, was to safeguard the mail, and he became the mascot of the Railway Mail Service, the train delivery network of the U.S. Post Office Department. Wherever he went, postal workers fed and sheltered him, showed him kindness and affection, and helped their occupational kin get started on his next adventure.

It became a practice to chronicle Owney's travels by attaching a leather or metal baggage tag to his collar with the name of the city he had visited written on it. Owney amassed a vast collection of tags—people attached labels and badges of all sorts—and the postmaster general of the United States ordered a harness to hold the lot. It must have been cumbersome for Owney to wear, but it offered a distinctive sight. The clanging of all the tags was rather noisy—like "the bells on a junk wagon," reported a New York newspaper in April 1894.

By the early 1890s Owney's fame was widespread. He attended all sorts of conventions and was honored by kennel clubs around the country and, of course, the railway mail clerks. Owney would always show up at these affairs and proudly collect the special engraved medals that would be placed around his neck or on his collar.

Owney was also an international tourist. He embarked on a world trip with the mail from the West Coast of the United States, traveling to the Orient, the Middle East, Africa, and other places. The canine tourist romped and played and sought adventure wherever he went and always managed to find his way safely to his next destination. Four months after he embarked on his worldwide jaunt, he returned safely by boat to New York City.

After several years of riding the mail cars, Owney began to experience health problems, and he was given permanent shelter in the Albany post office where his adventures as a mail dog all began. The sedentary lifestyle never appealed to Owney, however, not even in his enfeebled condition, and one day he hopped a train that landed him in Toledo, Ohio. Shortly after arriving he was provoked, and as a result he nipped a mailman. Word of this spread around, and some unknown gunman later fired a bullet into the dog, who passed away on June 11, 1897.

But Owney lives on! He was stuffed and mounted so that he might never be forgotten. The former canine ambassador to the world, who one night sought refuge from the cold inside a post office and subsequently found a world of adventure, continues to capture the public imagination.

LOCATION:　National Postal Museum, Washington, D.C.

The Wright Brothers' *Flyer*

<table>
<tr><td>DATE:</td><td>1903.</td></tr>
<tr><td>WHAT IT IS:</td><td>The first power-driven heavier-than-air machine ever to be flown successfully.</td></tr>
<tr><td>WHAT IT LOOKS LIKE:</td><td>The *Flyer* is a biplane, or two-winged plane, one wing above the other. At the front is the elevator (the device that controls the climb and descent of the airplane), and at the rear is the rudder. It has two propellers and a twelve-horsepower gasoline engine.</td></tr>
</table>

Orville and Wilbur Wright were not the first humans to defy the law of gravity. For more than a hundred years prior to their historic flights, men and women had flown in hot-air balloons, hydrogen balloons, steam-driven airships, and gliders. But the Wright brothers were the first to make a sustained, controlled, powered flight in a heavier-than-air machine. One of the extraordinary aspects of the Wright brothers' historic achievement is the relatively short period in which it was accomplished. The gliding experiments of German aeronautical inventor Otto Lilienthal fascinated the brothers, who owned a bicycle repair shop in Dayton, Ohio, but it wasn't until 1899 that the Wrights actually set to work in earnest to invent the airplane. Four years later they were airborne.

How did they do it so quickly? In a nutshell, it was their ability to grasp the nature of the critical problem, the need for control, and their understanding that an airplane is a collection of separate systems, all of which have to work in concert for the entire unit to function. Many of their contemporaries had focused on only one or a couple of these systems and for this reason had not been successful. The Wright brothers knew they had to develop and coordinate a control system, an efficient lifting system (wings), and an efficient propulsion system (propeller and engine).

Orville and Wilbur built a biplane kite with a five-foot span to test a wing-warping mechanism. They found that it worked reasonably well, so a year later, in 1900, they moved on, building a human-carrying glider based on the aerodynamic data of Otto Lilienthal. They needed a location to conduct flight tests that had strong, steady winds and wide open space, so they wrote to the U.S. Weather Bureau, which made several suggestions, and then to the postmasters and others in these cities. Based on the responses to their letters and the various locations' accessibility by train, the Wright brothers chose to do their glider testing in Kitty Hawk, North Carolina.

In terms of its lift, or ability to sustain itself aloft, the 1900 glider, which resembled a giant rectangular-shaped box kite, didn't perform as well as Orville and Wilbur had hoped, and in 1901 they returned to Kitty Hawk to test a new and—they hoped—improved glider. Although its performance was somewhat better than that of the 1900 model, it was still far below what their calculations had predicted. The disparity between the calculated performance and the actual performance caused the Wrights to gather their own aerodynamic data upon which to design the glider. To accomplish this, they decided to build a wind tunnel and a collection of different-shaped wings to determine which was the most efficient, generating the best lift for the least drag.

The wind tunnel was a wooden box six feet long with a fan at one end that generated a flow of air. The model wings were about six inches long and one inch wide, of different shapes and curvatures. As the wind blew down the tunnel and hit the model wings, which were mounted on small test stands or balances, lift and drag were measured. The pointer and scale of the balance recorded how much deflection, or lift, was being generated by each of these little surfaces. Through a series of calculations, the brothers were able to determine the efficiency of each shape: they made up approximately two hundred model wings of different shapes and curvatures.

In 1902, using what they had learned from the wind tunnel tests, the Wright brothers built a third glider. This design marked a large improvement over those of the 1900 and 1901 gliders. The wing surface was more efficient, and the Wrights had also worked out the problems with the wing-warping control system. The glider performed just as the brothers had predicted, making long, extended glides. Having achieved this success, Orville and Wilbur knew they had solved almost all the basic problems and were ready to build and fly a heavier-than-air powered machine.

The core of the Wright brothers' invention was their mechanism of three-axis control: roll (balancing the wings, or moving the airplane through an axis that runs from the nose to the tail), pitch (climb and descent, or bringing the nose up and down), and yaw (shifting the entire airplane from side to side or pivoting around the vertical axis that goes through the center of the airplane from top to bottom). Their development of an improved aerial propeller was also very original, drawing from their designs for efficient airfoils.

They began to construct their first powered airplane early in 1903. The parts were manufactured in Dayton and shipped by train to Elizabeth City, North Carolina. From there the crates were taken by boat to Kitty Hawk, where the brothers were assembling the plane in a work shed. By October they were almost finished, but problems, particularly with the engine, delayed the trial flight until December, when the brothers believed the plane was finally operating reliably.

The frame of the Wright brothers' biplane was made of spruce and ash and braced with wire; muslin fabric covered the wings and tail. There was no fuselage, or body, to the airplane, only an open frame. The elevator,

The Flyer *on December 17, 1903, the day it made aviation history when it was successfully flown.*

which controlled pitch motion, or climb and descent, was in the front, in what is called the "canard configuration." (As aviation technology advanced, airplane makers put the elevator and a horizontal stabilizer in the back because of less wind resistance, greater advantages for achieving particular control and flight parameters, and other factors.)

The plane had one engine mounted on the lower wing, just to the right of the pilot's station. This was connected by chain drives to two propellers mounted about midway out on the back of the wings. The function of propellers is to generate thrust; when enough thrust is generated, the airplane moves forward, and when it's moving fast enough to achieve flight, it rises into the air. In the Wright brothers' airplane, thrust was generated by two pusher propellers, as opposed to a tractor propeller. Because its propellers were mounted behind the wings, when they generated thrust they actually pushed the airplane forward by pushing air to the rear. The propeller on most modern-day airplanes is mounted in front of the wings, so when the propeller generates thrust, it pulls the airplane along; this is a tractor propeller.

For takeoff, the plane sat on a cradle, a two-wheeled dolly that rode down a sixty-foot wooden-rail track, which consisted of four fifteen-foot two-by-fours laid end to end on the ground. The airplane had no seats, being designed for the pilot to lie across the center of the bottom wing in a prone position. This was a carryover from the Wrights' earlier glider experiments in which the prone position reduced wind resistance at these critical low airspeeds.

The pilot lay in a hip cradle to which warping wires were connected; the pilot would swing his hips from side to side to control the roll of the airplane. Rudder control cables also were connected to the hip cradle and moved simultaneously with the wing warping, which controlled the airplane in roll.

The wing tip, or outer edge of the wing, could be twisted up on one side while being twisted down on the other. By creating a difference in the amount of lift on one side of the plane compared to the other, the balance of the airplane could be controlled.

The first try came on December 14, 1903. Who would fly, Orville or Wilbur? The brothers tossed a coin, and Wilbur won. Wilbur managed to get the plane aloft briefly, but it came close to stalling. Wilbur overcontrolled, and the plane hit the ground because it was so low. The aircraft sustained minor damage, so the brothers abandoned any further flights that day.

Three days after their first attempt, on December 17, the brothers were ready to try again. It was now Orville's turn to fly. This time history was made! The heavier-than-air machine stayed up twelve seconds and traveled 120 feet. Then Wilbur took a turn, flying 175 feet in 12 seconds. In the next flight Orville covered 200 feet in 15 seconds, and in the fourth and final flight, with Wilbur at the helm, the *Flyer* remained airborne for a whopping fifty-nine seconds and traveled 852 feet. Later that day, out on the sand dunes, a gust of wind caught the plane, cartwheeling it over the sand and badly damaging it. The plane was never flown again. But the Wright brothers had already achieved a monumental accomplishment: their *Flyer* was the first heavier-than-air machine to make a sustained and controlled powered flight.

To perfect their invention, the Wright brothers built two more airplanes over the next couple of years. They called all their aircraft simply "Flyers," distinguishing each by the year of its construction. Their first plane was called the *1903 Flyer* (it became popularly known as the *Kitty Hawk*, but this name eventually fell into disuse), their next year's plane the *1904 Flyer*, then the *1905 Flyer*.

After testing their 1905 plane the Wrights devoted themselves to protecting their invention and commercially marketing it. With the new flying machine greeted with tremendous excitement, people all over the world tried to build their own planes. Filing patent infringement suits, primarily against Glenn Curtiss in the United States, and against others in Europe, occupied much of the Wrights' time. In 1908 they demonstrated their plane, which now could fly over an hour without difficulty, both in the United States and Europe. In 1909, after having met various requirements of the U.S. government, including minimum distance and speed capability of the plane, they sold the government a plane they called the *Military Flyer* (National Air and Space Museum, Washington, D.C.). Following this sale, the Wrights began an aviation business. In the beginning the company didn't build and sell a great many airplanes, and much of its income was derived from its flying exhibition team, which performed at fairs and other outdoor events. But with aviation a burgeoning industry, the company's future as a manufacturer appeared promising until Wilbur, at the age of forty-five, suddenly developed typhoid fever and died in May 1912. Orville eventually decided he didn't want to run the company by himself and sold it to a group of investors in 1915.

Over the years Orville sat on company boards and came to be regarded essentially as an elder statesman of aviation until his death due to a heart attack in 1948. By that time, with sophisticated aircraft a regular part of the world, he was already regarded as a legend, having with his brother been the first to be airborne in a powered machine, their *1903 Flyer*. But in the years following their four historic flights on December 17, 1903, the machine that they worked so hard to perfect, the first airplane to fly, was largely ignored.

After its flights on December 17, the *1903 Flyer* had been immediately shipped back to Dayton, where it was kept in a crate in a back shed for several years. The crate wasn't opened until 1916, when Orville reassembled the plane for an exhibition at a new building at the Massachusetts Institute of Technology. It was displayed at a few other locations in the late teens and early twenties and reconditioned in 1927, the year before the plane went to the Science Museum in London.

In 1909 the Smithsonian Institution first asked the Wright brothers to donate a plane to the museum, but it wasn't the *1903 Flyer* that was requested. Rather, the Smithsonian wanted a current Wright brothers airplane, the type they were flying in 1909. The Wrights didn't have one available to give but offered either to rebuild the original 1903 plane from its pieces or to create a model of it.

The 1903 machine wasn't of interest to the Smithsonian, and this and other factors—including the institution's reluctance to credit the Wrights with building the first airplane, in view of the tests by the institution's secretary, Samuel Pierpont Langley, who built a machine that flew without a pilot—caused a rift between the Wrights and the Smithsonian. Recognition came only gradually through the years, and finally, the disagreement resolved, the Smithsonian requested the *1903 Flyer*. But at the time the plane was in England—Orville had sent it there as a gesture of protest against the Smithsonian—and it wasn't until after World War II ended, in 1948, that it was brought back to the United States and deposited in the Smithsonian.

The Wright brothers' landmark flights of December 17, 1903, received little news coverage, and the stories that were printed were highly exaggerated. One, for example, depicted a flight going six miles out over the ocean, which of course was untrue. In January 1904 the Wright brothers held a press conference to disclaim the exaggerated stories and explain precisely what they had done.

From its three-axis control to its lift and propulsion systems, the *1903 Flyer* embodied the fundamental elements required of all future airplanes. Indeed, with their remarkable flying machine, Orville and Wilbur Wright ushered in a new era, one that was to have profound effects on virtually every area of society, including transportation, commerce, and war.

LOCATION: National Air and Space Museum, Washington, D.C.

The Breast-Pocket Items That Saved the Life of Theodore Roosevelt

DATE: 1912.

WHAT THEY ARE: Two items that saved Theodore Roosevelt from an assassin's bullet: the typewritten pages of a speech and a metal eyeglass case.

WHAT THEY LOOK LIKE: The manuscript pages of the speech measure 8½ inches by 6½ inches. The eyeglass case measures a little more than 5 inches across and is maroon-brown. Both have bullet holes in them; because the speech was folded, it has bullet holes at the top and bottom of the pages.

It was the quintessence of serendipity—a deadly courier being obstructed by the casual impediments of habit. Ordinary objects, unwittingly but strategically placed by the intended victim of an assassination attempt, blocked the course of what would otherwise have been a deadly bullet.

October 14, 1912. Theodore Roosevelt was stumping in the Midwest as a Bull Moose candidate for the presidency of the United States. Roosevelt was vice president in 1901 when William McKinley was assassinated, and he ascended to the office of chief executive at the age of forty-two, the youngest president ever. His was a dramatically active presidency in basically uneventful times, and he was affectionately embraced by the public. But he stepped down in 1909 and was succeeded by his candidate of choice, William Howard Taft.

Taft made only halfhearted attempts in carrying out Roosevelt's policies, and progressive Republicans became disenchanted with the president. Roosevelt, always outspoken, broke with the Taft administration and decided he would run for office again. At the Republican convention of 1912, however, conservative Republicans nominated as their candidate the incumbent president, while progressive Republicans formed the Progressive, or Bull Moose, Party, with Roosevelt as their candidate.

In the early evening of October 14 Theodore Roosevelt had arrived in Milwaukee from Racine, Wisconsin. He had wanted to eat dinner in his car and proceed directly to the auditorium where he was to deliver his speech but was urged by local party leaders to greet the people of the city by riding through the streets and then to dine at the Gilpatrick Hotel. Those who traveled with him, including a physician, were concerned about the large crowds that always attended Roosevelt's appearances in public and about finding time for him to rest. But committeemen said the police would provide security and that this extra appearance would be beneficial. Along the route to the Gilpatrick, people were lined up and welcomed Roosevelt enthusiastically. At the hotel, Roosevelt rested briefly in a room and then had dinner. With a few others in his entourage, he emerged from the hotel into the darkness. A crowd of people around Roosevelt's car had gathered to cheer him. After he made it to his car, he stood up to bow and tip his hat in acknowledgment of the cheers. At the front of the crowd was a man holding a .38-caliber Colt, mounted on a .44-caliber frame, a weapon offering the user superior aim.

Unbeknownst to Roosevelt, a saloonkeeper from New York City named John Schrank had stalked him through eight states in an effort to seize the right moment to assassinate him. As Schrank would later claim in court proceedings (original transcripts at the Library of Congress, Washington, D.C.), the slain U.S. president William McKinley had appeared to him twice in dreams. The first was in September 1901 when McKinley rose from his coffin, pointed to Roosevelt, and claimed the vice president had murdered him. In September 1912 McKinley, in another dream, approached Schrank from behind, tapped his shoulder, and ordered him to avenge his murder.

At about 8:10 P.M., standing just six feet away from Roosevelt, Schrank raised his arm and fired his gun (now in private possession). The bullet was well aimed but encountered some unexpected obstacles. Let's trace its trajectory.

The bullet first penetrated the heavy overcoat Roosevelt was wearing. It ripped through the coat on the right side of his chest and plowed into his suit jacket at the breast-pocket level. Inside the pocket were two items

Teddy Roosevelt, just after John Schrank's assassination attempt.

that absorbed the impact of the bullet and undoubtedly saved Theodore Roosevelt's life. The first was a fifty-page speech folded in half into a wad one hundred pages thick. Behind this wad was a metal eyeglass case in which were Roosevelt's spectacles. Its force diminished but still lethal, the bullet traveled through Roosevelt's vest, then his outer shirt (Theodore Roosevelt Birthplace, New York, New York), his undershirt (Theodore Roosevelt National Park, Medora, North Dakota, on loan from the Theodore Roosevelt Association, Oyster Bay, New York), and finally punctured his skin, right below the nipple, and lodged in his chest just before reaching his lung.

After he was hit Roosevelt reeled a bit, then fell into the seat beneath him. Elbert Martin, Roosevelt's stenographer and a former football player, immediately jumped out of the car and ran to Schrank, who had his gun raised and appeared ready to fire again. Martin grabbed him from behind and wrestled him to the ground. Others rushed over as Martin, with his knee planted on the small of Schrank's back, yanked his head back. Roosevelt called for Martin not to hurt the gunman and to bring him near. Schrank tried to conceal the pistol under his left arm, but Martin grabbed it. When they made it to Roosevelt, Martin put his hand over Schrank's face and turned it toward the wounded man. There was much commotion by this time; the police came to maintain order in the crowd and take Schrank into custody.

Roosevelt was advised by his doctor and others to go immediately to a hospital, but he said he felt all right and emphatically insisted on making his speech. Roosevelt undoubtedly realized this was a supreme opportunity for a political candidate to make a great impact, and he wanted to grab it. He was wounded with a bullet in him; he could die. He figured the bullet hadn't hit his lung because he wasn't hemorrhaging. But if the wound required surgery, he would be incapacitated, and especially after being so vilified by the press in his campaign, he didn't want to pass up this chance.

People were lined up along the streets to Milwaukee Auditorium, where Roosevelt was to speak, and they applauded as he slowly drove by. Roosevelt's physician, Dr. Scurry L. Terrell, continued to try to talk the candidate into going to a hospital, but Roosevelt responded, "This is my big chance and I am going to make that speech if I die doing it."

At the auditorium before Roosevelt went on stage, he permitted Dr. Terrell to examine his wound. His advisers invited some local physicians to look at the wound so that it wouldn't appear as if the candidate was trying to hide anything. Roosevelt submitted to an examination and an interview. The doctors applied a handkerchief as a bandage and consented to Roosevelt making his speech.

It was an occasion to appeal to the audience's emotions, and Roosevelt rose gloriously to it. "I don't know whether you fully understand that I've just been shot," he began, "but it takes more than that to kill a Bull Moose." He showed his bullet-torn speech manuscript and declared it probably prevented the bullet from piercing his heart, and continued, "The bullet is in me now so that I cannot make a very long speech, but I will try my best."

Roosevelt in fact did make a rather long speech, speaking extemporaneously rather than reading from his manuscript. He made numerous references to the attempted assassination: "I have altogether too important things to think of to feel any concern over my own death"; "I cannot tell you of what infinitesimal importance I regard this incident as compared with the great issues at stake in this campaign"; "I am a little sore. Anybody has a right to be sore with a bullet in him. You would find that if I was in battle I would be leading my men just the same. Just the same way I am going to make this speech"; "I know these doctors, when they get hold of me, will never let me go back and there are just a few more things that I want to say to you"; "Don't you pity me. I am all right. I am all right and you cannot escape listening to my speech either." Roosevelt was interrupted a few times by his associates, who wanted him to conclude his remarks.

Shortly after the assassination attempt, Oscar King Davis, the press secretary of the Progressive Party, wrote, "I watched the Colonel very closely and it seemed to me that he had lost color and was laboring very hard to go on, so I stepped up to him and put my hand on his arm. He stopped

Lifesavers: the metal eyeglass case and speech that stopped a bullet from killing Theodore Roosevelt on the evening of October 14, 1912.

and glared at me ferociously and said, 'What do you want?' I said, 'Colonel, I want to stop you.' He said, 'No sir, I will not stop, you can't stop me nor anybody else.' Then he turned and went on with his speech." Ninety minutes after he began, Roosevelt concluded his speech.

When Roosevelt read a speech, he would typically hold it close to his face, for he was very nearsighted. When he finished with a sheet, he would frequently drop it, so that by the time he had completed delivering a speech the stage was littered with pages. People in the audience would rush to the stage and grab the sheets as souvenirs.

After his extemporaneous remarks at Milwaukee Auditorium, Roosevelt gave out some of his folded speech with the bullet holes to reporters seated in the first rows, as souvenirs. (One reporter later sold his page to the Smithsonian Institution.) Other pages were sent to Roosevelt's relatives and supporters as souvenirs.

Roosevelt was then driven to the Johnston Emergency Hospital, where physicians dressed his wound and took X rays, and Roosevelt telegraphed his wife, Edith. At 12:30 A.M. he was taken on a special train to Mercy Hospital in Chicago, where better care could be administered.

The doctors did not probe for the bullet. After President James A. Garfield was shot in 1881, doctors had probed for the bullet, and Garfield later died.

The physicians kept what was sometimes called a "death watch." If they observed a problem, they would take out the bullet and clean the wound. But since there were no antibiotics at the time and sterilization procedures were not always workable, there was a terrible risk of infection. Physicians finally decided not to remove the bullet. A week after being shot, Roosevelt was released from Mercy Hospital. He returned to his New York home in Oyster Bay, Long Island, for further recuperation, and was back campaigning on October 30.

Roosevelt lost the election of 1912—both he and Taft were defeated by Woodrow Wilson—but went on to lead a productive life. He explored and mapped a Brazilian river, wrote prolifically, and continued to speak out on and bring his influence to political matters. On January 6, 1919, Teddy Roosevelt died at his home in Oyster Bay at the age of sixty, with Schrank's bullet still in him. The next day, James Earle Fraser, the sculptor who designed the buffalo nickel, made a death mask (Theodore Roosevelt Home, Sagamore Hill National Historic Site, Oyster Bay, New York).

In the meantime, Roosevelt's almost-assassin, John Schrank, had been diagnosed as being a schizophrenic, clinically a dementia praecox paranoid. He was committed to an institution for the criminally insane, where he lived out his days. (He vowed to shoot President Franklin Delano Roosevelt if he were ever released.) Schrank died in 1943 at the age of sixty-seven.

Some interesting points may be made about the garments Roosevelt was wearing. The heavy overcoat, suit jacket, and vest seem no longer to be in existence; they were probably discarded.

The two shirts were used as evidence in the trial of John Schrank and were kept for a long time by the presiding judge of the trial. They were washed and bleached, but faint traces of bloodstains may be observed.

The eyeglass case and several pages of the speech survive, branded with bullet holes from the day when they resisted a lethal bullet marked for the twenty-sixth president of the United States, Theodore Roosevelt.

LOCATIONS: Metal eyeglass case: Theodore Roosevelt Birthplace National Historic Site, New York, New York.

Pages of the speech: eleven pages (now bound in a hardcover volume), Theodore Roosevelt Birthplace, New York, New York; one page, National Museum of American History, Washington, D.C.; other pages, privately owned.

Piltdown Man

DATE: 1912.

WHAT IT IS: Skull fragments and part of a jaw once thought to be from a newly discovered, ancient ancestor of humankind.

WHAT IT LOOKS LIKE: The parts of Piltdown Man are in separate pieces, all mahogany brown.

Mr. Dawson seemed surprised by the shard of "cocoa-nut" handed to him by a worker at the gravel pit.

He knew immediately it wasn't what the workers at Barkham Manor, a sprawling estate in the village of Piltdown in Sussex, thought it was. No, this wasn't a piece of edible fruit but a very old fragment of bone, possibly that of a human cranium.

Charles Dawson, a forty-four-year-old solicitor and amateur fossil collector, enthusiastically thanked the laborers who had brought this fragment to his attention. He frequently visited Barkham Manor, one of a few estates of which he was the steward, and told the men digging at the gravel pit there to keep a lookout for anything unusual; the pit just might yield something to feed his blazing passion for paleontology. The gravel bed—as well as all of Barkham Manor—was part of the Weald, a piece of countryside in southeast England girdled in the north and south by chalk hills known as the Downs. The region contained many sites associated with the study of human antiquity.

Over the next few years, Dawson reportedly returned to the pit, where he subsequently recovered further fragments of the very same broken piece—what he realized was part of a human skull of possibly great antiquity—found initially about 1910. In February 1912 he informed Arthur Smith Woodward, the keeper of geology at the British Museum (Natural

History) in London (later called the Natural History Museum), of these discoveries.

The gravel deposit at Barkham Manor was investigated further early in June 1912, when Dawson, accompanied by Arthur Smith Woodward and the French priest-paleontologist Pierre Teilhard de Chardin, searched the gravel bed for more finds. Based on the discoveries made that day, Woodward assisted Dawson in a more thorough search of the gravel deposit, which yielded further fragments of the cranium plus a section of a jawbone.

Woodward concluded that the bones were all from the same creature because of their color and their proximity to each other in the pit. The geology of the pit and other fossil remains (including the jaw) found in it indicated the site dated from the early Pleistocene epoch or earlier. This, of course, would mean the skull fragments were of great age, belonging to a truly primitive being, one that appeared to be human. The parietal bones were indeed human, and although the mandible was apelike, its canine tooth and molar teeth exhibited wear not characteristic of anthropoid apes but of humans.

Paleontologists of the day commonly believed that humans had descended directly from the apes (unlike the more modern theory that humans and apes have a common ancestor). Some transitional creature, they assumed, bridged the gap between "pure" ape and "pure" human. The bones found at Piltdown could very well be from such a creature. Even the jaw's apelike characteristics fit this theory. A transitional ape-to-man creature would develop a more advanced brain before its jaw became humanlike. Piltdown Man (dubbed *Eoanthropus dawsoni*), it was conjectured, was the "missing link"!

A skull was constructed from the cranial and mandibular fragments for presentation at a meeting of the Geological Society of London on December 18, 1912, by Dawson and Woodward. Those privy to Piltdown Man vowed secrecy, but almost a month before the meeting the *Manchester Guardian* somehow learned of the finds and reported the discovery of the supposedly prehistoric remains, trumpeting the possibility that they belonged to a progenitor of human beings.

News of the skull spread quickly around the world, and great excitement attended the meeting. The speakers included Woodward, Dawson, anatomy professor Grafton Elliot Smith, Royal College of Surgeons conservator Arthur Keith, and amateur geologist Alfred Kennard—each of whom subscribed to his own individual interpretation of the fragments

Piltdown Man was one of the greatest scientific hoaxes of all time. Pictured in this painting by John Cooke is an examination of the Piltdown skull by the "Piltdown Gang," with, from left to right in the front: Underwood, Keith, Pycraft, and Lankester; in the rear: Smith, Dawson, and Woodward.

and their age, but all of whom supported the belief that the fragments came from the same individual and that this individual belonged to a race that had descended from apes and was a predecessor to humankind.

From the time of Piltdown Man's public introduction, there were dissenters. Primarily, they contested the association of the apelike jaw with a human braincase. Although all these bones had been found in close proximity, a fact that supported the argument for their association, the dissenters argued against this on anatomical grounds. However, none of the skeptics questioned the authenticity of the remains.

Unable to prove or disprove the validity of the reconstruction, scientists continued to support the skull as belonging to an ancient form of humanity, though with mounting difficulty. Piltdown Man continued to withstand challenges to its authenticity, and because its origins were never proved conclusively, it became an anomaly, and as such hindered the progress of paleontology. Ultimately, however, the fluorine dating technique supplied the solution to this ongoing dilemma.

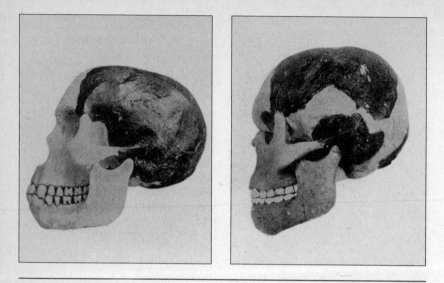

LEFT: *Apelike in jaw and of small brain capacity: the skull of the Piltdown Man as reconstructed by Dr. A. Smith Woodward.*

RIGHT: *Manlike both in jaw and in brain capacity: the skull of the Piltdown Man as reconstructed by Professor Arthur Keith.*

The technique of dating bones by determining their fluorine content was developed in the 1940s by British anthropologist Kenneth Oakley. When the Piltdown remains were dated with this technique in 1950, the results, while not resolving the issue of association, did indicate that the bones might be younger than expected, which only complicated the matter. Then, in 1953, Joseph Weiner, an anatomist at Oxford, put forward the hypothesis that the jaw belonged to an ape and had been artificially modified and stained. Convinced of the validity of Weiner's argument, Oakley requested a full investigation, which was sanctioned by the British Museum (Natural History) and which led to a complete resolution of the Piltdown controversy.

This investigation involved, among other things, a variety of physical and chemical tests, which determined the cranial bones were human whereas the jaw was undoubtedly a remnant of an ape. (Much later, it was confirmed that the jaw belonged to an orangutan.) Some portions of the Piltdown remains had been chemically stained and altered in other ways to make them appear to be ancient human fossils—and they were all less than one thousand years old.

What a revelation! For forty years, paleoanthropology had been misled, deliberately led astray. During this time other remains—discovered in South Africa and elsewhere—suggested an evolutionary scenario completely different from that indicated by the Piltdown Man remains. Those who had claimed that the Piltdown remains were incongruous were right, but little did they imagine the "finds" were a hoax. Someone—or more than one person—had methodically committed a fraud.

That Dawson was involved in the deception is virtually certain. But he was probably too scientifically uneducated to have pulled off the ruse alone. Someone else with a greater knowledge of anatomy was almost certainly behind it. But who?

It could have been any of the coterie of scientists who examined the remains before the public disclosure: Edwin Ray Lankester, a biologist and former director at the British Museum; James Reid Moir, an amateur archaeologist; Arthur Underwood, a dental surgeon; W. P. Pycraft, an anthropologist; or Edgar Willet, a retired hospital administrator. But many of the others associated in one way or another with Piltdown Man have been subsequently implicated in the forgery. In addition to Teilhard de Chardin, the priest-paleontologist, and Grafton Elliot Smith, the anatomy professor, they include: William Sollas, a geology professor; William Lewis Abbott, a jeweler and amateur archaeologist; Frank Barlow, a senior preparator at the British Museum (Natural History); and Arthur Conan Doyle, the Sherlock Holmes author and an acquaintance of Dawson. None of these cases have stood up to close scrutiny, however.

Of course, the conspirator(s) would have needed a motive. For Dawson, it was probably the recognition and glory that would provide him entry into the highly prestigious and venerable Royal Society, which would validate his interest in paleontology. But what about the co-conspirator? What induced the expert behind the scenes to doctor the remains planted in the Piltdown gravel pit?

The motivation could have been anything. It could have been the satisfaction of pulling off a joke (as it may only have been intended to be at the start) or discrediting Woodward (who almost certainly was an innocent victim) or any of the other Piltdown Man proponents, the prestige that would come with identifying the remains once the Piltdown Man thesis was accepted, an urge to upset the accepted beliefs of paleontology, or a desire to advance the evolutionary theory Piltdown Man supported.

The gallery of suspects has been examined exhaustively since the hoax was discovered. Arguments have been made for various persons associated with the hoax, including, notably, that of anthropologist Frank Spencer against Sir Arthur Keith, incorporating an investigation made by the late Australian scholar Ian Langham. Their case is a complicated one involving, among other things, contemporary documentary evidence. In particular, there is an entry from Keith's diary that identifies him as the author of an anonymous article on the unveiling of the Piltdown remains at the Geological Society in 1912. This article contains specific information on the location of the site, which was not revealed at the meeting. Furthermore, Keith's diary indicates that the article was written in advance of the meeting, so he must have had (unexplained) prior knowledge of the site and its history. Building on this, the Spencer-Langham case goes on to present an impressive string of other evidence implicating Keith as Dawson's co-conspirator. The case against Keith has been further strengthened by other circumstantial evidence uncovered by the South African anthropologist Phillip Tobias. His article published in the June 1992 issue of *Current Anthropology* provides a detailed summary and scholarly discussion of this intriguing case. However, as the discussions accompanying Tobias's article indicate, the case against Keith, though compelling, has not been proven beyond a reasonable doubt. In light of this, in all probability it is never going to be possible to present an iron-clad case with which everyone will be satisfied.

Clearly, the guilty players have taken their secret to their graves. But the mechanism of their deception, the device, the subterfuge, the object of all the commotion, sits quietly today, unflappable, unshakable.

Now if only that blasted skull could speak!

LOCATION: Natural History Museum, London, England.

Laddie Boy

DATE: 1926.

WHAT IT IS: A life-size replica of President Warren G. Harding's dog, cast from 19,314 copper pennies collected from newsboys around the United States.

WHAT IT LOOKS LIKE: The bronze statue measures 38½ inches long, 13¼ inches wide, and 20½ inches high with its pedestal.

The twenty-ninth president of the United States, Warren Gamaliel Harding, was devoted to his dog, an Airedale terrier named Laddie Boy, and the dog was quite fond of his master. Harding died suddenly and unexpectedly in 1923, while still president. As his funeral cortege proceeded down the driveway from the Harding home on Mount Vernon Avenue in Marion, Ohio, the dog was seen behind the screen door watching his master being carried away.

The Roosevelt Newsboys' Association of Greater Boston wanted to honor Warren Harding by commissioning a special statue of his favorite dog, Laddie Boy. The Boston newsboys regarded Harding as a friend because he took an interest in a Brookline memorial to a former local newsboy, Albert Scott, who died heroically in France during World War I, and because of Harding's background in the newspaper business. Harding and his wife, Florence, had been involved with newspapers for much of their lives. When he was seventeen, Warren began working for a newspaper in his hometown of Marion, Ohio. He eventually became the owner and editor of the *Marion Star* newspaper. Later, Florence essentially ran the paper and was very successful with it. And while she was running the *Star*, Florence Harding conceived the idea of having youths deliver newspapers to people's homes, a service that continues to this day. Indeed the

Newspaper boys across America collected pennies for this celebratory statue of President Warren G. Harding's Airedale terrier, Laddie Boy.

newspaper, which had been purchased for only a few hundred dollars, brought the Hardings $550,000—the bulk of their wealth—when they sold it six weeks before Warren's death.

To raise money to commission the statue, a poster was distributed around the United States asking for the help of other newsboys. Newsboy Leonard Poretsky of Revere, Massachusetts, wrote the prize essay on the poster:

> Fellow Newsboys:
>
> The country mourns the loss of that great, kindly, sincere man—Warren Gamaliel Harding,—and to the newsboys comes the reminder that he was one of the best friends they ever had.
>
> A man who worked in the game—a man who understood and loved the boys,—and a man to whom the newsboys of the country could give no greater honor than to erect a fitting monument to his memory.
>
> President Harding once said that the best article he ever wrote was a tribute to a dog. The plan is for every newsboy in the country to give one penny, which will be melted and modelled into a

life-size statue of "Laddie Boy," the President's dog. When completed, the statue will be presented to Mrs. Harding so that she may know how much we newsboys loved the Newspaperman-President—a monument which will live in history forever.

Circulation managers around the country collected more than nineteen thousand pennies from newsboys and sent them to the Roosevelt Newsboys' Association, which commissioned sculptress Bashka Paeff to fashion a bronze replica of Laddie Boy. The statue was to be presented to Mrs. Harding, but she died before it was completed. It came into the possession of Mrs. Harding's bodyguard, Robert Barker, of West Newton, Massachusetts.

The statue was first displayed to the public at the local Jordan Marsh department store, then was moved near the end of 1926 to the foyer of Keith's Theater in Washington, D.C.

The real Laddie Boy died on January 23, 1929, but thanks to the young news carriers of the United States in the 1920s, his image lives on.

LOCATION: National Museum of American History, Washington, D.C.

Babe Ruth's Sixtieth-Home-Run Bat

DATE: 1927.

WHAT IT IS: The bat with which Babe Ruth hit his sixtieth home run, setting the record for the most home runs hit in one season. (Ruth's sixtieth home run came in a 154-game schedule; in 1961 Roger Maris hit sixty-one home runs in a 162-game calendar. In 1991 Major League Baseball recognized Maris's sixty-one homers as the home-run record.)

WHAT IT LOOKS LIKE: The bat, a Hillerich and Bradsby Louisville Slugger is 35 inches long and weighs 39 ounces. It is light brown.

On Friday, September 30, 1927, the New York Yankees hosted the Washington Senators in the penultimate game of their season. Although the Bronx Bombers had clinched the American League pennant, the fans turned out in droves for the once-in-a-lifetime opportunity to witness one of baseball's greatest events. George Herman Ruth would try to break his own record of fifty-nine home runs in one season.

An electric excitement surged through the stands as the score remained low and tied. For seven innings, Ruth could not connect for that immortal hit; he drew a walk and hit a pair of singles. The tension grew nearly unbearable in the bottom of the eighth, when Ruth would come to bat for probably the last time in the game.

With one out and the score even at two all, Mark Koenig smacked a triple. Then the Sultan of Swat came to the plate, and the spectators cheered. Ruth knew what the fans wanted, and he wanted it, too. This

Babe Ruth hits his sixtieth home run in one season. The most famous baseball player ever clutches his bat as he watches the ball sail on into history.

The New York Yankees purchased bats for their players in 1927, when Babe Ruth hit his immortal sixtieth home run of the season with the bat shown above. It cost about five or six dollars and is probably made of ash.

was the showdown. There was incredible pressure to wallop the ball out of the field, but Babe Ruth had always thrived on pressure.

Tom Zachary, the Senators' fireball hurler, blazed the first pitch in for a strike. The next pitch came in above the strike zone, a ball. The count was one-and-one. Time was running out for the Babe. Two more strikes, and the game would be over.

Zachary fired his third pitch. It came in low as it reached the batter. Ruth arched back, clenched his bat tightly, and brought it around with his full strength. A cracking sound was heard, and all in the stadium craned their necks to watch as the ball sailed into the sun seats of the right-field bleachers. Having just witnessed baseball history, the fans leaped to their feet and roared with uncontrollable frenzy.

Babe Ruth had hit his sixtieth home run of the season—a feat no one thought possible a short while before—and the Yankees won the game 4 to 2. Ruth's record was monumental indeed. He alone hit more home runs that season than all but three entire major league baseball teams. The two National League home-run leaders, Cy Williams and Hack Wilson, hit thirty home runs each to combine for the total of Ruth's record. The following day, October 1, in the Yankees' final regular game of the season, Ruth was hitless. But it didn't matter. Along with his Louisville Slugger, he had already achieved the immortality that he and his faithful fans had hoped for.

Little is known of the history of the bat after Ruth hit his sixtieth home run with it, except that he probably gave it to someone who either held on to it or passed it on to another party. In any case, the bat was donated by James M. Kahn of the sports department of the *New York Sun* newspaper to its present home in 1939. The bat looks ordinary, to be sure, but it was with this slab of wood that the mighty Babe cracked a pitch out of Yankee Stadium at the end of the baseball season in 1927, and in so doing, immortalized himself and made his name forever synonymous with the game.

LOCATION: National Baseball Hall of Fame and Museum, Cooperstown, New York.

John Dillinger's Wooden Jail-Escape Gun

DATE: 1934.

WHAT IT IS: A "gun" carved out of wood by the notorious gangster John Dillinger, which he used to break out of jail.

WHAT IT LOOKS LIKE: The wooden object resembles a Colt .32 automatic. It's more or less flat, slightly rounded on top, and has a hammer carved on the back of it.

It was a daring escape. The jail was crawling with heavily armed guards. Any prisoner would need an iron nerve to attempt to bust out, but John Dillinger remained unfazed. He held up a piece of wood carved and painted to resemble a gun, threatened to kill with it, and began his bizarre odyssey to freedom.

For robbing and assaulting an elderly grocer in 1924, Dillinger spent almost nine years in prison. After his parole, he began a wild fourteen-month crime spree that was to be interrupted only by a brief stay in jail. He held up supermarkets and drugstores, robbed banks, and even relieved police officers of their weapons—inside police stations. There was no limit to the brazenness of this gangster, and he continually eluded both police and FBI agents—G-men, as they were popularly called back then. In the process he carved out a reputation that would become part of America's criminal folklore. What more could this Indiana farmboy named John Dillinger do to enhance his notoriety?

How about escape from jail using a fake gun? Wanted for bank robberies and killing a police officer during the commission of a robbery in East Chicago, Indiana, Dillinger was finally picked up in Tucson, Ari-

Legend grew that Dillinger could return anyone's stare for as long as the person felt comfortable. Dillinger's eyes were variably described as slate gray or yellow slate-gray.

zona, and transferred to the Lake County, Indiana, jail on January 30, 1934. Restless and fearless, he soon hatched a plan to get out. Escaping from jail wasn't all that novel for Dillinger. After all, he'd done it once before in September 1933 when his gang broke him out of the jail in Lima, Ohio, killing a sheriff in the process. This time Dillinger planned his ultimate ruse—escape with a wooden gun. Where Dillinger got the idea for this is not exactly known, but previously, in October 1933, a prisoner at Wisconsin State Prison tried to break out with a carved wooden gun.

Using a wooden gun that was probably smuggled in with the assistance of one or two jail guards,* John Dillinger, on the morning of Saturday, March 3, 1934, began his incredible odyssey to freedom from the Lake County jail at Crown Point. As a turnkey and two trusties opened his cell door, Dillinger sprang up and thrust his "gun" into the turnkey's stomach. The gun barely had a stub for a handle, but Dillinger disguised this with his grip. Holding his prisoners at "gunpoint," Dillinger forced them through the corridors and up to the warden's office, where he seized real firearms, including a submachine gun. To ensure his safe flight, Dillinger went around the jail locking up guards—more than twenty-five in total. Then he walked to a garage where he stole the sheriff's car and drove across the state border into Illinois.

*Credence is given the explanation offered by G. Russell Girardin in his 1994 book (with William Helmer) *Dillinger: The Untold Story* that Dillinger paid to have the gun smuggled in. Legend has it that Dillinger used his shaving razor blade to fashion the top rail of the washboard in his cell into a gun, blackening it with shoe polish and using either the barrel of a fountain pen or the handle of a safety razor as the barrel. He may actually have tried to do this and failed, but probably didn't use the rail in any modified way for his escape. A fake gun as opposed to a real one was smuggled probably because one or both of the guards was afraid of the repercussions of the latter.

John Dillinger's famous wooden gun with which he made a bold jailbreak in March 1934.

About two weeks later Dillinger sent his girlfriend to Maywood, Indiana, a suburb of Indianapolis, to give the wooden gun to his sister, Audrey Hancock. Some years later Dillinger's lawyer, Louis Piquett, along with a so-called investigator who worked with Piquett and who had served time in prison because of him, Arthur O'Leary, and a third man, wrote about the gun and borrowed it from Dillinger's sister to photograph and display it. Piquett wrote a note to O'Leary saying that when they were through with the wooden gun to make sure it was returned to the sister, but then the gun disappeared.

About forty years later, in the early 1980s, the owner of a house in Dubuque, Iowa, that was previously owned by Arthur O'Leary discovered something unusual in a first-floor closet. Underneath a section of the flooring was a tin box that extended into the basement. From the basement, the tin box looked as if it were part of the furnace ducting. The owner opened the peculiar tin box and found inside a wooden gun along with Louis Piquett's note to O'Leary to return the gun to Dillinger's sister. It was given for examination to Dillinger's sister, who was still alive at the time (residing in Maywood, Indiana), and she confirmed its authenticity and signed an affidavit to that effect.

Dillinger's jailbreak was an embarrassment to the officials and guards at the Lake County jail at Crown Point. They found wood shavings under the bed in his cell, presumably put there by Dillinger to make it look like he carved the wooden gun himself and acted alone. Following Dillinger's successful escape, two members of his gang serving time in an Ohio state prison for the killing of the sheriff in Lima carved pistols from soap and attempted to break out. Charles Mackley was shot and killed, Harry Pierpont was shot and later electrocuted.

For John Dillinger it not only took guts to attempt to break out of jail but required a kind of thespian finesse in a life-and-death situation to point a wooden object at armed officers and make believe—and make the officers believe—that the gun was real and potentially deadly. An infamous gangster who robbed, murdered, and stole, John Dillinger used a wooden gun as his first great escape prop. Unfortunately for him, it was his last.

A few months later Anna Sage, a whorehouse madam, tipped off East Chicago police as to John Dillinger's whereabouts, and the police in turn notified the Federal Bureau of Investigation. On July 22, 1934, as Dillinger was leaving the Biograph Theater in Chicago with Sage and his girlfriend, a waitress who sometimes worked for Sage, about two dozen G-men surrounded the theater and three gunned him down. Dillinger was thirty-one.

LOCATION: John Dillinger Museum, Nashville, Indiana.

Anne Frank's Diary

DATE: 1942 to 1944.

WHAT IT IS: The set of journals kept by a young girl while in hiding with her family and others during the Nazi occupation of the Netherlands in World War II.

WHAT IT LOOKS LIKE: The handwritten "diary" consists of an autograph-type album (in which the first entries were made), two exercise books (for later entries), and individual sheets of paper (on which the diary was being revised). The album is small, square, clothbound, and unlined; the exercise books have lined pages; and the loose sheets are colored and have no lines.

I feel as if I'm going to burst, and I know that it would get better with crying, but I can't. I'm restless, I go from one room to the other, breathe through the crack of a closed window, feel my heart beating, as if it is saying, "Can't you satisfy my longings at last?"

—Anne Frank,
February 12, 1944*

*Diary entries in this chapter from *Anne Frank: The Diary of a Young Girl* by Anne Frank. Copyright 1952 by Otto H. Frank. Used by permission of Doubleday, a division of Bantam Doubleday Dell Publishing Group, Inc.

A diary entry: "This is a photo of how I wish to be forever. Then I might still have a chance to go to Holywood. At present, unfortunately, most of the time I look different. Anne Frank, 10 Oct. 1942, Sunday."

The "Jewish Problem" had plagued the perverted leadership of the Nazi Party since their terrifying rise to power in the early 1930s. At first the Nazis liquidated Jewish businesses, segregated Jewish students, mandated Jews wear yellow stars on their arms, burned synagogues, and attacked Jews on the street. But then their violent hatred led them to their "Final Solution," the systematic extermination of the Jews, which they tried to achieve as efficiently as possible. The Nazis were scrupulous not only in rounding up Jews and collecting their valuables, but also in suppressing rebellions and destroying evidence of their own heinous acts. Yet there lives on the voice of one girl who was a victim of the genocide, whose poignant words would so deeply touch others, who would bear witness for all future generations to the living hell created by the Nazis.

Who has inflicted this upon us? Who has made us Jews different from all other people? Who has allowed us to suffer so terribly up till now?

—Anne Frank,
April 11, 1944

As conditions began to heat up in Hitler's Germany, a banker from Frankfurt, Otto Frank, took heed. Realizing that the very lives of Jews would soon be at stake, he, like other Jews, fled with his family. In December 1933 Otto Frank, his wife, Edith, and their daughter Margot settled in Amsterdam. Their youngest daughter, Anne, who was four, joined them there three months later.

Despite the persecution of Jews in other parts of Europe, the Franks lived a rather happy and peaceful life in Amsterdam. But Hitler continued to expand his empire, and by mid-May 1940 the Germans had conquered the Netherlands.

In his new country Otto Frank was a pectin manufacturer and trader. His business prospered, moving to different facilities until it finally settled at 263 Prinsengracht, a five-story building in Amsterdam. When the Germans took over, he had to transfer ownership of his business, but he was still very much admired by some of his employees.

When the Germans started deporting Jews, Frank devised a plan in which it would seem as though he had abandoned his business and fled with his family, but in reality they would hide in an annex, consisting of four rooms on two floors and an attic mainly used for the storage of food. On a warm July morning in 1942, a German Security Service call-up notice for Margot was delivered at the Franks' home; thousands of Jews, including many teenagers by themselves, were being summoned to report for emigration to concentration camps. This was a sign for Otto Frank that the time had come for him and his family to go into hiding. They "disappeared" into the annex of 263 Prinsengracht, their temporary haven of safety, where an intense drama would unfold over the next couple of years.

Four more protagonists were added to the annex: Friedrich Pfeffer, a dentist; and Mr. and Mrs. Hermann van Pels and their son, Peter. The staircase leading to the annex was blocked by a bookcase that concealed a door that had hooks to lock it. Food obtained from phony ration cards was provided daily for the residents. The four employees in the building, including Miep Gies and her husband, looked after the occupants of the annex with devotion.

"Prison" may be a more apt way of describing the lives of the occupants, because they truly felt like captives in their limited surroundings. For over two years they lived in forced proximity, not able to make a sound in the daytime, only able to break out of their hutch on evenings and on weekends. For all this time they could not venture outdoors in the daytime and feel the sun warm their faces. Instead, they had to be quiet, contain their moods and emotions, and get along as well as they could, all under the looming threat that at any moment the merciless Nazis could storm their confines and send them to someplace even worse.

> Again and again I ask myself, would it not have been better for us all if we had not gone into hiding, and if we were dead now and not going through all this misery, especially as we should be sparing the others. But we all recoil from these thoughts too, for we still love life, we haven't forgotten the voice of nature, we still hope, hope about everything. I hope something will happen soon now, shooting if need be—nothing can crush us more than this restlessness. Let the end come, even if it is hard; then at least we shall know whether we are finally going to win through or go under.
>
> —Anne Frank,
> May 26, 1944

For her thirteenth birthday on June 12, 1942, Anne Frank had been given an autograph album, which she used as a diary. Anne was a pretty girl, with black hair, a tender smile, and expressive eyes. Although she had not shone above her classmates in school, she was intelligent and had an eye for detail, and a simple but thorough and warm way of expressing herself. She wanted to become a writer or a journalist.

During her time in the annex, Anne blossomed from a girl into a young woman. In her diary she recorded not only the difficulties of being sequestered for so long with people of different personalities and how they lived under the pall of terror, but the painful transition of a girl on the verge of womanhood. She wrote of her conflicts with her mother, of her physical awakening, of her love for Peter. She addressed her entries to a fictional girl named "Kitty."

Adolescence is a period of confusion, of self-doubt. In her diaries Anne sought refuge and comfort from the hardships of her life and bared her soul, using code names for the other occupants as well as herself. She wrote in Dutch and filled nearly three journals. In March 1944 she heard the Dutch minister of education, art, and science in a radio broadcast from London say that descendants of the nation would best understand its struggle for freedom through ordinary documents such as letters and diaries. Excited by the prospect of making her contribution and proving herself as a journalist, Anne began revising her diary.

June 6, 1944, was D-Day; the Allies launched a massive attack on the Germans. At last, liberation seemed imminent! Despite their long and arduous confinement, the hidden Dutch occupants of 263 Prinsengracht were optimistic that they would soon resume normal lives. In her diary Anne wrote about the "Great commotion in the 'Secret Annex.' Would the long-awaited liberation that has been talked of so much, but which seems too wonderful, too much like a fairy tale, ever come true?"

Unfortunately, not for her and the others. Sometime after ten o'clock on the morning of August 4, 1944, a number of armed officers of the German Security Service came to arrest the Jews. Someone—perhaps a person they knew—had betrayed the inmates of the attic. The police ordered the bookcase moved and ascended the stairs. In the rooms above they found their bounty: eight Jews. The officers ravaged the room, confiscating valuables but ignoring Anne's papers, which fell to the floor along with books and magazines. The Jews were told to gather some personal items. Anne did so but left her diaries behind. In the early afternoon a truck came to take the prisoners away. A few days later they were transferred to Westerbork, a Jewish transit camp, or waiting room for the death camps in the east.

With more than a thousand other men, women, and children, the Franks were transported by train to Auschwitz. Like other families, they were split up. Edith and Otto stayed on at Auschwitz; less than two months later Margot and Anne were sent on to Bergen-Belsen. All except Otto would perish: Edith succumbed in Auschwitz; Margot and Anne were swept away by typhus. Anne's corpse was put into a mass unmarked grave, and to this day her burial spot is unknown. The other occupants of the annex fared equally tragically in the camps. Dr. Pfeffer died in Neuengamme, Mr. and Mrs. van Pels in Auschwitz, and young Peter in Mauthausen.

After the war Otto Frank returned to Amsterdam and lived for a few years with Miep Gies and her husband. About two months after his arrival, Otto Frank received news of the Frank girls' deaths. Miep Gies then presented to Otto his daughter Anne's papers. She had gathered them off the floor after the Nazis had left with their prey and had hoped to return them to Anne one day.

When the smoke of World War II cleared, the world learned about Hitler's concentration camps and the incomprehensible crimes committed by the Nazis. Living eyewitnesses to the reign of terror were few; six million Jews died. One such victim was Anne Frank. In her diary, which her father brought to publishers' attention, she conveys the plight of the Jews better perhaps than other, more direct accounts of the Holocaust. Her spirit persists, and her faith in the good of humanity will continue to reverberate in our hearts.

On April 4, 1944, about a year before she died at the age of fifteen, Anne Frank wrote, "I want to go on living, even after death!" With her heartrending diary, a work that evokes so splendidly both the courage and pathos of war, she has indeed achieved immortality.

LOCATION: Netherlands State Institute for War Documentation, Amsterdam, the Netherlands. (The autograph album, Anne Frank's first diary, is exhibited every so often at the Anne Frank House in Amsterdam.)

The *Enola Gay*

DATE: 1945.

WHAT IT IS: The aircraft that dropped the most devastating bomb ever unleashed upon a warring nation.

WHAT IT LOOKS LIKE: It is a four-engine, multiseat Boeing B-29 Superfortress bomber that measures 99 feet long and has a 141-foot wingspan. It has a pressurized crew compartment while at altitude and is made entirely of metal.

On August 6, 1945, the atomic age was graphically introduced to the world when the release mechanism within a single aircraft some thirty-one thousand feet above ground was activated, and a container packed with uranium fission material that could produce the equivalent of a twenty-thousand-ton TNT explosion fell toward Earth. The instrument of this historic apocalypse was the *Enola Gay*.

By July 1945 the United States had devised a weapon of unprecedented explosive power: the atomic bomb. At this point in World War II, Germany had already surrendered, but fighting continued with Japan, and both sides were suffering heavy casualties. The Potsdam Proclamation was broadcast on July 26, calling for the "unconditional surrender of all Japanese forces," with the alternative being "prompt and utter destruction." Two days later Prime Minister Kantarō Suzuki answered that Japan would disregard the proclamation. After Japan continued to show no signs of capitulating, plans were set in motion to drop the bomb.

• • •

The Glenn L. Martin Company of Omaha, Nebraska, was one of three manufacturers selected by the U.S. government to build B-29s during World War II, when about four thousand of these bombers were built. Of the Martin-built airplanes, twenty were selected to be reconfigured under a special project named Silverplate for anticipated deployment in the Pacific—namely, dropping the atomic bomb. All twenty of these planes, of which the *Enola Gay* was one, were delivered to a nearby air force modification center, where the gun turrets were removed in order to improve performance of the airplane, leaving only the twenty-millimeter tailgun, and the bomb bay was reconfigured for single-point suspension. All twenty of the Silverplate planes had the capability of dropping an atomic bomb; since the atomic age was new and the destructive power of the bomb wasn't known with certainty, this quantity of bombers ensured that atomic warfare could be continued if necessary.

While the modifications were being made, no one knew which of the twenty planes would be used—assuming the atomic bomb was produced successfully—if it was deemed necessary to drop the bomb. Nor did anyone know which among them would drop another atomic bomb (based on plutonium fission) on Nagasaki a few days later. The lot of aircraft was delivered to the U.S. Army Air Forces on May 18, 1945, and was accepted for service less than a month later.

Shortly afterward, one of the planes was selected to carry out the historic Hiroshima mission—should it be given a green light. The man designated to fly the plane was Colonel Paul W. Tibbets, Jr., a decorated bomber pilot. Tibbets named the aircraft after his mother, calling it the *Enola Gay*.

In mid-June 1945 the *Enola Gay* was ferried to the 393rd Heavy Bombardment Squadron at the air force base at Wendover, Utah, and two weeks later, after intensive training of its crew, it departed for Tinian, part of the Mariana Islands in the western Pacific Ocean. Regular bombing missions began early in July with the dropping of twenty conventional-type five-hundred-pound bombs that had been loaded into the *Enola Gay*, which then raided Marcus Island with several other planes. A total of four more training missions followed.

Two types of atomic bombs were used by the B-29s: "Fat Man" and "Little Boy." These descriptive names were based on the bombs' shape and method of detonation. The Fat Man was an implosion-type bomb, meaning that the detonation was set off so that it worked inwardly rather

The Enola Gay *lands at Tinian, Mariana Islands, on August 6, 1945, after having dropped the atomic bomb on Hiroshima.*

than outwardly to compress for fusion to yield an atomic explosion. The Little Boy had a gun-type mechanism that fired a detonator into the implosion substance to cause the explosion. (A Little Boy was dropped on Hiroshima by the *Enola Gay*, and a Fat Man was discharged on Nagasaki by the *Bockscar* [United States Air Force Museum, Wright-Patterson Air Force Base, Ohio].)

For the *Enola Gay*'s four practice runs, Fat Man–shaped practice bombs called "pumpkins" were used that would simulate the same fall trajectory as the real weapon. Two of these missions were flown against protruding rocks in the Pacific Ocean; two others were dropped upon pinpoint objects in target areas in Japan. Four caricatures of Fat Man are painted in black on the nose of the aircraft to mark these practice missions. Symbolizing the actual drop is a fifth and identical caricature painted in red. A Little Boy figure painted red would be more appropriate, but no one knows why this wasn't the figure used.

In July 1945 the components of the first atomic bomb to be used for warfare began their journey to Tinian, the point of assembly. From the secret research lab at Los Alamos, New Mexico, came the inner cannon that the USS *Indianapolis* would transport out of San Francisco. Other parts were sent by air.

Early on the morning of August 6, a crew of twelve men took off in the *Enola Gay* from the air base at Tinian on one of the most important and dangerous Allied missions of World War II. In the belly of the plane was a bomb weighing more than nine thousand pounds. Should the plane crash on takeoff—a not-uncommon occurrence for bombers at the time—or be attacked in the air, it could mean instant death for all on board. Besides the pilot, the thirty-year-old Colonel Tibbets, there was copilot Robert W. Lewis, weapons officer William Parsons, proximity fuse specialist Morris Jeppson, radar officer Jacob Beser, flight engineer Wyatt Duzenbery, bombardier Thomas W. Ferebee, radio operator Richard Nelson, tail gunner George R. Caron, radio operator Joseph A. Stiborik, flight engineer Robert Shumard, and navigator Theodore van Kirk.

At 8:15 A.M. the *Enola Gay* unleashed its lethal cargo into the skies above Hiroshima. As its crew donned special goggles to protect them from the blinding flash below, the *Enola Gay* banked steeply to the right to avoid being over the point of detonation. In the ensuing explosion and conflagration, 80,000 to 150,000 people died, either immediately or from subsequent radiation poisoning. No other single strike of a weapon ever took more lives, caused greater destruction, or had grimmer repercussions. Many survivors would suffer permanently from the radiation, and even their unborn would become casualties.

The plane returned to Tinian and three months later was flown to Roswell Air Force Base in New Mexico. By that time the plane had acquired considerable notoriety, but it wasn't retired yet. In April 1946 the plane was flown by Tibbets to Kwajalein, one of the Marshall Islands, where it served as a standby airplane in Operation Crossroads, in which further tests of atomic weapons were conducted.

The following July, the plane was flown back to the United States, and on August 30, 1946, it was placed in storage at the Davis-Monthan Army Air Force Base in Tucson, Arizona. Three years later the *Enola Gay* became part of the collection of the Smithsonian Institution and its National Air and Space Museum. It was ceremoniously flown on July 3, 1949, by Tibbets to the Smithsonian's gathering facility for museum aircraft in Park Ridge, Illinois, where it joined a myriad of other warplanes.

In December 1984 the National Air and Space Museum began restoration on the *Enola Gay.* One of the obstacles to the project was rebuilding the original release device, which no longer exists. The few photographs and drawings of the original were still classified, so the Smithsonian had to get them declassified in order to reconstruct it.

Over the years, much debate over whether the atomic bombing of Japan was necessary has ensued, especially around the time of the fiftieth anniversary of the bombings, in 1995. Two events planned for that year precipitated a heated international public reaction: the Smithsonian Institution's forthcoming exhibit on World War II and the atomic bomb (U.S. military veterans protested its initial sympathetic position to the Japanese), and the U.S. Postal Service's plan to issue a commemorative stamp picturing an atomic mushroom cloud, with the caption "Atomic bombs hasten war's end, August 1945." Essentially, the controversy pitted those who believe the atomic bomb was necessary to bring a quick end to the war against those who believe that atomic warfare was not justified.

Numerous questions have been debated since the bombings of Hiroshima and Nagasaki: Was there any other way the Allies could have proceeded? Would a conventional invasion of Japan by the Allies have saved more lives? How much longer would fighting have gone on if the United States didn't drop the bombs? Could the United States have targeted areas without civilian populations? Should the United States have demonstrated in some other way the lethal nature of its new atomic weapon to persuade the Japanese to surrender? Was President Truman prompted by racism in dropping the bomb? Did Japan's attack on Pearl Harbor, its abominable treatment of Allied POWs, and its commission of other atrocities and mass murders of innocent people during World War II show that it was a belligerent nation willing to stop at nothing to win? These and many other questions have been argued vigorously by people with different political ideologies. As far as the fiftieth anniversary commemorations were concerned, the Smithsonian ran a minimal exhibition, with a display of the forward fuselage of the *Enola Gay*, and the U.S. Postal Service scuttled its plan to issue the mushroom-cloud stamp.

In the end, one can only weigh the facts, and the two most essential facts are these: tens of thousands of people died as a result of the atomic bombs dropped on Japan, and eight days after the *Enola Gay* dropped the bomb over Hiroshima, Japan transmitted its unconditional surrender to the Allies, bringing to an end the most destructive conflict in humankind's history. Were the bombings justified? That question may never be resolved, but the *Enola Gay* will serve to remind future generations of the devastation of war.

LOCATION: Paul E. Garber Restoration, Preservation and Storage Facility, Suitland, Maryland. The *Enola Gay* will be moved for permanent exhibition to an extension site of the National Air and Space Museum after funding has been approved by Congress and the facility has been built.

Einstein's Brain

DATE: 1955.

WHAT IT IS: Brain matter from the great twentieth-century scientist Albert Einstein.

WHAT IT LOOKS LIKE: The brain is in several pieces, the largest of which measures approximately 3 inches by 2 inches. There are also thinly cut sections of brain tissue on microscopic slides.

At approximately eight o'clock on the morning of April 18, 1955, a forty-two-year-old pathologist stood before a corpse lying on a table in the morgue of Princeton Hospital in Princeton, New Jersey. As he prepared to make his first incision he glanced at the body, the famous face, and the bountiful snowy mane. The genius that had once resonated within this lifeless form had been extinguished less than seven hours before by a ruptured aneurysm.

As news of the man's death spread and members of the press converged on the hospital, the pathologist lifted his scalpel. Otto Nathan, a close friend of the deceased, stood at the foot of the table. The room was quiet, pin-drop still.

A tinge of excitement crept through the pathologist. Might this post-mortem uncover some secret of human intelligence, decode some labyrinthine oracle of cerebral ordination? For the pathologist was planning to extract and examine the brain of Albert Einstein.

Einstein's work was so abstruse that it was (and still is) beyond the grasp of most human beings. In his special theory of relativity he described how space and time in one frame are not absolute but functions of space and time in another frame. He demonstrated that light, previously regarded as a wave phenomenon, could also, paradoxically, be thought of as a stream of particles. His studies on statistical mechanics, Brownian motion, quantum physics, and radiation were all brilliant. And his theory of general relativity revolutionized scientists' concepts of gravity, space, time, mass, energy, and motion.

The first widespread acceptance of the German-born physicist's genius came in 1919 when astronomers tested his prediction that the force of gravity deflects starlight by a certain value, demonstrating space was "curved" by matter. On May 29, during a total eclipse of the sun, expeditions of British astronomers in equatorial Africa and South America observed and measured the bending of light waves coming from the stars. When they analyzed their work, they found that Einstein's calculation of the degree of deflection was almost exact. As a result, Einstein immediately received worldwide acclaim and was elevated to the pantheon of geniuses inhabited by the likes of Socrates, Aristotle, and Newton.

Only a handful of geniuses of the caliber of Einstein come along every millennium. It was even said that Einstein was the most brilliant being ever to have graced this Earth. The pathologist marveled: here was the opportunity of a hundred lifetimes! What benefits to humankind might result from the study of Einstein's brain?

The pathologist's name was Thomas Stoltz Harvey. Born in 1912 in Kentucky, he showed little interest in a medical career as a youth, although he did develop an early interest in nature. As a boy he would rise early in the morning to look for birds in the woods and creek near where he lived at the edge of Indianapolis. He graduated from West Hartford High School in 1930 and went on to college at Yale, where he majored in economics. Graduating in 1934 at the height of the Depression, he decided a career in business might not be the most prudent choice; he spent a year taking the requisite premed courses and in 1935 entered Yale Medical School.

The man who admitted Thomas Harvey to Yale was Milton Charles Winternitz, dean of the medical school and a professor of pathology. Dr. Winternitz was to be a strong influence in Harvey's later decision to become a pathologist.

In his senior year in medical school, Harvey came down with tuberculosis. At the time, there were no drugs to treat this disease, and the prescribed treatment was admittance to a sanatorium.

Harvey left medical school to convalesce, returning in time to graduate in 1941. Because of his health, Dr. Harvey had to find an internship that

Einstein's name may be synonymous with the word genius, *but he was also a great humanitarian.*

wouldn't require him to wake in the middle of the night. Under Winternitz's tutelage he became a pathologist and held positions in research, clinical medicine, and teaching.

In 1952 Harvey was hired by Princeton Hospital. Since the 1930s, Princeton, New Jersey, had been the home of Albert Einstein. Einstein had emigrated from Europe to work at the Institute for Advanced Study, and by the time Harvey arrived was already a living legend. As Einstein's health deteriorated in the 1950s, he was closely monitored by his personal physician, Guy Dean. Dr. Dean had occasionally requested Princeton Hospital to run lab tests on Einstein's blood, and Dr. Harvey would dispatch technicians to the scientist's house to draw his blood.

On one occasion, however, Harvey decided to go himself and meet the icon. He was conducted to a second-floor bedroom, where the renowned scientist was lying in bed.

Einstein looked up. On previous occasions, the technicians who came to draw his blood had all been women. The pajama-clad legend was surprised to see a male visitor at his door.

"I see you have changed your sex," Einstein noted wryly.

Harvey laughed. After a brief conversation, the doctor began to draw blood from Einstein's left arm. About fifteen minutes later Harvey left, elated to have had a pleasant chat with the great man. He never dreamed that the next time he saw Einstein, it would be at a morgue table, with Harvey making preparations to remove his brain.

The autopsy on the seventy-six-year-old mathematical wizard was conducted just as any other, the torso opened first, then the head. Dr. Harvey made an incision across the scalp, from behind one ear to the other, peeling the skin of the front half forward down over the face. Then he peeled back the skin remaining on the skull. He sawed through the bone and revealed Einstein's brain.

Harvey took great care not to damage the brain; to remove it was a delicate process. Otto Nathan, Einstein's friend, the executor of Einstein's estate and a professor of economics at New York University, continued to observe silently in the thirty-by-thirty-foot room on the ground floor in the back of Princeton Hospital.

Dr. Harvey cut the various blood vessels and nerves around the brain and the spinal cord. Finally, he reached into Einstein's open cranium and put his hands on the brain. It was soft and pink and felt like semisolid Jell-O. Then, holding his breath, he withdrew it.

Harvey immediately placed the brain on a spring scale hanging from the ceiling. The normal range in weight of the human male brain is 1,200 to 1,600 grams. (It is slightly less for females because of their smaller body size.) Einstein's brain weight of 1,230 grams fell into the normal male range, immediately casting in doubt a long-held theory that brain size and intelligence were correlated.

With a formaldehyde solution Harvey injected the arterial system of the brain to "fix," or harden and preserve, it. He then gently placed it in a large jar filled with a solution of formaldehyde. This immersion completed the fixing process.

Dr. Harvey finished the autopsy around 10:00 A.M. and met with a throng of reporters an hour later. He reported on the cause of death and announced his plans to examine the physicist's brain.

Einstein's body was to be cremated, pursuant to his wish. His family had requested that no one should know what time his corpse was going to arrive at the crematory, and workers there had a bit of difficulty getting the body in unnoticed by the photographers and reporters.

At around noon Einstein's body was deposited in a retort, and his flesh and bones turned to ashes. The ashes were placed in a cardboard container furnished by the crematory. The cost of the cremation was seventy-five dollars. It was two or three months before a professor from Princeton University came to pick up the remains, and he would not disclose where they were spread.

At the hospital, before proceeding to investigate the secrets of Einstein's brain, Dr. Harvey examined microscopically the tissues he had removed from the scientist's body during the autopsy. They showed arterial disease. Einstein had had a severe atherosclerosis of his abdominal aorta, which had finally ruptured. He had bled to death.

Harvey had had no conversations with Einstein prior to his death about removing his brain for study. Nor did he speak with Einstein's family about this, although in an article in the *New York Times* on April 20, two days after Einstein died, Otto Nathan reported that Einstein's son, Hans, had requested a scientific examination of the brain.

When the family was contacted by Nathan, according to Dr. Harvey, they were surprised to learn that the brain had been removed. They had wanted Einstein's entire body to be cremated. But once they were in-

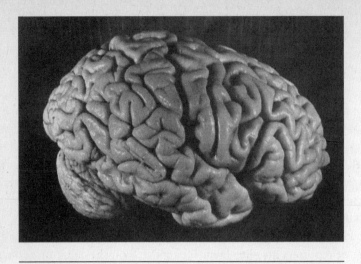

Einstein's brain shortly after it was removed during his autopsy.

formed of the nature and scope of Harvey's planned study, they gave their permission for the work to proceed, provided the results would be reported in scientific journals and no attempts would be made to sensationalize the findings.

Harvey had a plan for his investigation of the brain: he would section the brain into numerous pieces from which he would prepare microscopic slide sets, and these he would distribute to a handpicked group of top-notch medical experts for study. But first he took measurements and photographed the brain from different angles, with and without the meninges (the membranes that envelop the brain). When it was time to make the microscopic preparations, Harvey took the brain to the University of Pennsylvania laboratory in Philadelphia, where he had worked before Princeton.

It was in this laboratory, located in a medical school building in back of the UP hospital at Thirty-fourth and Spruce, that Thomas Harvey first cut Einstein's brain, sectioning it into approximately 170 pieces—far more than usual, but Dr. Harvey wanted a comprehensive study. The process was painstaking and took more than three months. The pieces were numbered, charts were drawn indicating the location of each segment, and the pieces were all photographed before and after the cutting. The technicians could handle only so much of the process at a time, and Dr. Harvey had to shuttle back and forth between Princeton and Philadelphia.

From these pieces, microscopic sections were cut. The sections were embedded in celloidin, a chemical that hardens tissue and is used for sectioning thin specimens to be examined under a microscope.

The tissue preparations were made by Marta Keller, a German histology technician with extensive experience in cutting brains. Keller used a tissue-cutting instrument called a microtome to slice thin sections of the celloidin blocks. The sections were mounted on glass slides and then stained so they could be examined under a microscope. Keller made a dozen sets of slides, each consisting of over one hundred slides.

Photographs were taken through microscopes of the various areas of Einstein's brain. Most were in black and white, but some were in color.

Although just tiny slices of inert material now, the slide specimens represented an exciting scientific treasure. If genius had any organic manifestation, it would certainly be here. What would Einstein's brain reveal?

Of the dozen sets of slides, Harvey retained two, which he took back to Princeton, and he distributed the remainder to his handpicked specialists. The key players were Gerhard Von Bonin and Percival Bailey, professors of neuroanatomy at the University of Illinois; Walli Nauta, a professor of neuroanatomy at MIT; Hartwig Kuhlenbeck, a professor of anatomy at Women's Medical College in Philadelphia; and Harry Zimmerman, of Montefiore Hospital in New York City and a Columbia University professor of pathology.

The recipients of the microscopic slide sets had no mandate from Harvey. They were given full rein to study the brain using their own methods and report back to Harvey at their convenience. Their general modus operandi would be to examine under the microscope the configuration, or cell architecture, of Einstein's brain and compare it with that of other human brains.

Anticipating good research, Harvey resumed his work at Princeton Hospital. He stayed there until 1962, when he left to do research at the New Jersey Neuropsychiatric Institute near Princeton.

Over the next decade or so, Harvey worked part-time in the psychiatric hospital systems of various New Jersey state hospitals. At the same time, he ran a commercial medical lab he started at Princeton, which he later moved when he changed jobs, until he finally sold it. He took Einstein's brain with him wherever he moved, keeping it at home or in his office.

Through the years, rumors abounded about Einstein's brain being investigated, but little was known publicly about it, and the research was all done in relative secrecy. Harvey, ever patient and hopeful, stayed in touch with the recipients of the microscopic slides, but strangely, there was never any announcement from them, nor was their work published. Eventually, Harvey came to expect that no startling differences would be found. Some researchers, such as Gerhard Von Bonin, who later moved to California, died. Harvey does not know what became of the slide sets used by these late investigators.

In 1975 Dr. Harvey accepted a job offer to run a large medical laboratory in Wichita, Kansas. He worked there for three years, then, in 1978, retired from laboratory work and moved to Weston, Missouri, to go into general practice. He practiced in Weston for a decade, also serving as the physician of the Kansas State Penitentiary near Leavenworth.

In the early 1980s Marian Diamond, a professor of physiology and anatomy at the University of California at Berkeley, contacted Harvey after her students sparked her interest in Einstein's brain. A science magazine had run a photo of Einstein's brain in a cardboard box sitting beside a desk, and Diamond's students mounted the picture on a classroom wall. It hung there for months. After seeing it day after day, Diamond, unaware of Harvey's ongoing investigation, finally said, "Nobody else has studied it and we have a database of [comparative information from normal human males], so why not take a look at it?"

Diamond, who had been studying brains for over forty years and had a special interest in how the environment can change the structure and function of the brain, had been conducting a study on the normal human male brain. She was investigating the neuron-glial ratios in the main association cortices, specifically in certain areas that are thought to be some of the most highly evolved parts of the human brain. (Glial cells are the structural and metabolic support cells for the nerve cells.) Diamond wanted to compare these same areas in Einstein's brain with the areas she had been studying in other human brains. She contacted Thomas Harvey and requested samples of Einstein's right and left superior frontal and right and left inferior parietal lobes. In a small mayonnaise jar, Harvey sent the requested four pieces of Einstein's brain embedded in celloidin.

Although this was now more than twenty-five years after the brain had been extracted, its cells were well preserved. Harvey's technique of fixing the brain had worked well.

Diamond and her assistants sliced and stained the pieces, counting the nerve cells and the glial cells. It was tedious work. Unlike chemistry research, in which tissue can be ground up, placed in a solution, and analyzed in a spectrophotometer, counting cells with the human eye (which can make better decisions regarding densities than scanners) is painstaking and can take several months or longer.

After months and months of counting cells, Diamond concluded that in all four areas—the right and left superior frontal and the right and left inferior parietal—Einstein had more glial cells per neuron than the average male, but in only one area, the left inferior parietal cortex, was the variation statistically significant. This, she believed, constituted the major difference between Einstein's brain and that of the ordinary human.

Although this would seem to be of significance, Diamond expressed caution about her findings. Scientists don't do research on one specimen and declare their results conclusive. Ten genius specimens would be needed, ten Einsteinian brains with the same results, to affirm a scientific truth. Diamond's work on Einstein's brain supports what she has found in more than thirty years of research on rats: that rats that use their brains actively (in what scientists call an "enriched environment") have more glial cells per neuron.

Diamond reported her findings in 1985 in *Experimental Neurology*, a professional journal. She is the only investigator to date to publish scientific research on Einstein's brain.

Harvey asked Diamond if she wanted to continue studying Einstein's brain, but she declined. She had no other databases from human brains with which to compare other aspects of Einstein's brain.

Although she has no future plans for studying Einstein's brain, Diamond has retained the four pieces, storing them in a slide box.

Einstein's brain continued to be itinerant over the next several years, as Harvey moved around, taking the brain with him and keeping it in his home or office.

In 1988 Harvey moved to North Carolina to work in hospital emergency rooms. He stayed only a year, then returned to live in Leavenworth, Kansas. Now retired from the medical field, he and his wife moved a short time later to Lawrence.

Today Harvey keeps the blocks of Einstein's brain in his home. The microscopic slides are in boxes that sit on a shelf, and the larger pieces are kept in jars. One small piece, from which no microscopic sections were made, is immersed in formaldehyde.

Indeed, within these boxes and jars rests the gray matter of one of history's all-time geniuses. When Einstein was alive, its cells were throbbing with the electrical and chemical signals that represented the "raw" form of $E = mc^2$. The extracted brain matter may be said to carry the imprint, the specter, the ghost of that primal formula of energy, which continues in the cells of millions of other brains today as an icon of scientific triumph.

The microscopic sections that were made consumed only a small portion of the brain. Dr. Harvey has kept all the pieces save a few he has sent to medical research laboratories to examine. Of the almost 170 blocks of Einstein's brain in Harvey's possession today, the largest is three inches by two inches, from the area of the frontal lobes. Harvey continues to diligently research Einstein's brain and plans one day to bequeath the blocks to a medical center.

Curiously, much of the material Princeton Hospital had on Einstein's autopsy disappeared. The whereabouts of the clinical record of his illness and the autopsy protocol are not known. And the specimens from Einstein's body that Harvey cut away during the autopsy for anatomical studies are gone too.

Although Einstein died in 1955, his brain tissue is still good and holds the promise of future revelations. With new scientific methods and equipment constantly being developed, new avenues of opportunity will no doubt arise for unlocking the physiological secrets of genius.

And there is always the fantastic possibility that in the future Einstein's brain could be cloned. Science has not yet identified the physiological basis of genius, so whether there is a genetic component of cerebral nerve cell chromosomes that could be cloned cannot be determined at the moment. But in the end, would it make a difference?

According to Harvey's investigation, Einstein's brain was not significantly different from any other human brain. It would indeed be a monumental discovery if some hidden ingredient were found in Einstein's brain that would reveal the secret of genius. But if not, the nature of genius remains all the more elusive.

"The most beautiful thing we can experience," Einstein once wrote, "is the mysterious." With his own brain matter shedding little light on why he was so blindingly intelligent, Einstein was the quintessential example of his own philosophy.

LOCATIONS: Approximately 170 pieces of the brain and two sets of slides: Lawrence, Kansas.

Four pieces of the brain: University of California at Berkeley (Lawrence Hall of Science).

Several pieces and slides: Japan, Australia, and Germany.

The Rifle That Killed
President Kennedy

YEAR: 1963.

WHAT IT IS: The weapon identified by the Warren Commission as the one used to assassinate John F. Kennedy.

WHAT IT LOOKS LIKE: It is a Mannlicher-Carcano 6.5-millimeter rifle with a telescopic sight and measures over forty inches long. It has various inscriptions on it, including the serial number C2766.

It was a day all those of a certain age can remember: where they were when they first heard the news, their shock, their grief. And the images that were continuously rebroadcast are indelibly imprinted in the minds of all Americans who lived through the harrowing event—the grassy knoll, the presidential motorcade winding through downtown Dallas, the smiling, waving president.

November 22, 1963, Dallas, Texas. *Air Force One* had landed late in the morning at Love Field, carrying President John Fitzgerald Kennedy, his wife, Jacqueline, and a small entourage. The airport was mobbed with people carrying welcome signs and cheering the president on his way to drive through the city and deliver a speech at the Trade Mart.

At about 11:50 A.M. central standard time, the presidential motorcade departed from Love Field. The president sat in the backseat of an open-top Lincoln limousine with Mrs. Kennedy. In front of them in the jump (pull-out) seat were Texas governor John B. Connally and his wife, Nellie, and in the front seat were two Secret Service agents, one of whom was the driver. In several vehicles behind the president's were additional armed Secret Service agents, Vice President Lyndon Johnson, members of the press corps, and various local VIPs.

When the trip was planned and the motorcade route through downtown Dallas chosen on November 1 at the White House, there was concern that the president might find antagonistic crowds in the Lone Star State and perhaps should not make the trip there. The anti-Kennedy sentiment in Texas ran deep, and just the week before, on October 24, Adlai Stevenson, the U.S. ambassador to the United Nations, was physically and verbally abused in Dallas after delivering a speech on the UN. But the president thought that going to Texas might boost his popularity in the state and infuse energy into the troubled Democratic Party there, which could be helpful in the upcoming 1964 election.

In his two years and ten months in office, President John F. Kennedy had had his share of successes and failures. Among his successes was the Soviet dismantling of nuclear missile bases in Cuba after he quarantined the island from receiving offensive military equipment, entering into a treaty with the Soviets to ban nuclear testing in the air and under water, establishing a Peace Corps to send American men and women overseas to help foreign countries, and establishing a ten-year program called Alliance for Progress to help countries south of the United States. The president's most notable failure was the Bay of Pigs debacle, in which CIA-trained anti-Castro Cuban exiles failed miserably in an attempt to take over Cuba in a surprise attack. But John F. Kennedy, America's youngest elected president, had an engaging charm and charisma about him that electrified the nation, and in the spirit of the Kennedy regime's glamour and vigor and quest for peace in the world, his administration was dubbed Camelot. Although Kennedy hadn't really been president long enough for history to judge his ability in the role, he resolutely desired a second term in office; given the challenges he faced, he thought it would not be too soon for him to begin campaigning for reelection.

With local newspapers having announced the route of the motorcade over the past few days, the streets of downtown Dallas were now lined with people waiting to catch a glimpse of the handsome young president; above the crowd, curious onlookers were peering out the windows of many buildings. The charge of excitement grew as the caravan of vehicles cruised into the area. Along Main Street the people cheered wildly, and the president and Mrs. Kennedy smiled and waved. There were more uproarious greetings on Houston Street. It was a warm autumn day in the South, and the president was not only relieved to find the crowds warm and friendly but thrilled that they received him so enthusiastically.

But as the Kennedys' car turned left onto Elm Street, it moved slowly toward disaster. Six floors above the ground, in the Texas School Book Depository building, a man was waiting by a window to shoot the president. Arranged behind him were stacks of cartons to prevent anyone on the floor from seeing him carry out his deadly mission. From his high perch, he could see the motorcade travel on Houston Street and turn onto Elm. As he observed the president's limousine approach in front of him, he peered through the telescopic sight of the rifle he held.

With the rifle supported on three cartons at the window at the southeast corner of the sixth floor, the sniper, later identified by the Warren Commission as Lee Harvey Oswald, focused on his moving target. The president was engaging in casual conversation in the car, enjoying the day, while Secret Service agents, planted on the side running boards of their backup vehicles, scanned the crowds for potential danger.

Without warning, at 12:30 P.M., cracks sounded and two bullets struck the president. One tore through the lower back of his neck and came out the front of his neck. Another entered the back of his head, splattering blood and brain tissue over the car; he then collapsed onto his wife, Jacqueline, seated to his left. Governor Connally, sitting on the right side of the limo directly in front of the president, was also wounded by a bullet. Jacqueline Kennedy cried out. People on the sides screamed and ran for cover or hit the ground. The scene was one of pandemonium. Mrs. Kennedy, apparently disoriented, turned and started crawling over the trunk of the limo just as a Secret Service agent jumped onto the rear of the vehicle. Mrs. Kennedy climbed back into her seat, and the vehicle, with the Secret Service agent now draped over President and Mrs. Kennedy, sped away.

As the president was being rushed to Parkland Memorial Hospital, Lee Harvey Oswald walked calmly out of the Texas School Book Depository (its name was changed in 1980 to the Dallas County Administration Building), which had been identified as the origin of the shots. He was empty-handed; the assassination rifle would be found later between boxes near the stairwell at the northwest corner of the sixth floor. Within minutes, a description of the suspected sniper—a witness claimed to have seen a gunman in the building—was broadcast. The police quickly zeroed in on the sixth-floor window of the building as the location from which the shots had been fired, but the gunman was already at large. At 1:00 P.M., after a hopeless effort by doctors to keep him alive, President John Fitzgerald Kennedy was pronounced dead. A Catholic priest administered last rites.

Lee Harvey Oswald was on the move. After leaving the Texas School Book Depository, he took a bus and cab to a street near his boarding-house, then walked to it, entered his room, and after staying there for only a few minutes, left. Then, walking along East Tenth Street, he was spotted by J. D. Tippit, a policeman who thought Oswald fit the assassin's description. As Tippit alighted from his car and approached him, Oswald drew a revolver and opened fire, immediately killing the officer.

By now, news of the forty-six-year-old president's death had reached across the nation, and people wept. It was almost inconceivable that the United States president was cut down in the prime of his years, in the full bloom and glory of his remarkable career. The New York Stock Exchange immediately shut down; businesses closed; schools let out early—the shock was incredible. Just as quickly, the news traveled around the world, and the outpouring of grief was tremendous.

Meanwhile, in Dallas, police continued the manhunt for the suspect, now a double murderer. Oswald made his way over to the Texas Theater, which he slipped into without paying, and took a seat (Texas Theater, Dallas, Texas). On the screen was the movie *Cry Battle*, which with *War Is Hell* composed a double feature. Before long, Oswald was surrounded by police, who converged on the theater after someone phoned in a tip. With the theater lights turned on, the police quickly identified the suspect, and after a brief scuffle—Oswald reached for his gun—he was apprehended and taken to police headquarters. Two days later, on November 24, Lee Harvey Oswald was to be transferred to the county jail. As he was being led through the basement corridor of the Dallas Police build-ing—the proceeding being televised live to the nation—a nightclub owner, Jack Ruby, stepped out from the crowd, thrust a gun to Oswald's stom-ach, and fired. Like JFK only days before, Oswald was rushed to Park-land Memorial Hospital, where he died shortly after 1:00 P.M. Ruby himself died at the same hospital in January 1967, succumbing to cancer before his second trial for the murder of Oswald.*

---

*After a long dispute over who owned the gun used to kill Oswald, a .38-caliber Colt Cobra, a jury in November 1990 awarded the weapon to the Ruby family. The execu-tor of Ruby's estate, Jules Mayer, claimed the gun belonged to him. In December 1991 Ruby's gun was sold at an auction in New York City for $220,000 to a private col-lector.

Who killed President Kennedy? On September 24, 1964, the Report of the President's Commission on the Assassination of President John F. Kennedy, also known as the Warren Commission Report, was presented to President Lyndon B. Johnson. From the evidence before it, the Warren Commission concluded that Lee Harvey Oswald fired the shots that killed John F. Kennedy and that he acted alone. That finding has long been the source of controversy; in September 1978 the House Select Committee on Assassinations (HSCA) opened hearings on the killings of President Kennedy and civil rights leader Martin Luther King, Jr. Regarding the Kennedy assassination, the committee reported that the three shots fired at Kennedy came from the sixth floor of the Texas School Book Depository and were triggered by Lee Harvey Oswald. From the acoustical evidence, mainly the recording of a police motorcycle's transmission, however, the committee concluded there were two gunmen involved in a conspiracy to kill the president. This evaluation was struck down in 1982 when the National Research Council, which studied the HSCA's acoustical evidence, questioned the conclusions of the HSCA, finding that its examination of the tape did not support the idea of two shooters.

A new American president, Lyndon Baines Johnson, came on board with the mission to lift the nation out of its throes of anguish and plot a course for the future. And with the new guard, new seeds were planted and new routes navigated that might not have been charted by the fallen president. For although Kennedy had brought Americans to the shores of Vietnam, he is said to have confided to close associates that after the 1964 election, he would withdraw troops in what he saw as a potentially futile war. Clearly, this changing of the guard marked the end of one era and the beginning of another.

Through the years numerous theories have been put forth attributing the assassination of John Kennedy to one conspiracy or another. Among the many culprits named have been the Mafia, Fidel Castro, Cuban exiles, Lyndon Johnson, the KGB, and the CIA. Many of the theories don't deny Lee Harvey Oswald as the assassin or as one of the assassins; it's just that, they tell us, he was merely a pawn in a large and complex game. In any case, the evidence is overwhelming that Lee Harvey Oswald shot John F. Kennedy on November 22, 1963, and that the rifle recovered on the sixth

The weapon that changed twentieth-century history. This rifle (with its scope), which cost less than twenty dollars, was used to assassinate President John F. Kennedy.

floor of the Texas School Book Depository was the weapon used to assassinate the president. As such, this weapon becomes a source of intrigue: How did Oswald acquire it and how was it determined that it was in fact the weapon from which the fatal bullet was fired?

As the Warren Commission Report tells us, shortly after the assassination and the discovery of the weapon, a Mannlicher-Carcano 6.5-millimeter rifle with the serial number C2766, FBI agents canvassed firearms dealers in Dallas for information on the rifle. They were told that the Mannlicher-Carcano, a rifle made in Italy, was distributed by a company in New York City called Crescent Firearms. The night of the assassination, November 22, law enforcement agents in New York City perused Crescent's records to find out to whom the C2766 was sold. An invoice showed that it went to Klein's Sporting Goods Company, located at 227 West Washington Street in Chicago, Illinois.

With the rifle bearing an uneffaced serial number and documentation existing from its original source of distribution, it wasn't difficult for law enforcement officials to follow the weapon's paper trail. An examination of the records of Klein's Sporting Goods, a firm that sold rifles by mail order, revealed to whom the rifle was shipped. A Klein's shipping order form showed that the C2766 was sold, with a nightscope, for $19.95 plus $1.50 for shipping, or $21.45 in total, to an A. Hidell, at P.O. Box 2915, Dallas, Texas. The purchaser remitted a U.S. postal money order made out to Klein's Sporting Goods in the amount of $21.45 and stamped with the date March 12, 1963. It was enclosed with a coupon from the magazine *American Rifleman*, on which the purchaser's name and address (a post office box) were written, as they had also been on the postal money order.

Post Office Box 2915 was in the Oak Cliff Station of Dallas. The application for this box showed that it was taken out on October 9, 1962, by a Lee H. Oswald (whose signature appears on the document) of 3519 Fairmore Road, Dallas, Texas. The "A. Hidell" name, as Dallas police found, was a pseudonym used by Lee Harvey Oswald. When he was arrested, he had identification on him using the Hidell name, including a Selective Service card signed by "Alek J. Hidell" with Oswald's photograph on it, and other identification was later found in his boardinghouse room with the Hidell name or a variation of it.

There was even more evidence that Oswald used the Hidell alias to order the rifle and that it was he who picked up the rifle mailed to Post Office Box 2915. Both the writing on the post office box rental application and on the rifle order form with the name A. Hidell were compared by handwriting experts with writing known to be in the hand of Lee Harvey Oswald, and their conclusion was that the writing on the rental application and on the order form was Oswald's. This was the same Lee Harvey Oswald who worked at the Texas School Book Depository and was seen in the Depository building on the day John F. Kennedy was assassinated, who was identified as the shooter of J. D. Tippit, and who was arrested later in the Texas Theater after putting up a struggle.

Shortly after the C2766 rifle was shipped by Klein's on March 20, 1963, Oswald asked his wife, Marina, a twenty-one-year-old woman from Russia, to take a photograph of him holding a rifle and some other objects. At the time the Oswald family—the couple had a young daughter—was renting a house on Neely Street in Dallas, and Oswald, as Marina later testified, had not owned any other rifle since she immigrated to the United States with him in 1962. Marina took two photographs of him, which since the assassination have been reproduced in a plethora of publications. The pictures show Oswald holding his rifle, as well as two different newspapers (they were radical political newspapers sold by subscription), and having a gun at his right side in a holster. From the dates of the newspapers, mailing intervals, and Marina's testimony, it was determined that the photos were taken around the end of March 1963. An FBI agent with expertise in photography took pictures of the C2766 rifle duplicating its position and the lighting conditions of the photos taken by Marina Oswald, and concluded that the rifle Oswald held was

Did Lee Harvey Oswald, pictured above, plan to kill President John F. Kennedy when he posed for this picture around the end of March 1963? Oswald asked his wife Marina to take this picture in the backyard of their Dallas home less than 8 months before Kennedy was killed.

either the same rifle recovered at the Depository after the assassination or another 6.5-millimeter Mannlicher-Carcano just like it. Comparing a negative of a picture he snapped with a camera that Marina Oswald testified she used to take the two pictures of her husband holding the rifle, and the surviving negative of one of the two Marina Oswald photographs, the agent concluded also that Marina's photos came from the camera she testified she used and that her two photos were not retouched.

Other evidence was examined by leading investigators to identify Lee Harvey Oswald as JFK's assassin. On the day of the assassination Oswald was seen carrying a paper bag (presumably with the disassembled rifle) into the Texas School Book Depository; a paper bag found near the alleged shooting window contained Oswald's fingerprint and palm print; Oswald's fingerprints were found on cartons near the same window. For two months prior to the day of the assassination, Oswald kept his rifle wrapped in a blanket in the garage of Ruth Paine, a woman who lived near Dallas with whom Marina had been staying. When police came to the Paine home and looked at the blanket in the garage, the rifle was missing.

Of course the C2766 was examined for fingerprints. Dallas police found it and dusted it for prints before forwarding the rifle to the FBI. An FBI latent print expert concluded that the fragments of fingerprints he lifted were insufficient for identification purposes, but a palm print had been lifted by a Dallas police lieutenant and it was positively identified as the palm print of Lee Harvey Oswald. (Palm prints, like fingerprints, are unique to individuals and can be used for identification purposes.)

Additionally, a comparison was made of fibers found on the rifle and on the shirt Lee Harvey Oswald was wearing when he was arrested, and an expert concluded that based on color, fabric, freshness, and other characteristics, they could have come from the same shirt. (A definite match can normally not be made in such circumstances; since more than one shirt of a certain kind is normally manufactured, one cannot say that fibers found as evidence came from a specific item of clothing.)

Ballistics tests were carried out by firearms experts (mostly from the FBI) to determine if the bullet fragments, cartridge cases, and an almost intact single bullet that were recovered came from the rifle found on the sixth floor of the Texas School Book Depository. When a rifle discharges a bullet, it leaves a unique imprint, or signature, on it that may be compared to those of bullets known to have been fired from the same weapon. If the markings on the bullets (or fragment of the bullet in question) match, the bullets can be positively identified as emanating from the same weapon. Cartridge cases may be tested in the same way, for they are

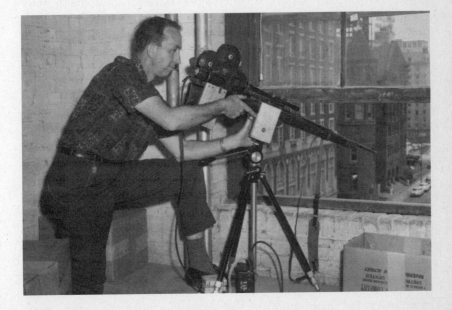

Using a 16-millimeter motion picture camera mounted on the rifle allegedly used by Lee Harvey Oswald to shoot President Kennedy, Special Agent Lyndal Shaneyfelt photographs the street scene below during a reenactment of the assassination conducted by the FBI on May 24, 1964.

also left with distinctive markings on their bases after being fired. Various items were recovered: three spent cartridge shells from the floor around the sixth-floor southeast corner window; bullet fragments from the vehicle the president rode in; a nearly intact bullet that presumably fell out of the stretcher on which Governor Connally was carried into Parkland Memorial Hospital. Ballistics tests revealed that the recovered materials were fired from the Mannlicher-Carcano C2766 rifle found on the sixth floor.

There were bullet wounds in the back and side of Kennedy's head and in the back of his neck (the wound at the front of his neck had been obliterated by the tracheotomy performed at Parkland Memorial Hospital). It is important for law enforcement authorities to know which wounds are points where a bullet entered the body and which are points where a bullet exited, because this information can be helpful in revealing the location of the shooter, as well as in disputing locations of shooters alleged by witnesses or others. Experts determined that the rear head and rear neck wounds on President Kennedy were points of entry, and the side head wound was where the bullet that entered his skull exited, leading them to conclude that the president was shot from behind. Based on various series of tests, experts also concluded that John Kennedy's head wounds were consistent with those produced by 6.5-millimeter bullets, and the alleged assassination weapon, and from the distance of the window from which the shots were allegedly fired.

Two bullets struck President Kennedy, and one hit Governor Connally, allegedly from the sixth-floor southeast corner window of the Depository. To confirm the trajectory of the bullets and the location of the victims—as supported by medical evidence, eyewitness accounts, and films taken on home movie cameras by some bystanders, the most famous of which is the 8-millimeter film taken by Abraham Zapruder—the assassination scene was re-created. A similar vehicle substituted for the original, stand-ins appeared for President Kennedy in the rear seat and Governor Connally in front of him, and the C2766 rifle with a motion picture camera attached to it was positioned at the sixth-floor southeast corner window of the Texas School Book Depository. Frames of the Zapruder film enabled law enforcement authorities to determine when the victims were struck. With the rifle and camera focused on the wounds of the "victims" (the stand-ins with wounds marked on their bodies in the spots where Kennedy and Connally were hit), the angles were measured and were

The Rifle That Killed President Kennedy

shown to match the trajectories of the bullets that caused the wounds of the real-life victims.

As mentioned, an analysis of the Zapruder film showed the approximate frames when President Kennedy was struck by each bullet. It also helped show that the bullet that struck Governor Connally was the same one that pierced the back of the president's neck. According to firing tests made with the C2766, this bullet exited the front of Kennedy's neck at a velocity of almost 1,800 feet per second, before striking Connally, who was sitting in the jump seat. These findings were also confirmed by the reenactment.

The number of shots fired varied according to the eyewitnesses, ranging from two to six. Various acoustical phenomena resulting from the firing of a weapon can account for people perceiving more shots fired than were actually discharged, and tests, film analyses, and other factors led experts to conclude that at least two shots were fired, each hitting President Kennedy (one of which struck Governor Connally), and that probably a third shot was fired, missing all the occupants of the vehicle. The order of the shots—which one missed the occupants, which struck the president in the back of the neck, and which one hit him in the back of the head— could not be determined.

In contemplating the immensity of the crime allegedly perpetrated by Lee Harvey Oswald, one might consider the unlikelihood of a number of serendipitous events in his favor: the serendipity that led him to the location where he pulled the trigger, the serendipity that the Secret Service did not prevent him from shooting the president, the accurate precision with which he hit his target six stories down on the street below.

Regarding the firing of deadly shots from the sixth floor, firearms experts testified that that would not be difficult for a sharpshooter, which was what Oswald had become when in the marines in the 1950s. The distance from the rifle pointed out the sixth-floor southeast corner window to the spot where Kennedy was sitting—determined through eyewitness accounts and an analysis of the frames of the motion pictures taken by bystanders at the time the shots were fired—was calculated to be just over 265 feet. Although his target was moving slowly, Oswald, as a sharpshooter, should have had no difficulty hitting a mark under three hundred feet with the aid of a telescopic sight.

Law enforcement guidelines are often made after a terrible event, and at the time of the assassination Secret Service agents did not make thorough searches of buildings for potential dangers to the president, nor was it against policy for the president to ride in an open-top limousine. President Kennedy, in fact, had ridden in open-top limousines in motorcades on several previous occasions—both in the United States and in foreign countries—sometimes standing or sitting high out of the rear of the vehicle. Although Kennedy was aware of the potential danger of this routine, he accepted it as a necessary hazard of politicking.

Among the more remarkable, if not downright bizarre, circumstances of the assassination is the extraordinary coincidence that led Oswald to be working at the Texas School Book Depository at the very time when the motorcade route was being planned. One could conceivably pick any point in a person's life to begin an examination of the random occurrences that led the person to a certain place at a certain time, but an apt point to focus on for purposes of a cursory examination of Oswald would be October 14, 1963. In a way, this is a pivotal date in the random occurrences that led President Kennedy's assassin to the post from which he would carry out his execution.

It was on October 14, 1963, that Ruth Paine of Irving, Texas, informed the unemployed Lee Harvey Oswald that he might be able to find a job at the Texas School Book Depository on Elm Street in Dallas. At the time, Oswald's wife, Marina, was staying with Paine until he found work. But while Oswald was ostensibly looking for work—the previous April he went to New Orleans and found a menial job—he was also carrying on questionable political activities. In New Orleans he handed out literature supporting Fidel Castro (as a result of this he got into a fight and was arrested, and he even requested an interview with the FBI), and in September he took a bus to Mexico City and visited the Cuban and Soviet embassies there to obtain visas to travel to these two countries.

Unsuccessful in obtaining the visas, Oswald returned to Dallas, where he continued his job search and rented a room in a boardinghouse, visiting his wife, who would continue to stay at the Paine house until he could find employment. Marina was a Russian whom Oswald had met in the Soviet Union early in 1961 after he was granted permission to stay in the country—he attempted to commit suicide there the previous October after being denied Soviet citizenship—and married a short time later. After the Oswalds resettled in Dallas, where Lee's mother and brother lived, they met Ruth Paine, who took a liking to Marina and wanted to help her while her husband was unemployed.

On October 14, after having been told by a friend of a possible job opening, Ruth Paine called the Texas School Book Depository to inquire about it. She told Oswald, who interviewed for the job the next day; two days later, on October 16, he began work there as a shipping clerk.

When Oswald started working at the Depository he may have already harbored a desire to kill the president. (It would not be his first attempt at murder. On April 10, 1963, Oswald had fired a shot into the ground-floor window of a retired army general and devout anti-Communist, General Edwin A. Walker.) But whether he had the idea or not, at some point between October 16 and November 22, he firmly decided that he wanted to kill John F. Kennedy. Undoubtedly the decision was hastened by the announcement that the president was coming to Dallas, but regardless of when the idea materialized, it was sheer serendipity for Oswald, if you will, that he was only recently hired to work in a building that happened to be along the motorcade route chosen for President Kennedy when he was in town.

As mentioned earlier, over the years elaborate conspiracy theories for the assassination of President Kennedy have been put forward, advancing the involvement of gangsters, heads of foreign governments, secret police, and high-level U.S. government officials and officeholders. But what if the assassination was all the work of one person? It is disconcerting to think that in modern times such a tremendous crime could be perpetrated by a single determined, if deranged, individual. But while the question of whether others were involved will undoubtedly continue to be debated— the various theories set forth embraced by members of the public—there has been no hard-core, concrete evidence to dispute the findings of the Warren Commission. The evidence as it stands overwhelmingly points to President John Fitzgerald Kennedy being shot from the sixth-floor southeast corner window of the Texas School Book Depository by Lee Harvey Oswald, who took aim through his $7.17 nightscope and fired with his $12.78 Mannlicher-Carcano 6.5-millimeter rifle.

Today the C2766 rifle, along with the clothes John F. Kennedy wore on November 22, 1963, Abraham Zapruder's motion picture camera, a piece of the curbstone along Elm Street which is believed to have been struck by a bullet that missed Kennedy, and numerous other remnants of one of the grimmest episodes of American history, lies sequestered in a locked shelving section within a locked room that may only be accessed by certain National Archives staff members. The rifle is stored in a custom-made acid-free box built by National Archives conservators and will not shift around and possibly sustain damage when the box is handled.*

LOCATION: National Archives, College Park, Maryland.

---

*Abraham Zapruder's 8-millimeter color film of the assassination is maintained in cold storage in a separate vault with limited access at the National Archives.

Voyager 1 and Voyager 2's Gold-Plated Phonograph Record for Extraterrestrials

DATE:	1977.
WHAT IT IS:	A two-sided metal record containing pictures, music, Earth sounds, and multilingual Earth greetings for any creature or civilization that may find it in outer space and thereby gain an understanding of life on Earth in the twentieth century. All the information is encoded on a single disk playable at 16⅔ revolutions per minute. The same record is aboard the spacecraft *Voyager 1* and *Voyager 2* and is accompanied on each ship by a stylus and cartridge.
WHAT IT LOOKS LIKE:	The record has a diameter of twelve inches and is made of copper and coated with gold. It is actually two metal discs pressed together to form a single record. An aluminum jacket protects the record, which is mounted to the outside of the spacecraft.

As time marches on here on Earth, twin spacecraft are speeding through the cosmos bearing not just the normal complement of scientific instruments but also a very special cargo: a quintessential collection of images and sounds of life on Earth. The phonograph record on which these are encoded is intended to serve as an emissary of the human race in the event that the spacecraft are encountered sometime in the future by the intelligent inhabitants of a distant solar system.

The vehicles bearing this ambassador to the cosmos are two identical robotic spacecraft that were launched in 1977 to survey the solar system's four large outer planets—Jupiter, Saturn, Uranus, and Neptune—and

Greetings from Earth! *As each second passes, the spacecraft carrying this metal record embodying images and sounds of life on the third planet travel deeper into space.*

their moons, rings, and magnetic fields. The mission took advantage of an uncommon alignment of the outer planets at the time, enabling the spacecraft to use a technique called "gravity assist" to go from one planet to the next in a relatively short period. With this technique, a spacecraft's path is bent as it flies by a planet, and its speed increased to send it to the next heavenly body in its flight path.

Voyager 2 was launched first, on August 20, followed by *Voyager 1* on September 5. *Voyager 2* encountered Jupiter on July 9, 1979, Saturn on August 25, 1981, Uranus on January 24, 1986, and Neptune on August 25, 1989. *Voyager 1* made its closest approach to Jupiter on March 5, 1979, and Saturn on November 12, 1980; then its trajectory caused its path to be bent, and it ejected from the plane in which the planets orbit the sun. The spacecraft performed their missions superbly, sending back to Earth data and pictures of their encounters with the planets and their satellite systems, and gave scientists the opportunity to make some spectacular discoveries.

The *Voyager*s are the creation of the National Aeronautics and Space Administration's Jet Propulsion Laboratory, which is managed by the California Institute of Technology. About eight months before the launch of *Voyager 2*, Dr. Carl Sagan, a distinguished astronomer, author, and professor at Cornell University who was responsible for the interstellar messages put on the plaques placed aboard the Jupiter-probing spacecraft *Pioneer*s 10 and 11 in the early 1970s, was assigned the prodigious task of collecting the images that, in the limited space of a two-hour long-playing phonograph record, would reveal to interested extraterrestrial life-forms the nature and history of humans and the planet we live on.

Sagan and his team of compilers and consultants enthusiastically embraced the project. They needed all their enthusiasm because the entire collection had to be assembled within such a short time. The challenge was to make a representative selection of the vast visual and audio repertoire of Earth and its inhabitants. Sagan and his collaborators decided to include information in four categories: music, natural Earth sounds, pictures, and greetings.

Because the selections were meant to represent all the people of Earth, the compilers were judicious in their choices to avoid limiting the record's content to any particular human society. Overall, the final selections are characterized by their generic quality.

The pictorial portion of the record attempts to present the kinds of animal and plant life of the planet, the varieties of human life, man-made structures, technology, and the planet itself. Images showing humans fighting, suffering from illness, or living in squalor were avoided, as were any with political implications. The visual images were converted by sophisticated equipment into analog audio signals that were cut into the record.

Among the 118 images including some labeled diagrams and silhouettes collected by artist and writer Jon Lomberg were a DNA molecule, cell division, human sex organs, human fertilization and birth, a mother and her baby, a father and his son, and a family; people from around the world, a schoolroom, a person looking through a microscope, people consuming food, and a barn-building scene; different kinds of houses, the Great Wall of China, the United Nations, and an observatory; a highway, a bridge, an airplane, a train, and a rocket; a sheet of music, a book page, and an abbreviated mathematical dictionary; a diagram of continental drift, a valley, a seashore, sand dunes, a river, and a harbor; a forest, a sequoia tree, a leaf, and a daffodil; an insect, a family of chimpanzees, a crocodile, a toad, a fish, and a school of dolphins.

The goal in gathering the music was to find inspiring selections that reflected the various cultures on Earth. The diverse musical menu of twenty-seven pieces amassed by writer Timothy Ferris and his collaborators included: the "Queen of the Night" aria from Mozart's opera *The Magic Flute*; Bach's "Gavotte en rondeaux" and the first movement of the Bach Brandenburg Concerto No. 2 in F; "El Cascabel," a Mexican mariachi tune; "Cranes in the Nest," a Japanese tune played on a bamboo flute; "Melancholy Blues," played by Louis Armstrong; "Sacrificial Dance," from Stravinsky's *Rite of Spring*; a puberty rite song of female Mbuti pygmies from Zaire; "Kinds of Flowers," a piece performed by a Javanese orchestra and singers; Chuck Berry's "Johnny B. Goode"; the first movement of Beethoven's Fifth Symphony; a Peruvian wedding song; and a Navajo Indian chant.

The spectrum of natural Earth sounds compiled by Ferris and novelist Ann Druyan included a volcano, thunder, rain, wind, and surf, the clip-clop of a horse, a dog barking, a chimpanzee shrieking, a bird singing, and a cricket chirping; footsteps, heartbeats, laughter, an infant crying, and a kiss; a car, bus, train whistle, trucks, jet, rocket liftoff, and a tonal sequence mathematically representing planetary motion.

The "greetings" portion of the *Voyagers*' record, compiled by Linda Salzman, demonstrated the friendly nature of humans and the variety of spoken languages on Earth. This portion was also intended as an invitation to extraterrestrials to communicate with Earthlings.

Among the greetings—in fifty-five languages and ranging from a single word to a few sentences—were the following: Luganda, "Greetings to the inhabitants of the universe from the third planet Earth of the star the sun"; Serbian, "We wish you everything good from our planet"; Welsh, "Good health to you now and forever"; French, "Good day to the entire world"; Persian, "Hello to the residents of far skies"; Nguni, "We greet you, great ones. We wish you longevity"; Greek, "Greetings to you, who-ever you are. We come in friendship to those who are friends"; English, "Hello from the children of planet Earth"; Hungarian, "We are sending greetings in the Hungarian language to all peace-loving beings in the uni-verse"; Latin, "Greetings to you, whoever you are. We have goodwill to-ward you and bring peace across space"; Amoy, "Friends of space, how are you all? Have you eaten yet? Come visit us if you have the time"; He-brew, "Peace."

Engraved on the aluminum cover protecting each record are instruc-tions in the form of scientific drawings that explain how the record may be played with the stylus and cartridge. The aluminum covers should pro-tect the records in interstellar space, which is an almost perfect vacuum, for at least a billion years.

The chance of either *Voyager* spacecraft being met by extraterrestrials is remote, at least in the near future. With their set flight paths, it may be billions of years before they enter another planetary system. At present, they are both racing out of our solar system at a speed of about 38,000 miles per hour. They are expected sometime after the year 2000 to pass the edge of the solar system, which according to many scientists lies not at the outermost planet but far beyond, in what is called the heliopause (this is where the sun's influence in space ends, and may be thought of as an invisible line between the end of the sun's magnetic field and interstellar space). Both *Voyager 1* and *Voyager 2* will eventually plunge into the darkness of outer space and cruise endlessly in the heavens. In interstellar space, since the stars move much faster than the *Voyager* spacecraft, the stars will move past the *Voyager*s rather than the other way around.

It will take both *Voyager*s about 20,300 years to travel one light-year. In the year A.D. 8751, *Voyager 2* will be 4.03 light-years (one light-year is approximately six trillion miles) from Barnard's Star. Its next encounter will be in the year 20,319, when it will pass 3.21 light-years from Proxima Centauri, the star nearest to Earth after the sun (it is 4.28 light-years from our planet). Its next stellar flyby, within 3.47 light-years of Alpha Centauri, will take place in 20,269. In 23,274, it will be 4.6 light-years from the Star of Lalande; in 40,176, it will be 1.65 light-years from Ross 248, a star in the constellation Andromeda; and in the year 957,963, *Voyager 2* will zoom by the star DM+27 1311 at a distance of 6.62 light-years.

In 40,000 years *Voyager 1* will be 1.6 light-years from star AC+79 3888, which is in the constellation Camelopardalis. This will be about the same time that *Voyager 2* is approximately 1.65 light-years from Ross 248.

Even if the records, titled *The Sounds of Earth*, are never found by intelligent alien beings, one cannot help but wonder whether, millions of years in the future, some child of humankind on an intergalactic cruise will spot *Voyager 1* or *Voyager 2* moving silently along in its orbit of the Milky Way and be curious enough to retrieve the record. At that point in the future, Earth will most likely be a lifeless ball of molten rock, burned out by the expansion of the dying sun. Of all that humans have ever created, of all the manifestations and symbols of freedom, technology, culture, and creativity, this ancient record bearing sounds, pictures, music, and greetings may be one of the very few remaining artifacts of Earth history.

LOCATION: Outer space.

ACKNOWLEDGMENTS

Grateful acknowledgment is made to all those who kindly shared their special expertise in history or in a particular artifact or object with me. These people are listed below, with expanded acknowledgments for those whose assistance was thoroughly invaluable.

Introduction:
Dr. James F. Strange, University of South Florida; Terence C. Charman, Imperial War Museum; Marjorie L. Caygill, British Museum; Dr. B. C. Benedikz, University of Birmingham; David Meschutt, West Point Museum; Folger Shakespeare Library; Dr. John Langellier, Gene Autry Western Heritage Museum; Magen Broshi, Israel Museum; Dawn Whitman, Welcome Museum of the History of Medicine, Science Museum; George Tselos, Edison National Historic Site; Gail DeBuse Potter, Nebraska State Historical Society; Mark J. Meister, Archaeological Institute of America; Dr. Eva Hanebutt-Benz, Gutenberg-Museum; Joe Pinkston, John Dillinger Museum; Thomas Sworenzer, University of Kansas; Bernard S. Finn and Harry Hunter, National Museum of American History.

Black Stone of the Ka'bah:
Islamic Center, Washington, D.C.; Mohammed Magid; Imam Dr. Mohammed Shamsher Ali; Dr. Abdel-Rahman Osman.

Lucy the Hominid:
Dr. Eric Meikle, Institute of Human Origins, Berkeley, California.

Code of Hammurabi:
Annie Caubet, Musée du Louvre, Paris.

Black Obelisk:
Dr. Irving Finkel, British Museum, London.

Rosetta Stone:
Dr. Robert Brier, Long Island University (C. W. Post campus, Brookville, New York); Col. Armand J. Gelinas, M.D.; Society of Antiquaries, London; Carol A. R. Andrews, assistant keeper, British Museum.

Veil of the Virgin:
Abbé Joseph Hercouët, Cathédrale Notre-Dame de Chartres, Chartres, France; Dr. Chuck Talar; Paul C. Maloney; Ken Cavanagh.

Crown of Thorns:
Dr. Chuck Talar; Paul C. Maloney.

Holy Lance:
Rene M. Querido, Rudolf Steiner College, Fair Oaks, California; Dr. Peter Knotz; Paul C. Maloney; Arch. Pierluigi Silvan, Fabrica di S. Pietro in the Vatican; Ken Cavanagh.

Shroud of Turin:
For this chapter I am very much indebted to Paul C. Maloney, general projects director for the Association of Scientists and Scholars International for the Shroud of Turin, Ltd. (ASSIST), Garnerville, New York, and author/editor of *The Shroud of Turin: A Case Study in Document Authentication* (Binghamton, N.Y.: Haworth Press, in preparation). He provided much valuable information, proofread the manuscript, and suggested rewrites at numerous points, many of which were incorporated in the body of the text. Mr. Maloney was a constant source of information for many other chapters, continually answering questions and providing a wealth of facts. I cannot overstate my gratitude for his kind and generous help.

Rubens Vase:
Dr. Gary Vikan, Walters Art Gallery, Baltimore.

Antioch Chalice:
Dr. Marlia Mundell Mango; Dr. Gary Vikan; Thomas Hoving.

Book of Kells:
I am most grateful to the late Archbishop George Simms of Dublin, Ireland, one of the most eminent modern authorities on this work. Also Daithi O'Ceallaigh, consulate general of Ireland in New York City, and Bernard Meehan and the Trinity College Library, Dublin, Ireland.

Bayeux Tapestry:
Sylvette Lemagnen, conservateur de la Bibliothèque municipale et de la Tapisserie de Bayeux, Bayeux, France.

Holy Child of Aracoeli:
Father Bernardino Di Prospero, Convento S. Maria in Aracoeli, Rome, Italy.

Columbus's Books of Privileges:
Rosemary Fry Plakas, the Library of Congress's American history specialist in its Rare Book and Special Collections Division, made me aware of these volumes and told me the story of the volume in the Library of Congress in Wash-

ington, D.C. An authority on Columbus's Books of Privileges, she proofread the chapter and filled in gaps; I am very grateful to her. Also Rosario Parra Cala and María Antonia Colomar of Archivo General de Indias in Seville, Spain; Dr. Flavia Sartore, director of the Comune di Genova in Italy; Monique Constant, chief conservator in the History Division at the Ministère des Affaires Étrangères, Paris; Juan Guillén Torralba, director of the Biblioteca Columbina y Capitular, Seville.

Cantino Map:
I am grateful to Dr. Ernesto Milano, director of the Estense Library, Modena, Italy, who provided much valuable information in his letters to me.

Hope Diamond:
Generous assistance for this chapter came from Mary Winters, formerly a research assistant at the National Museum of Natural History, Washington, D.C., and one of the great experts on the Hope Diamond; Russell C. Feather, Department of Mineral Sciences, National Museum of Natural History; Elise B. Misiorowski and the Gemological Institute of America, Santa Monica, California.

Edmond Halley's Astronomical Observation Notebooks:
I was fortunate to have the kind assistance of Adam J. Perkins, the Royal Greenwich Observatory archivist, Department of Manuscripts and University Archives, Cambridge University Library, Cambridge, England. Not only did Mr. Perkins provide the relevant information, he always responded to my letters promptly and comprehensively. Also Professor A. Boksenberg, Royal Greenwich Observatory, Cambridge.

Declaration of Independence:
Dr. Gerard Gawalt, Library of Congress (Manuscript Division); Elissa O'Loughlin and Milton O. Gustafson, National Archives, Washington, D.C.

George Washington's False Teeth:
I am especially indebted to Dr. H. Berton McCauley, 1991 president, American Academy of the History of Dentistry, Baltimore, Maryland. Valuable assistance also came from Dr. Andrew Christopher; Dr. Gardner Patrick Henry Foley, who sent me a box full of old notes, newspaper clippings, pictures, and other materials relating to Washington's dentures from his collection; Christine Meadows, Mount Vernon Ladies' Association; Barbara Easton, National Museum of Dentistry, Baltimore; Jonathan Evans, Royal London Trust.

Crypt of John Paul Jones:
James W. Cheevers, United States Naval Academy Museum, Annapolis, Maryland.

HMS Victory:
Colin S. White, chief curator, Royal Naval Museum, Portsmouth, Hampshire, England.

Vice Admiral Lord Nelson's Uniform Coat:
P. M. Blackett Barber, curator of uniforms, medals and weapons, National Maritime Museum, Greenwich, London.

Star-Spangled Banner:
Dr. Harold D. Langley, curator of naval history, National Museum of American History, Washington, D.C.; Scott S. Sheads, Fort McHenry National Monument and Historic Shrine, Baltimore; Francis O'Neill, Maryland Historical Society, Baltimore. Dr. Langley noted that scholars such as Walter Lord, Scott Sheads, P. W. Filby, and Edward G. Howard have greatly advanced our understanding of the Fort McHenry battle, the flag known as the Star-Spangled Banner, and Francis Scott Key's lyric poem of the same name.

Napoleon's Penis:
I am especially grateful to the distinguished Napoleon authority Col. J. Armand Gelinas, M.D., retired; Gayle L. Petty, Library Company of Philadelphia; Leslie Morris, Rosenbach Library, Philadelphia; Bruce Gimelson; Dr. John K. Lattimer; Robert M. Snibbe and the Napoleonic Society of America, Clearwater, Florida.

London Bridge:
Elrose M. Dussault, former historian of Lake Havasu City.

Jeremy Bentham:
I am most grateful to Philip Schofield of University College London, who kindly provided information and answers to my many questions and suggested revisions to the chapter. He is part of a team of scholars working on the Bentham Project, a research program dedicated to bringing out scholarly editions of the works of Jeremy Bentham. There will be about sixty-five volumes in total, based in part on the approximately seventy thousand sheets of Bentham's manuscripts that are deposited at the library at University College London; Tarique Shakir-Khalil of the University of London Union.

One-Cent Magenta:
Irwin Weinberg.

John Brown's Bible:
Ralph A. Pugh and Olivia Mahoney, Chicago Historical Society; Bruce Noble, Harpers Ferry National Historic Park. It should be noted that the park owns a John Brown family Bible, in which the abolitionist also made notations.

Captain Danjou's Wooden Hand:
Adjutant-chef Glaziou, conservateur du Musée de la Légion étrangère, Aubagne, France.

Major General Daniel E. Sickles's Leg:
Robert Montgomery, National Museum of Health and Medicine, Washington, D.C.; John Heiser, Gettysburg National Military Park, Gettysburg, Pennsylvania.

Gettysburg Address:
Dr. John R. Sellers, specialist, Civil War and Reconstruction, Library of Congress, kindly explained to me the issues at hand in the controversy over Lincoln's reading copy of the Gettysburg Address and was indispensable to me in my writing of this chapter. He also helped graciously with many other chapters.

Appomattox Surrender Tables:
Ronald G. Wilson, supervisory park ranger, Appomattox Court House National Historical Park, Appomattox, Virginia; Dr. John Y. Simon, Ulysses S. Grant Association, Southern Illinois University, Carbondale, Illinois; Olivia Mahoney, Chicago Historical Society; James Hutchins, National Museum of American History.

Bed Lincoln Died In:
I would like to express my utmost appreciation to Michael Maione, historian at Ford's Theatre National Historic Site, Washington, D.C. Maione possesses an encyclopedic knowledge of the Lincoln assassination, and he always courteously, comprehensively, and zealously shared that with me.

Michael Maione reviewed my various drafts of this chapter and asked that I avoid using the famous quote attributed to Lincoln's secretary of war, Edwin M. Stanton, after Lincoln expired: "Now he belongs to the ages." Because, as Maione astutely pointed out, although the quote has been reproduced in many books and articles, it did not appear in print until 1890, twenty-five years after the assassination of Abraham Lincoln, so if Stanton had said those exact words, they would have invariably been printed earlier and reprinted often and attributed to Stanton. The quote first appeared in the ten-volume work *Abraham Lincoln: A History* by John Nicolay and John Hay. Stanton did not write his memoirs, so there is no direct evidence that he said this when Lincoln died.

I would also like to thank Frank Hebblethwaite, former acting curator at Ford's Theatre; Olivia Mahoney, Chicago Historical Society; the Lincoln Museum in Fort Wayne, Indiana, especially Ruth Cook; John Sellers; Herbert Collins, formerly of the National Philatelic Collection; Alan Hawk and Dick Levinson, National Museum of Health and Medicine; Tom Swarz, curator, Lincoln Collection of the State of Illinois; Studebaker National Museum, South Bend, Indiana, especially Edna Kaeppler; Lincoln's Tomb Historic Site, Oak Ridge Cemetery, especially Linda Bee; and Marilyn Higgins, National Museum of American History.

Little Sorrel:
Lt. Col. Keith Gibson, Virginia Military Institute Museum, Lexington.

Robert Browning's Reliquary:
Philip Kelley is a renowned authority on the Brownings, and I was fortunate to have his generous assistance. I also appreciate the help of Sir Joseph Cheyne, formerly of the Keats-Shelley Memorial House, Rome, Italy; Bathsheba Abse, Keats-Shelley Memorial House; Keats-Shelley Association of America, particularly Dr. Donald Reiman and Doucet Fisher; Carl and Lily Pforzheimer Foundation, Inc., New York City; Gayle L. Petty, Library Company, Philadelphia; Dr. Dallas Pratt.

Elephant Man:
Professor Sir Colin Berry, London Hospital Medical College; David Nunn, London Hospital Medical College (Museum Department); Dr. D. T. D. Hughes, consultant physician, and Jonathan Evans, district archivist, Royal London Trust. I would like to thank Dr. G. R. Seward for supplying the pho-

tographs of Joseph Carey Merrick that had been published in the *British Dental Journal*. Dr. Seward is a renowned authority on the Elephant Man, and his several *BDJ* articles on Joseph Carey Merrick were based on his lectures given at the Royal London Hospital bicentenary celebrations.

Owney, the Canine Traveler:
James H. Bruns, director, National Postal Museum, Washington, D.C.; Herbert R. Collins.

Wright Brothers' Flyer:
Dr. Peter L. Jakab, National Air and Space Museum, Washington, D.C.; Robert C. Mikesh.

Breast-Pocket Items That Saved the Life of Theodore Roosevelt:
John Gable, Theodore Roosevelt Association, Oyster Bay, New York; James M. Shea, Theodore Roosevelt Birthplace, National Historic Site, New York City; Bruce Kay, Theodore Roosevelt National Park, Medora, North Dakota; Herbert R. Collins.

Piltdown Man:
Dr. Frank Spencer, Queens College, a noted authority on Piltdown Man, provided much valuable information and proofread my drafts of this chapter. I am also grateful to Robert Kruszynski, Natural History Museum (Human Origins Group), London.

Laddie Boy:
Herbert R. Collins; Marilyn Higgins, National Museum of American History.

Babe Ruth's Sixtieth-Home-Run Bat:
Peter Clark, National Baseball Hall of Fame and Museum, Cooperstown, New York.

John Dillinger's Wooden Jail-Escape Gun:
John Dillinger Museum, Nashville, Indiana, particularly curator Joe M. Pinkston and researcher Tom Smusyn.

Anne Frank's Diary:
Yt Stoker, Anne Frank Stichting, Amsterdam, the Netherlands; Anne Frank Center, New York City; Cordula Bartha, consulate general of the Netherlands, New York City.

Enola Gay:
Robert C. Mikesh, aviation author and former senior curator, aeronautics, National Air and Space Museum, was extremely helpful. His knowledge of aviation is vast and I am most grateful to him for sharing some of it with me.

Einstein's Brain:
Dr. Thomas Harvey gave me the story firsthand, spending hours on the phone, and politely answering all my questions; Dr. Marian C. Diamond, director, Lawrence Hall of Science, University of California, Berkeley; Robert Schulmann, director, Einstein Papers Project, Boston; Dr. Philip Schewe, American Institute of Physics; Ewing Cemetery Association, Trenton, New Jersey.

Rifle That Killed President Kennedy:
Steve Tilley, National Archives, College Park, Maryland; "The Sixth Floor," Dallas, Texas; John F. Kennedy Library, Boston, Massachusetts.

Voyager 1 *and* Voyager 2:
Timothy Ferris; Mary Hardin and Edward McNevin, Jet Propulsion Laboratory at the California Institute of Technology, Pasadena, California; National Aeronautics and Space Administration.

I am very much indebted to the editor of this book, David Sobel, both for making it a reality and for superbly editing it. His keen critiques and editorial suggestions prompted me to flesh out the histories in this book and make numerous other improvements. I also appreciate the excellent work of editorial assistant Jonathan S. Landreth.

As always, I am indebted to my literary agents, Lynn Chu and Glen Hartley. I am honored to be represented by two such fine people, whose enthusiasm for this project also helped make it a reality.

Marisa Nadell translated Italian for me; Fred Steins and Dr. Peter Knote translated German; Alvin Nesbot, Janet Nesbot, Victoria Delgado, and Dr. Blance N. Vazquez translated Spanish.

Many invaluable suggestions for improving the manuscript were made by my friend Judith Stein.

Stephanie Long, James Morgan, Gretchen Worden, Alan Hawk, Rabbi Mordecai Kamenetzky, Agnes Dubin, Max Dubin, Sally Schiller, Pearl Bernstein, Henry Bloomstein, Jeff Burke, Morris Sivak, Sarah Sivak, Lorraine Katz, Susan Healy, Pastor Ken Cavanagh, and John Barilla all were helpful in one way or another.

Nancy Constantine and Paulette Kloepfer adeptly handled the typing of the manuscript and were always a pleasure to work with.

I enjoy a close relationship with my three brothers and their families, and they were constant sources of inspiration during the writing of this book. I extend my heartfelt appreciation to Steven and Jeanne Rachlin, Gary and Lauren Rachlin, Craig and Sharon Rachlin, and nieces Stephanie, Aimee, Amanda, and Serena. The same gratitude is expressed to my parents, Philip and Mazie Rachlin.

I would like to thank my family—Marla, Elyssa, Lauren, and Glenn—for hanging in there during my long periods of isolation spent researching and writing this book.

Finally, I would like to say that this book was truly a labor of love. Delving into the fascinating events and episodes of the past described here was thoroughly enjoyable, and during the research I used to love to share the bizarre or unusual stories I uncovered with friends and strangers alike, as these would always evoke an amused, if not incredulous, response. History needn't be boring. It can truly be fun and exciting, inspiring and intriguing. It is for me, and I hope it is for you, too.

SOURCES AND BIBLIOGRAPHY

There were several volumes I used extensively throughout my research for this book. Rather than reproduce their titles in the chapters that follow, they are listed here as general reference sources: *The Book of Knowledge* (New York: Grolier Society, 1928); *The Concise Dictionary of National Biography: From the Beginnings to 1930* (London: Oxford University Press, 1939); *Encyclopedia Americana International Edition* (Danbury, Conn.: Grolier, 1988); *Encyclopaedia Britannica* (Chicago: Encyclopaedia Britannica, 1963); *The World Almanac* (New York: World Almanac, Pharos Books, 1990); *The World Book Encyclopedia* (Chicago: Field Enterprises Educational Corporation, 1958; Chicago: World Book, 1989). Two magazines I also found very useful were *Archaeology* and *Biblical Archaeology*.

Introduction

Begley, Sharon, and Louise Lief. "The Way We Were, Our Ice Age Heritage: Language, Art, Fashion, and the Family." *Newsweek*, November 10, 1986.
Geck, Elisabeth. *Johannes Gutenberg*. Berlin: Brüder Hartmann, 1968.
Lamar, Howard R., ed. *The Reader's Encyclopedia of the American West*. New York: Crowell, 1977.
Lossing, Benson John. *The Pictorial Field Book of the War of 1812*. New York: Harper and Brothers, 1868.
Vacquier, J. *Souvenir de Napoléon Bonaparte*. Kahn: Strasbourg, 1928.

The Black Stone of the Ka'bah

Farwell, Byron. *Burton: A Biography of Sir Richard Francis Burton*. New York: Viking Penguin, 1988. First published by Longmans, Green, 1963. Source of the quote attributed to Sir Richard Francis Burton (page 14).

Gibb, H. A. R., and J. H. Kramers, eds. *Shorter Encyclopedia of Islam*. Ithaca, N.Y.: Cornell University Press, 1965.

Hughes, Thomas Patrick. *A Dictionary of Islam*. Delhi, India: Oriental Publishers, 1973.

Rice, Edward. *Captain Sir Richard Francis Burton: The Secret Agent Who Made the Pilgrimage to Mecca, Discovered the Kama Sutra, and Brought the Arabian Nights to the West*. New York: Scribner's, 1990.

Sharafuddin, Abdus-Samad. "Is the Black Stone an Idol? Is Pilgrimage a Pagan Rite?" Pamphlet. Bombay, India: Ad-Darul-Qayyimah, 1975.

Lucy the Hominid

Johanson, Donald, and Maitland Edey. *Lucy, the Beginnings of Humankind*. New York: Simon and Schuster, 1981.

Science Year: The World Book Science Annual, 1973. Chicago: Field Enterprises.

Science Year: The World Book Science Annual, 1979. Chicago: World Book–Childcraft International, 1978.

The Code of Hammurabi

Kramer, Samuel Noah, and the Editors of Time-Life Books. *Cradle of Civilization*. New York: Time-Life Books, 1967.

Oppenheim, A. Leo. *Ancient Mesopotamia: Portrait of a Dead Civilization*. Chicago: University of Chicago Press, 1964.

Pritchard, James B. *Archaeology and the Old Testament*. Princeton, N.J.: Princeton University Press, 1958.

The Contents of King Tutankhamen's Tomb

Carter, Howard, and A. C. Mace. *The Tomb of Tut-Ankh-Amen*. 2 vols. London: Cassell, 1923.

———. *The Discovery of the Tomb of Tutankhamen*. With a new introduction by John Manchip White. New York: Dover, 1977.

Carter, Michael. *Tutankhamen, the Golden Monarch*. New York: McKay, 1972.

Cottrell, Leonard. *The Secrets of Tutankhamen's Tomb*. Greenwich, Conn.: New York Graphic Society Publishers, 1964.

"Debunking Tut 'Curse.'" *Newsday* (from *The London Observer*), September 21, 1993.

Glubok, Shirley. *Discovering Tut-Ankh-Amen's Tomb*. Abridged and adapted from *The Tomb of Tut-Ankh-Amen* by Howard Carter and A. C. Mace. New York: Macmillan, 1968.

The Black Obelisk

Biblical Archaeology Review, January/February 1991.

Layard, Austin Henry. *Nineveh and Its Remains: With an Account of a Visit to the Chaldaean Christians of Kurdistan, and the Yezids, or Devil-Worshippers; and an Inquiry into the Manners and Arts of the Ancient Assyrians.* 2 vols. New York: Putnam, 1849. It is Layard's eloquent account of his excavations upon which I have based my story of his unearthing of the Black Obelisk.

Millard, Alan. *Treasures from Bible Times.* Belleville, Mich.: Lion Publishing, 1985.

Pritchard, James B. *Archaeology and the Old Testament.* Princeton, N.J.: Princeton University Press, 1958.

Tenney, Merrill C., general ed., and J. D. Douglas, revising ed. *The New International Dictionary of the Bible.* Grand Rapids, Mich.: Zondervan Publishing, 1987.

The Siloam Inscription

Great People of the Bible and How They Lived. Pleasantville, N.Y.: Reader's Digest Association, 1974.

Magnuson, Magnus. *Archaeology of the Bible.* New York: Simon and Schuster, 1977.

Millard, Alan. *Treasures from Bible Times.* Belleville, Mich.: Lion Publishing, 1985.

Pearlman, Moshe. *Digging Up the Bible.* New York: Morrow, 1980.

"Please Return the Siloam Inscription to Jerusalem." *Biblical Archaeology Review*, May/June 1991.

Pritchard, James B., ed. *The Ancient Near East: An Anthology of Texts and Pictures.* Princeton, N.J.: Princeton University Press, 1958.

The Rosetta Stone

Andrews, Carol. *The British Museum Book of the Rosetta Stone.* New York: Peter Bedrick Books, 1981.

Belloc, Hilaire. *Napoleon.* New York: Halcyon House, 1932.

Budge, Sir E. A. Wallis. *The Rosetta Stone in the British Museum.* London: Religious Tract Society, 1929.

Cottrell, Leonard, ed. *The Concise Encyclopedia of Archaeology.* 2nd ed. New York: Hawthorn Books, 1971.

Cronin, Vincent. *Napoleon Bonaparte: An Intimate Biography.* New York: Morrow, 1971.

Guérard, Albert. *Napoleon I: A Great Life in Brief.* New York: Knopf, 1956.

Ludwig, Emil. *Napoleon.* Translated by Eden Paul and Cedar Paul. New York: Modern Library, 1953.

Pearlman, Moshe. *Digging Up the Bible.* New York: Morrow, 1980.

Quirke, Stephen, and Carol Andrews, eds. *The Rosetta Stone*. New York: Abrams, 1989.

Turner, Major General Tomkyns Hilgrove. "An Account of the Rosetta Stone." Letter dated May 30, 1810. In *Archaeologia: or Miscellaneous Tracts Relating to Antiquity*, vol. 16, page 214. London: Society of Antiquaries of London, 1812. Source of the Turner quote.

Williams, Walter G. *Archaeology in Biblical Research*. New York: Abingdon Press, 1965.

The Portland Vase

Biblical Archaeology Review, July/August 1990.

Harden, Donald B., Hansgerd Hellenkemper, Kenneth Painter, and David Whitehouse. *Glass of the Caesars*. Milan: Olivetti, 1987.

Haufmann, George M. *Roman Art*. Greenwich, Conn.: New York Graphic Society, n.d.

Shenker, Israel. "A Celebrated Roman Vase Has Become a 20th-Century Phoenix." *Smithsonian*, July 1989.

Strong, Donald, and David Brown, eds. *Roman Crafts*. New York: New York University Press, 1976. Specifically, I referred to the chapter entitled "Glass" by Jennifer Price.

Tait, H., ed. *Five Thousand Years of Glass*, 2nd ed. London: British Museum Press, 1995.

"A 2,000-Year-Old Vase to Be Broken (to Fix It)." *The New York Times*, June 6, 1986.

Von Holst, Niels. *Creators, Collectors, and Connoisseurs*. New York: Putnam's, 1967.

The Veil of the Virgin

Delaporte, Yves. *Le Voile de Notre Dame*. Chartres: Maison des Clercs, 1927. My main source of information here.

The Holy Bible Containing the Old and New Testaments Translated Out of the Original Tongues. New York: Thomas Nelson and Sons, 1901.

The Crown of Thorns

Durant, Will, and Ariel Durant. *The Story of Civilization*. New York: Simon and Schuster, 1966.

Hartman, Louis F. *Encyclopedic Dictionary of the Bible*. Translation and adaptation of A. van den Born's *Bijbels Woordenboek*. New York: McGraw-Hill, 1963.

The Holy Bible Containing the Old and New Testaments Translated Out of the Original Tongues. New York: Thomas Nelson and Sons, 1901.

The Interpreter's Dictionary of the Bible. 4 vols. New York: Abingdon Press, 1962.

Neil, William, ed. *The Bible Companion.* New York: McGraw-Hill, 1960.

"Les Reliques de la Passion à Notre-Dame de Paris" (The Relics of Notre-Dame of Paris). Pamphlet. N.p., n.d.

Steinfels, Peter. "For Both the Faithful and the Skeptics, Relics Hold Their Mysteries." *The New York Times,* November 9, 1988.

Temko, Allan. *Notre-Dame of Paris: The Biography of a Cathedral.* London: Secker and Warburg, 1976. Source of King Louis IX's relics parade.

The Holy Lance

The Holy Bible Containing the Old and New Testaments Translated Out of the Original Tongues. New York: Thomas Nelson and Sons, 1901.

Krása, Josef, commentator, and Peter Kussi, translator. *The Travels of Sir John Mandeville: A Manuscript in the British Library.* New York: Braziller, 1983.

Labarte, Jules. *Histoire des Arts Industriels au Moyen Age et a l'Époque de la Renaissance.* Vol. 2. Paris: A. Morel, Libraires-Éditeurs, 1873.

National Archives. Ardelia Hall Collection. Record Group 260, Boxes 32–34.

Trnek, Helmut. "The Holy Lance." In *The Secular and Ecclesiastical Treasuries (Illustrated Guide).* Vienna: Kunsthistorisches Museum, 1991.

Young, Brigadier Peter. *The World Almanac Book of World War II.* New York: World Almanac, 1981.

The Shroud of Turin

Heller, John H. *Report on the Shroud of Turin.* Boston: Houghton Mifflin, 1983.

Lavoie, B. B., G. R. Lavoie, D. Klutstein, and J. Regan. "In Accordance with Jewish Burial Custom, the Body of Jesus Was Not Washed." *Shroud Spectrum International,* June 1982.

Maloney, Paul, ed. *The Shroud of Turin: A Case Study in Document Authentication.* Binghamton, N.Y.: Haworth Press, in preparation.

Meagher, Paul Kevin, Thomas C. O'Brien, and Sister Consuelo Maria Aherne. *Encyclopedic Dictionary of Religion.* Washington, D.C.: Sisters of St. Joseph of Philadelphia, Corpus Publications, 1974.

Stevenson, Kenneth E., and Gary R. Habermas. *Verdict on the Shroud, Evidence for the Death and Resurrection of Jesus Christ.* Ann Arbor, Mich.: Servant Books, 1981.

Walsh, John. *The Shroud.* New York: Random House, 1963.

Wilcox, Robert K. *Shroud.* New York: Macmillan, 1977.

Wilson, Ian. *The Shroud of Turin: The Burial Cloak of Jesus Christ?* Garden City, N.Y.: Doubleday, 1978.

For further research:

Shroud Spectrum International
Indiana Center for Shroud Studies
1252 N. Jackson Branch Ridge Road
Nashville, Indiana 47448

This is the single best journal source in the English language for researchers to find scholarly articles on the science, medicine, history, art, theology, exegesis, and botanical and textile studies of the Shroud of Turin.

The Blood of Saint Januarius

Catholic University of America (editorial staff), Washington, D.C. *New Catholic Encyclopedia*. 17 vols. New York: McGraw-Hill, 1967.

Cross, F. L., and E. A. Livingstone, eds., 2nd ed. *The Oxford Dictionary of the Christian Church*. Edited by F. L. Cross. London: Oxford University Press, 1974.

Meagher, Paul Kevin, Thomas C. O'Brien, and Sister Consuelo Maria Aherne. *Encyclopedic Dictionary of Religion*. Washington, D.C.: Sisters of St. Joseph of Philadelphia, Corpus Publications, 1974.

Nature, vol. 353, October 10, 1991.

Newsday, October 10, 1991.

Newsweek, October 21, 1991.

Thurston, Herbert. "The 'Miracle' of Saint Januarius." *The Month*, vol. 149 (1927), pp. 119–29.

———. "The Blood Miracles of Naples." *The Month,* vol. 155 (1930), pp. 44–55. Source of the Father Landi and Thurston's Pozzuoli quotes.

The Rubens Vase

Bankers Almanac 1881. Haywards Heath, England: Thomas Skinner Directories, 1882.

Schoettler, Carl. "The Vase." *Baltimore Sun*, May 6, 1980.

Vikan, Gary. "A Vase and a Chalice." Paper delivered at the Curator's Choice dinner on June 9, 1986, at the Walters Art Gallery, Baltimore, Maryland. Source of quotes and Marvin Chauncey Ross anecdotes.

The Antioch Chalice

Eisen, Gustavus E. *The Great Chalice of Antioch*. New York: Kouchakji Frères, 1923. My source for some of the history of the Antioch Chalice, including its oxidation cleaning in Paris and then being sent to New York for safekeeping. Also my source for much of the artistic study of the object.

Maltin, Leonard, ed. *Leonard Maltin's TV Movies and Video Guide, 1989 Ed*. New York: Penguin/NAL, 1988. Source of Paul Newman movie debut.

Mango, Marlia Mundell. *Silver From Early Byzantium*. Baltimore: Walters Art Gallery, 1986. Much of my account is based on Mango's chapter, "The Stuma, Riha, Hama, and Antioch Silver Treasures: Their Modern History."

Vikan, Gary. "A Vase and a Chalice." Paper delivered at the Curator's Choice dinner on June 9, 1986, at the Walters Art Gallery, Baltimore, Maryland.

The Book of Kells

Book of Kells. Facsimile edition. New York: Abrams, 1991.

Brown, Peter. *The Book of Kells*. London: Thames and Hudson, 1980.

Lewis, Paul. "Rare Manuscripts from the Public." *The New York Times*, January 25, 1987.

"The Long Room and the Book of Kells." Pamphlet. Dublin: Trinity College Library, n.d.

Schoeffling, Conrad. "The Book of Kells." Pamphlet. C. W. Post College, Long Island University, Brookville, N.Y., 1990.

Simms, G. O. "The Book of Kells." Manuscript essay. N.d.

———. *The Book of Kells: A Selection of Pages Reproduced with a Description*. Chester Springs, Penn.: Dufour, 1972.

The Bayeux Tapestry and the Domesday Book

Bernstein, David J. *The Mystery of the Bayeux Tapestry*. Chicago: University of Chicago Press, 1986.

Bertrand, Simone. *The Bayeux Tapestry*. English edition. Ouest France, 1978.

Douglas, David C. *William the Conqueror: The Norman Impact Upon England*. Berkeley: University of California Press, 1964.

Finn, R. Welldon. *Domesday Book: A Guide*. Chichester, England: Phillimore, 1973.

Galbraith, V. H. *Domesday Book: Its Place in Administrative History*. London: Oxford University Press, 1974.

La Tapisserie de Bayeux. Réalisation Édition. Ville de Bayeux: Artaud Frères.

Wood, Michael. *Domesday: A Search for the Roots of England*. New York: Facts on File, 1986.

The Holy Child of Aracoeli

"The Holy Bambino of Aracoeli." Pamphlet. N.p., n.d.

"Il S. Bambino di Aracoeli." Pamphlet. Rome: Convento Aracoeli, 1970.

Lo Bello, Nino. "A Christ Child of Roman Lore." *Newsday*, December 2, 1990.

Rothermund, B. *Traduzione Del Tedesco da "Guedeureiche Jesuleire."* 1982.

Santa Maria in Aracoeli: Album Guide. Rome: n.p., n.d.

Columbus's Books of Privileges

Bradford, Ernle. *Christopher Columbus*. New York: Viking, 1973.

Davenport, Frances G. "Texts of Columbus's Privileges." *American Historical Review*, vol. 14 (1909), 764–76.

Granzotto, Giani. *Christopher Columbus: The Dream and the Obsession*. Garden City, N.Y.: Doubleday, 1985.

"The Letters of Cristopher Columbus and the 'Codice del Privilegi' (Privilege Code)." Pamphlet. Genoa, Italy: Comune di Genova, 1991.

Morison, Samuel E. *Admiral of the Ocean Sea*. Boston: Little, Brown, 1942.

Pérez-Bustamante, Don Ciriaco. *Libro de los Privilegios de Almirante Don Cristobal Colon (1498)*. Madrid: Real Academia de la Historia, 1951.

Plakas, Rosemary. Information sheet on "Colombo, Cristoforo, Codice Diplomatico Columbo-Americano." Washington, D.C.: Library of Congress, n.d.

Stevens, Benjamin Franklin, compiler and ed. *Christopher Columbus: His Own Book of Privileges, 1502, Photographic Facsimile of the Manuscript in the Archives of the Foreign Office in Paris, Now for the First Time Published with Expanded Text Translation into English and an Historical Introduction*. With an introduction by Henry Harrisse. London: B. F. Stevens, 1893.

Thacher, John Boyd. *Christopher Columbus: His Life, His Work, His Remains*. 3 vols. New York: Putnam's, 1903.

Welter, H., ed. *À Propos d'un Manuscript du Ministère des Affaires Etrangères*. Paris, 1894.

The Cantino Map

Frabetti, Pietro. *La "Charta Del Navicare" Del Cantino*. Modena: ARBE, n.d. My account is based on this pamphlet.

Milano, Ernesto. *La carta del Cantino e la rappresentazione della Terra nei codici e nei libri a stampa della Biblioteca Estense e Universitaria*. Modena: Il Bulino, 1991.

Wilford, John Noble. *The Mapmakers*. New York: Knopf, 1981.

The Hope Diamond

American Philatelist, May 1986. Source of the postage paid to mail the Hope to the Smithsonian.

Block, Maxine, ed. *Current Biography, Who's News and Why, 1943*. New York: H. W. Wilson, 1944.

Crowningshield, Robert. "Grading the Hope Diamond." *Gems and Gemology*, vol. 25, no. 2 (Summer 1989), pp. 91–94.

Current Biography, 1947. New York: H. W. Wilson, 1948.

Dickinson, Joan Younger. *The Book of Diamonds*. New York: Crown, 1965.

James, Edward T., ed. *Dictionary of American Biography* (Supplement Three, 1941–1945). New York: Scribner's, 1973.

McLean, Evalyn Walsh, with Boyden Sparkes. *Father Struck It Rich*. Boston: Little, Brown, 1936. Source of the McLean quotes. Bad luck objects, p. 175; Monsignor Russell, p. 179.

Notable American Women, 1607–1950: A Biographical Dictionary. Cambridge, Mass.: Belknap Press, 1971.

Patch, Suzanne. *Blue Mystery: The Story of the Hope Diamond*. Washington, D.C.: Smithsonian Institution Press, 1976. An excellent book to read for a full story of the Hope Diamond.

Rogers, Frances, and Alice Beard. *5,000 Years of Gems and Jewelry*. Philadelphia: Lippincott, 1947.

Winters, Mary. "The Hope Diamond" (G3551). Printed information of the National Museum of American History, Washington, D.C., 1989.

Winters, Mary, and John White. "George IV's Blue Diamond." *Lapidary Journal*, December 1991 (part 1), pp. 34–40, and January 1992 (part 2), pp. 48–52.

Edmond Halley's Astronomical Observation Notebooks

Asimov, Isaac. *Asimov's Guide to Halley's Comet*. New York: Walker, 1985.

Branley, Franklyn M. *Halley: Comet 1986*. New York: Lodestar/Dutton, 1983.

Flaste, Richard, Holcomb Noble, Walter Sullivan, and John Noble Wilford. *The New York Times Guide to the Return of Halley's Comet*. New York: Times Books, 1985.

Langwell, W. H. *The Conservation of Books and Documents*. London: Sir Isaac Pitman and Sons, 1957.

The Declaration of Independence

Bell, Whitfield J., Jr. *The Declaration of Independence, Four Versions: Jefferson's Manuscript Copy, The First Official Printing by John Dunlap, The First Newspaper Printing, A Unique Printing on Parchment by John Dunlap*. Reprint, Philadelphia: American Philosophical Society, 1986.

Donovan, Frank. *Mr. Jefferson's Declaration: The Story Behind the Declaration of Independence*. New York: Dodd, Mead, 1968.

Fitzpatrick, John C. "The Travels of the Declaration of Independence." *Daughters of the American Revolution Magazine*, vol. 57, no. 7 (July 1923), pp. 389–97.

Gustafson, Milton O. "The Empty Shrine: The Transfer of the Declaration of Independence and the Constitution to the National Archives." *The American Archivist*, vol. 39, no. 3 (July 1976), pp. 271–85.

Hazelton, John. *The Declaration of Independence, Its History*. New York: Dodd, Mead, 1906.

Maeder, Jay. "1776's Pride Is Worth 2M." *The New York Daily News*, June 14, 1991.

Mearns, David C. "The Declaration of Independence: The Story of a Parchment." Washington, D.C.: Library of Congress, 1950. Reprinted from the *Annual Report of the Librarian of Congress for the Fiscal Year Ending June 30, 1949*, 36–55. Source of the Richard Rush, *Historical Magazine*, and James McCabe quotes.

Meyer, Alfred. "Daily Rise and Fall of the Nation's Revered Documents," *Smithsonian*, vol. 17 (October 1986), 134–36.

Molotsky, Irving. "Let Us Now Celebrate the Second." *New York Times*, July 2, 1986.

Wright, Chapin. "$4 'Declaration' Auctioned for $2.2M." *Newsday*, June 14, 1991.

George Washington's False Teeth

Bird, Aldine R. "Washington Smiled at Own Risk as False Teeth Stuck." *News*, Baltimore, Md., February 15, 1940.

"A George Washington Relic: A Monstrous Set of False Teeth the First President Used Is in a Museum Here." *Baltimore Sun*, July 18, 1954.

Gustaitis, Joseph. "George Washington's False Teeth." *American History Illustrated*, February 1989.

"Historic Teeth: Those of George Washington in Baltimore Dental College Museum." *Baltimore Sun*, July 10, 1904.

Hoffmann-Axthelm, Walter. *History of Dentistry*. Chicago: Quintessence, 1981.

"It's No Lie: George Got Teeth From Hippopotami." Associated Press article in *Providence Journal*, March 22, 1980.

Locke, Robert. "Down in the Mouth: Tale of George Washington's Wooden Teeth May Have Been Tongue in Cheek." *Philadelphia Inquirer*, March 22, 1980.

"Maryland University to Show George Washington's False Teeth." *The Washington Post and Times Herald*, February 23, 1956.

McCauley, H. Berton. "George Washington's Teeth and Dentistry in 18th Century America." Paper delivered at Fraunces Tavern in New York City on February 6, 1986. (I would like to record Dr. McCauley's own documentation, which appears at the end of his paper: "The material from which the substance of this presentation is derived may be found in the work of Bernhard Wolf Weinberger, *An Introduction to the History of Dentistry in America*, 2 vols., C. V. Mosby Co., St. Louis, 1948. Also in the publication of Curt Proskauer and Fritz H. Witt: *Pictorial History of Dentistry*, Verlag M. DuMont Schauberg, Koln, 1962. Further in *The Foundation of Professional Dentistry* by J. Ben Robison, Waverly Press, Baltimore, 1940. And more recently in *Heritage and History* of the Baltimore College of Dental Surgery, 1978; and in *Dentistry: An Illustrated History* by Malvin E. Ring, C. V. Mosby Co., St. Louis, 1985.")

Rice, Howard C., Jr. *Travels in North America in the Years 1780, 1781, and 1782 by the Marquis De Chastellux*. Vol. 1. Chapel Hill: University of North Carolina Press, 1963.

Schaden, Herman. "Admiral Brushing Up on Washington's Teeth." *The Evening Star*, Washington, D.C., October 27, 1967.

Sognnaes, Reidar F. "President Washington's Most Famous Dentures Stolen from the Smithsonian." *Journal of the American Dental Association*, February 1983.

Weinberger, Bernhard Wolf. "George Washington's Dentures." Reprint from February 1934 issue of *Dental Survey*.

———. "Washington's Missing Dentures: Solving the Mystery." *Journal of the American Dental Association*, May 1960.

Who Was Who in America: Historical Volume 1607–1896, Revised Edition. Chicago: Marquis Who's Who, Incorporated, 1967.

Additional sources include notes of the First District Dental Society held April 11, 1893, at the New York Academy of Medicine and *The Illinois Dental Journal, 1932–1933*; numerous letters of George Washington and John Greenwood located at the American Academy of the History of Dentistry, Baltimore; numerous newspaper clippings of the eighteenth and nineteenth centuries from the *New York Observer, St. Louis Republic, Virginia Gazette, New York Sun*, and other publications.

The Crypt of John Paul Jones

Malone, Dumas, ed. *Dictionary of American Biography*. Vol. 3. New York: Scribner's, 1935.

Morison, Samuel Eliot. *John Paul Jones: A Sailor's Biography*. Boston: Atlantic Monthly Press/Little, Brown, 1959.

Stewart, Charles W., compiler. *John Paul Jones Commemoration at Annapolis April 24, 1906*. Washington, D.C.: Government Printing Office, 1907; reprinted 1966. This book contains General Horace Porter's detailed account of his search for Jones, on which my account is based. Other material in this book that was of use included John Paul Jones's report of his engagement on the *Bonhomme Richard* with the *Serapis*; General Porter's description of the battle given in his address on April 30, 1908, at the U.S. Naval Academy; and Captain John Stone's recollection of seeing Jones's corpse when he was in Paris in 1905.

Walsh, John Evangelist. *Night on Fire*. New York: McGraw-Hill, 1978.

HMS *Victory* and Vice Admiral Lord Nelson's Uniform Coat

Beatty, William, M.D. *Authentic Narrative of the Death of Lord Nelson*. 3rd ed. London: W. Mason, 1825. Source of the Beatty quote in "Vice Admiral Lord Nelson's Uniform Coat," pp. 17–19.

Bennett, Geoffrey. *Nelson the Commander*. New York: Scribner's, 1972.

Hattersley, Roy. *Nelson*. New York: Saturday Review Press, 1974.

Hedges, A. A. C. *Admiral Lord Nelson*. Norwich, England: Jarrould Colour Publications, n.d.

Howarth, David, and Stephen Howarth. *Lord Nelson: The Immortal Memory.* New York: Viking, 1988.

Nicolas, Sir Nicholas Harris. *The Dispatches and Letters of Vice Admiral Lord Viscount Nelson.* Vol. 7. London: H. Colburn, 1844; reprinted 1845.

Warner, Oliver. *Victory: The Life of Lord Nelson.* Boston: Atlantic Monthly Press/Little, Brown, 1958. Source of the Coleridge quote (from S. T. Coleridge, *The Friend*, essay 6).

Wilton-Smith, Jane, ed. *HMS Victory: Souvenir Guidebook.* Andover, England: Pitkin Pictorials, 1988.

The Star-Spangled Banner

Filby, P. W., and Edward G. Howard, compilers. *Star-Spangled Books.* Baltimore: Maryland Historical Society, 1972. Source of the advertisement of the first public singing of "The Star-Spangled Banner" on October 19, 1814, p. 16.

"Fort McHenry." Pamphlet. Washington, D.C.: National Park Service, U.S. Department of the Interior, 1990.

La Cour, Art. *Proudly We Hail: The Story of Our National Anthem.* West Orange, N.J.: Economics Press, 1965.

Lord, Walter. *The Dawn's Early Light.* New York: Norton, 1972.

Sheads, Scott S. *The Rockets' Red Glare: The Maritime Defense of Baltimore in 1814.* Centreville, Md.: Tidewater, 1986.

"The Star-Spangled Banner." Leaflet. Washington, D.C.: National Museum of American History of the Smithsonian Institution, n.d.

Napoleon's Penis

Castelot, André. *Napoleon.* Translated from the French-language edition by Guy Daniels. New York: Harper and Row, 1971.

"Catalogue of Printed Books, Manuscripts and the Celebrated Vignali Collection of Napoleon Relics removed from Saint Helena and Other Items of Napoleonic Interest from Various Sources." Printed by Christie, Manson & Woods for auction in London on October 29, 1969. My source for the items in the Abbé Vignali collection.

Cronin, Vincent. *Napoleon Bonaparte: An Intimate Biography.* New York: Morrow, 1971.

A Description of the Vignali Collection of Relics of Napoleon. Philadelphia: Rosenbach, 1924.

Guérard, Albert. *Napoleon I: A Great Life in Brief.* New York: Knopf, 1962.

Korngold, Ralph. *The Last Years of Napoleon. His Captivity on St. Helena.* New York: Harcourt, Brace, 1959.

Ludwig, Emil. *Napoleon.* N.p., n.d.

Martineau, Gilbert. *Napoleon's St. Helena.* Translated from the French-language edition by Frances Partridge. Chicago: Rand McNally, 1968.

Saint Denis, Louis Etienne. *Napoleon: From the Tuileries to St. Helena.* New York: Harper, 1922.

Wolf, Edwin II, and John F. Fleming. *Rosenbach: A Biography.* Cleveland: World Publishing, 1960.

London Bridge

Dussault, Elrose M. "History of the London Bridge and Lake Havasu City." Leaflet. 1987.

Elmer, Carlos. *London Bridge in Pictures.* Kingman, Ariz.: Carlos H. Elmer, 1971, 1983.

Johnson, Roger A. "New City, Old Bridge." Booklet. Media Specialist, 1981.

McGrath, Ron. "London Bridge Spans Time and Space to Awe Millions of Visitors at Lake Havasu." In *Visit Lake Havasu City, Arizona,* Lake Havasu Area Chamber of Commerce, 1988.

Shepherd, C. W. *A Thousand Years of London Bridge.* New York: Hastings House, 1971.

Jeremy Bentham: A Philosopher for the Ages

Bentham, Jeremy. "Auto-Icon; or, farther uses of the dead to the living. A Fragment From the Mss. of Jeremy Bentham. [Not published]."

Marmoy, C. F. A. "The Auto-Icon of Jeremy Bentham at University College, London." Reprinted from *Medical History,* vol. 2, no. 2 (April 1958).

Richardson, Ruth, and Brian Hurwitz. "Jeremy Bentham's Self Image: An Exemplary Request for Dissection." *British Medical Journal* (July 18, 1987), 195–98, 295.

The One-Cent Magenta

"1847 Stamps Sold for $3.3M." Reuters dispatch in *Newsday,* November 4, 1993.

Ilma, Viola. *Funk and Wagnalls Guide to the World of Stamp Collecting.* New York: Crowell, 1978.

India's Stamp Journal, September 1970.

Kernan, Michael. "The $5 Million Stampede." *Washington Post,* April 7, 1980.

Lidman, David, and John D. Apfelbaum. *The World of Stamps and Stamp Collecting.* New York: Scribner's, 1981.

Williams, M., and L. W. Williams. *Rare Stamps.* New York: Putnam's, 1967.

John Brown's Bible

Boyer, Richard O. *The Legend of John Brown.* New York: Knopf, 1972.

Chicago Historical Society materials: Letters from B. D. Gibson to F. G.

Logan, dated December 21, 1892, and January 10, 1893. Notarized documents executed in the State of West Virginia, County of Jefferson, dated January 5, 1893 (Charles C. Conklyn and George W. Engle, signees; B. D. Gibson, notary public); January 5, 1893 (Lewis M. Blessing, Herbert S. Blessing, Alice V. Blessing, Laura F. Blessing, signees; B. D. Gibson, notary public); January 5, 1893 (Emily Jane Blessing, signee, B. D. Gibson, notary public); January 9, 1893 (G. F. Mason, signee, B. D. Gibson, notary public); January 9, 1893 (Daniel B. Lucas, signee, B. D. Gibson, notary public); notarized document in the District of Columbia, City of Washington, dated January 5, 1893 (John E. Hilbert, signee, George Finckel, notary public).

Downes, Olin, and Elie Siegmeister. *A Treasury of American Song.* New York: Knopf, 1943.

Oates, Stephen B. *To Purge This Land with Blood: A Biography of John Brown.* New York: Harper and Row, 1970.

Captain Danjou's Wooden Hand

Boca, Geoffrey. *La Légion: The French Foreign Legion and the Men Who Made It Glorious.* New York: Crowell, 1964.

"The Foreign Legion." Brochure. N.d.

Keating, Susan Katz. "Legion Marches into the Spotlight." *Insight* magazine, May 7, 1990.

Mercer, Charles. *Legion of Strangers.* New York: Holt, Rinehart and Winston, 1964.

Wellard, James. *The French Foreign Legion.* Boston: Little, Brown, 1974.

Major General Daniel E. Sickles's Leg

Brandt, Nat. *The Congressman Who Got Away With Murder.* Syracuse: Syracuse University Press, 1991.

Dowling, Tom. "The Sunday Murder at Lafayette Square—and Afterwards." *The Washington Star*, September 15, 1976.

Maclean, Don. "Shinbone Connected to the Toe-Hold." *The Washington Daily News*, June 13, 1956.

Moyer, William J. "The Fantastic Career of Daniel E. Sickles." *The Washington Star Journal Pictorial Magazine*, March 1, 1953.

National Museum of Health and Medicine, Washington, D.C. File cards. N.d.

Swanberg, W. A. *Sickles the Incredible.* New York: Scribner's, 1956.

The Gettysburg Address

Commager, Henry Steele, and Allan Nevins. *Heritage of America.* Boston: Little, Brown, 1949.

Kunhardt, Philip B., Jr. *A New Birth of Freedom, Lincoln at Gettysburg*. Boston: Little, Brown, 1983.

Long, E. B., with Barbara Long. *The Civil War Day by Day: An Almanac, 1861–1865*. Garden City, N.Y.: Doubleday, 1971.

Luthin, Reinhard H. *The Real Abraham Lincoln*. Englewood Cliffs, N.J.: Prentice-Hall, 1960.

Mearns, David C., and Lloyd A. Dunlap. *Long Remembered: Facsimiles of the Five Versions of the Gettysburg Address in the Handwriting of Abraham Lincoln*. Washington, D.C.: Library of Congress, 1963.

Mitgang, Herbert, ed. *Abraham Lincoln: A Press Portrait*. Chicago: Quadrangle Books, 1971.

Nevins, Allan, ed. *Lincoln and the Gettysburg Address: Commemorative Papers*. Urbana: University of Illinois Press, 1964.

Press Release No. 63-5. Library of Congress, Washington, D.C., September 21, 1962.

Randall, J. G. *Lincoln, the President: Springfield to Gettysburg*. Vol. 2. New York: Dodd, Mead, 1945.

Thomas, Benjamin P. *Abraham Lincoln*. New York: Knopf, 1952.

Trueblood, Elton. *Abraham Lincoln: Theologian of American Anguish*. New York: Harper and Row, 1973.

Wills, Garry. *Lincoln at Gettysburg: The Words That Remade America*. New York: Simon and Schuster, 1992.

The Appomattox Surrender Tables

America: Great Crises in Our History Told by Its Makers (A Library of Original Sources). Vol. 8, *The Civil War, 1861–1865*. Chicago: Americanization Department, Veterans of Foreign Wars of the United States, 1925.

Appomattox Court House: Appomattox Court House National Historical Park, Virginia. Washington, D.C.: National Park Service, U.S. Department of the Interior, 1980.

"Appomattox Furniture." *Furniture South*, July 1961.

"The 'Appomattox' Table in Chicago." *Chicago Tribune*, July 23, 1887.

"Appomattox Table Story." Sheets of the Chicago Historical Society, circa 1920.

Bowman, John S. *The Civil War Almanac*. New York: World Almanac, Bison Books, 1983.

Cadawallader, Sylvanus. *Three Years with Grant: As Recalled by War Correspondent Sylvanus Cadawallader*, ed. Thomas Benjamin. 1955. Reprint, Westport, Conn.: Greenwood Press, 1980.

Cauble, Dr. Frank P. *The Proceedings Connected with the Surrender of the Army of Northern Virginia, April 1865*. 1962. Reprint, H. E. Howard, 1987.

Chesley, A. H. Letter to Charles Gunther, March 22, 1887. Chicago Historical Society.

Chicago Historical Society. Accession records.

Dunlap, Lloyd A. "The Grant-Lee Surrender Correspondence: Some Notes and Queries." *Manuscripts*, Spring 1969, pp. 78–91.

Freeman, Douglas S. *R. E. Lee*. Volume 4. New York: Scribner, 1935.

Grant, Julia. Letter to Mrs. E. O. C. Ord, January 26, 1887. Chicago Historical Society.

Grant, Ulysses S. *Personal Memoirs of U. S. Grant*. Vol. 2. New York: Charles L. Webster, 1886. Source of Grant and Lee letters, pp. 289, 290, 292.

"Historic Furnishings Report and Plan Appomattox Court House National Historical Park." Prepared under contract by William Seale, Harpers Ferry Center, 1984.

"A National Shrine Is Dedicated, 'Surrender House' Becomes 'Peace House.'" *The Iron Worker*, vol. 13, no. 3 (Summer 1950), pp. 1–5.

"Notebook of James Kelly." New York, circa 1892.

Ord, Mrs. E. O. C. Letters to Charles Gunther, January 12, 1887; March 10, 1887; March 24, 1887; July 20, 1887. Chicago Historical Society.

Simon, John Y., ed. *The Papers of Ulysses S. Grant*. Vol. 14, *February 21–April 30, 1865*. Carbondale, Ill.: Southern Illinois University Press, 1985. Source of the terms of surrender letter, pp. 373–74; permission to reproduce granted by John Y. Simon and the Ulysses S. Grant Association, Frank J. Williams, president.

The Bed Lincoln Died In

Bailey, J. O. *British Plays of the Nineteenth Century*. New York: Odyssey Press, 1966.

Bishop, Jim. *The Day Lincoln Was Shot*. New York: Harper and Brothers, 1955.

Borreson, Ralph. *When Lincoln Died*. New York: Appleton-Century, 1965.

Buffalo–Erie County Historical Society sheet on the Lincoln railroad funeral car. N.d.

Chicago Historical Society. Accession records.

"The Funeral!" *The World*, New York (April 20, 1865).

Historic Structure Report of Ford's Theatre. Washington, D.C.: Government Printing Office, 1963. Source of the Frank Ford quote.

Hobbies—The Magazine for Collectors, February 1948, 127.

Johnson, Geoffrey. "Souvenir of Sorrow." *Chicago*, April 1990.

Leale, Charles A., M.D. "Lincoln's Last Hours." From *Address Delivered Before the Commandery of the State of New York Military Order of the Loyal Legion of the United States* at the regular meeting, February 1909, City of New York, in Observance of the One Hundredth Anniversary of the Birth of President Abraham Lincoln. New York, 1909.

Luthin, Reinhard H. *The Real Abraham Lincoln*. Englewood Cliffs, N.J.: Prentice-Hall, 1960.

McMurty, Gerald R., ed. "The Lincoln Funeral Car." *Lincoln Lore*, no. 1431 (May 1957), pp. 1–4.

Medical and Surgical History, War of the Rebellion, Surgical History, vol. 2, part 1, Washington, D.C., 1870, pp. 305–6.

Oldroyd, Osborn H. *The Assassination of Abraham Lincoln.* Washington, D.C.: O. H. Oldroyd, 1910. Source of the William T. Clark quote.

Olszewski, George J. *The House Where Lincoln Died: Furnishing Study.* Washington, D.C.: U.S. National Park Service, Office of Archaeology and Historic Preservation, 1967.

Steers, Edward, Jr. *The Escape and Capture of John Wilkes Booth.* Brandywine, Md.: Marker Tours, 1983.

Taft, C. S. "Last Hours of Abraham Lincoln." *Medical and Surgical Reporter*, Philadelphia, April 22, 1865.

Taylor, Tom. *Our American Cousin: The Play That Changed History.* With an introduction by Welford D. Taylor. Washington, D.C.: Beacham, 1990.

Thomas, Benjamin P. *Abraham Lincoln.* New York: Knopf, 1952.

White House Historical Association with the cooperation of the National Geographic Society. *The White House, An Historic Guide.* Washington, D.C.: The White House Historical Association, 1987.

Little Sorrel, Stonewall Jackson's Charger

Bowman, John S. *The Civil War Almanac.* New York: World Almanac, Bison Books, 1983.

Davis, Burke. *They Called Him Stonewall: A Life of Lt. General T. J. Jackson, C.S.A.* New York: Rinehart, 1954.

Dooley, Louise K. "Little Sorrel: A War-Horse for Stonewall." *Army*, April 1975, pp. 34–39.

Henderson, G. F. R. *Stonewall Jackson and the American Civil War.* New York: Grosset and Dunlap, 1937.

Rhinesmith, Donald W. "Traveller, 'Just the Horse for General Lee.'" *Virginia Cavalcade*, vol. 33, no. 1 (Summer 1983), pp. 38–47.

Riggs, David F. "Stonewall Jackson's Raincoat." *Civil War Times Illustrated*, July 1977, pp. 35–41.

Wheeler, Richard. *We Knew Stonewall Jackson.* New York: Crowell, 1973.

Robert Browning's Reliquary

Cameron, Kenneth Neill, ed. *Shelley and His Circle, 1773–1822.* Vol. 3. Cambridge, Mass.: Harvard University Press, 1970.

Garrod, H. W., ed. *Keats: Poetical Works.* London: Oxford University Press, 1956. Source of "On Seeing a Lock of Milton's Hair."

Kelley, Philip, and Betty A. Coley, compilers. *The Browning Collections: A Reconstruction with Other Memorabilia.* Winfield, Kans.: Wedgestone Press, 1984.

Kelley, Philip, and Scott Lewis. *The Brownings' Correspondence, Vol. 11.* Winfield, Kans.: Wedgestone Press, 1984. Source of Elizabeth and Robert's correspondence in November and December 1845.

The Library Company, Philadelphia, materials: A description of the frame of a lock of Washington's hair signed by Joseph Crout, dated February 1860, and minutes of a meeting dated August 6, 1829.

Origo, Iris. "Additions to the Keats Collection." *Times Literary Supplement*, April 23, 1970.

Stack, V. E., ed. *How Do I Love Thee: The Love Letters of Robert Browning and Elizabeth Barrett*. New York: G. P. Putnam's Sons, 1969.

Stephens, James, Edwin L. Beck, and Royall L. Snow, eds. *English Poets Romantic, Victorian, and Later*. New York: American Book, 1934. Source for the excerpt from *Sonnets from the Portuguese*, p. 847.

The Elephant Man

Angier, Natalie. "Scientists Discover the Gene in a Nervous System Disease." *The New York Times*, July 13, 1990.

Graham, Peter W., and Fritz H. Oehlschlaeger. *Articulating the Elephant Man: Joseph Merrick and His Interpreters*. Baltimore: Johns Hopkins University Press, 1992.

Howell, Michael, and Peter Ford. *The True History of the Elephant Man*. London: Allison and Busby, 1980. The definitive book on the Elephant Man. Much of my discussion is based on Sir Frederick Treves's essay "The Elephant Man," which appears in Howell and Ford's book, and which is from Treves's *The Elephant Man and Other Reminiscences* (London: Cassell, 1923); and "The Autobiography of Joseph Carey Merrick" as it appears in Howell and Ford.

Montagu, Ashley. *The Elephant Man: A Study in Human Behavior*. New York: Dutton, 1979. This book contains a reproduction of "Report on the Inquest of John Merrick," *The Times* (London), April 16, 1890, which was used as a resource.

Seward, G. R. *The Elephant Man*. London: British Dental Association, 1992. An excellent medical analysis of Joseph Carey Merrick.

"What the Elephant Man Really Had." *Newsweek*, February 29, 1988.

Owney, the Canine Traveler

Bruns, James, compiler. "Owney, Mascot of the Railway Service." Washington, D.C.: The National Philatelic Collection of the Smithsonian Institution, 1990.

The Wright Brothers' *Flyer*

Crouch, Tom. *The Bishop's Boys: A Life of Orville and Wilbur Wright*. New York: Norton, 1989.

Hallion, Richard P. *The Wright Brothers: Heirs of Prometheus*. Washington, D.C.: Smithsonian, 1979.

Howard, Fred. *Wilbur and Orville: A Biography of the Wright Brothers.* New York: Knopf, 1987.

McMahon, John R. *The Wright Brothers: Pioneers of Flight.* New York: Grosset and Dunlap, 1930.

Walsh, John Evangelist. *One Day at Kitty Hawk: The Untold Story of the Wright Brothers and the Airplane.* New York: Crowell, 1975.

Wright Brothers National Memorial, North Carolina. Washington, D.C.: U.S. Government Printing Office, 1961; reprinted 1985.

The Breast-Pocket Items That Saved the Life of Theodore Roosevelt

Abbott, Lyman, ed. in chief. "The Assault on Theodore Roosevelt." *The Outlook*, October 26, 1912.

Davis, Oscar King. Letter telegraphed from Chicago, Illinois, to George Perkins, national chairman of the Progressive Party, in New York City, October 15, 1912. Theodore Roosevelt Birthplace, National Historic Site, New York, N.Y.

Donovan, Robert J. "Annals of Crime." *The New Yorker*, November 6, 1954.

Gores, Stan. *Wisconsin Stories: The Attempted Assassination of Teddy Roosevelt.* Madison: State Historical Society of Wisconsin, 1980. Reprinted from *Wisconsin Magazine of History*, vol. 53 (Summer 1970).

Lorant, Stan. *The Life and Times of Theodore Roosevelt.* Garden City, N.Y.: Doubleday, 1959.

McCullough, David. *Mornings on Horseback.* New York: Simon and Schuster, 1981.

Remey, Oliver E., Henry F. Cochems, and Wheeler P. Bloodgood. *The Attempted Assassination of Ex-President Theodore Roosevelt.* Milwaukee: Progressive Publishing, 1912.

Roosevelt, Theodore. *Social Justice and Popular Rule: Essays, Addresses, and Public Statements Relating to the Progressive Movement (1910–1916)*, from *The Works of Theodore Roosevelt*, by Theodore Roosevelt. © 1925 by Charles Scribner's Sons/Macmillan. My source for lines quoted from the Theodore Roosevelt speech given after the assassination attempt.

Theodore Roosevelt Birthplace National Historic Site, New York City. Accession records, catalog cards, restoration contracts, and memos. The birthplace has possession of the Perkins paper cited above.

This Week Magazine, March 21, 1965, 12–13.

Piltdown Man

Blinderman, Charles. *The Piltdown Inquest.* Buffalo: Prometheus Books, 1986.

Shipman, Pat. "On the Trail of the Piltdown Fraudsters." *New Scientist*, October 6, 1990.

Spencer, Frank. *Piltdown: A Scientific Forgery*. London and New York: Natural History Museum Publications, Oxford University Press, 1990.

————. *The Piltdown Papers, 1908–1955: The Correspondence and Other Documents Relating to the Piltdown Forgery*. London: Oxford University Press, 1990.

Wilford, John Noble. "Mastermind of Piltdown Hoax Unmasked?" *The New York Times*, June 5, 1990.

Laddie Boy

Boston Transcript, August 5, 1926.

Carvan, Anthony (head curator, Department of Civil History, Smithsonian Institution). Letter to William M. Hall, October 1960. National Museum of American History, Washington, D.C.

Russell, Francis. *The Shadow of Blooming Grove: Warren G. Harding in His Times*. New York: McGraw-Hill, 1968.

Babe Ruth's Sixtieth-Home-Run Bat

Ruth, Babe, as told to Bob Considine. *The Babe Ruth Story*. New York: Dutton, 1948.

"Ruth Crashes 60th to Set New Record." *The New York Times*, October 1, 1927.

John Dillinger's Wooden Jail-Escape Gun

Cromie, Robert, and Joseph Pinkston. *Dillinger: A Short and Violent Life*. Evanston, Ill.: Chicago Historical Bookworks, 1990.

Girardin, G. Russell, with William J. Helmer. *Dillinger: The Untold Story*. Bloomington: Indiana University Press, 1994.

Nash, J. Robert, and Ron Offen. *Dillinger: Dead or Alive*. Chicago: Henry Regnery, 1970.

Toland, John. *The Dillinger Days*. New York: Random House, 1962.

Anne Frank's Diary

Barnouw, David, and Gerrold van der Stroom, eds. *The Diary of Anne Frank: The Critical Edition*. Prepared by the Netherlands State Institute for War Documentation. New York: Doubleday, 1989.

Frank, Anne. *Anne Frank: The Diary of a Young Girl*. Garden City, N.Y.: Doubleday, 1952.

The Works of Anne Frank. Introduction by Ann Birstein and Alfred Kazin. Westport, Conn.: Greenwood Press, 1959.

The *Enola Gay*

Thomas, Gordon, and Max Morgan Witts. *Enola Gay*. New York: Stein and Day, 1977.

Young, Peter. *The World Almanac Book of World War Two*. New York: World Almanac, Bison Books, 1981.

Einstein's Brain

Garbedian, H. Gordon. *Albert Einstein: Maker of Universes*. New York: Funk and Wagnalls, 1939.

Hoffman, Banesh, with Helen Dukas. *Albert Einstein: Creator and Rebel*. New York: Viking, 1972.

Lawren, Bill. "Slam Dunks and Einstein's Brain." *Longevity*, April 1993.

Levy, Steven. "My Search for Einstein's Brain." *New Jersey Monthly*, August 1978.

The Rifle That Killed President Kennedy

Four Days: The Historical Record of the Death of President Kennedy. Compiled by United Press International and *American Heritage* magazine. New York: American Heritage (distributed by Simon and Schuster), 1983.

O'Donnell, Kenneth P. and David F. Powers, with Joe McCarthy, *"Johnny, We Hardly Knew Ye."* Boston: Little, Brown, 1972.

Posner, Gerald. *Case Closed: Lee Harvey Oswald and the Assassination of JFK*. New York: Random House, 1993.

Rachlin, Harvey. *The Kennedys: A Chronological History: 1823–Present*. New York: World Almanac, Pharos Books, 1986.

Report of the President's Commission on the Assassination of President John F. Kennedy. Washington, D.C.: United States Government Printing Office, 1964.

Voyager 1 and *Voyager 2*'s Gold-Plated Phonograph Record for Extraterrestrials

Begley, Sharon, and Mary Hager. "A Fantastic Voyage to Neptune." *Newsweek*, September 4, 1989.

Cooke, Robert. "The Voyager Legacy." *Newsday*, August 28, 1989.

Fact Sheet: Voyager 2 Encounter of Neptune. Pasadena: Jet Propulsion Laboratory, National Aeronautics and Space Administration, 1989.

Sagan, Carl, F. D. Drake, Ann Druyan, Timothy Ferris, Jon Lomberg, and Linda Salzman Sagan. *Murmurs from Earth: The Voyager Interstellar Record*. New York: Random House, 1978. Source of the greetings that appear in this chapter, pp. 134–43.

The Voyager Neptune Travel Guide. Pasadena: Jet Propulsion Laboratory, National Aeronautics and Space Administration, 1989.

"Voyager Will Carry 'Earth Sounds' Record." NASA News press release. National Aeronautics and Space Administration, Washington, D.C., 1977.

Wilford, John Noble. "Target of Four Spacecraft: Edge of the Solar System." *The New York Times*, August 28, 1989.

INDEX

ILLUSTRATION CREDITS

Worshiper kissing Black Stone: Mehmet Biber (Ajans Biber); *Black Stone of the Ka'bah*: copyright Robert Azzi/Woodfin Camp & Associates; *Lucy—field*: Neg./ Trans. no. 338315, courtesy Department of Library Sciences, American Museum of Natural History; *Lucy—skeleton*: Institute of Human Origins; *Code of Hammurabi*: 85 EN 366, copyright Cliché des Musées Nationaux—Paris; *Carter/ Mace—King Tut*: Griffith Institute, Ashmolean Museum, Oxford, England; *Death Mask—King Tut*: copyright Egyptian Museum; *Black Obelisk*: copyright British Museum; *Gihon Spring, Siloam Pool*: Israel Government Press Office; *Siloam Inscription*: Israel Museum; *Rosetta Stone*: copyright British Museum; *Portland Vase—Side One, Portland Vase—Side Two, "The Portland Museum"*: copyright British Museum; *Veil of the Virgin*: Courtesy Editions Houvet "La Crypte"; *Crown of Thorns—Portrait of Jesus*: Alinari/Art Resource, New York; *Crown of Thorns—wreath*: Gérard Boullay; *Holy Lance*: Kunsthistoriches Museum, Vienna; *Positive and negative images of Shroud of Turin, Positive image of the face on the Shroud, Negative image of the face on the Shroud*: courtesy of the Holy Shroud Guild, Esopus, New York/Photo: G. Enrie; *Blood of Saint Januarius*: Chiesa Cattedrale di Napoli; *Rubens Vase*: The Walters Art Gallery, Baltimore; *Antioch Chalice*: All rights reserved, The Metropolitan Museum of Art, New York; *Book of Kells*: The Board of Trinity College Dublin; *Bayeux Tapestry—panel one, Bayeux Tapestry—panel two*: Centre Guillaume le Conquerant, Bayeux; *Domesday Book*: Crown copyright reproduced with the permission of the Controller of Her Majesty's Stationery Office; *Holy Child of Aracoeli*: Basilica S. Maria in Aracoeli; *Columbus's Book of Privileges, Columbus at court*: Library of Congress; *Cantino Map*: Biblioteca Estense ed Universitaria; *Hope Diamond*: Smithsonian Institution Photo No. 78–8853; *Edmond Halley's notebook page*: Royal Greenwich Observatory; *Declaration of Independence—Second Continental Congress, Declaration of Independence—the document*: National Archives, Washington, D.C.; *George Washington's false teeth*: courtesy of the New York Academy of Medicine Library; *Washington face portrait*: painting by Gilbert Stuart, gift of Thomas Jefferson Coolidge IV in memory of his great-grandfather, Thomas Jefferson